The Government and Politics of Ireland

Third Edition

Basil Chubb

LONGMAN
London and New York

Longman Group UK Limited,
Longman House, Burnt Mill, Harlow,
Essex CM20 2JE, England
and Associated Companies throughout the world

*Published in the United States of America
by Longman Publishing, New York*

First edition published 1970
Second edition 1982
Third edition 1992

British Library Cataloguing in Publication Data

A catalogue record for this book is
available from the British Library

Library of Congress Cataloging in Publication Data
Applied for

Set by 7 in 10pt Times

Produced by Longman Singapore Publishers (Pte) Ltd.
Printed in Singapore

CONTENTS

LIST OF TABLES AND FIGURES

TABLES

FIGURES

GLOSSARY OF IRISH TERMS

Some, but by no means all, Irish political institutions are commonly called by their Irish names. For the convenience of non-Irish readers, a list of such terms used frequently in this book is given here.

Bunreacht na hÉireann. The Constitution of Ireland. This term is usually applied only to the Constitution enacted in 1937 and still in force.

Dáil (full title, *Dáil Éireann*). Chamber of Deputies. The popularly elected legislative assembly.

Éire. Ireland. Article 4 of Bunreacht na hÉireann says that the name of the state is 'Éire, or in the English language, *Ireland*'. The name Éire is often used outside Ireland to denote the present state, which extends *de facto* over part, though the largest part, of the island of Ireland.

Fianna Fáil (Soldiers of Destiny). The title of the largest party, founded by Eamon de Valera in 1926.

Fine Gael (Tribe of the Gaels). The successor of Cumann na nGaedheal (League of Gaels), the pro-Treaty party. In 1991 the second largest party.

Gaeltacht (plural, *Gaeltachtaí*). Irish-speaking areas. Most of these are situated on the western seaboard, in Donegal, Mayo, Galway, and Kerry.

Garda Síochána. The Civic Guards, Police.

Oireachtas. Parliament.

Seanad (full title, *Seanad Éireann*). Senate.

Sinn Féin (We Ourselves). Originally a nationalist political movement founded by Arthur Griffith in 1905. In 1917 a number of separatist groups coalesced under the title of Sinn Féin, pledged to the achievement of an independent republic. The movement split over the terms of the Treaty with the United Kingdom (December 1921). Organizations calling themselves Sinn Féin have existed ever since.

Taoiseach (plural, *Taoisigh*). Prime Minister.

Teachta Dála (plural, *Teachtaí*). Deputy (literally messenger or delegate to the Dáil). Abbreviated to TD.

PREFACE TO THE THIRD EDITION

Once again, I have had to rewrite many parts of this book for the third edition. The reasons are precisely those that, as I stated in the Preface to the second edition, made it necessary for me then to rewrite extensively. In the last ten years, Ireland has continued to change as fast as it did in the previous fifteen. As important, political scientists have proliferated and political science has burgeoned, with the result that the quantity and quality of writing on Irish politics have improved immeasurably. In addition, government departments themselves have begun to publish more factual and explanatory material than previously and students of Irish government have benefited greatly.

Some topics, however, have still attracted little attention, and in respect of these, as previously, I have had to rely on personal enquiries directed to the practitioners. I am again indebted to many more people than I can mention here, particularly those civil servants whom I have bothered more than most of my contacts. The market research organizations have been generous in making material available: in particular, I am grateful to Jack Jones and Áine of the Market Research Bureau of Ireland Ltd for their generous help over many years.

I thank my academic colleagues in political science and law who have unfailingly responded to my buttonholing over the years. I acknowledge gratefully also the help of Miriam Nestor, Teresa Mulroy and Shauna Curran, who have worked with me at some time or another during the preparation of this edition, and of Geraldine O'Dea who prepared the index.

B.C.

ULSTER

CONNACHT

LEINSTER

MUNSTER

Londonderry

DONEGAL

BELFAST

Donegal Bay

Sligo

SLIGO

MONAGHAN

LEITRIM

CAVAN

Dundalk

MAYO

Westport

ROSCOMMON

LONGFORD

LOUTH

Drogheda

IRISH SEA

WESTMEATH

MEATH

DUBLIN

GALWAY

Athlone

DUBLIN

Dun Laoghaire

Galway

OFFALY

KILDARE

Galway Bay

R. Shannon

WICKLOW

*ATLANTIC
OCEAN*

CLARE

LAOIGHIS

Carlow

CARLOW

Limerick

TIPPERARY

Kilkenny

LIMERICK

Tipperary

KILKENNY

WEXFORD

Clonmel

Tralee

Waterford

Wexford

KERRY

CORK

WATERFORD

St. George's Channel

Killarney

Cork

Bantry

50 Miles

CHAPTER 1
Basic Influences

I

The state with which this book is concerned is in the words of its Constitution called 'Éire, or in the English language, *Ireland*'.[1] We shall call it 'Ireland' and its people 'Irish'. However, Ireland, the state, does not extend over the whole island of Ireland, nor does it include everyone who calls himself or herself Irish or everyone who might be reckoned to be Irish. Both inside the state and especially outside, it is often called by other names – Éire, the Republic of Ireland, the Irish Republic. In this book, whenever the use of 'Ireland' would be ambiguous or confusing, the term 'Republic of Ireland' will be used.

II

The Irish are a peripheral people: their homeland is on the fringe of the British Isles, which in turn is on the edge of Europe. They are, too, a not very numerous people. After well over a century of population decline – in 1841, 6.5 million people lived in the area now known as the Republic of Ireland – the population, then below 3 million, began slowly to increase from the middle of this century and in the late eighties was about 3.5 million. The overwhelming majority – 93 per cent in 1981 – were Roman Catholic and all but a tiny minority ordinarily speak English.

This population, which is small for a sovereign state, has a large rural element and with 50 people per square kilometre is the least densely populated of the countries in the European Communities. Only in the late 1960s did the number of people living in 'towns' (defined as places with a population of 1,500 or more) rise above that living in rural areas. In 1981 four out of ten people were rural dwellers. Outside Dublin City and County and the southern region (the counties of Cork, Waterford, Limerick, and South Tipperary), the population is still overwhelmingly rural; as many as three-quarters in the western seaboard counties. Many people who today are counted as urban were born and reared as country people; many more have country-bred parents; and more again have relations who still live in rural areas. Dublin and environs, with 1 million people (about 30 per cent of the population), is the only large conurbation. Cork, the second largest city, has about 175,000 inhabitants (5 per cent); the other towns are mostly small regional centres serving and attuned to the farming people of their hinterlands.

The proportion of the work force engaged in agriculture (about 15 per cent) is large compared with the highly industrialized countries of the European Communities and in this respect Ireland more resembles the southern European peripheral countries like Spain, Portugal and Greece. However, more important for understanding the country, are the facts that only forty years ago half the work force was in agriculture and that farming was, and to a large extent still is, on small units. The picture which the traveller gets in the countryside is overwhelmingly of scattered small farms.

The land reforms initiated by British governments in the late nineteenth century and completed in the first decade of independence in the twenties, effected a rural revolution and quickly produced a class of owner-occupiers who came to dominate Irish politics. In 1981 over half of all farms were of less than 50 acres. By the standards of late twentieth century Western Europe with its ever more commercial farming and rising living standards, farms of this size have become increasingly less viable. Today 'less than one third of Irish farmers operate commercially viable enterprises'.[2] In the west almost all are unviable.

The existence of a large agricultural sector of small farmers means that Ireland is a peripheral country in another, the economist's, sense of that word. It is 'one of the small peripheral societies of capitalist Europe. . . . Ireland's affinities in the European context are with those societies – like Greece, Portugal, Spain and Finland – that evolved within a sub-region in the shadow of a powerful centre, and for whom economic development remains incomplete'.[3] Ireland's is a small, open economy with all that that implies. Notwithstanding a rapid pace of industrialization from about 1960 onwards and a consequent big growth in professional and technical employment, white-collar positions, and skilled manual jobs, Ireland lags behind the most industrialized countries of Western Europe. Gross domestic product per head in 1988 was £8,297. Although this put Ireland among the rich countries of the world with a highly literate population enjoying high standards of social services, it amounted to only 42 per cent of the figure for Denmark, the richest of the Community countries, and 71 per cent of the neighbouring United Kingdom. It rated ninth place in the Community league table with only Portugal, Greece and Spain less wealthy. In the absence as yet of effective Community policies to redress the differences between the members, Ireland's position relative to the developed industrialized members is not likely to alter materially in the near future. Emigration, both a social safety valve and a debilitating haemorrhage, was for a century and a half a feature of Irish life. Fluctuating between 5 and 15 per

1,000 of population from independence to the mid-1960s, it was halted and reversed for a short period, but resumed in the eighties, and in 1989, at 13 per 1,000, it was almost as high as it had ever been.

III

Identification of the basic political attitudes of a community is largely a matter either of impressionistic generalization or of drawing inferences from survey data. What is perceived or adduced can often be explained only by reference to the past, for contemporary perceptions, beliefs, and attitudes are inevitably to some extent the product of the conditions and events of the past. They are, moreover, changing continuously, sometimes slowly as in Ireland between independence and the early 1960s; at other times more rapidly, as was the Irish experience from 1960 onwards to today. This period was one of rapid industrialization, and 'industrial societies unquestionably introduce a rate of social change previously unparalleled in history'.[4]

Again, these generalizations can often be little more than statements about 'most people', for even in a comparatively homogeneous community like that in the Republic, there exist groups, such as the tiny Protestant minority, that have an outlook that is to some extent different from the outlook of the majority. Of more political significance, the attitudes and values of town people are likely to be different in some respects from those of rural people. If, as is the case in Ireland, there is a continuous movement from the countryside to the town, there will be urban dwellers who are but slowly becoming town people: perhaps they never will be, though their children probably will. Even to talk of an urban culture and a rural culture is misleading, if doing so suggests that everyone can be placed in one or the other of two identifiable groups, for this is to ignore the stance of great numbers of people who are in-between. Obviously, in times of comparatively rapid change such as Ireland has been experiencing, generalization is particularly hazardous. In these circumstances, it might be best first to identify the cultural influences contributing to the making of the Irish of the middle twentieth century, which was culturally a comparatively stable period. These are the 'basic influences' which are the subject of this chapter. Thence, in Chapter 2, an attempt is made to determine what are the social changes which have induced, and continue to induce, cultural change and which are reshaping the political culture of Irish people.

The British influence

Geography and history combine to make the British influence the most important in determining the pattern of much of Irish political thought and practice, both in the past and still, though less so, today. This is a simple matter of the geographical propinquity of a large national group and a small one, and the historical facts of political dominion, social and economic domination, and cultural blanketing. Ireland, like Scotland and Wales, became an English province in medieval times, its politics and its economic and cultural life dominated by, and oriented to, England.

The process of assimilation was aided both by the settlement in Ireland of people of English and Scottish origins who were Protestants and by the emergence of an elite class whose members gave loyalty to Britain, in many cases their place of recent origin and in all cases the guarantor of their political and economic power. The 'plantations' – that is, the placing of English and Scottish families as farmers in Ireland – in the sixteenth and seventeenth centuries and the Irish wars of the seventeenth century resulted in massive transfers of property. In 1641, nearly 60 per cent of Irish land was owned by Catholics; by 1703, only 14 per cent. The province, for that was what Ireland was, particularly after the Act of Union (1800), was dominated by a Protestant landowning class until the late nineteenth century. If this class and the better-off Catholics who identified with them had specific Irish interests, they were nevertheless essentially provincials, London being their metropolis as it was for the Welsh and the Scots. The nineteenth century, moreover, saw the rise of the English-dominated, London-centred 'United Kingdom of Great Britain and Ireland' to the status of a world imperial power, engendering in its people and particularly its English ruling class the belief that their values and habits were in all respects excellent. Lesser breeds, among whom they included the Irish, could by espousing them hope to tread the same path of progress.

Inevitably, in these circumstances, Irish people acquired much of the culture, including much of the political culture, of the British and more particularly of the English. The substitution of the English language for Irish was especially important. During the seventeenth and eighteenth centuries the number of people speaking Irish declined very rapidly. By 1851, less than 30 per cent of the population could speak it; by 1871 less than 20 per cent. Although significant (but diminishing) numbers in the west continued to speak Irish, in Dublin and the east, which dominated social and economic life, only 5 per cent or less could speak it from the middle of the nineteenth century. The process of absorption of English ways and values was most complete in Dublin, the bigger towns, and the east of the country generally. In addition, Ireland enjoyed, and came to expect, the standards of public services, including education, health, and welfare services, comparable in general with those of Great Britain.

As in the case of the white communities of the British Commonwealth, many of the currently held political traditions and values were inculcated and absorbed during a most critical and formative period: the period of the advent of mass democracy. Extensions of the franchise (the right to vote) in Britain were followed by extensions, with modifications, in Ireland; and Irish people acquired democratic habits and values. Political ideas were almost wholly expressed in British categories, for, from Daniel O'Connell to Charles Stuart Parnell and beyond, the political experience of many Irish leaders was gained in British political life, and they practised the parliamentary ways of Westminster. However, Ireland, geographically and in other ways more peripheral than Wales or Scotland, was never integrated to the extent that they were, because of the survival in greater measure of a pre-industrial rural society and the centrifugal pull of national feeling and consequent nationalism made stronger by religious differences. Yet even Irish nationalism itself was a 'revolution within and against a democracy and could not help using many of that system's institutions and procedures'.[5]

There is no better way to illustrate Irish acceptance of democratic values and British forms than by the history of the independence movement and the formation and consolidation of the new state. Although, with the founding of Sinn Féin in 1905, Irish nationalism turned away from parliamentary methods, the parliamentary tradition and the belief in the legitimacy of a democratically elected assembly can be seen to have been strongly ingrained in both the leaders and the majority of the population. By 1916, in Brian Farrell's words, 'modern Ireland already existed . . .; most of its political values – as well as its political structures – were not merely modern but were articulated in a distinctively British way'.[6] The revolutionary Dáil of 1919, legitimized by election, continued in being as a parliamentary assembly through revolution and war. If it did not in fact control the situation, nevertheless it claimed the right to do so, and those who sustained it recognized its importance in the eyes of a people, many of whom had imbibed liberal-democratic values. Farrell concluded from his study of its origins and record that it was 'as intent on maintaining the framework of an established society and its associated values as with attempting to change it'.[7] The general acceptance of the most important norms of democracy is well shown by the widespread recognition of the duly elected government in 1922 despite its rejection by Eamon de Valera and his supporters, by the rapid acceptance of this group when they abandoned force (which was getting them nowhere) for constitutional and parliamentary methods, and, finally, by their transformation into a majority government at the election of 1932.

Political independence did not automatically bring economic or cultural independence. The Irish economy was not a balanced and viable whole, the less so because of the retention by the United Kingdom of the north-eastern part of the island, which included Belfast, the only industrial city. Agriculture, in so far as it was market-orientated, was wholly geared to British needs. Banking, insurance, industry, and trade were largely British-dominated and almost wholly British-orientated and only slowly became centred upon Dublin. Britain was, and still is, Ireland's biggest customer and its main supplier. As recently as 1968, 70 per cent of Irish exports went there and over half of its imports came from there. Only from the seventies, with Ireland's accession to the European Communities, did this pattern change quickly.

The boundaries of the Irish state were from the beginning highly permeable. People and ideas have always passed freely across them. The newly independent Irish Free State, as it was at first called, was a member of the British Commonwealth and as such its citizens were not classed as aliens in the United Kingdom or in Commonwealth countries. Even when, later, Ireland left the Commonwealth, this situation was not altered. Passports have never been necessary to travel in either direction, and citizens of each country can settle in the other without any formalities whatsoever. Much of Irish emigration was always to Great Britain; today there might be well over half a million persons living in Great Britain who were born in the Republic. They and their families, together with seasonal and short-term migrants, have always moved freely between the two countries on a large scale, the larger as growing affluence increased the propensity to take holidays 'at home'. Although Ireland has a full range of home-produced newspapers and its own radio and television services, British newspapers and magazines circulate freely; British radio transmissions can be received throughout the country; British television is available to people in the north and east of the country (three-fifths of Irish television sets can receive it); and most of the books read in the country are published in Great Britain.

Britain not only influenced the Irish, it also insulated them. In the words of Jean Blanchard, 'L'Irlande est une île derrière une île'.[8] Little of continental European thought or experience was directly tapped or assimilated by the Irish. Knowledge of continental European languages has always been very poor by the standards of most Western European countries. Because of the irredentist obsession of the political leaders of the past with the problem of the six northern counties still in the United Kingdom and consequent neutrality in and after the Second World War, Ireland was cut off to a considerable degree from the mainstream of Western European life from independence until the 1960s. Only the prospect of membership in the European Communities, and its actuality ten years later in 1973, led to widening horizons as the Irish government and Irish business and agricultural organizations began to operate in a broader context than before. An increase in foreign travel had the same effect and, reflecting all this, the media expanded their coverage.

The influence of Britain upon Irish politics has been pervasive. The British legacy to the new state was enormous, as we shall see throughout this book. The constitutional forms adopted were those of

British parliamentary democracy; the governmental system was based on the Westminster model; the administrative system, on the Whitehall model. The main lines of many public services had been laid down under the aegis of the British government and parliament in the formative period of the welfare state in the late nineteenth and early twentieth centuries. These services continued barely touched by the takeover by a native government and parliament. Because of this and because the country had comparable educational standards and a fully fledged Civil Service on British lines, it was not only wholly equipped for statehood but could embark on it with no break at all in continuity.

That the political institutions then established and the services then taken over continued largely unaltered in basic design was due, first, to the conservatism of the community and its leaders; second, to the continued cultural impact of British contacts at almost as high a frequency as hitherto; and, third, to a long-continuing ignorance of the experience of other countries. Ireland settled down politically independent but, like the white Commonwealth countries, with institutions closely modelled upon those of the imperial power from which its freedom had been won. It was only after Ireland joined the European Communities that the horizons of politicians, administrators, and eventually ordinary people, extended to continental European countries and the influence of Britain and the British began to wane.

Nationalism.

Since the British influence was so great, it may well be asked why Ireland did not settle down politically as a British province. The answer lies in the fact that it was more peripheral to England than were Wales and Scotland and, notwithstanding considerable cultural penetration, was less assimilated. The preservation of a separate identity was greater because the religion of the masses continued to be Roman Catholicism and because a pre-industrial society persisted in rural areas, particularly in the west. In time, nationalist feeling evolved, asserted itself, and grew stronger:

Irish nationalism, as it took organized mass political form in the last quarter of the nineteenth century, had its core of support in that part of the Irish population which was isolated by all these divisions: the Gaelic, Catholic, agrarian, peasant community which was the largest element in Irish society outside of eastern Ulster.[9]

The state itself owes its existence to the successful outcome of a typical nationalist movement for independence.

When a national movement succeeds, people are very self-conscious about their statehood, however passive many of them may have been before. If the state is small and weak, anxiety about its continued existence and integrity is inevitably reflected in a heightened self-consciousness. For the first forty years of the state's existence, memories of the struggle for independence and the myths of Irish nationalism were continually revived by political leaders who, having won power by evoking nationalist feeling, continued to exploit it.

In the Irish case, also, the emergence of the Irish Free State was not the end of the matter. Some national issues were still unresolved. Nationalist feeling remained high because the break with Great Britain was not complete. The new state had Commonwealth status, but for some people this was not sufficient. For the majority, the fact that the country was partitioned and the state did not extend over the whole island of Ireland meant that the job had not been finished. Irish nationalism continued in the form of a typical irredentist movement, doomed to sterile frustration because of the true nature of the Northern Ireland problem – arising from the fact that the majority of the unredeemed did not and do not, see themselves as such – was simply not recognized, running counter as it did to one of the strongest of nationalist myths, namely, that the people of the island are one people.

For forty years from independence, the manifestation of nationalism altered very little. Constitutional issues and the problem of 'the border' never ceased to obsess political leaders, who assiduously kept them alive in the public mind. Those leaders who survived the successful independence struggle, and their kinsmen, virtually monopolized political leadership positions for thirty years and dominated politics for even longer. Their appeals to old and familiar issues paid them dividends in terms of electoral support; and their differences, which concerned these same issues, were the basis of party allegiance and rivalry. Hence there was great political stability, which in time became sterility. A largely rural electorate, set in its ways and slow to change, was exposed to unvarying appeals. Ireland became a thoroughly conservative society whose leaders until the mid-1950s hardly attempted to tackle many of its social and economic problems, let alone solve them. Likewise, there was a tendency to ignore international issues other than those related to the traditional nationalist problems, a tendency increased by the insulating effect of the nearness of Britain and by Ireland's small size and limited interests. Foreign policy, except in relation to the United Kingdom, usually evoked little or no interest and played no part in parliamentary or electoral politics.

This situation began to change slowly from the mid-1950s. Age eventually caught up with the first generation of political leaders, the veterans of the national struggle, and they gave way to new and in many cases less obsessive men. Ireland, hitherto barred from the United Nations because it was neutral during the Second World War, was admitted in 1955, and its soldiers joined peacekeeping forces in Cyprus and the Congo. The challenge of the European Communities was slowly apprehended and its opportunities and implications recognized. By the 1960s, when the country embarked on industrial expansion and enjoyed a period of economic growth and prosperity of unprecedented proportions, nationalism began to wither. Although the onset of civil war in Northern Ireland from 1969 brought old issues back to the centre of politics again, the reaction of people in the Republic made it quite clear that nationalist fires were almost extinct, the burning of the British embassy in Dublin in 1972, a surrogate for real action, notwithstanding. By the late 1960s many people and most politicians were at last coming to recognize the Northern Ireland problem for what it was – a struggle between two deeply divided communities in the North itself, not soluble simply by British withdrawal. Seen in this light, the nature of Irish nationalism, if not its eventual objective, was bound – eventually – to change.

Traditionally, Irish nationalism involved being anti- British, and that changed little over the years. Cooperation with the powerful neighbour was emotionally unpalatable and politically unrewarding. Of course, the connections built up over time and the exigencies imposed by propinquity could not be ignored. Considerable conformity and cooperation with public authorities and other organizations in the United Kingdom were, and are, obviously necessary and beneficial. Many of the advantages now accruing to citizens of the states of the European Communities were always enjoyed by Irish people in Great Britain. It was obviously to their considerable benefit that they should be able to enter the professions and the labour market and generally to enjoy the benefits of being treated like British citizens. Because of this, because of the continuing penetration of British ideas and standards, and because of emigration, which led to many Irish families having relatives 'across the water', a curiously ambivalent attitude to Britain developed. On the one hand, there was willingness (besides often a necessity) to go there and live there, a personal friendliness for British people as individuals, and a propensity to accept British standards and values. On the other hand, there was an almost ritualistic antipathy to 'the Brits', and particularly to manifestations of British military power or symbols of British monarchy – uniforms, warships, the Union Jack, members of the Royal Family, even statues, monuments, and buildings. Although the intensity of anti- British sentiment slowly lessened from the middle of the century onwards, twenty years of trouble in Northern Ireland notwithstanding, this ambivalence to some extent still persists.

Equally persistent has been the cultural nationalism that developed in typical fashion to support the independence movement in the late nineteenth century. The Gaelic League and the literary movements were intended to be non-political, though they, and particularly the first, became so. From the beginning the language was a highly political subject in independent Ireland. The problems of reviving it, its place in education, its use in everyday business and for official purposes, and the treatment of those dwindling communities whose mother tongue it was, were exacerbated because the most ardent nationalists insisted on identifying the language with Irishness, thus making rational appraisal impossible and rational solutions politically inexpedient. It was well into the second half of the century before Irish governments were able or willing slowly to adopt less emotionally charged and more practical policies.

The other gaelicizing force in the independence movement was very different and very effective. The Gaelic Athletic Association, founded in 1884 to promote national – that is, Gaelic as opposed to 'foreign' – games, 'was a mass movement, unintellectual and positively grounded in militant separatism from the outset'.[10] Its branches formed a countrywide network that embraced large numbers of people. Its strongly nationalist and exclusive policies did much to socialize generations of Irish people. Many of the country's political leaders came from its ranks.

The rapid disappearance of the ascendency, the former ruling class, and a marked thinning of the ranks of middle-class Protestants after independence opened the way for the emergence of a bourgeois Catholic elite. Protestant domination of business, commerce, and the professions declined; and although the number of Protestants with large farms did not fall, the social and political leadership of the 'West British' gentry had finally ended. These had been the leaders of the most significant minority community in the country. Although it could be said that a Protestant subculture still exists today, based upon religious, educational, but only occasionally social, separation, this small minority of less than 5 per cent has been to a considerable extent almost everywhere absorbed into the larger community.

Because of the numbers involved, political divisions along religious lines were not to be a general feature of politics in independent Ireland as they were in Northern Ireland. Of far greater importance was the cleavage that resulted from the division in the nationalist movement over the terms of the treaty of December 1921 with the British and led to civil war. The split in Sinn Féin and, subsequently, in the country as a whole into Treaty versus anti-Treaty factions polarized Irish politics with tremendous consequences. There is much evidence to suggest that this division at first reflected regional and socio-economic divisions as well as political and personal differences. Certainly, it aggravated, if it did not cause, great conflict in Irish society. It was reflected in social life, in nationalist associations and ceremonials, and in politics. In politics it was the major polarizing agent and formed the basis of party division: Fianna Fáil and Fine Gael, the two biggest parties, derive from it. By the time the issues that led to the split were removed from the political agenda, the parties which it threw up had developed their own life and momentum. If they do not now polarize politics in the way they once did, they continue to dominate it: between them they attracted between 71 per cent and 85 per cent of first preferences votes at general elections in the eighties.

Although the major groups involved in the split of Sinn Féin eventually learned to live together, the extremists could not be assimilated. De Valera, for all his republican principles, entered constitutional politics when his circumstances required it. Others were not so practical. A tradition of extreme republican movements continually produced people who did not recognize the government or the state and who resorted to force and to outrage. Such people are now very few, the less since the centre of IRA power shifted to Northern Ireland. They have, too, become increasingly estranged from the community, but they epitomize a small element of republican radicalism that continues to exist mainly in parts of the west and the border counties and among members of certain social groups, particularly urban workers and very small farmers. It might almost be said that these extreme republicans constitute a distinct but tiny subculture.

The reservoir from which this tiny stream of extremists came was sizeable. Up to 1980, it could be measured in double figures. Among the secondary-school pupils whom they surveyed, in the early seventies, Pfretzschner and Borock discovered

a sizeable minority of students who do not . . . display a confidence in the system . . . they do not exhibit a high regard for democracy . . . and are attracted to violence as an acceptable means to the solution of political problems. Our analysis suggests that roughly one-third of the students falls into this . . . category.[11]

No less than 40 per cent of their respondents favoured the use of force 'if necessary' to end British rule in Northern Ireland. Davis and Sinnott, in a controversial study published in 1979, concluded that 'the stark fact remains that 21 per cent of the population emerge as being in some degree supportive in their attitude to IRA activities'.[12] The proportion today is less than this.

A dying pre-industrial society

Ireland was for long a fringe province of the United Kingdom. Like West Wales, Cornwall, and the highlands and islands of Scotland, it lacked the essential minerals of the industrial revolution and was geographically remote. The development of an industrial society in the British Isles touched such areas last and least; the further west, the more delayed and the smaller were its effects.

Although the dominance of Britain during the formative period of modern mass politics ensured that the values of an industrial, urbanized, liberal-democratic society would prevail, Ireland's traditional social-geographic pattern continued to survive. For hundreds of years, the country exhibited what Erhard Rumpf called 'das allgemeine Ost–West Gefälle', an east–west gradient corresponding to the degree of anglicization.[13] Thus the cultural history of the country after the industrial revolution was one of modern urban values permeating an older peasant society inexorably but to differing degrees – more and faster in the towns than in rural areas, and more in the east than in the west. Although the decline of the one culture through the permeation of the other is now almost complete, the impact of the older culture on the politics of independent Ireland was enormous. In the past, Irish politics was dominated by the countryman, more particularly the small-scale farmer whose characteristics and attitudes to some extent continued to reflect the older, pre-industrial society.

We can label this rural culture a 'peasant' culture, but we should do so with reservations. Some Irish scholars, indeed, have challenged the very concept of a single peasant political culture in pre-modern Ireland. Even if one does not go that far, the very term 'peasant' must be used cautiously. A 'peasant society' proper, according to Teodor Shanin, consists of

small producers on land who, with the help of simple equipment and the labour of their families, produce mainly for their own consumption and/or the fulfilment of their duties to the holders of political and economic power. . . . The family farm is the basic unit of peasant ownership, production, consumption and social life.[14]

As Shanin goes on to point out, the ties of family and the land and the wide variety of tasks to be performed, which causes the peasant to operate at a relatively low level of specialization, lead to many of the distinguishing characteristics of peasant life and thought: 'The peasantry is a pre-industrial social entity which carries into contemporary society specific, different and older elements of social inter-relation, economics, policy and culture.' The impact of a money economy, of towns and of modernization, however, is relentless and makes inroads into this culture. Gradually, the peasant becomes an agricultural producer. 'This pattern of development of the peasantry into a cohesive, increasingly narrowing and professionalized occupational group of farmers is seen clearly in most parts of North-Western Europe'.[15] In broad outline Irish experience was along the lines indicated by Shanin. The land reforms of the late nineteenth and early twentieth centuries produced a class of highly conservative small owner-occupier farmers. Although they were increasingly concerned with producing for the market, their type of farming and their life styles retained some peasant characteristics.

The outlook on life of a farming community of this sort has been dubbed 'rural fundamentalism', defined by Patrick Commins as:

a set of values and beliefs by which a positive view was taken of

– the family-owned farm as the basic unit of agricultural production
– having a numerous class of landowners

- farming as an occupation
- agriculture as the basis of national prosperity
- farm or small-town living.[16]

This outlook was retained at least for a generation by the increasing numbers who year after year left farming and rural life for the towns. It thus infused Irish society generally and continued to infuse it despite the decline in the rural population. To this day, for many, farmers and non-farmers alike, land is by no means simply a resource to be exploited and managed.

The values of this class influenced the pattern of development of the newly independent Irish state in the twenties and beyond. It was one of the bases of de Valera's philosophy of life and clearly inspired part of Article 45 of his creation, Bunreacht na hÉireann, (the Constitution of Ireland), the 'Directive Principles of Social Policy'. As late as the mid-sixties, A. J. Humphreys could say that 'small farm families, taken collectively, hold and exercise the largest measure of power in the rural community'.[17] At that time, be it remembered, the rural population still out numbered the town dwellers.

Among the predominant values of the countryman are a concern for, and loyalty to, family and neighbours. David Schmitt in 1973 noted that 'virtually every writer about Irish society has observed the importance of close personal connections among community and family members'.[18] Country people are strongly locally oriented, and they set great store by face-to-face contact. In the past, even the recent past, Mass on Sunday, Fair Day, the cooperative creamery, all had significance far wider than their primary purposes for a people who were dispersed on their own small family farms, who were not very mobile until they got cars (from the late sixties) and who acquired TV sets in considerable numbers only during the seventies. An important characteristic of such a society is 'personalism' – that is, 'a pattern of social relations in which people are valued for who they are and whom they know . . . where extreme personalism exists, family and friends determine one's chances for success'.[19] These features lead to a great emphasis upon the personal and local in politics. They have been clearly reflected, as we shall see, in the selection of candidates for elections, in electoral behaviour, in the role of elected representatives, and in representatives' relationships with their constituents.

The dominance of the small farmer was also largely the cause of the static conservatism that marked Irish politics so strongly for the first forty years of independence. Only in the poorest areas on the periphery did poverty and discontent spawn a measure of peasant radicalism that issued in extreme republicanism. Elsewhere, smallholders, with their little farms secure but undercapitalized, were conservative, shrewd in the short run, but unimaginative in their attitudes both to their livelihood and to politics. In these circumstances, productivity was low and the rural population declined as emigration drained off the young, the loss being particularly severe from the poorest areas. Although emigration obviated the development of a more radical type of rural politics, it left a sad legacy in the areas most affected. There hung over such areas a torpor that was death to initiative.

Although Ireland experienced unprecedented economic expansion for a decade from the early 1960s and continued thereafter to develop economically, though with occasional hiccoughs, the growth was almost wholly in the urban, industrial sector. When the climate in rural Ireland changed, as it did in the 1970s, it was largely the result of membership of the European Communities, which benefited farming, whether efficient or otherwise, greatly. Both the effects on rural prosperity of the Community's agricultural policy and the impact of television-set ownership in rural areas grew rapidly from the end of the 1960s. The increased prosperity of the young people was immense. By 1980, the life styles and values of the rural young, both those who stayed at home and those who worked in Dublin but could now afford to go home regularly, began to approach more closely those of their urban counterparts than they ever had been. This was a generational change that has since been consolidated.

The persistence of a peasant culture until well into the second half of the twentieth century was the greater because it was identified by late-nineteenth-century nationalists with the Gaelic tradition. In turn, the Gaelic peasantry came in those same eyes to epitomize the Irish nation. 'The whole national movement . . . fused with the cause of maintaining the integrity of the peasant tradition against an insidiously destructive colonial power'.[20] Once established, the new state was concerned to preserve not only its political but also its cultural integrity. Irish leaders, and in particular de Valera, cherished a vision of a rural Gaelic Ireland and pursued it as a political objective. Not until after he and his generation left politics – de Valera finally retired from active politics in 1959 – were old myths discarded and more realistic and materialistic objectives accorded priority. This, then, is another of the bases of the static Ireland of the first half of the century that began to crumble increasingly quickly from the sixties onwards.

Irish Catholicism

The persistence of older traditions and conservative attitudes, which owed much to the identification of the nation with the peasantry, was still further strengthened by their identification in turn with Catholicism, more particularly the Catholic church in Ireland. This symbiosis, accomplished by the end of the nineteenth century, was to have enormous political consequences. In Emmet Larkin's words: 'What really evolved . . . in the making of the Irish state was a unique constitutional balance that became basic to the functioning of the Irish political system.' More specifically, 'the price Parnell paid . . . for the accommodation of the Church . . . was to make his *de facto* Irish state essentially a confessional one: it was left to de Valera to make it formally confessional'.[21]

Ninety-three people out of a hundred in the Republic of Ireland are Roman Catholics. The attachment of most people, Catholic and Protestant, to their church has traditionally always been very strong. As late as the early seventies, a national survey conducted by the Irish Episcopal Commission for Research and Development showed

a high level of religious belief and practice among Catholics in the Republic of Ireland. Nine out of ten Catholics fully believed in God, Christ's Resurrection, Our Lady's Immaculate Conception, Our Lady's Assumption, Transubstantiation and that sins are forgiven in Confession. The level of religious practice was also high with nine out of ten attending Mass at least once a week, and Communion and Confession at least once a year.[22]

Even today, most Irish people are conscious of religious differences between individuals. A person's religion is almost always recognized and mentally noted on first acquaintance. Education was always, and continues to be, organized to a great extent on confessional lines. So, too, were some forms of social intercourse, though these are mostly now integrated. Until recently, mixed marriages were uncommon and disapproved of by many in all denominations.

Traditionally, Irish Catholicism was an austere and puritanical variety, somewhat cold and authoritarian and rather cut off from continental influences. It was a folk church geared to what it saw as the needs and limitations of a peasant people. Many of its clergy themselves came from that background. In 1967, a teacher in a theological seminary explained the situation thus: 'The traditions of the Irish Church bear the marks of a settled rural based culture which changed remarkably little over centuries. The measured pace of rural life gave a tone to the Church and its liturgies and in its style of government.' He was able to add that 'There did not appear to be any good reason why the old ways should not persist until recently'.[23]

The power and influence of the Roman Catholic church increased considerably during the nineteenth century. Its position was further enhanced because it 'managed to build itself into the very vitals of the nation by becoming almost at one with its identity'.[24] The parish clergy, too, were community leaders, the more so since many of them identified themselves – sometimes despite the Hierarchy – with the agrarian and nationalist aims of the country people, and because the church, not being a great landowner, was not a source of envy to land-hungry men. The political effects of this dominant position were immense. The Irish state was from the beginning ostentatiously Catholic. Bunreacht na hÉireann (the Constitution of Ireland), which replaced the negotiated Irish Free State Constitution of 1922, was a self-conscious attempt to combine the liberal-democratic tradition of

Great Britain with Catholic social teaching. The impact of Catholic teaching was always evident in the content of public policy on marriage and divorce, contraception, censorship, health services, and, above all, education. In other areas of policy 'the church' did not exert an influence on a wide range or large number of issues. Surveying more than half a century from independence to 1979, John Whyte concluded that 'the hierarchy is more than just one interest group among many; but it is not so powerful that Ireland must be considered a theocratic state. Some middle view has to be worked out'.[25] There can be no doubt, however, that when the church deemed it vital to its interests, its intervention was conclusive and there was no doubt either about the direction in which its weight was cast. It was almost always conservative: those seeking social change would have dubbed it 'reactionary'.

What kept Irish society so unchanged for so long, however, was neither the political power of the hierarchy nor the social control exercised by the clergy. Rather, it was the wholehearted acceptance by the vast majority of the people of a seemingly immutable set of Catholic ideological and social values. A. J. Humphreys, who was an American Jesuit priest and a sociologist, identified these 'traditional Catholic beliefs' as 'a special brand of Catholicism' – namely, Augustinianism. He found them strongly inculcated in the 'New Dubliners' – that is, country people recently come to the city – whom he studied. These values survived largely unaffected by urbanization. He described this ideology thus:

By comparison with other orthodox views within the general framework of Catholic doctrine, the Augustinian tradition lays relatively greater emphasis on the weakness and evil to which human nature is prone as a result of original sin. By the same token, it attributes relatively less efficacy to natural knowledge and human action and relatively more validity to God's revelation and more power to the action of God's grace. Under the impact of this particular Catholic conception of life, aided and abetted by the traditionalism characteristic of the rural areas, the Irish countryman has acquired a more than average distrust of native human reason. . . . The tradition he inherits tends towards a certain historical and theological positivism in regard to the major truths and values of life, and, together with the other historical factors, has led him to an intensified reliance upon the teaching power of the Church as voiced by the clergy. . . . He inclines to a jaundiced view of sex and a generally ascetic outlook which places a high premium upon continence, penance and, in most spheres of life, on abstemiousness.[26]

It was the persistence of these attitudes and values, their inculcation in generation after generation, and their resilience in the face of individualist, rationalist, and secularist attitudes of the invading industrial urban culture that explain the slow pace of social change and legislative reform. Likewise, it has been the gradual erosion of these attitudes and values which eventually began to take place from the sixties that has more than anything else opened the way to radical changes in Irish society. Although, as we shall see, the intervention of the church, when the need arises, can still be conclusive, its position has begun to change and so, too, its attitudes. Here, as elsewhere, industrialization, urbanization, and modernization generally are altering the Irish situation, and nowhere more than here is that change largely a generational one.

Authoritarian attitudes

A society dominated by values and attitudes such as those described by Humphreys is a society that tends not to question authority. 'Throughout Irish history, social institutions have been highly authoritarian' and, in David Schmitt's view in the early 1970s 'most remain substantially so today'.[27] Authoritarianism traditionally manifested itself particularly in family life, where deference to males, parents, and the elderly was a marked feature; in the church, which was and still is run on hierarchical lines and where deference to the clergy was in the past extreme; and in the school system, where the clergy controlled many aspects of education because the management of elementary schools was almost universally in their hands until 1975, and secondary schools were almost all owned, managed, and largely staffed by them. Charles McCarthy identified the national (elementary level) schoolteacher as the principal socializing agent in the inculcation of the authoritarian attitudes that he described in the late 1960s.[28]

The effect of socialization into authoritarian attitudes could still be seen in survey evidence in the seventies. For example, Father Michael MacGréil's study of Dubliners, which included questions designed to establish 'the extent of authoritarianism as a personality type', showed in his view 'a relatively high degree of authoritarianism among the respondents – when taken as a unit' (see Table 1.1).[29] At about the same time, both Raven and Whelan, in respect of adults, and Pfretzschner and Borock, in respect of secondary school students, found considerable intolerance and a willingness to use force in certain circumstances.[30]

Authoritarian attitudes, it has often been maintained, are not conducive to the successful practice of democracy. However, despite some signs of paternalism on the part of some politicians and bureaucratic attitudes on the part of some public servants, Ireland has been as successful a democracy as many other states that claim to be so. Once the state was established, democratic government was never seriously threatened. In a tense period in 1932 and 1933, when de Valera came to power, there was a threat of the development of rival paramilitary organizations. In the 1930s, also, there were a few signs of activity by individuals with fascist leanings. These manifestations

Table 1.1 **Authoritarian attitudes in Dublin, 1972**

Statement summary	Per cent agreeing (N = 2,271–2,282)
Prostitution is a crime	51.7
Communism should be outlawed in Ireland	53.6
A thing is either right or wrong	48.4
Obedience to clergy is the hallmark of a good RC	44.7
Homosexual behaviour between consenting adults is a crime	39.9
Skinheads should be locked up	39.2
Gardaí (police) should be armed always	31.9
There should be very strict control of Radio Telefís Eireann	28.8
Student protest should be outlawed	25.2
The dole should be abolished	22.8

Source: Derived from M. MacGréil, *Prejudice and Tolerance in Ireland* (Dublin, 1977), p. 413. MacGréil classifies these items as 'authoritarian and "fascist-type" '.

are noteworthy only to illustrate how firmly democratic rather than authoritarian ideas have dominated politics. Seeking to explain this apparent paradox, Schmitt suggested that deferential attitudes helped maintain stability in the early days of the new state's existence. In the Irish case, people were willing to accept the authority of the government in power as legitimate despite the military action of de Valera and his colleagues against it. Thus Schmitt concluded: 'Ironically, authoritarian and personalistic norms have facilitated democratic political development in Ireland'.[31]

More obvious than authoritarianism in politics, however, were the manifestations of other characteristics that were undoubtedly connected with the influence of the church but also with the national and agrarian struggles of the past, and perhaps with the continuing survival of a rural society. These were loyalty and a marked anti-intellectualism in Irish life.

Loyalty

In traditional rural society 'the bases of man's behaviour . . . were kinship, friendship, loyalty and obligation'.[32] In the nationalist movement, loyalty to the concept of the Irish nation became identified for most with faithfulness to one's religion and to the church. The fierce partisanship evoked by the split over the Treaty and the civil war that ushered in the new state put a further premium upon fidelity to one's leaders. Thus, loyalty became and remained an especially important feature in Irish political life. Old comrades who had become political leaders remained loyal one to another. Adherence to one's party was for most a matter of being faithful to its leaders. Throughout his political career, de Valera continued to prefer and stand by his civil war comrades – and their sons.

This loyalty was to persons and institutions rather than to ideas. It reinforced powerfully the natural tendency of people generally in the past to adopt the political affiliations of their parents and to support their chosen parties consistently. Pfretzschner and Borock in 1972 found that seven out of ten of their secondary-school respondents who declared for Fianna Fáil reported a Fianna Fáil father and/or mother, and six out of ten who declared for Fine Gael had a Fine Gael father and/or mother.[33] Today the young are politically more volatile and less inclined to identify closely with a particular political party. Given the circumstances of the origins of the state, party loyalty and strictly adversary politics were inevitably the major features of parliamentary life and became part of the Irish political style. Loyalty, of course, evokes recognition, and the need and desire to reward it led to another feature of political life, the expectation that it would be acknowledged by preferment or a reciprocal service. Such an expectation continues to be experienced by those Irish people who have hardly yet abandoned wholly the norms of traditional rural life.

Anti-intellectualism

The historical and social factors that led to authoritarian attitudes and a stress on the virtue of loyalty also produced in Irish society a marked anti-intellectualism which persisted well into the second half of the century. The church, cut off to a large extent and for a long time from continental European Catholic life and thought, maintained its traditional ways and attitudes to a considerable degree. It was not given to speculation on the great issues that engaged continental Catholics. Maynooth College, its major intellectual centre, was described by Jean Blanchard, a French Catholic writer, in 1958 as 'très conservatrice'.[34] Irish writers and artists in the past were in all too many cases driven to Britain or further afield not only by economic necessity but by the uncongenial and unsympathetic intellectual climate, reflected in phenomena such as ubiquitous signs of tastelessness, censorship, and the cold suspicion of the church typified in this passage from the Archbishop's 1967 *Lenten Regulations for Dublin Diocese:* 'They who give themselves the title of intellectuals have grave need of being constantly warned that a common danger exists that no one may disregard, and that artistic or literary merit does not excuse indulgence in sensuality'.[35]

Inevitably, the process of *aggiornamento* initiated by Pope John XXIII and the Second Vatican Council (1962–65) brought a particularly agonizing reappraisal for the Irish clergy, and they were reluctant to embark upon it. It failed at first to produce the intellectual ferment that was engendered in some other Catholic countries. Many of the clergy, while anxiously awaiting authoritative pronouncements giving them their marching orders to new positions that they earnestly hoped would be very little distance away, preferred to argue that nothing had changed. Much had changed, of course, and those changes were gathering pace all around them. By the late sixties an increasing number of the younger clergy and some of their seniors with wider horizons than their colleagues recognized this and, as we shall see, became part of it.

In politics, a similar anti-intellectualism was for long evident. After the emergence of the new state, a rural, nationalist, and Catholic community neither felt the need for, nor got, bold new initiatives from its leaders. At first, these leaders were absorbed in establishing and consolidating the state on conservative lines. Until the late 1950s, they were more concerned with the outstanding constitutional issues than with new ones. From the 1920s to the 1960s, few enquiries of any depth were made into social and economic problems, and even those were mostly of pedestrian quality or, like the *Report of the Commission on Vocational Organization* (1943), by common consent were ignored. New social services and new legislation tended to follow, *mutatis mutandis*, the existing British pattern. Neither public servants (politician or professional) nor the universities provided new ideas, and there were few attempts to observe and adapt the experience of countries other than the United Kingdom. This anti-intellectual conservatism began to change in the 1960s. The new climate was epitomized in the series of reports on economic and social matters put out by the National Industrial Economic Council and its successor, the National Economic and Social Council, both influential advisory bodies appointed by governments desirous of engaging in economic planning, itself a sign of changed times, and of formulating their policies on as firm a factual basis as possible. When, in 1977, Fine Gael, the second largest political party and traditionally the most conservative, chose Dr Garret FitzGerald, an intellectual pledged to a social-democratic programme, as its new leader, it was obvious that times were indeed changing.

IV

In an article entitled 'Creating a new Irish identity', Desmond Fennell wrote of an 'agreed self image . . . that attained its full and definitive form in the first half of this century'.[36] It was an image of Ireland as

an ancient, virtuously rural, self-sufficient nation, democratic and republican in its politics, comprising (in all but political fact) all the inhabitants of the island, and scattered widely beyond seas and oceans; an anti- imperialist and neutral nation, with a long history of freedom struggle; Gaelic essentially, and engaged in reviving its Gaelic language, while in the interim speaking English; Catholic, in a fundamentalist and missionary manner that stressed the dangers of modern immorality and atheism, but proudly including Protestants and Jews and holding some of these in high honour.[37]

Fennell considered that 'from the end of the fifties onwards it came under sustained and increasing internal assault'.[38] Other writers on Irish society also date the onset of rapid economic, social, and cultural changes from that time. Throughout this chapter we, too, have noted changes from the traditional patterns from mid-century or after. Evidently, Irish society, having remained comparatively stable throughout the entire previous history of the state, began to alter quite quickly. This could be expected to have its impact upon politics. These changes are the subject of the next chapter.

Notes

1   Bunreacht na hÉireann (the Constitution of Ireland), Article 4. The Republic of Ireland Act (1948), Article 2, declares that 'the description of the State shall be the "Republic" of Ireland'.
2   R. Breen, D. F. Hannan, D. B. Rottman and C. T. Whelan, *Understanding Contemporary Ireland: State, Class and Development in the Republic of Ireland* (Dublin, 1990), p. 98.
3   *Ibid.*, p. 8.
4   A. Giddens, *The Class Structure of the Advanced Societies*, (London, 1973), p. 17.
5   J. G. A. Pocock, 'The case of Ireland truly stated: revolutionary politics in the context of increasing stabilisation' (Unpublished paper, Department of History, Washington University, St. Louis, Mo., 1966).
6   B. Farrell, *The Founding of Dáil Éireann: Parliament and Nation-Building* (Dublin, 1971), p. xv.
7   *Ibid.*, p. 78.
8   J. Blanchard, *Le droit ecclésiastique contemporain d'Irlande* (Paris, 1958), p. 11.
9   A. W. Orridge, 'Explanations of Irish nationalism: a review and some suggestions', in *Journal of the Conflict Research Society*, 1 (1977), p. 49.
10 O. McDonagh, *Ireland: The Union and its Aftermath* (London, 1977), p. 73.
11 P. A. Pfretzschner and D. M. Borock, 'Political socialization of the Irish secondary school student', in J. Raven *et al.*, *Political Culture in Ireland: the Views of Two Generations* (Dublin, 1976), p. 132.
12 E. E. Davis and R. Sinnott, *Attitudes in the Republic of Ireland Relevant to the Northern Problem* (Economic and Social Research Institute, Dublin, 1979), p. 149. Their findings were strongly challenged by politicians and some of their professional colleagues.
13 E. Rumpf, *Nationalismus und Sozialismus in Irland* (Meisenheim am Glan, 1959), p. 67.
14 T. Shanin, 'The peasantry as a political factor', *Sociological Review*, 14 (1966),p. 7.
15 *Ibid.*, pp.10 and 17.
16 P. Commins, *Ireland: a Sociological Profile in* P. Clancy, S. Drudy, K. Lynch and L. O. Dowd, (eds.), (Dublin, 1986), p. 52.

17   A. J. Humphreys, *New Dubliners: Urbanization and the Irish Family* (London, 1966), p. 12.
18   D. Schmitt, *The Irony of Irish Democracy* (Lexington, 1973), p. 55.
19   *Ibid.*
20   P. M. Sacks, *The Donegal Mafia: an Irish Political Machine* (New Haven and London, 1976), p. 28.
21   E. Larkin, 'Church, state and nation in modern Ireland', *American Historical Review*, 80, (1975), pp. 1267 and 1276.
22   T. Inglis, 'How religious are Irish university students?' *Doctrine and Life*, 30 (1978), p. 404. Detailed results of the survey are given in Marie Nic Ghiolla Phadraig, 'Religion in Ireland – preliminary analysis', *Social Studies*, 5 (1976), pp. 113–80.
23   Rev. Patrick J. Brophy, Professor of Dogmatic Theology at Carlow Theological Seminary, quoted in *Sunday Independent*, 29 Oct. 1967.
24   E. Larkin, 'Church, state and nation in modern Ireland,' *American Historical Review*, 80 (1975), p. 1244.
25   J. Whyte, *Church and State in Modern Ireland, 1923–1979*, 2nd edn (London and Dublin, 1980), p. 370.
26   Humphreys, *New Dubliners,* p. 26.
27   D. Schmitt, *Irony of Irish Democracy* p. 44.
28   See C. McCarthy, *The Distasteful Challenge* (Dublin, 1968), p. 109.
29   Micheál MacGréil, *Prejudice and Tolerance in Ireland* (Dublin, 1977), p. 525.
30   See J. Raven, C. T. Whelan, P. A. Pfretzschner and D. M. Borock, *Political Culture in Ireland: the Views of Two Generations* (Dublin, 1976), pp. 50 and 127.
31   Schmitt, *Irony of Irish Democracy*, p. 3.
32   Sacks, *The Donegal Mafia,* p. 48.
33   In Raven *et al.*, *Political Culture in Ireland*, p. 107.
34   Blanchard, *Le droit ecclésiastique contemporain d'Irlande*, p. 86.
35   Quoted in *Irish Times*, 6 Feb. 1967.
36   *Studies*, 75, p. 395.
37   *Ibid.*, p. 396.
38   *Ibid.*, p. 395.

CHAPTER 2

The Changing Face (and Mind?) of Ireland

I

In Chapter 1, we attempted to identify the major influences that contributed to the formation of the political culture of the Irish in the middle of this century and beyond. Time and again it was noted that, in the second half of the century, the traditional, stable attitudes associated with nationalism and with the lingering pre-industrial society, together with the values and life style inculcated by an austere and authoritarian church, began to be eroded. Changed circumstances and new influences increasingly undermined these three foundation pillars on which that stable society had rested. In this chapter, we shall explore the changing face (and mind?) of Ireland. 'Changing' because, although Irish people to varying degrees have become assimilated to the ways of life and thought characteristic of Western European industrialized countries, the metamorphosis is still not complete. Although they are much weakened and eroded, the pillars have not yet collapsed completely.

II

Richard Breen and his colleagues, in *Understanding Contemporary Ireland* (1990), characterized it as 'a country which industrialized late and rapidly'.[1] Whereas much of war-torn Western Europe had to be renewed after 1945, the neutral, insulated Irish did not experience their post-war modernization until much later. The publication of the *Programme for Economic Expansion* in 1958 is often cited as marking the end of one era in Irish life and the beginning of the next. Appropriately so: the work largely of civil servants endorsed by their political masters, it advocated and evoked a major change in political and administrative thinking about economic and social development. Keynesian economics came – belatedly – into favour, and the state itself began actively to promote industrialization and trade and, in particular, to encourage foreign investment. Aided by favourable conditions in Western Europe generally and later, from 1973, membership of the European Economic Community, Ireland experienced a period of economic growth more rapid than anything in its previous history. Economic and social indicators which, significantly, now began to assume great importance in the minds of politicians, administrators, and journalists, illustrate the extent and speed of these changes.

In the decade 1961–70, industrial production grew at an annual average rate of 6.6 per cent, as fast as the best of those Western European countries with which Ireland was to be associated in the EEC. In the decade 1971–80, the annual average growth was 4.5 per cent, almost twice that of the Community average; and in the eighties it was yet faster. Exports of goods and services, on which the country relies more than most of its neighbours, averaged 36 per cent of gross domestic product between 1961 and 1970; 44 per cent in 1971–80; and in 1989 it was 67 per cent. With growth of this order the country prospered despite the decline of agriculture, itself cushioned by the benefits of the Common Agricultural Policy (CAP). Gross domestic product per head of population rose at an anual average rate of 4.3 per cent in the sixties; 4.5 per cent in the seventies – one and a half times that of the Community as a whole – and though it grew less fast in the recession-hit eighties, economic growth in the thirty years from 1960 was such that the standard of living of most people was transformed. Prosperity can be measured by such outward and visible indices as television-set ownership, telephones and cars (see Table 2.1), and more generally by overall consumption patterns such as those used in Table 2.2.

Table 2.1 *Telephones, motor vehicles, and television licences, 1962 and 1984, 1987 and 1988 respectively*

	1962	1984	1987	1988
Telephones	172,340	894,138	–	–
Motor vehicles	354,905	–	959,753	–
TV licences	92,675	–	–	759,711

Source: *Statistical Abstracts of Ireland* (Central Statistics Office, Dublin 1989).
These are the latest figures available at the time of going to press.

Table 2.2 *Percentage increase in consumption expenditure 1970–1984*

Food, drink, and tobacco	14
Recreation, education, culture	26
Housing	23
Transport and communications	31

Source: Derived from *Europe in Figures*, 1989–90 edition, Eurostat (Luxembourg, 1989).

Rapid industrialization and rising prosperity (for most though not for all) hastened the movement from country to town and from agriculture to industrial and service occupations. In 1966, the population was half urban, half rural: by 1986, almost two-thirds of the population lived in towns. The flight from the land, which had been gradual though inexorable from the first days of the state until the middle of the century, increased in pace. Just after the 1939–45 war, nearly half of Irish work people were in agriculture: in 1990, about 15 per cent.

Industrialization, economic expansion, and urbanization on this scale, together with a massive decline in agricultural employment could not help but alter the pattern of social stratification. In the view of Richard Breen and his colleagues: 'the underlying processes of class formation were sufficient to engineer a new class structure'.[2] They have identified and measured these changes (see Table 2.3).

Table 2.3 **Changes in employment opportunities by class, 1951–81**

Class category		1951/61	1961/71	1971/81
1	Small farmers (<50 acres)	−55,000	−51,500	−47 400
2	Agricultural labourers	−30,200	−24,500	−14,500
3	Unskilled manual labourers	−16,500	−67,000	−18 800
4	Skilled manual labourers	+ 2,200	+35,400	+35,000
5	Upper non-manual	+11,200	+25,600	+44,000
6	Lower non-manual	−1,900	+18,900	+23,000
Total decline (1+2+3)		−101,700	−143,000	−80,700
Total increase (4+5+6)		+11,500	+79,900	+102,000

Source: R. Breen *et al.*, *Understanding Contemporary Ireland; State, Class and Development in the Republic of Ireland* (Dublin, 1990), p. 60.

They comprised, on the one hand, a large growth in professional and technical middle-class employments and in skilled manual labour; and, on the other, the creation of two groups of stranded 'residuals', the one urban, the other rural. The first are farmers on small and unviable farms, anomalies in a world of commercial farming and a rapidly urbanizing society: the second are workers without skills, a large proportion of whom are unemployed due to a combination of inadequate educational opportunities and the industrial development policies of the state.[3] The emergence of a new pattern of social stratification such as this could be expected to have social repercussions and, perhaps, political consequences.

This industrial revolution typically encompassed another social transformation. Once it got under way, there was a dramatic increase in the number of women in the labour force. Of course, women on family farms had always worked at agricultural tasks: now, as they

hastened to leave the rigours of farm and rural life, they joined the
increasing number of women generally going into industry and the
services. Participation by women in the labour force which had been
very low by the standards of Western industrialized countries
increased from 5 per cent in 1961 to 8 per cent in 1971 and then
rapidly to 20 per cent in 1984 and, thence, to 32 per cent in 1990, the
increase among young married women being 'particularly dramatic'.[4]
This development, made possible by the increase in employment
possibilities as new industries and services were started, was both a
cause and a result of great changes in the position of women in Irish
society. Like class changes, these too might be expected to have social
and political consequences.

III

Demographic, social, and economic changes of this order and at this
pace cannot but have a considerable impact upon a people's culture. It
will be the greater if, as happened in the Irish case, they coincide with
other changes that widen people's experience and enlarge their
horizons. Not the least were those that occurred in the Roman Catholic
church following the Second Vatican Council (1962–65) and the
significant reforms there initiated. The Second Vatican Council
touched on topics that had hitherto not been regarded by most Irish
people as matters even for discussion, let alone being open to change –
matters involving the liturgy, relations between the clergy and the laity,
marriage, divorce, contraception, attitudes to other religions, and the
role of the state. Urban middle-class people in particular began to
question the existing rules of their church and to adopt a new, more
independent attitude to their clergy as they rejected rules and
relationships that they thought suited only to a rural, peasant society.
So, too, gradually did more and more of the growing industrial work
force with its increasing proportion of women of child-bearing age.
The consequences were seen in an increased number of marriages at
an earlier age than hitherto and, with the rapid spread of contraception,
a marked decline in the fertility rate. These were accompanied by
demands for the kinds of policy reforms that have troubled many
countries far less traditional and religion-dominated than Ireland.

The prospect, and from 1973 the fact, of membership of the
European Communities was yet another engine of change. The country
was brought face to face with unpleasant economic realities, but at the
same time possibilities of growth and prosperity were opened up.
Ireland would henceforth move in the same direction and at roughly
the same pace as the other Community countries. It was no longer
'une île derrière une île' insulated from continental Europe: on the
contrary, inevitably though slowly, the Community would envelop it.
This was yet another process that was bound to have considerable

social and political consequences. Irish people began to notice, many for the first time, what was happening and how people lived 'on the continent'. Foreign travel (from the sixties), student militancy (at the end of the sixties) and women's liberation were associated phenomena.

The legal obligations of membership of the Communities had a considerable effect on Irish economic and social life, not least in respect of rights issues in employment, non-discrimination, and equal pay. Immediately obvious were the material benefits to farmers of the Common Agricultural Policy. Rises in agricultural incomes were dramatic for the commercial sector of farming, though membership only served to confirm and hasten the 'marginalization' of the unviable sector.

The addition of a continental European dimension to Irish life had its converse in a waning of the British influence. The prospect of this was indeed one of the reasons adduced for joining the Communities by some leading proponents. Although the timing of Ireland's accession was governed by British entry, the step was a major constitutional and political change to which for the first time in Irish experience the United Kingdom had contributed little. The Community treaties, in particular the Economic Community Treaty, became in effect a second Irish Constitution. Henceforth, the imperatives of European Community law and policies, and because Ireland was relatively so disadvantaged, the impact of a great in-flow of Community funds would increasingly displace the influence of British attitudes and practice.

The impact of Community membership was nowhere more obvious than in trade and finance. The structure of trade altered markedly. In 1958, 77 per cent of Irish exports went to the United Kingdom; in 1988, 35 per cent. The break in the link between the Irish punt and the British pound and the linking of the Irish currency with the European Monetary System in 1979, together with the development of an Irish stock exchange and money market, went a long way to complete the process of fiscal and financial reorientation from London to Dublin which had begun a half century before. Nevertheless, the British connection is still strong: the United Kingdom is still Ireland's biggest customer and its main supplier; British interest rates are still as important for Irish business as those of the Community countries; what happens to the British pound still matters as much as the movement of the Deutschmark. More generally, in 1990, 35 per cent of Irish TV viewers watched British programmes; the Dublin–London route had Europe's second largest number of air passengers; the readership of British newspapers was actually increasing again; and so on: the list was endless.

When it comes to basic political issues such as defence, neutrality, and sovereignty which have now to be viewed in a European Community context, it is obvious that the decoupling process is still far from complete. In particular, as always, Northern Ireland, the unfinished business on the Irish nationalist agenda, continues to have a distorting influence on the normal development of Anglo-Irish relations. In the late 1960s, the problem of the North was exacerbated with the outbreak in the province of guerrilla war and civil disobedience that have continued ever since.

Although people in the Republic have never ceased to show an irredentist concern about the position of Northern Catholics, not least those in British gaols, it is clear that nationalist perceptions have altered and the intensity of feeling has lessened. From the late 1960s, there was a slowly growing awareness that the core of the problem lies in the existence on the island not of one community with a dissident minority, mostly aliens, but of two communities each with its own traditions, loyalties, and legitimate aspirations. People in the Republic came increasingly to realize that if a united Ireland is ever to become a reality, it must be with the consent of Unionists and will require changes in those of their laws and social conditions that most affront Northerners. This involves jettisoning some nationalist shibboleths and modifying measures that reflect specifically Catholic attitudes and values.

Notwithstanding the fact that Northern Ireland is continuously on the political agenda, the more so as a result of the constant political consultation and cooperation under the Anglo-Irish Agreement, poll evidence suggests that it came very low in the political priorities of most people in the late eighties. At the 1989 general election it was mentioned among important issues by less than 3 per cent of respondents. Although many people would still like to see a united Ireland – in 1987, 67 per cent of the respondents in a Market Research Bureau of Ireland (MRBI) survey viewed it as 'something to hope for' – 60 per cent saw this as 'unlikely ever to happen or not for at least 100 years'. The percentage of both those who hope and expect it to happen was in continuous decline.[5]

So also is extreme nationalism. *The Irish Report of the European Value Systems Study*, the field work for which was done in 1981, identified a very small group of extreme nationalists, people who display a high level of political activism and a readiness to resort to violence, who constituted less than 2 per cent of the sample. They were mostly in unskilled manual jobs or unemployed.[6] In *The Dynamics of Irish Politics* (1989), Paul Bew and his colleagues concluded that 'continued modernization and realignment in the policies of the Republic . . . threatens finally to consign militant republicanism to the ghettos of Northern Ireland'.[7] The vote for Sinn Féin, the political wing of the IRA, fell from 1.9 per cent at the 1987 general election to 1.2 per cent in 1989. The tiny subculture of which we spoke in Chapter 1 does still exist, though. Occasional incidents during the eighties showed that 'safe houses' were still available for Republican extremists 'on the run', and that in some places near the Northern Ireland border significant numbers of people supported paramilitary activities.

If industrialization and urbanization were the parents of the rapid cultural changes that are the subject of this chapter, television was the midwife. The importance of TV lies in its ability to project new ideas and influences right into the home in a particularly insistent manner, together with the blandishments of the advertisers of the consumerist society. Just as industrialization came late but rapidly to Ireland, so too did television: a national service was not begun until 1962. Although people in rural areas, especially the poorer farmers, were slower than the urban population to acquire sets, ownership and viewing had reached saturation by 1980.

'Television has without doubt been a major instrument in Ireland's conversion to consumerism.'[8] Programmes reflected to a considerable extent the urban metropolitan values of the majority of the broadcasters and programme makers. From the first, they 'tended to adopt both the style and some of the independence they detected in the neighbouring British model' with whom they were in competition for viewers.[9] Furthermore, 'there was a conscious iconoclasm that breached at least some of the established conventions of Irish society; the mere fact that those in authority were seen to be asked questions (no matter how deferentially) was an important advance'.[10] The impact on politics was considerable, as we shall see, and as in some other Western countries there developed a state of continuous tension between broadcasters and politicians that continues to this day.

IV

The agents of change identified in the preceding section appear to a considerable extent to have reinforced one another in their impact upon Irish social life and – what is our particular concern – its politics. Although Ireland would have to change a great deal more than it has so far before it could be labelled 'a pluralist society', let alone 'a secular society', this is the direction in which it is undoubtedly moving. The pace of the change, however, is problematic and its extent has often been overestimated. The political experiences of the eighties and particularly the referenda of 1983 (on abortion) and 1986 (on divorce) demonstrated the limited extent of the changes in public opinion up to that time and showed dramatically how liberals, particularly wishful-thinking, urban liberals and even some leading politicians, could misjudge the state of opinion in the community.

Secularization is 'that process by which many sections of society and culture are removed from the influence of religious values, institutions and symbols'.[11] In a secular society there is a decline in religious practice, and individuals decide for themselves what is right and wrong. These attitudes were increasingly being displayed in Ireland from the sixties, the lead being taken by middle-class intellectuals, particularly those working in broadcasting, journalism and teaching, and by more and more young people in each generation. Indices such as attendance at Mass, the extent of religious belief and confidence in the church provide some measure of this phenomenon (see Table 2.4). What is notable perhaps is not how great but how modest these changes were: and for a very good reason. Ireland, as we have observed, is one of those countries (Poland is another) where the church has been closely identified with nationalism and, as David Martin points out, such countries 'remain areas of high practice and belief. . . . The myth of identity is strengthened further wherever the dominated group have been at the border with another faith.'[12] In these circumstances, the tendency of modern societies to become secularized is slowed down by the continuing hold of religion upon the people. Inevitably, that hold will eventually be loosened, and as this takes place signs of strain in the community will be apparent. Recent Irish experience demonstrates this process and, in the words of Professor Liam Ryan, 'the years from 1960 . . . can best be described in sociological language as years of "tension management", tension between the old and the new . . . between the ways of God and the ways of the world'.[13]

Table 2.4 *Practice of religion, beliefs and confidence in the church (in percentages)*

		Age groups						
Church going	All.	18–24,	25–34,	35–44,	45–54,	55–64,	65–74,	75+
Weekly or oftener	82	76	72	81	91	90	93	90
Beliefs								
Life after death	76	67	69	74	83	82	89	90
There is only								
one true religion	46	31	36	44	54	55	67	70
Confidence in the church								
A great deal	52	27	43	49	64	62	79	85
Quite a lot	26	36	26	30	23	27	12	7
Not very much/none	22	36	31	21	12	11	9	6

Source: Derived from M. Fogarty, L. Ryan and J. Lee, *Irish Values and Attitudes: the Irish Report of the European Value Systems Study* (Dublin, 1984), Tables 1(ii), 2(i) and 2(ii).

Of course, the church too was changing. Beginning in the sixties, the process of *aggiornamento* brought an increasing tolerance of other religions and ecumenical attitudes. The fact that the Catholic church no longer sought special recognition from the state nor a special status had particular relevance for Ireland. The pressure of modernization upon the church's hold on the community was exacerbated by the worsening of the Northern Ireland situation in the late sixties and the growing recognition of Southerners that the Protestant traditions and mores of the majority community there had to be accommodated. To do this involved reforms directed towards creating a pluralist society. They were spelled out by Garret FitzGerald in 1972 in *Towards a New Ireland*, and included among others the removal from the Constitution of a section of Article 44, the 'special position' clause, and the bar on divorce legislation; the removal of the ban on the import and sale of contraceptives; and the relaxation of the censorship laws. In any case, liberal reformers like FitzGerald himself argued that these were necessary reforms to create a pluralist society in the context of the Republic itself in order belatedly to do justice to its non-Catholic minority.

Some of these reforms could be made wholly within principles now accepted by the modernizing Roman Catholic church. The 'special position' clause was removed from the Constitution in 1972, Cardinal Conway having signalled the church's consent, which, significantly, he gave in a specifically Northern Ireland context.[14] A redefinition of the church's view on church–state relations followed in 1973:

There are many things which the Catholic Church holds to be morally wrong and no one has ever suggested, least of all the Church herself, that they should be prohibited by the State. . . . What the legislators have to decide is whether a change in the law would, on balance, do more harm than good, by damaging the character of the society for which they are responsible. . . . We emphasise that it is not a matter for the bishops to decide whether the law should be changed or not. That is a matter for the legislators, after a conscientious consideration of all the factors involved.[15]

The application of this principle was another matter, however, when it came to contraception, divorce, and abortion. The Irish bishops viewed with alarm the trends in Western society: in Rome, too, opinion was hardening. When in the middle eighties issues concerning divorce and abortion were put to the people in referenda, the bishops and clergy, as was their right and duty, made it abundantly clear to politicians and people where Catholic duty lay. In doing so, not all of them confined themselves within the 1973 principle and some spoke in distinctly pre-Vatican II terms. For most people, the clergy's signals were conclusive. The outcomes in the two referenda in 1983 and 1986 were strikingly similar: two-thirds of Irish voters paid heed to their clergy when Catholic values were an issue. As data collected by the MRBI in 1983 and 1987 suggest, 'home and Church are seen as the main sources of influence on marriage and family life; the Church itself followed by the home, are most influential on divorce and abortion' (See Table 2.5).[16] In Michael Fogarty's words: 'Ireland remains an outstandingly religious country',[17] and in this respect still stands, in marked contrast with most of the other Community countries. To the question in the *Eurobarometer* survey of November 1989, 'In your opinion in this list [displayed], which are the great causes which nowadays are worth the trouble of taking risks and making sacrifices for?', 35 per cent of Irish respondents chose 'religious faith' as compared with the Community average of 12 per cent.[18]

Table 2.5 *Sources of influence on matters of marriage and family, divorce, and abortion, 1983 and 1987 (percentages)*

		Home & family	Church	Media	Government & politicians	Don't know
Marriage and family	1983	55	31	7	1	6
	1987	58	29	7	1	5
Divorce	1983	23	40	17	4	16
	1987	33	40	14	3	10
Abortion	1983	23	39	16	7	15
	1987	28	47	12	2	11

Source: *Éire Inniu: an MRBI Perspective on Irish Society Today*, Market Research Bureau of Ireland (Dublin, 1987), p. 13.

Although 'there is no tidal wave of modernization in the Republic', as Paul Bew and his colleagues put it,[19] there is evidence that the tide is in fact changing generation by generation. In 1984, Fogarty and his colleagues concluded from their data that there is a 'shift across generations from stronger to weaker acceptance of orthodox beliefs and religious practice and of the authority of the Church'.[20] Likewise, the MRBI 1987 survey results suggested a marked decline in the influence of the church upon younger people. It is in data like those in Table 2.6 that we can see the changing mind of Ireland.

Table 2.6 **The church as a source of influence**

	Age				
	18–24	25–34	35–49	50–64	65+
On marriage and family life	16	22	29	38	47
On abortion	4	39	46	55	62
On divorce	27	35	41	49	56

Source: Derived from *Éire Inniu: an MRBI Perspective on Irish Society Today*, Market Research Bureau of Ireland (Dublin, 1987), Table 1B2

V

Evidently, modernization has not as yet taken the Irish far down the road to being a genuinely pluralist and secular society, with all that this implies for political policies and practices. It might be thought, however, that the impact of the 'new class structure' identified by Breen and his colleagues (see above p. 25) would be bound to change attitudes. If such change is to be measured by evidence of a developing class basis in politics, the conclusion must be: 'not so far'.

Although Irish party politics have been strongly partisan and adversarial, differences were not based on ideologies to any great extent. Political behaviour during the period of modernization does not suggest that there have been fundamental changes in popular opinion. Coalition governments comprising the Labour Party, a comparatively unideological, mildly left-wing party, and Fine Gael, the party which is generally considered to have a strong conservative wing in its membership, were in office for four periods during the seventies and eighties. Fianna Fáil, the biggest party by far, had become a 'catch-all party' by the middle of the century and it remained so, attracting support from all classes. Industrialization and urbanization have not so far had the effect of strengthening the left. Survey evidence consistently shows that Fianna Fáil attracts more working-class support than the left parties (the Labour Party and the Workers' Party) put together. The upper and lower limits of 'left' votes in the six general elections between 1977 and 1989 (10–15 per cent) were still within the upper and lower limits experienced between 1932 and 1977 (8–17 per cent). Even the recession and mounting unemployment of the eighties did not alter the pattern significantly.

The fact that the Irish trade-union movement does not have a strong class-based ideology deprives left parties of what in many industrialized countries is a natural reservoir of committed left supporters. It is the absence of such class-based cleavages that goes far to explain the persistence of traditional attitudes. Paul Bew and his colleagues summed up the experience of the last quarter of a century accurately: 'neither economic growth nor crisis helped the left'.[21]

Not only has there been no marked development of class cleavages in the modernizing Ireland but, on the contrary, there has been a marked disposition to conceptualize economic growth and development in national rather than class terms. This was to continue and develop an approach advocated and pursued by Seán Lemass, de Valera's first lieutenant and successor, from the middle of the century. A decade of 'National Wage Agreements' in the seventies was followed by two 'National Understandings' and, in the late eighties, a 'Programme for National Recovery'. All involved the state, employer organizations, and the Irish Congress of Trade Unions in tripartite or corporatist-type structures and procedures (see below, p. 126–128).

It is the same story so far as the position of women is concerned. The pace of the changes triggered by the influx of women into the work force that came with industrialization reflected a culture that was not in revolution but only slowly adapting. A Commission on the Status of Women in 1972 sought to have the position of Irish women brought up to the levels generally obtaining in industrialized Western Europe. The position of women became and remained a permanent item on the political agenda in the seventies and eighties, a sign as much of slow progress in this area as of quickly changing attitudes. In 1990, it was necessary to set up another inquiry into the status of women. Not surprisingly: the average wage of women industrial workers as a proportion of that of men in 1990 was still only 59 per cent. In 1990 also, Gemma Hussey, then Minister for Education, publicly withdrew her acceptance of an invitation to speak at the Charter Day dinner of the Royal College of Surgeons in Ireland when she learned of its 'male only' guest rule.[22] It was no wonder that an MRBI survey in 1987 found that over two-thirds of Irish women believed that 'women are not treated equally with men' (and perhaps no wonder, either, that four out of ten men thought that they were!).[23] No wonder either that the *Eurobarometer* inquiry in the same year into people's perceptions of the ideal roles of husband and wife indicated that the proposition that 'husband has a job: wife runs the home' was favoured by more Irish people (39 per cent) than by the people of any other member country save Luxembourg.[24] In the light of these attitudes, one would not expect to find women making great inroads into politics. Between 1922 and 1977, 4 per cent of those elected to Dáil Éireann were women: at the 1989 general election thirteen women (8 per cent) were returned. Paul Bew and his colleagues concluded that, although 'feminism was an important liberalizing influence on the dominant moral and social values . . . it did not always translate into the legislative area, remaining principally an urban – if not south Dublin – phenomenon'.[25]

VI

At the beginning of the 1980s, Michael Fogarty concluded that the findings of the *Irish Values and Attitudes* study demonstrated 'the continuing quality and solidity of so much of Irish life' although there might be 'cracks in the fabric'.[26] At the end of the decade, Paul Bew and his colleagues came to the same conclusion:

The profound changes in social and economic life over [the 1970s and 80s] were not reflected in the emergence of radical politics, industrial militancy or in any fundamental change in the nature of Irish society. Ireland remained a conservative society imbued with the values of Catholicism, nationalism and ruralism, although less stridently so than in earlier periods.[27]

This solidity (Fogarty) or conservatism (Bew) seems to embrace values that are important for politics as for so much else. However, survey findings such as those we have cited in this chapter ought to be viewed with caution. Whatever their intrinsic value might be, too much should not be inferred from them. What is important is how people behave. The question upon which we should concentrate is: how well do the people of the Republic with their particular combination of characteristics and traditions practise democracy? This book aims to present some of the evidence upon which an answer to this question might be based. It concentrates upon the institutions and procedures of government and the practice of politics. A major artefact of such practice is a democratic constitution that provides a framework of limited government. The Constitution is therefore a natural starting place and the subject of the next chapter.

Notes

1 R. Breen, D. F. Hannan, D. B. Rottman and C. T. Whelan, *Understanding Contemporary Ireland: State, Class and Development in the Republic of Ireland* (Dublin and London, 1990), p. xi.
2 *Ibid.*, p. 6.
3 *Ibid.*, p. 59 and pp. 155 ff.
4 *Ibid.*, p. 117.
5 *Éire Inniu: an MRBI Perspective on Irish Society Today*, Market Research Bureau of Ireland Ltd (Dublin, 1987), p. 48. For evidence of the decline, see Charts 5A(i) and 5B(i).
6 See M. Fogarty, L. Ryan and J. Lee, *Irish Values and Attitudes: the Irish Report of the European Value Systems Study* (Dublin, 1984), p. 70.
7 P. Bew, E. Hazelkorn and H. Patterson, *The Dynamics of Irish Politics* (London, 1989), p. 224.
8 T. Brown, *Ireland, a Social and Cultural History, 1922–79* (London, 1981), p. 261.
9 B. Farrell, 'The mass media and the 1977 campaign', in H. R. Penniman (ed.), *Ireland at the Polls: The Dáil Elections of 1977* (Washington, DC, 1978), p. 106.
10 *Ibid.*
11 L. Ryan in Fogarty *et al.*, *Irish Values and Attitudes*, p. 104.
12 D. Martin, *A General Theory of Secularization* (Oxford, 1978), p. 107.
13 In Fogarty, *Irish Values and Attitudes*, pp. 101–2.
14 See *Irish Times*, 23 Sept. 1969.
15 Statement of the Irish Episcopal Conference, 25 Nov. 1973.
16 *MRBI 21st Anniversary Poll*, Market Research Bureau of Ireland (Dublin, 1983), p. 15. See also *Éire Inniu, an MRBI Perspective on Irish Society Today* (Dublin, 1987), p. 13 and Table 1 B/2 in the Statistical Tables.
17 Fogarty, *Irish Values and Attitudes*, p. 8.
18 *Eurobarometer, Public Opinion in the European Community*, Special Study on Racism and Xenophobia (Commission of the European Communities, Brussels, Nov. 1989).
19 Bew *et al.*, *The Dynamics of Irish Politics*, p. 217.
20 Fogarty, *Irish Values and Attitudes*, p. 12.
21 Bew *et al.*, *The Dynamics of Irish Politics*, p. 197.
22 See G. Hussey, *At the Cutting Edge: Cabinet Diaries 1982–1987* (Dublin, 1990), pp. 141–2.
23 *Éire Inniu*, p. 11.
24 *Eurobarometer*, no. 27 (June 1987), Table A 38.

25 Bew *et al.*, *The Dynamics of Irish Politics*, p. 185.
26 Fogarty, *Irish Values and Attitudes*, pp. 89 and 91.
27 Bew *et al.*, *The Dynamics of Irish Politics*, p. 185.

CHAPTER 3

The Framework of Limited Government

I

The desire to limit the power of public authorities and to define the rights and duties of the citizens is a characteristic feature of the liberal-democratic world. To effect such a limitation involves formulating and formalizing the basic and most important of these powers, rights and duties in rules of law that have special significance and status. Thus, 'the constitution for most countries in the world, is a selection of legal rules which govern the government of that country and which have been embodied in a document'.[1] In Ireland, as in most countries, such a document is regarded as being both the fundamental law of the state and 'a kind of higher law'.[2] It is both an instrument by which public authorities can be controlled and a point of reference in disputes over rights and duties.

A constitution thus defined is, however, no more than a *selection* of rules that define the functions and powers of public authorities, govern the more formal political procedures and relationships and enunciate the basic rights and duties of the citizens. At best, it will define only the general pattern of political and legal organization and relationships. The day-to-day operations of government will make necessary both the creation of a body of law dealing with matters too detailed to include in the constitution and the development of an ever-growing collection of laws or other legal instruments, court rulings, and statements of practice or norms that are not formal rules at all. For lawyers and political scientists this collection, too, is part of 'the constitution' in a second and wider sense of the word. There is merit in this: no selection of rules embodied in a document can be operated in isolation. The document is thus only a part, albeit the key part, of the whole system of government.

Unless a country is governed by an alien power that ignores indigenous traditions, its constitution at the time it is written is likely to reflect the political beliefs, values, and standards of the inhabitants, or at least those of the dominant group. Thus it might well be an important source of information about the political beliefs, values, and standards of its makers and those for whom they spoke. Going further, one might judge the worth of a constitution at any time by the extent to which it does reflect the political beliefs, values, and standards of the community. In so far as it does, it is a political force of considerable influence.

However much a constitution at its inception mirrors the basic values of a community, changes in the community's values and in the pattern of its social and political life, and new ideas about the rights and duties of citizens, will cause the original wording of the document to fit less well in places. Then, new meanings are given to the words; they might be stretched by ingenious judges to cover situations never contemplated by its authors. Additions and subtractions might have to be made. Unless it is constantly changed, whether by way of judicial interpretation or by formal amendment, a constitution will increasingly contain matter that is outmoded or inappropriate. Sometimes, if a constitution was never 'a good fit' or if times change radically, a new constitution altogether might be needed.

As it happens, the constitution in force in Ireland today, Bunreacht na hÉireann (the Constitution of Ireland), did, when it was enacted in 1937, and to a great extent still does, reflect the values of the great majority of the people in the state. One can easily detect in it many of the 'basic influences' that we identified in Chapter 1. Equally, some of the changes made in it by the courts and by amendment reflect changes in Irish society that have occurred since 1937 and particularly in the last twenty-five years. By 1990, more than fifty years since its enactment, changes were being increasingly canvassed.

The accession of Ireland to the European Communities in 1973 brought the state into 'a new type of international organization with much greater powers over member countries than those traditionally given to international institutions'.[3] A new body of law, including the Treaties of Accession themselves and the fruits of fifteen years of Community activity, had to be received into Irish law. Community institutions have continued to make laws that either apply directly in Ireland or necessitate compliance by the Irish government and parliament by the enactment of appropriate domestic legislation. Community law, to which Irish law, including Bunreacht na hÉireann, must be adapted, adds another dimension to the framework of limited government within which the Irish government operates. It can hardly fail to have an impact upon the development of the Constitution itself.

A constitution, though a collection of basic rules and a point of reference, should be viewed as an adaptable instrument of government. In fact, the constitution in force today – Bunreacht na hÉireann – was itself an adaptation of earlier constitutions; its enactment marked an important stage in the evolution of the state. To understand both the occasion for it and its contents, it is necessary to see it as the successor of two previous constitutions – the Constitution of Dáil Éireann (1919) and the Constitution of the Irish Free State (1922). All three were the products of the same process of emancipation from British rule and influence. Each succeeding version reflected another stage reached in the evolution of an Irish state with constitutional symbols and international status broadly acceptable to the majority of the population. They thus reflected evolution rather than revolution. Perhaps that evolution is still not complete. Many Irish people still see unfinished business in Northern Ireland. Ireland's next constitution, like its predecessors, might be occasioned by a change in the position of Northern Ireland and in Anglo-Irish relations. Such developments, if they ever occur, will require changes on such a scale that might well necessitate recasting Bunreacht na hÉireann.

II

The Sinn Féin candidates who were elected at the general election to the United Kingdom parliament in December 1918 and who constituted themselves Dáil Éireann in January 1919 were members of an independence movement engaged in active struggle. Their political tactics involved establishing at least the basic structures of a government and administration and inducing their fellow countrymen and women, with the help of the military wing as required, to give allegiance to these and to repudiate British government. The formation and operation of a 'government' and the meetings of the Dáil itself were part of their campaign; so, too, was their constitution, the Constitution of Dáil Éireann.[4] In such circumstances, the Dáil Constitution was not seriously intended to meet all the needs of an effectively operating independent state; rather, it was essentially part of a publicity exercise. It was short, its five sections covering the appointment of a chairman, the competence of the Dáil, the appointment of a Prime Minister and a government and their powers, the provision of funds, and the audit of expenditure. In addition, the Dáil passed a 'Declaration of Independence' and a 'Democratic Programme' of rights and duties that reaffirmed and elaborated what had been contained in the proclamation of the Republic on Easter Day, 1916.

These enactments reflected the democratic and republican nature of the independence movement. The Dáil Constitution made no mention of a republic, and there was no provision in it for a president to represent the state. Nevertheless, it was clearly intended to be a provisional constitution for an independent republic, which the representatives hoped to make a reality. At the same time, continuity was also very evident; these enactments showed how much of the British and how little of any other foreign tradition the independence movement had absorbed. In the words of Brian Farrell: 'Irish political culture was already developed into an established and sturdy parliamentary mould prior to political independence.' There was, Farrell thought, 'a considerable consensus in Ireland on what the process of representation and government was about. There was never any serious dispute; a familiar and acceptable model – the Westminster model – was available and was simply taken over.'[5] In fact, this was a takeover, not a revolution.

The pattern of government envisaged was cabinet government in the British style. The Prime Minister and other ministers were to be members of the Dáil, chosen by it and answerable to it. Perhaps other provisions reflected the desire of some Dáil members to lean more to parliamentary government than to cabinet government; if so, their hopes were not realized. In general, during the period of operation of the Dáil Constitution, from 1919 to 1922, 'the Cabinet controlled the Dáil. It had a secure majority, no organized opposition and the advantage of a war situation to stimulate consensus.'[6] The Democratic Programme, covering the ownership of property and matters such as the right to education, social welfare services, and equality, and stressing international cooperation, no doubt reflected Sinn Féin principles; but it also had a strong early-twentieth-century socialist flavour, being the work of leaders of the more left-wing elements in the independence movement. It was probably not really acceptable to the majority of Dáil members and certainly not to some of the leaders, including de Valera himself. One of them afterwards doubted 'whether a majority of the members would have voted for it, without amendment, had there been any immediate prospect of putting it into force'.[7]

The Constitution of the Irish Free State marked the success of the independence movement. In contrast with its predecessor, it was a constitution for an effective sovereign state, but a state that had perforce to remain in a special relationship with the United Kingdom. The Provisional Government that took over in January 1922 was greatly constrained in preparing a constitution by the terms of the Treaty that had just been signed and by undertakings given during negotiations. The most important of these constraints was that the Irish leaders had to accept both then-current British ideas of the proper arrangements for emergent colonies – that is, Commonwealth status – and also a number of safeguards for defence and for the protection of the Protestant minority left in the new state. Consequently, the Irish Free State Constitution reflected two different political theories. One was the theory of popular sovereignty, which was couched in dogmatic assertions about the rights of the people, intended by Irish leaders to mark the break with Britain. The other was British constitutional theory, for the break was not complete. The state was to be a member of the British Commonwealth and, at British insistence, the Constitution provided for the symbols and institutions of government considered at that time to be necesary and appropriate for such membership; namely, recognition of the Crown, a governor general, an oath of loyalty, and the constitutional fictions connected with the concept of 'His Majesty's government'.

The provisions for political organization and procedures expanded the sketchy arrangements of the Dáil Constitution considerably, following quite closely the existing British patterns. However, although the British cabinet system and the Westminster model generally were the basis of the machinery of government, attempts were made to correct what some Irish leaders of the time thought were imperfections in British government. Included in the Constitution of the Irish Free State were devices intended to increase popular and parliamentary control and to prevent the development of a strong cabinet backed by a majority party from establishing hegemony over the Oireachtas (parliament). The Constitution contained provisions for referendum, the initiative, and 'Extern Ministers', that is, ministers elected directly by the Dáil, who did not need to be members of the Dáil and were not members of the cabinet. Confidence in the power of constitutional devices to modify British-style government was quickly seen to have been unfounded. Within five years, all such devices were removed or inoperative. Indeed, modification had never been desired by some of the state's first leaders. In the circumstances of the time, strong government was needed to establish the state successfully in the face of civil war and guerrilla activity both within the state and on its northern border.

The need for constitutional declarations of rights and duties was as foreign to early-twentieth-century British constitutional theory and Commonwealth practice as assertions of popular sovereignty, but the constitutions of most other countries, following American and French precedents, do include them. In any case, the independence movement had social as well as national aims, to which the enactment of the Democratic Programme in 1919 had borne witness. The Irish Free State Constitution guaranteed a catalogue of rights and provided for judicial review of legislation 'having regard to the provisions of the Constitution'. Included were personal rights such as habeas corpus, freedom to practise any religion, freedom of association, the right to free elementary education, and the inviolability of the citizen's home. Notwithstanding a statement that all the natural resources of the country belonged to the state, the tone of this Constitution was less socialistic than the statements of 1919, reflecting the conservative stance of the surviving leaders and their acceptance of the British liberal-democratic tradition and British legal concepts. In its prohibition of the endowment of any religion and of discrimination on account of religious beliefs, both conditions required under the terms of the Treaty, the Constitution was secular in tone.

The result of the Irish leaders having to meet their treaty obligations was that the Constitution contained a mixture of two different and incompatible political traditions; the republican with its basis in popular sovereignty, and the British political tradition combining constitutional monarchy, with all its necessary formal fictions, and Commonwealth status. These inconsistencies symbolized deep disagreements, both political and personal, among Irish leaders that had tragic and lasting consequences. They precipitated a civil war that in turn generated the major political cleavage that has run through Irish politics ever since.

The Irish Free State Constitution was much amended. Until 1932, most changes were confined to the machinery of government, for the leaders of the pro-Treaty party (which became Cumann na nGaedheal), then in power, felt bound by the Treaty. With the coming to power of de Valera, the leading opponent of the Treaty, a radical revision of the whole position in respect of the Commonwealth was certain, for this was what he had stood and fought for. If the substance of independence had been sufficient for the moment for many in 1922 – and was in any case the best that could be got – the majority accepted the need for revision. Many who had helped elect de Valera had done so to enable him to carry it out. Such a revision involved, first, the removal from the Irish Free State Constitution of all signs and symbols of Commonwealth status and, then, the construction of an entirely new constitution 'unquestionably indigenous in character'.[8] This constitution would stress the republican and popular nature of the state, superseding the Commonwealth concept entirely. It did so, as we shall see, without actually mentioning the word 'republic' at all.

III

Bunreacht na hÉireann was almost literally de Valera's constitution.[9] He drafted it or supervised its drafting, clearing its principles with his government and taking advice from officials and others, including a number of the Catholic clergy. He personally piloted it through Dáil Éireann – there was no senate at that time – and presented it to the people in a radio broadcast. It does not follow, however, that it embodied his ideal vision of the Irish state. This would have been a state that was unequivocally republican, with thirty-two counties, Catholic and Gaelic. Fifteen years on from the Treaty he recognized the constraints within which he had to operate in respect of links with the United Kingdom for security and economic reasons. He recognized also the problems he faced in seeking to include Northern Unionists in an all-Ireland state. The consequence was that Bunreacht na hÉireann, like its predecessor, embodied compromise and equivocations.

The state that is provided for is in essentials a republic. The basis of all governmental authority, including the authority to enact the Constitution itself and to change it, is the people. In the words of the Preamble, 'We, the people of Éire . . . do hereby adopt, enact, and give to ourselves this Constitution.' It is important to notice that the people here referred to are in principle the people of the whole island. Article 2 makes clear that 'the national territory consists of the whole island of Ireland, its islands and the territorial seas'. However, in Article 3 the *de facto* situation is recognized, for, 'pending the reintegration of the national territory', the laws of the state are declared to have effect in only twenty-six counties. In place of the symbols of British Commonwealth status, provision is made for an elected president, the symbol of republican status. Yet nowhere in the Constitution is Ireland declared to be a republic. Article 4 says only that the name of the state 'is Éire, or in the English language, Ireland'; not, be it noted, Poblacht na hÉireann (the Republic of Ireland), the name used in the Proclamation of the Republic at Easter 1916. Likewise, the following article, Article 5, says only that 'Ireland is a sovereign, independent, democratic state'. Surprising as this may seem, it was a deliberate omission, reflecting the evolutionary approach to the development of Ireland's constitutional status in general and de Valera's policy of 'external association' and his hopes of acquiring the six Ulster counties in particular.

Formally to have declared the state a republic in 1937 would have involved a complete break with the Commonwealth, the members of which, it was thought at the time, were linked by a common allegiance to the British Crown and could not include a republic. Such a break would be seen as deliberately removing all possibility of eventually wooing Northern Ireland into an all-Ireland state. De Valera made no bones about his motives: 'If the Northern problem were not there . . . in all probability there would be a flat, downright proclamation of a republic in this Constitution.'[10] He provided instead in obscure language (in Article 29.4.2°) for the continuation of arrangements devised at the abdication of King Edward VIII in 1936. At that time, opportunity had been taken to remove mention of the Crown from the Irish Free State Constitution and to reinstate it in an ordinary statute, the Executive Authority (External Relations) Act, as an organ or instrument that might be used by the Irish state for some purposes in the conduct of external affairs. These arrangements, de Valera hoped, would constitute 'a bridge over which the Northern Unionists might eventually walk'.[11]

It was a forlorn hope, but the arrangements made in 1937 had the advantage, as de Valera pointed out, of allowing for further evolution of Ireland's status without the need to change one word of the Constitution. Thus, when in 1948 John A. Costello's 'Inter-Party' government decided that the time had come to declare Ireland a republic, the deed was done by ordinary legislation in the Republic of Ireland Act, which declared that 'the description of the State shall be the Republic of Ireland', and cancelled the arrangement for the use of the British monarch provided for in the Executive Authority (External Relations) Act. On Easter Day 1949, Ireland became formally and unequivocally a republic.

The enactment of the Republic of Ireland Act and the symbolic declaration of a republic on Easter Day, 1949, though salutary, were full of irony. Firstly, it marked the end of the policy of external association. Yet, at this very time, the possibility of establishing an intimate relationship between a republic and the British Commonwealth, first explored by de Valera and now extinguished, was being pursued with some success by other countries emerging from British control to independence. Secondly, it is bitterly ironic to recall that the leaders involved hoped that this move would 'take the gun out of Irish politics'. Events in Northern Ireland since 1948 have shown how tragically wrong they were: never have there been more guns in Irish politics.

Ireland's status in the world of states was now finally fixed *de jure* as it had been *de facto* in December 1921. Nevertheless, the realities of its position in relation to the United Kingdom had perforce still to be recognized. It was, and still is, neither convenient nor practicable for the United Kingdom to regard Ireland as a foreign state. Under the Ireland Act (1949), the Republic of Ireland, as the state was in future to be known in the United Kingdom, was not to be a foreign country, not were its citizens to be classed as aliens. Instead, they were to continue to enjoy the exemption from that status accorded in the British Nationality Act (1948) and to have all the privileges of Commonwealth citizens. Today, they are even more privileged, for the restrictions applied to the entry of Commonwealth citizens to the United Kingdom under the Commonwealth Immigrants Act do not apply to Irish people. In this way, as in many others, the unique association of the two countries is constantly demonstrated.

The dissatisfaction of de Valera and Fianna Fáil with the Irish Free State Constitution did not extend to the system by which the country was governed. On the contrary, the trend towards a system of the British type, operating in a similar manner, was confirmed after 1932. To a large extent Bunreacht na hÉireann continued what already existed formally or in practice. Some of its words and phrases were identical with, or very similar to, those used in the 1922 Constitution. The most important changes were intended to increase the status and power of the Prime Minister (now called Taoiseach), but even this was to some extent only to make formal what was in fact the practice, at least since the accession of de Valera. Otherwise, changes were comparatively minor. The occasion was taken to make yet another – not very successful – attempt to solve the difficult problem of the composition and powers of Seanad Éireann (the Senate). The Irish language was declared to be 'the first official language' with English recognized as 'a second official language'. Provision could be made by law for the exclusive use of Irish under Article 8, but unless de Valera and his government were prepared to take draconian measures – as governments elsewhere have sometimes done – there was little more that he could realistically do. As he himself lamented many years later, 'the nation as a whole had not yet put its back into it'.[12]

In general, the machinery of government provided for in Bunreacht na hÉireann followed the British model, and the similarity is the greater because of the persistence of similar working practices. These similarities extend to government–parliament relationships, parliamentary procedure and behaviour, the forms of administrative organization at both the national and the local level, the structure and working of the Civil Service, and to much else besides. There are differences, of course. Because there is a great disparity in scale, Irish government is less complex. Because there are social and cultural differences resulting from the fact that the political traditions and culture of the Irish contain elements other than those derived from Britain, the conduct of government and the political behaviour of those involved are by no means always similar. To a great extent, what this study of Irish government is concerned with is precisely the working of British-type institutions in a cultural setting that, though it owes much to Britain, is very different.

IV

If the enactment of Bunreacht na hÉireann marked another stage in the progress of the Irish state to an international status that satisfied its inhabitants, it also heralded the formal recognition that this was a Catholic state. The Cumann na nGaedheal governments of the first decade had carried through a programme of legislation reflecting an austere Catholic outlook. The 1937 Constitution confirmed the acceptance of Catholic principles as guidelines for the country's political life and institutions and for its social policies. John Whyte called it 'the coping stone of this development'.[13] Thus, mixed with liberal and democratic elements derived from the British tradition were principles and precepts drawn from Catholic social theory and, in particular, papal encyclicals.

This mixture is mostly to be seen in Articles 40–44, the articles dealing with the rights of the citizens, and in Article 45, which is entitled 'Directive Principles of Social Policy'. Elsewhere, the 1937 Constitution, though clearly Christian in tone, is not especially Catholic, except in Articles 15, 18, and 19. Those articles, taking up a political idea put forward by Pope Pius XI in the encyclical *Quadragesimo Anno* (1931) and much in vogue among Catholic publicists for a few years, make provision for occupational or, as they called it, 'vocational' representation.

This mixture of liberal-democratic and Catholic principles seems on the whole to have been successful, and certainly it satisfied the vast majority of the citizens of the Republic, at least until recently. In hindsight it is easy to see that it would not evoke the support or inspire the loyalty of the Protestant population of the six counties of the North. However, most people in the twenty-six counties were unable or unwilling to recognize that at the time, or to accept that, this being the case, an all-Ireland republic was not possible because the Northern Protestant majority could not be coerced.

Article 40, entitled 'Personal Rights', enunciates many of the personal and civil rights that are the product of the liberal tradition. It declares citizens to be equal before the law and to have the right of habeas corpus. Citizens' homes are not to be forcibly entered 'save in accordance with law'. It also guarantees the right of free expression 'including criticisms of government policy', the right of peaceful assembly, and the right to form associations and unions – all 'subject to public order and morality'. It expressly forbids political, religious, or class discrimination. Elsewhere in the Constitution, notably in Articles 15.5 and 34–39 (the articles that deal with the courts), other liberal rights connected with legal processes are laid down.

Although Article 40 is an important vehicle of the liberal inheritance, the Constitution is not very explicit when it comes to protecting the citizen against the State: on the contrary, its wording seems to have been well able to accommodate the need to provide the police and other authorities with discretionary powers and the right to act in emergencies and protect the security of the state. It has been the courts in recent years which have stretched the Constitution and done much to operationalize citizens' rights in respect of access to the courts, 'due process', and treatment of people by the Gardaí (police), and to whittle away the state's claims to privilege in legal processes.

If Article 40 as originally enacted reflects the liberal tradition, Articles 41, 42, and 43, which deal with the family, education, and property, are Catholic in content and tone. So, too, is the important addition to Article 40 itself, made by the Eighth Amendment of the Constitution Act 1983, which was intended to copper-fasten the existing legal prohibition on abortion in a specifically Catholic fashion. Article 41 declares that 'the State recognizes the Family as the natural primary and fundamental unit group of Society, and as a moral institution possessing inalienable and imprescriptible rights, antecedent and superior to all positive law'. The integrity of the family is, therefore, carefully protected by constitutional safeguards. The state guarantees to guard the institution of marriage, and the enactment of laws granting a dissolution of marriage is forbidden, a prohibition confirmed very explicitly by the defeat in 1986 of a proposed amendment designed to permit legislation providing for divorce in some circumstances. Further, Article 41 provides that a person who has been divorced in another country and whose marriage is 'a subsisting valid marriage' in Irish law may not legally remarry in the Republic while the original spouse is alive. Similarly, even persons whose marriages have been 'annulled' by Catholic Church authorities may not legally remarry in the Republic.

In Article 42 the family is recognized as 'the primary and natural educator of the child'. Parents have the right and the duty to provide education for their children, but they may, if they wish, provide it in their own homes; the state steps in only in default. The enunciation in Article 43 of the right to possess property and its qualifications are also expressed in unmistakably Catholic terms: 'The State acknowledges that man, in virtue of his rational being, has the natural right, antecedent to positive law, to the private ownership of external goods.' The state, therefore, will pass no law attempting to abolish the right of private ownership or the right to bequeath or inherit it. However, the exercise of property rights is to be regulated by 'the principles of social justice', and the state may 'delimit by law the exercise of the said rights' for 'the common good'.

In Article 44, which deals with religion, de Valera – for it was his solution to a difficult problem – made a brave attempt to reconcile contemporary Catholic teaching on the treatment of religions by the state with his aspirations, and those of the majority, for a united Ireland.[14] The desire to end partition, which involved allaying the fears of 'Rome rule' held by the Protestant majority in Northern Ireland and the need, for the same reason, to renew the guarantees on religion given in the Irish Free State Constitution, required that contemporary Catholic principles be not strictly applied. This turned out to be the most contentious article in Bunreacht na hÉireann: it was attacked at first for not being Catholic enough and, later, after the church at the Second Vatican Council had changed its stance and no longer sought a privileged position, for being too rigidly Catholic. It is one of the few articles to have been amended.

In Article 44, in its original form, which remained the law until 1972, the state acknowledges the duty to respect and honour religion and 'recognizes the special position of the Holy Catholic Apostolic and Roman Church as the guardian of the Faith professed by the great majority of its citizens'. It also recognizes the other religious denominations that existed in the community at the time of the enactment, and it safeguards 'freedom of conscience and the free profession and practice of religion'. Article 44 guarantees not to endow any religion, not to impose any disabilities on religious grounds, not to discriminate in providing aid for schools, and not to take over church property compulsorily except for 'necessary works of public utility and on payment of compensation'.

In the late 1960s, this article came under attack, largely in the context of Northern Ireland but also by those promoting a more pluralist state and society. In 1967, an all-party committee on the Constitution recommended the removal of two sections, but it was the declaration of the Primate, Cardinal Conway, in 1969 that he personally 'would not shed a tear if the relevant subsections of Article 44 were to disappear' that gave a clearance for the Fifth Amendment of the Constitution Bill in 1972. This amendment removed sections 2 and 3 of Article 44.1; that is, the 'special position' clause and the clause according recognition to named religions.

As in Articles 41–44, so too in Article 45, entitled 'Directive Principles of Social Policy', the precepts of Catholic teaching are much in evidence. The principles enunciated in this article supplement the fundamental rights in Articles 40–44, for they consist of a collection of welfare-state aims 'for the general guidance of the Oireachtas'. The state is bidden to seek 'a social order in which justice and charity shall inform all the institutions of the national life' and so to organize affairs that all men and women 'may through their occupations find the means of making reasonable provision for their domestic needs'. The state should have special care for the weaker in the community. Concerning property, the Catholic position is once again stated: the public must be protected against 'unjust exploitation' and 'the state shall favour and, where necessary, supplement private initiative in industry and commerce'.

Finally, we should notice in Article 45 an enunciation of the idealistic dream of a rural, peasant-owner society so dear to the heart of de Valera. The state is directed to secure 'that there may be established on the land in economic security as many families as in the circumstances shall be practicable'. The figures of the numbers engaged in farming, of population movement, and of emigration from Ireland show how far this dream was from the realities of the ensuing half century.

Article 45 was addressed to the Oireachtas. The application of the principles set out therein 'shall not be cognisable by any Court'. Notwithstanding the apparent finality of this wording , the High Court in 1972 decided that, although the application of the principles enunciated in the article are 'in the care of the Oireachtas exclusively and shall not be cognisable by any court', the wording does not mean that 'the courts may not take it into consideration when deciding whether a claimed constitutional right exists'.[15]

V

However well suited a constitution might seem to be when it first comes into effect, the inevitable changes that time brings will lead to a need and desire to alter or develop it. Such modifications can be made by the courts if they have the power to review and invalidate any action of any governmental agency on constitutional grounds, as the Irish courts have. Changes can also be made by amendment, which very often requires a special procedure that in Ireland's case involves enactment by the Oireachtas followed by popular approval at a referendum. These are the principal methods by which to develop a constitution which, as we have suggested, (see above, p. 37), consists of both a document and an ever-increasing penumbra of authoritative principles and rules added item by item as circumstances arise. Thus, both judges (in the courts) and politicians (in the Oireachtas and subject to the agreement of the electorate) have a role as constitutional developers.

After a tidying up period from 1938 to 1941, during which time two amendment acts were passed by ordinary legislation as provided

for in 'Transitory Provisions', Bunreacht na hÉireann was hardly
developed at all either by interpretation or by amendment for a quarter
of a century. Its enactment had evidently given Ireland what Karl
Loewenstein called a 'normative' constitution – that is, a constitution
that was 'not only valid in the sense of being legal but also real in the
sense of being fully activated and effective'.[16] In the eyes of its
author, de Valera, and of the country as a whole, it suited Ireland's
traditions and expressed its aspirations. It tended, therefore, to be
regarded as a finished product and not as a developing instrument of
government. This was especially so both because its author dominated
politics for most of the next quarter of a century, and because the
judiciary had for even longer a diffident attitude towards their power
to review and a conservative bias when it came to interpretation.

Since neither war nor revolution afflicted the country to precipitate
the kinds of social and economic change that many Western European
countries experienced after 1939, Ireland was very conservative until
the 1960s. After this comparatively negative period, during which time
Irish lawyers trained in the British tradition were slow to put their new
powers of review to creative use, judicial interpretation of the
Constitution became bolder. From that time, judges of the High Court
and the Supreme Court, on whom falls the task of interpreting the
Constitution, were prone to take a broader approach towards
interpretation, seeking guidance from a range of sources wider than the
mandatory clauses. In their deliberations they considered the Preamble,
Article 45, the nature of the Irish state, and even, in the words of Chief
Justice O'Higgins, 'concepts of prudence, justice and charity which
may gradually change or develop as society changes and develops, and
which fall to be interpreted from time to time in accordance with
prevailing ideas'.[17] In particular, the judges enlarged the range of
personal rights. In an important judgement in the case of *Ryan* v.
Attorney General, Mr Justice Kenny enunciated a concept of
'undisclosed human rights', declaring that 'the personal rights which
may be invoked to invalidate legislation are not confined to those
specified in Article 40 but include all those rights which result from
the Christian and democratic nature of the state'.[18]

This line of thought received considerable support from some of his
colleagues and the results were, and continue to be, far-reaching.
Unspecified and hitherto unrecognized rights so identified have
included the right to bodily integrity, the right to work, the right to
belong to a trade union, the right of a union member to take part in the
decision-making processes of his union, the right to a career, the right
to free movement, the right to marry, and a general right to privacy.
Equally important, procedural safeguards and personal rights for those
involved in court proceedings and rules for the treatment of accused
persons have been formulated and redefined this way.

Important and even necessary as this judicial process is for
constitutional development, it has potential dangers. Innovative

judgements, especially if they flow from seemingly vague or novel principles and are given in politically sensitive matters, might bring the judges who make them to the centre of the political stage with undesirable consequences. The judicial system can only be harmed if people begin to question the impartiality of judges or if political considerations come into the appointment process. Again, this kind of judicial activism can have the effect of allowing politicians to leave politically sensitive issues to the courts to decide and thus relieve themselves of their responsibilities. The record of constitutional amendment shows that this has been the case in Ireland. In 1986, the Chairman of the Bar Council summed up the situation by saying: 'I conclude that the legislature has been disposed to vacate certain areas of their legislative functions where unpopular decisions were for one reason or another unavoidable.'[19]

Ironically, the first use of the amending procedure served to show how important it is, not in getting changes made, but in preventing governments from making changes that they desire though the public does not. Both in 1959 and 1968, attempts to replace proportional representation by a single transferable vote with the 'first-past-the-post' system at elections were rejected at the referendum. It was not until 1972 that the first amendments were made under the full procedures laid down in the Constitution. A survey of the eight amendments made up to 1991 shows how meagre has been the politicians' response to their obligation to keep Bunreacht na hÉireann up-to-date and congruent with social and political realities. Membership of the European Communities required two amendments, both to Article 29. The Third Amendment Act in 1972 allowed Ireland to join, and the Tenth Amendment Act in 1987 authorized the state to ratify the Single European Act, which modified and extended the original Treaty (of Rome). The Tenth Amendment and another, the Sixth (on adoption) were made necessary by court decisions which forced the government and Oireachtas to act.

Not all of the other changes by any means can be viewed as the results of politicians carrying out their constitutional development duties. Those that were – the reduction of the voting age to eighteen (the Fourth Amendment); an extension of the graduate franchise in Seanad (Senate) elections (the Seventh Amendment) that was not put into operation; and the extension to non-citizens of the vote at Dáil elections (the Ninth Amendment) – were uncontentious acts of modernization. The remaining two amendments were very different affairs. Both were important and both owed their origins to Catholic interests. The first, the deletion of the 'special position' clause was triggered, as we have noted (see above p. 47), by Cardinal Conway, and the second, the so-called 'right-to-life' amendment (the Eighth Amendment), resulted from a campaign by Catholic pressure groups. The attempt to alter the constitutional ban on divorce legislation owed its failure to the same pressures. This is a thin record for a period of more than fifty years during which time the country underwent a process of considerable industrialization and modernization. It serves, too, to suggest a major reason for the politicans' inhibitions in one policy area. One of them put it succinctly when he referred to the dangers to politicians 'in entering as it were the radiation zone of possible episcopal wrath'.[20]

The continuous discussion from the early seventies about the need to change the Constitution was almost always in the context of Northern Ireland. It centred on the changes needed to suit a state that would embrace all Ireland and on whether or not it was advisable to make those changes before such a state was under active discussion. The need for other changes, not least those arising from membership of the European Communities, did not attract much attention. In the future it might well be Community imperatives that will be as powerful an engine of change as Northern Ireland.

VI

The legal framework within which Irish public authorities operate is not confined to domestic law. Ireland's accession to the European Communities had the effect of superimposing on domestic constraints and treaty obligations (which are entirely matters within the competence of the government and the Oireachtas to decide) another body of law that not only governs member states but applies in part directly to individual citizens. Potentially, the constraining effect of European Community law upon the actions of public authorites is enormous. In the words of a British judge, it is 'like an incoming tide. It flows into the estuaries and up the rivers. It cannot be held back'.[21]

Bunreacht na hÉireann, being a product of the interwar years when the possibility of international organizations with powers of this sort was not contemplated, could not encompass such a development without amendment. Article 29.6 states that 'no international agreement shall be part of the domestic law of the State save as may be determined by the Oireachtas'. The obligations of membership in the Communities require otherwise, and the Third Amendment of the Constitution – a simple addition of one subsection to Article 29.4 – both permitted accession and declared that

no provision of this Constitution invalidates laws enacted, acts done or measures adopted by the State necessitated by the obligations of membership of the Communities or prevents laws enacted, acts done or measures adopted by the Communities, or institutions thereof, from having the force of law in the State.

Following this enabling amendment, the European Communities Act (1972) provided that 'the Treaties governing the European Communities and the existing and future acts adopted by the institutions of those Communities shall be binding on the State and shall be part of the domestic law thereof'.

The same procedure was necessary in 1987, when a major extension of Community activities, together with measures to strengthen Community institutions, all embodied in the Single European Act, came up for ratification. Following a Supreme Court decision that part of that act would require a constitutional amendment, the Tenth Amendment of the Constitution Act 1987, provided for another addition to Article 29.4.3°, the subsection inserted in 1972: 'The State may ratify the Single European Act signed on behalf of the Member States of the Communities at Luxembourg on the 17th day of February, 1986 and at the Hague on the 28th day of February 1986.' Thus European law has been welded on to Irish law and Article 29.4.3° together with the provisions of the European Communities Act 1972, provide the legal conduit through which Community law flows into Irish law and provides an important part of the framework of limited government (see Chapter 17 below).

Notes

1   K. C. Wheare, *Modern Constitutions* (London, 1966), p. 2.
2   S. A. de Smith, *Constitutional and Administrative Law*, 3rd edn, (Harmondsworth, 1977), p. 16.
3   J. Temple Lang, *The Common Market and the Common Law* (Chicago and London, 1966), p. xi.
4   The definitive text of the Constitution of Dáil Éireann is in Irish and is published in Dáil Éireann: *Minutes of the Proceedings of the First Parliament of the Republic of Ireland*, 1919–21 (Dublin, 1922), p. 13. An English version published in the press on 22 Jan. 1919 is reproduced in D. Macardle, *The Irish Republic*, 4th edn (Dublin, 1951), pp. 923–4.
5   B. Farrell, *The Founding of Dáil Éireann: Parliament and Nation-Building* (Dublin, 1971), pp. 83 and xviii.
6   B. Farrell, 'The legislation of a "revolutionary" Assembly: Dáil Decrees 1919–22', in *Irish Jurist*, 10 (1975) n.s., p. 116.
7   P. Béaslai, *Michael Collins and the Making of a New Ireland*, Vol. 1 (London, 1926), p. 259.
8   N. Mansergh, *Survey of British Commonwealth Affairs: Problems of External Policy, 1931–39* (London, 1952), p. 289.
9   *Bunreacht na hÉireann (Constitution of Ireland)* (Government Publications Office, Dublin).
10   *Dáil Debates*, Vol. 68, col. 430 (14 June 1937).
11   C. O'Leary, *Irish Elections, 1918–77: Parties, Voters and Proportional Representation* (Dublin, 1979), p. 29.
12   The Earl of Longford and T. P. O Neill, *Eamon de Valera* (Dublin and London, 1970), p. 459.
13   J. Whyte, *Church and State in Modern Ireland, 1923–1979*, 2nd edn (London and Dublin, 1980), p. 50.
14   De Valera's work on this article and his difficulties with it are described by the Earl of Longford and T. P. O'Neill in *Eamon de Valera*, pp.

295–8. There is also a full account based on a study of the de Valera papers by D. Keogh in F. Litton (ed.), *The Constitution of Ireland 1937–1987* (Dublin, 1988), pp. 4–84.
15 Mr Justice Kenny in *Murtagh Properties* v. *Cleary* [1972] IR 330 at pp. 335–6.
16 K. Loewenstein, 'Reflections on the value of constitutions in our revolutionary age', in H. Eckstein and D. E. Apter (eds), *Comparative Politics* (Glencoe, 1963), p. 154.
17 *State (Healy)* v. *Donoghue* [1967] IR 347.
18 [1965] IR 294.
19 Quoted in *Irish Times*, 18 Aug. 1986.
20 Michael O'Leary quoted in *Irish Independent*, 4 Oct. 1985.
21 Lord Justice Denning in *H. P. Bulmer Ltd.* v. *J. Bollinger SA* [1974] 1 ch. 401 at 418.

CHAPTER 4

Political Communications and the Mass Media

I

One of the most fruitful approaches to the study of politics is to see it as a system of communications involving a network of channels of information and institutions for transmitting ideas, demands, and orders. Some of this communication is 'horizontal' – ministers of state conferring together or with community leaders, men talking in a bar, children learning, as they once used to, to sing 'Kevin Barry' or 'Derry's Walls' at school. Those who, because of their elite status in the community, can communicate horizontally in a direct manner with members of a government or other political leaders or senior public servants are likely to be comparatively well informed and influential. For most people, political information, ideas, and values are communicated either horizontally at a low level within the family, school, religious group, or work place, or vertically from the top or source downward and by more formal media. Conversely, some, but regrettably much less, information about public attitudes and demands passes vertically upward to political leaders. Obviously, in a modern society, television, radio, newspapers, and to a lesser extent other printed material are powerful means of wholesale vertical communication – thus the term 'mass media'.

So important are the mass media that their ownership, direction, and standards are commonly and rightly regarded as matters of crucial public importance and, hence, proper for governments to control. In regimes based upon a totalitarian ideology, state regulation is inevitably directed to fostering and reinforcing the political system and the rulers who interpret the ideology. In Western democracies, views differ about the proper role of the state *vis-à-vis* the media. One view sees the media as being, properly, business enterprises that should be free to serve the market. The state's role is to hold the ring, protect individuals and groups from the excesses of commercialism and enforce so far as possible the maintenance of the standards of the community. A second sees them as a 'fourth estate'. This is the view that journalism is an autonomous activity carried on in a competitive context by professionals whose unfettered power to expose public authorities enables them to be held to account and allows the people to get at the truth about public affairs. A third view that came to prevail in many democratic countries as the press becomes concentrated in fewer and fewer hands and broadcasting more often than not was a monopoly, was that the media have a social responsibility that it is the duty of the state to nurture and enforce.

This duty has turned out to be difficult to perform, not least because the would-be controllers, the politicians, are also clients and users of the media and are properly regarded with suspicion by journalists. It has become the more difficult, on the one hand, because of the trend in many countries towards a declining number of newspapers with ownership concentrated in the hands of a few, and, on the other, because of the enormous changes in broadcasting which are part of the communications explosion. Governments everywhere are faced with difficult policy choices that have important consequences for the future of their communities, not least their politics.

It is clear, therefore, that although it is legitimate and convenient to treat the structure, functioning, and outputs of the media at any given time as an important part of the context of politics, influencing the very kind of politics a country experiences, it must be recognized that they are themselves influenced by political decisions. In a broad and general way, their pattern is governed by the dominant ideology of the community, and the translation of that ideology into laws. It falls inevitably to the government of the day to formulate state policy towards the mass media. Perhaps, given the transnational nature of satellite developments in recent years, that government will be but one voice in an international forum.

II

Although there is no denying the importance of the mass media for politics, it is essential to an understanding of how political attitudes are formed and behaviour is shaped to recognize that the mass channels – the press and other print media, radio, and television – are by no means the only suppliers of political information and ideas. Political communications in advanced countries like Ireland consist of 'a fusion of high technology and special, professionalized processes of communication with informal, society-based and non-specialized processes of person-to-person communication'.[1] Although this chapter is mainly concerned with the 'special, professionalized processes of communication' (the mass media), these might make surprisingly little impact upon the basic political attitudes of most consumers. Face-to-face contacts and informal communications might be of much greater importance.

In any case, there can be no doubting the pre-eminence of basic social groups such as the family, religious groups, school, and peer groups, in the political socialization of individuals and in holding them fast. Some social scientists investigating the impact of mass media claim that 'opinions and attitudes which are important to an individual's image of himself, or to his picture of society, cannot easily be changed by a fusillade of communications, however persuasive . . . such opinions are often anchored and shielded by a person's primary group affiliations – "ensconced in protective group cocoon" '.[2] Whatever is said about the mass media must not obscure this most important political fact.

III

A free, private-enterprise press was established in Ireland parallel with its establishment in Great Britain. Mass-readership daily papers, produced in Dublin and reflecting a number of shades of opinion, were well established with strong traditions of independence before the First World War. Independent Ireland emerged with an established free press, home-produced and privately owned and operated. It embraced the full range of newspaper and journal production. British newspapers, journals, and magazines continued to circulate in small but significant numbers. Furthermore, many of the books read in Ireland were (and are) produced in the United Kingdom.

The industry is still largely based on the major groups that had their origins before independence – Independent Newspapers, Irish Times Ltd and the Cork Examiner – together with the Irish Press Group founded in 1931 by de Valera. Three of them have national daily newspapers; the *Irish Independent* and its associated tabloid the *Star*; the *Irish Press*, since 1988 a tabloid; and the *Irish Times*. The *Cork Examiner* is a regional paper with 99 per cent of its readership in the province of Munster. Traditionally, these groups competed for the biggest share they could get of a small total market that was comparatively homogeneous in outlook. Hence there developed a considerable uniformity in the amount and proportion of space given to various types of material and in the treatment of news and comment. Their morning newspapers were all 'serious' papers, although their styles and images were different one from another. The associated Sunday newspapers, however, resembled more closely the British popular Sunday papers, as also did the evening papers. Even so, the situation was not the same as that in Great Britain where, to a considerable extent, the politically influential read one kind of newspaper (the 'quality' papers) and the working class the other (the 'popular' papers).

From the late seventies, commercial pressures – the impact of new owners and managers, the need to counter the loss of advertising to television and commercial radio – led to an erosion of this uniformity. The coming of the tabloids increased this tendency. The position in the early nineties was that at one end of the spectrum the *Irish Times* remained a quality newspaper; at the other end, the tabloids by their very nature and because of the competition between them were unable to perform the functions of a 'serious' newspaper, though one of them, the *Irish Press*, was still trying – not very successfully – to do so. The *Irish Independent* was still a 'serious' newspaper, albeit with a different style from that of the *Irish Times*, as befitted a paper with a big readership in all socio-economic groups. (During the 1989 general election 60 per cent of its total column centimetres were devoted to the election: the figure for the *Irish Times* was 45 per cent.)[3] Given its ownership, management, readership, and commercial problems, however, it could easily move towards the popular end of the spectrum.

Because we know little about the effect upon people of consuming what the media produce, the data on newspaper readership (as on listening and watching) have to be viewed with caution. We may speculate that they might be important in explaining people's political attitudes and behaviour, and, if so, it is useful to know what they are.

The circulations of newspapers in the Republic are shown in Table 4.1. During the eighties, circulations generally dropped. Only the *Irish*

Table 4.1 **Newspaper circulations, 1989–90**

Irish morning newspapers

Broadsheets		Tabloids	
Cork Examiner	58,000	Irish Press	64,000
Irish Independent	153,000	Star	74,000
Irish Times	92,000		

Irish evening newspapers

Cork Evening Echo	32,000		
Evening Herald	105,000		
Evening Press	105,000		

Irish Sunday newspapers

Sunday Independent	224,000		
Sunday Press	216,000		
Sunday Tribune	97,000		
Sunday World	347,000	(includes Northern Ireland)	

British newspapers with the largest circulations

Daily Mirror	62,000	News of the World	171,000
The Sun	26,000	Sunday People	82,000
		Sunday Mirror	70,000
		Sunday Times	27,000

Note: Figures are approximate and rounded.
Source: Derived from information supplied by the Institute of Advertising Practitioners of Ireland.

Times and some of the British papers increased their readership. The Independent group, however, successfully launched a tabloid morning paper to further strengthen its leadership. The Irish Press Group was less successful: it lost readers for all its products and, in an effort to stem the tide, converted its morning daily, the *Irish Press*, to a tabloid. By the end of the decade, however, the circulation was only two-thirds of what it had been at the beginning and the group was in difficulties, which were still persisting in 1992.

Although the Sunday papers still attract the largest readership by far, it is perhaps the morning daily papers that are the most important politically since, with the important exception of the *Sunday Tribune*, it is in this category that the serious newspapers are to be found. These are the papers that are likely to have an impact upon the politically active and influential. In 1989, 57 per cent of all adults saw an Irish morning paper, a proportion that had not changed in twenty years. In contrast to the past, regional differences were quite small. On the other hand, differences according to socio-economic status continued to be large, as Table 4.2 shows. The poorest in both town and country were the least likely to see a daily paper, a striking contrast to television viewing, for about eight people out of ten in all classes saw some television each day.

Data on who reads the various morning papers are displayed in Table 4.3. By the end of the eighties the people of the Republic were as never before divided into two groups of newspaper readers. There were those, nearly a half, who read a broadsheet morning daily together perhaps with the *Sunday Tribune* (15 per cent) and one or more of the popular Sunday papers; and there were those whose diet consisted of a selection of one or more of a 'popular' Sunday paper, an evening paper, an Irish morning tabloid (22 per cent) or a British tabloid. These two groups were likely to be getting rather different pictures of the world, although the differences were still probably not as great as that which obtains between the two readership worlds in Britain. The half who read the Irish broadsheet dailies were still probably getting a fairly uniform picture of the world produced by a profession that inherited and has by and large carried on a long tradition of serious and responsible journalism. In the future, this profession might find itself harder pressed than it was in the eighties by commercial pressures. From the point of view of healthy democratic politics, the changes forced by such pressures might well be for the worse.

The morning daily newspaper readership is dominated by the *Irish Independent*, which is read by over a quarter of all adults. It has the largest circulation among the lower middle class, the working class, and the farming community, groups that together comprise about 70 per cent of the adult population. It dominates also both in town and countryside and regionally, except in Munster, where the *Cork Examiner* reigns supreme. It is surpassed in the small but significant

Table 4.2 **Adult population reading Irish Newspapers 1988–89 (Per cent)**

Category	Any morning newspaper	Any evening newspaper	Any Sunday newspaper
All	57	33	80
Region			
Dublin	54	62	79
Rest of Leinster	58	24	84
Munster	63	24	79
Connacht & Ulster (part)	49	14	82
Social class			
Upper middle & middle class (AB)	78	29	86
Lower middle class (C1)	71	41	84
Skilled working class (C2)	54	45	82
Other working class (D)	49	38	78
Those at lowest levels of subsistence (E)	32	35	59
Farmers or farm managers on holdings of 50 acres or more	61	12	86
Farmers with farms of less than 50 acres and farm workers	45	9	77

Source: Derived from *Joint National Media Research, 1988–89*, Vol. 1 (Dublin, 1989), made available by Market Research Bureau of Ireland Ltd.

AB groups (the upper middle and middle class) by the *Irish Times*. Although the circulation of the *Irish Times* was only 60 per cent of that of the *Irish Independent* in 1989, this readership is thought by many to be of particular importance. Formerly the unofficial organ of the Protestant and Unionist minority, it long ago became a politically independent, liberal, middle-class paper with a European reputation. Transformed from a private company into a trust in 1974, it proceeded to capture a growing proportion of the middle class and it has, in the

Table 4.3 **Adult readership of the principal morning daily newspapers by socio-economic status, 1988–89 (per cent)**

| | Broadsheets | | | Tabloids | |
	Irish Independent	Irish Times	Cork Examiner	Irish Press	The Star
All	27	12	9	13	9
Upper middle & middle class (AB)	34	47	8	9	3
Lower middle class (C1)	37	26	10	14	6
Skilled working class (C2)	23	6	8	13	15
Other working class (D)	20	3	10	13	14
Those at lowest levels of subsistence (E)	11	2	10	13	10
Farmers or farm managers on holdings of 50 acres or more	39	4	12	11	3
Farmers with holdings of less than 50 acres and farm workers	23	2	6	15	5

Source: Derived from *Joint National Media Research 1988–89*, Vol. 1 (Dublin, 1989), made available by Market Research Bureau of Ireland Ltd.

jargon of the advertising world, a distinctly up-market profile. It carries the widest news coverage, particularly of foreign news, the largest amount of space given to parliamentary reports and the biggest number of surveys of social, economic, and political topics. It sees itself as the 'newspaper of record' and carries Law Reports and full or edited versions of all politically important documents.

Besides the national newspapers and the Cork regional papers, there is a thriving local press, mainly weeklies. In 1990, there were forty-six firms producing fifty-three titles. Most were still independent units owned by individuals or by small companies producing a single paper. A few were grouped in chains under a common ownership; one such was owned by the Independent Group. Many of the local newspapers flourished in a modest way by concentrating on local news, including 'parish pump' politics and local advertisements, and by using their presses for miscellaneous commercial printing besides the production of a newspaper. They had an extraordinary continuity based on a loyal readership, and they were of great importance in the localities they served. The following tabulation shows circulation figures for those that made them available:[4]

Below 5,000	0	20,000–24,999	2
5,000–9,999	9	25,000–29,999	3
10,000–14,999	14	30,000–39,999	3
15,000–19,999	17	Over 40,000	0

The local papers cover political events in their own districts and any national political news that has local significance – for example, the parliamentary questions and other interventions in debate offered by the local parliamentary representatives. They feature reports of the proceedings of local authorities, health boards, and other public bodies. Such a focus might well reinforce the strong local orientation of many country people, and it certainly contributes to the local bias that is a feature of Irish politics.

The Irish press is a free press. That does not mean that editors can print anything they choose under all circumstances. What it does mean, however, is that editors have a very wide freedom to print news, comment and opinion that is unpalatable to the government without danger of penalties, legal or other. Of course, there are legal limitations, but these do not usually operate to restrict the publication of political news or comment on matters of current political moment. The Censorship of Publications Act forbids the publication of matter that is 'indecent or obscene' or that 'advocates the unnatural prevention of conception', both prohibitions arising from a zealous regard for Catholic morality. The libel laws, which are still patterned after the comparatively severe British code, and the laws concerning contempt of court are perhaps the most important editorial inhibitors, but only infrequently do these operate to prevent publication of matter of political significance.

The principal legal restrictions which might have consequences for politics are the Official Secrets Act and the Offences Against the State Act 1939. So far as is known, Irish governments have only rarely tried, as British governments do, to use the Official Secrets Act to prevent publication of material for security reasons or because it derives from unauthorized leaks or improperly acquired documents. An unsuccessful attempt was made in 1977 to suppress information about the value of the Bula mines in which the state had an interest, and in 1984 the editor of the *Irish Independent* and his newspaper were fined derisory sums for publishing confidential identikit pictures.[5] Some journalists say that pressure is occasionally exerted secretly and, more important, that fear of possible consequences leads to self-censorship. The restrictions contained in the Offences Against the State Act 1939, are more specific but as little used. Under sections 2 and 10 of this act, newspapers are forbidden to refer to organizations declared illegal under the act, in other words, to the Irish Republican Army. In practice, newspapers have never been inhibited from reporting or commenting on the activities of the IRA. When, as happened once or twice in the sixties, the government of the day decided to enforce the law, the papers simply substituted the term 'an illegal organization'. Since, in any case, the neighbouring British and Northern Ireland press, radio, and television were not so prohibited, this was an appropriate Irish solution to an Irish problem. As we shall see, the print journalists' experience contrasts markedly with the experience of broadcasters (see below, p. 69–70).

Another potential external influence upon newspapers is commercial pressure. The influence that advertisers have upon editorial material is a subject of much speculation. It is increasingly obvious that the amount of space given to various types of material and their juxtaposition are influenced by the need to win and hold advertising, but this is not likely to affect the treatment of political matter. Perhaps this is more a matter of self-censorship. Advertisers are interested in large circulations and in minority newspapers only if these have a solid middle-class business and professional readership. In both cases, this means papers with a conservative rather than a radical approach. Consequently, fundamental criticism or 'alternative' views of society have less chance of being publicized. Nevertheless, there are vehicles for radical journalism in Ireland and their importance might be out of all proportion to their circulations. The most important in 1989 were *Phoenix*, a fortnightly with a 4 per-cent readership and *Magill* (now defunct), a monthly with an 8 per-cent readership, both of mostly urban middle-class people, many of them probably intellectual liberals.[6] More important, the *Sunday Tribune* with a 15 per-cent readership in 1989 is also aimed at this kind of reader. This group, together with television journalists working on current affairs programmes, were the pioneers of investigative journalism of a more pointed kind than the traditional.

Editors (and other newspeople) are inevitably subject to representations and appeals from ministers, senior officials, and other political leaders and their advisers. In recent years there has been a marked increase in the use by leading politicians of professional public relations experts. In public, press conferences and press releases and, in private, requests to 'kill', soft-pedal, or give prominence to items are all part of the everyday business of the journalist. Potentially more dangerous is the increase in entertainment, free trips, and the like. On the whole, however, contacts are carried on to well-understood conventions and exist for mutual convenience. A few might result in political interference. Threats, for example to withhold advertising, have been uncommon. All in all, legal and other outside restrictions on editors publishing political material are few, and newspapers are well placed to resist *outside* pressure and influence if they wish. Whether they are well placed to acquire information from a government and administration that are, in the British tradition, inclined to cagey secrecy is another matter. Unlike some Western democracies, Ireland does not have a Freedom of Information Act. What restrictions or irresistible pressures, if any, there are on editors in political matters arise not so much from the law or from importuning by politicians or business interests, but from *inside* – from the owners and boards of the papers and, in recent years, sometimes from trade unions.

If Irish newspapers enjoy considerable freedom from outside pressures, it might be thought that there is no cause for concern on democratic grounds. If that were so, Ireland would be out of step with much of the rest of the democratic world. There, the story has been of contraction in consumption and ownership, of takeover by big business, of mergers, and of a widespread tendency to see information as a commodity to be traded. Wherever these things have occurred, they have evoked public concern and, ironically, demands for state intervention by way of tax advantages, loans, and direct subsidies from public funds. The state is increasingly expected to guarantee the operation of an independent press with an adequate number of organs, for it is said – rightly – that democracy needs a thriving newspaper industry as part of the political communications network if it is to work well. On the other hand, governments are not disinterested parties and state intervention has obvious dangers.

As yet, however, the press in Ireland has not had to face this dilemma. Until 1985 it was alone among the European Community countries in not having VAT (Value Added Tax) concessions on its newsprint and it still has none of a range of other concessions, let alone direct grants or loans, such as they enjoy. Nevertheless, between the dangers, on the one hand, of becoming, in T. P. Coogan's words, 'appendages to conglomerates and big business' with the 'whey-faced clerks . . . moving into the seats of power' and, on the other, of the possible implications of state aid, however well-intentioned, the press in Ireland faces a difficult future.[7]

IV

Whereas the press in Ireland is essentially an industry whose activities are not greatly restricted by the law and hardly if at all inhibited by political pressure, broadcasting has from the beginning been in the public sector. In Ireland, as in most other countries, 'broadcasting became a prime exemplification of the social responsibility theory: too powerful, too scarce a resource to be allowed to operate completely unfettered'.[8] In fact, it was from the beginning a state monopoly and remained so until recently: until 1961, it was under direct ministerial control. As Anthony Smith pointed out, in Ireland's case, this monopoly was operated under particularly unfavourable circumstances – and these still obtain at a time when a private sector is struggling to get established – a small population undergoing rapid cultural changes; a population that is too small and too poor to produce enough revenue whether by licence fees or advertising income; a population that possesses two languages, one of which is viewed with indifference by the majority and the other of which is the broadcasting language of its inconveniently close and overpoweringly large neighbour.[9]

The first broadcasting authority, Radio Éireann (1925–61), was a branch of the Department of Posts and Telegraphs. Its staff were civil servants, and its activities were open to detailed parliamentary scrutiny like all other services operated by the central administration. The effect of this was not to subject broadcasting to party political pressures but rather the reverse, to insulate it entirely from politics. The station took a strictly neutral position simply by broadcasting no political material at all. The introduction of a television service in 1961 coincided with a rapid development of more forthright political programmes by the rival British broadcasting organizations, whose programmes could be received in some parts of the Republic, and inevitably altered this state of affairs greatly.

The Broadcasting Authority Act 1960 was intended to give broadcasting a more autonomous status than it had had hitherto. It created Radio Telefís Éireann (RTE) in the form of a 'state-sponsored body' – that is, a public authority with statutory functions and powers whose governing body is appointed, and can be dismissed, by its sponsor minister. (For a discussion of state-sponsored bodies, see Chapter 14.) This act and its successor, the Broadcasting Authority (Amendment) Act 1976, were the most important statutes governing radio and television until the coming of a new era in broadcasting in the late eighties. The Radio and Television Act 1988 and the Broadcasting Act 1990 provided for private enterprise broadcasting and for a framework within which 'public service' and 'independent' broadcasting will operate in the nineties.

The 1960 Act was in some respects modelled upon British practice. It charged the Broadcasting Authority with providing both radio and television services, and gave it the right to receive licence fees and to sell commercial advertising. Although RTE was given a legal persona and some autonomy, the governing principle of the Broadcasting Authority Acts is the concept of social responsibility, which it is the duty of the state to ensure. Consequently, RTE operates under statutory constraints and is subject to certain government controls. The most important of these relate to programming and the circumstances in which the minister may intervene. Over the years these controls have often been the cause of friction between governments and the Authority, leading to political debate and acrimony.

RTE is, thus, like most European broadcasting organizations of the time, a 'public service broadcasting' system. To quote the Authority itself: a major aim of public service broadcasting is to support and develop its audience's national identity and sense of community. It regards its listeners and viewers as members of a specific community with particular loyalties, culture and values.'[10] The Authority contrasts this with commercial broadcasting, which is 'a commodity to be sold to as many people as possible by the use of marketing techniques'.[11]

As part of the fabric of a democracy, RTE has specific obligations, which are set out in the legislation governing its operations. In carrying out its functions it is required in its programming to:

(a) be responsive to the interests and concerns of the whole community, be mindful of the need for understanding and peace within the whole island of Ireland, ensure that the programmes reflect the varied elements which make up the culture of the people of the whole island of Ireland, and have special regard for the elements which distinguish that culture and in particular for the Irish language;

(b) uphold the democratic values enshrined in the Constitution, especially those relating to rightful liberty of expression;

(c) have regard to the need for the formation of public awareness and understanding of the values and traditions of countries other than the State, including in particular those of such countries which are members of the European Community.[12]

News must be 'reported and presented in an objective and impartial manner and without any expression of the Authority's own views'. The same applies to the treatment of current affairs, which must in addition be 'fair to all interests concerned'.[13] The Authority is specifically prohibited from publishing in any form 'anything which may reasonably be regarded as being likely to promote, or incite to, crime or as tending to undermine the Authority of the state'.[14]

Besides imposing upon RTE the ordinary obligations of a state-sponsored body, such as to present an annual report and accounts to the minister and to give him information as required, the law empowers the minister 'to direct the Authority in writing to allocate broadcasting time for any announcements by or on behalf of any Minister of State in connection with his functions'.[15] In addition: 'Where the Minister is of the opinion that the broadcasting of a particular matter or any matter of a particular class would be likely to promote, or incite to, crime or would tend to undermine the authority of the State, he may by order direct the Authority to refrain from broadcasting the matter.'[16]

The story of broadcasting since the inception of television is peppered with controversy and incidents. RTE's difficulties were the greater because politicians and the public in general believed that television had tremendous power to influence, even brainwash, viewers. The evident concern shown in the legislation and in RTE's domestic procedures to ensure fair and balanced programmes reflects this belief in the enormous impact of broadcasting and the cagey suspicion that politicians have of journalist broadcasters. From their point of view the need to do so is evident when one considers the proportion of RTE's output that is or might be important from the standpoint of politics and the size of its audiences for these programmes.

Table 4.4 shows the proportions of RTE's radio and television programmes that were devoted to news, current affairs, and other information programmes in 1988. They were a little less than those of a decade before. They were also, in the case of TV, as Table 4.5 indicates, lower than those of the other members of the European Communities.

Table 4.4 **Percentage of RTE television and radio programmes devoted to news, current affairs and other information, 1988**

	Radio	Television
News	7.55	6.49
Current Affairs	⎫	2.95
	⎬ 8.57	
Other information	⎭	9.87
Total	16.12	19.31

Source: Information supplied by Radio Telefís Éireann Audience Research.

Table 4.5 **Percentage of television programmes devoted to news, current affairs and other information in Ireland and a number of other European Countries in 1986**

Station	News	Information Current affairs	Information Information	Total News & info.
BRT (Belgium)	7.8	2.9	14.1	24.8
DR (Denmark)	8.0	9.4	11.5	28.9
A2F (France)	16.9	3.3	–	20.2
FR3 (France)	7.9	5.4	16.0	29.3
ZDF (Germany)	8.7	13.8	6.7	29.2
RTE (Ireland)	6.4	3.3	9.1	18.8
NOS (Netherlands)	7.3	3.0	17.0	27.3
IBA (United Kingdom)	15.0	13.0	1.5	29.5
BBC (United Kingdom)	4.4	22.7		27.1

Source: Information supplied by Rado Telefís Éireann Audience Research.

The audiences for these programmes tend to be comparatively high. Almost everyone has access to a radio. In 1990, three-quarters of all adults listened to RTE radio programmes at some time during the day and 40 per cent to one or other of the private enterprise stations. Radio 1's 'Morning Ireland', a one-hour news and current affairs programme, was heard by almost one-fifth of adults, as was the lunchtime news and current affairs programme. The 9 a.m. news was heard by almost one-quarter. Audiences for the shorter and lighter newscasts broadcast by RTE Radio 2 FM and the privately owned Century Radio together totalled less than 10 per cent.[17]

In 1990 also, 91 per cent of homes had a TV set and 55 per cent of those were capable of receiving British (including Northern Ireland) programmes. Television viewing in Ireland is high, and higher in the provinces and rural areas than in Dublin, as Table 4.6 shows. It shows also that British programmes had a considerable attraction particularly for Dubliners and people in provincial areas where these broadcasts were available. Rural farming people and the people of Munster generally did not see them because they could not.

Table 4.6 **Television viewing by adults[a]in Ireland, 1989 (per cent)**

Category	Viewing yesterday Any TV at all	RTE	All other stations[b]
All	79	70	38
Region:			
Dublin	75	57	57
Rest of Leinster	83	72	40
Munster	82	79	18
Connacht & Ulster (part of)	77	71	36
Community:			
Urban	78	65	50
Rural	80	70	22

Notes: [a] 'Adult' means age 15 and over.
[b] BBC and Independent Television broadcast from both Northern Ireland and Great Britain. People who watched both RTE and some other station are included in this category.

Source: Derived from *Joint National Media Review 1988–89*, Vol. 1, made available by Market Research Bureau of Ireland.

The audiences in early 1990 for some of the programmes that were most likely to have an important political content are set out in Table 4.7. Perhaps because more people now have available alternative stations to RTE 1, the proportion of the population viewing them was lower than a decade ago. *Today Tonight*, the major current affairs programme was attracting only half the audience of its predecessor ten years before. Nevertheless, it was still among the programmes with a large audience. Similarly, party political broadcasts: an average of 19 per cent of the population watched them during the 1989 election campaign.[18]

Table 4.7 *Audiences for RTE's main evening news and current affairs programmes, 29 January to 25 March 1990 (per cent)*

	Average TAM Rating[a]	Highest average TAM Rating[a]	Lowest average TAM Rating[a]
Early evening news (RTE 1)	17	17	15
Mid evening news (RTE 1)	25	27	23
Network news (Network 2)	7	8	6
Today Tonight (RTE 1)	16	22	13
For comparison	*TAM Rating*		
Glenroe (soap opera) 21 Jan. 1990	44		
The Late Late Show 12 Jan. 1990	38		

Note: [a] Audiences are measured by Irish TAM Ltd. The population base for these measurements was an estimated 3,103,000 individuals aged four and over resident in private homes equipped with television in the Republic. A rating of e.g. 50 for a programme means that 50 per cent of the population base were viewing that programme.

Source: Data made available by Radio Telefís Éireann Audience Research.

Undoubtedly the introduction of television marked a watershed in Irish mass communication. The most conservative elements in a very conservative community found television coverage disturbing. Surveying the troubled history of Irish broadcasting, Desmond Fisher concluded that 'it was from the programming itself and from the evolution of broadcasting's new relationship to the state, to government and to the different elements in Irish society, itself going through a period of rapid and sometimes painful adjustment, that difficulties developed'.[19] Powerful interest groups like the Catholic church and national language and sporting organizations – all foundation pillars of Irish society – complained frequently in the early days at what they considered RTE's sins of omission or commission and occasionally still do so. 'It was, however, in the political field that the biggest problems arose.'[20] In this respect Ireland was not alone. In the early sixties when RTE began to broadcast programmes, television, in Anthony Smith's words, 'had seemed for a moment to escape from all its bonds and become a free and international medium, operated by an almost autonomous profession *despite* its legal and constitutional background'.[21] However, as he pointed out, by the end of the seventies 'the most important change which appears to have taken place is the realisation everywhere that the practices of television will inevitably and necessarily be subjected to political scrutiny and politically imposed change. The genie has been put back in the bottle'.[22] This was precisely the experience in Ireland, and it was a painful one.

From the mid-1960s, there were a number of clashes between the Broadcasting Authority and ministers or other politicians, and they have recurred on and off ever since. From the beginning, 'senior politicians did not share the ideal of an independent service free from government interference'.[23] At its most vulgar this came down to the view of some politicians that RTE, being a state body, should treat all public representatives with respect; report their speeches, whether important or not; and never ask them awkward questions. More serious was the view that RTE was 'an instrument of public policy', put forward in 1966 by the Taoiseach of the day, Seán Lemass, during a Dáil discussion on an incident involving the station and a minister:

Radio Telefís Éireann was set up by legislation as an instrument of public policy and as such is responsible to the Government. The Government have overall responsibility for its conduct and especially the obligation to ensure that its programmes do not offend against the public interest. . . . To this extent the Government reject the view that Radio Telefís Éireann should be, either generally or in regard to its current affairs and news programmes, completely independent of Government supervision.[24]

This was a strong expression of the social responsibility theory. Although Lemass's statement was made in the context of pressure by a minister to alter a news item, it was probably not intended to cover petty interference. It was, however, in respect of the treatment of events in Northern Ireland after 1969, an altogether more serious subject, that the matter was put to the test.

In its desire to report developments in Northern Ireland in a full, balanced, and rounded way, RTE considered that it should report the views of republican organizations such as the IRA as expressed by their spokesmen. Governments took the contrary view, that such reporting would give undesirable publicity and encouragement to organizations whose aim was to subvert the state and perhaps would imply that their spokesmen had some status. In 1971, the Fianna Fáil Minister for Posts and Telegraphs directed the Authority under section 31 of the Broadcasting Authority Act 'to refrain from broadcasting any matter that could be calculated to promote the aims and activities of any organization which engages in, encourages or advocates the attaining of any particular objective by violent means'. Disagreement arose over the interpretation of this directive; and when, in November 1972, after growing political criticism, RTE broadcast a reporter's account of an interview with a provisional IRA leader, the Authority itself was dismissed. Disagreement over section 31 has continued ever since, with each succeeding government of whatever persuasion in its turn renewing the ban, and journalists and others incessantly grumbling and occasionally campaigning to have it removed.

This experience – and there is a similar and continuing history of tension between British broadcasters and British governments – demonstrates clearly that when it comes to sensitive matters, broadcasters are not going to be left free to treat them according to their own standards or be permitted to interpret the requirement to be 'objective and impartial' in their own way. Of course, broadcasters chafe at this. They have the more reason to do so because politicians, particularly those in office, continue to be prone, on the one hand, to petulant sensitivity and, on the other, to seeking to influence or thwart broadcasters for immediate political advantage. Sometimes the broadcasters spoil their own case by claiming too much. As John Horgan has pointed out, the claim of broadcasters to journalistic freedom (specifically the removal of the ban under section 31) on the grounds that the public have an absolute right to know, is really to claim that journalists have an absolute right to decide what the public should and should not know, which is 'a proposition that is less glamorous, and less self-evident'.[25] Journalists in the print medium, as also those in private enterprise – so-called 'independent' – broadcasting, know well that 'freedom exists, in the actual world, primarily for owners, controllers and proprietors, as journalists who offend them find out fairly rapidly'.[26]

In the context of broadcasting as an activity that made use of a very scarce resource, only a very small number of frequencies being available, Michael Tracey was right when he observed that

broadcasting organizations as institutions within society have no actual autonomy and in that sense they have never possessed a legitimate membership of the 'fourth estate'. . . . That fundamental absence of legitimacy as autonomous entities has always defined the political reality of political broadcasting.[27]

However, that reality is now changing because the context of broadcasting has itself changed radically. These changes might well render sterile the debate between broadcasters and politicians, certainly in the terms in which it has been conducted for the last twenty years or so. More seriously, they also have the effect of threatening public service broadcasting with even greater, perhaps insuperable, problems.

These changes are part of the great revolution in tele-communications and the media. They have been well characterized by the RTE Authority itself:

Technological advances have enabled a much greater volume of radio and television programming to be offered to the public. Programmes can now be transmitted by satellite or microwave distribution systems direct to people's homes or carried by cable systems. As a result, the old 'scarcity of frequencies' argument which was the traditional reason for State control of broadcasting is now no longer valid. . . .

Broadcasting is being incorporated into the wider field of communications where innovations are so rapid and far-reaching that they have given rise to what has been called, with some justification, 'the communications explosion'. Because of this integration process and because nearly all of the innovations in communications have been developed, and are being operated, by private enterprise, there is a growing insistence that State monopolies in broadcasting should be scrapped and the airwaves opened to commercial interests.[28]

The response of Irish governments to these changes was at first uncertain and inadequate. Until the late eighties they were both unwilling to deal with the existence of illegal but popular radio stations and slow to take up the wider problem of devising a structure within which public service and private enterprise broadcasting systems would operate side by side. The Radio and Television Act 1988 and the Broadcasting Act 1990 were intended to do this, and they marked the beginning – the official beginning, at least – of a new era in Irish broadcasting.

The Radio and Television Act 1988 provided for the establishment of the Independent Radio and Television Commission to arrange for the setting up and surveillance of private sector broadcasting. The act provides a framework, firstly, for sound broadcasting services, including a national channel. The Commission lets contracts to private enterprise and the Minister for Communications issues licences to broadcast. The act places specific public service broadcasting obligations upon the independent stations. They are required to devote a minimum of 20 per cent of broadcasting time, including two hours between 07.00 and 19.00, to the provision of news and current affairs, unless they are granted a derogation by the Commission. They are bound by the same kind of rules about objectivity and fairness as is RTE and, similarly, may not put out material that undermines the authority of the state or express their own views. They may transmit party political broadcasts but must not give 'unfair preference' to any political party. By 1990, both the national station and local stations were operating under these rules.

The Act provides, secondly, for a private enterprise television service. It empowers the Authority to enter into a contract with a private operator for a new national television service. The new service has statutory obligations in respect of its programming. It must include 'a reasonable proportion of news and current affairs programmes' in its output, and in its programmes generally it is bound by exactly the same rules as RTE (see above, p. 65).[29] This third channel (RTE has two channels) had not begun to broadcast by the end of 1991.

The other act, the Broadcasting Act 1990 was the end-product of a long and acrimonious debate between – and perhaps within – the government, other politicians and parties, the RTE Authority, broadcasters, and private interests. Among its provisions there are arrangements for allocating the all-important revenues, the sources of which are licence fees and advertising. Without these, on the one hand, RTE, the public service broadcasting organization, could not continue to fulfil its social – and legal – responsibilities; and, on the other, the private sector could not make money and survive. The government's original intention to direct some of the licence fee revenue to the private sector to help finance their public service obligations was abandoned during the passage of the bill in a massive U-turn in the face of political, trade-union, and public pressure, as was a blatant attempt in the interests of private enterprise to neuter RTE's popular radio channel, 2FM, by requiring it to cease being a predominantly 'pop' channel and, thus, a big advertising revenue earner. The act did, however, 'cap' RTE's advertising revenue by relating it to the amount it receives in licence fees, a sum governed by the Minister for Communications, and by setting limits to the amount of advertising that can be broadcast. Clearly, the intention was to provide the opportunity for the private enterprise sector to get a bigger share of advertising revenue than it otherwise would. Some, however, saw in these provisions a more sinister objective, an attempt to bring RTE 'to heel'.[30] By the end of 1991, it was widely held that the 1990 Act had been a failure and would have to be modified.

If 'independent' broadcasting is to be able to survive and prosper alongside a public broadcasting organization, some arrangements governing both programming and financing clearly have to be made. Inevitably, the attempt to make them exposes a government to charges of favouring private interests and what the leader of the Labour Party on this occasion called 'the smell of political cronyism and jobbery'.[31] From the point of view of the successful operation of democracy, what matters most is whether the arrangements that are made permit public service broadcasting of the standard which the country has hitherto enjoyed to be maintained. This is a problem that faces many countries. In 1989, the RTE Authority in its document on this subject, *Change and Challenge: the Future for Broadcasting in Ireland,* posed it thus:

How public service broadcasting organisations in particular will finally adjust their programme schedules in response to the new situation has still to become clear. In most European countries where competition has already intensified, the interim response has been to schedule like against like – that is to increase the amount of mass audience programming such as quiz and game shows, serials, films and so on.

The danger is that in trying by these means to win a ratings battle the public service broadcaster could end by losing the war. . . .

The Authority believes that only a properly integrated national policy for communications can ensure that in the wake of deregulation the public service ethic in broadcasting is retained.[32]

In 1991, Ireland was a long way from having such a 'properly integrated national policy'. If the quality of the debate and the uncertainty of the decision-making in the case of the 1990 Act is to characterize future policy formulation in this area, the outlook is not hopeful for public service broadcasting. Perhaps even a *national* policy might not be sufficient. With satellite broadcasting, the dangers of transnational activities and the limited possibilities for any one country to cope with them, since they require international agreement, were in 1991 far from being adequately elucidated and assessed.

V

The effect of the mass media upon political attitudes and behaviour is a subject that is widely recognized as among the most perplexing in politics. A Market Research Bureau of Ireland survey in 1987 produced suggestive data on the media as sources of information and influence, and their findings were in general quite similar to the results obtained by them in 1983.[33] Three-quarters of their respondents declared themselves either 'very interested' or 'fairly interested' in current affairs: over a half perceived – unprompted – television to be the source of 'the most interesting comments and viewpoints': another 21 per cent mentioned radio; and daily newspapers were favoured by 16 per cent. The proposition that 'I rely on newspapers to keep me informed' secured the agreement or strong agreement of 55 per cent, with rural people above that figure and young people below it. When it came to influence, however, there was a clear difference according to issues. Over half of their respondents named the media as being the main source of influence on their 'thinking and opinions' about Northern Ireland, the Third World and the threat of nuclear war but, when it came to more personal matters, it was overwhelmingly their primary group affiliations, the church and the family, that were the significant influences (see Table 2.5, p. 32 above).

We may suspect that the mass media actually communicate less to politicians about the feelings and desires of the public and less to the public about the whys and wherefores of ministerial action than either politicians or newspeople like to believe. Rudolf Klein once argued that

Newspapers and politicians have an almost incestuous relationship: they tend to have closer ties with each other than the newspapers have with their readers and politicians have with their voters. The result is that they both tend to overestimate their influence on the country at large – when, in fact, their main influence is often on each other. [34]

The same might be said of broadcasters and politicians. However, we know so little about the impact of the political inputs effected by way of the mass media that we can hardly even begin to assess their influence upon the outputs – that is, people's political behaviour – in any systematic way. Consequently, there is a formidable gap between this chapter and the rest of the book, the measure of our lack of understanding of political behaviour.

Notes

1   L. Pye, *Communications and Political Development* (Princeton, 1963), p. 26.
2   J. G. Blumler and J. Madge, *Citizenship and Television* (London, 1967), p. 7.
3   See D. Farrell, in *How Ireland Voted 1989* M. Gallagher and R. Sinnott (eds.) (Dublin, 1990), p. 40.
4   Information supplied by Provincial Newspapers Association of Ireland.
5   See *Irish Times,* 7 March 1977; 27 Aug. 1983 and 8 Feb. 1984.
6   Readership figures are derived from *Joint National Media Review 1988–89,* Vol. 1, made available by the Market Research Bureau of Ireland.
7   T. P. Coogan, 'Can the media survive the growing challenge?' in *Irish Broadcasting Review*, No. 4, (Spring, 1979) p. 53.
8   M. Tracey, *The Production of Political Television* (London, 1977), p. 24.
9   A. Smith, in *Irish Broadcasting Review,* No. 2 (Summer 1978).
10   *Change and Challenge: the Future for Broadcasting in Ireland*, issued by the RTE Authority (Dublin, 1989), p. 14.
11   *Ibid.*
12   Broadcasting Authority (Amendment) Act 1976 (No. 37), s. 13.
13   *Ibid.*, s. 3.
14   *Ibid.*
15   Broadcasting Authority Act 1960 (No. 10), s. 31.
16   Broadcasting Authority (Amendment) Act, 1976 (No. 37), s. 16.
17   Derived from Joint National Listenership Research Report: April–May 1990, made available by Market Research Bureau of Ireland.
18   Figures made available by Radio Telefís Éireann Audience Research. See also David M. Farrell, 'Campaign strategies and media coverage' in *How Ireland Voted 1989* M. Gallagher and R. Sinnott (eds.) (Galway, 1990). pp. 37–41.
19   D. Fisher, *Broadcasting in Ireland* (London, 1978), p. 29.
20   *Ibid.*, p. 31.
21   A. Smith (ed.), *Television and Political Life: Studies in Six European Countries* (London, 1979), pp. 232.
22   *Ibid.*, p. 233.

23 B. Farrell in *Ireland at the Polls: the Dáil Election* of *1977*, H. R. Penniman (ed.) (Washington DC, 1978), p. 106.
24 *Dáil Debates*, Vol. 224, cols. 1045–6 (12 Oct. 1966).
25 J. Horgan, 'Broadcasting and the politician' in *Irish Broadcasting Review*, No. 11 (Summer 1981), p. 17.
26 *Ibid.*, p. 15.
27 Michael Tracey, *The Production of Political Television* (London, 1977), p. 231.
28 *Change and Challenge: the Future for Broadcasting in Ireland*, issued by the RTE Authority (Dublin, 1989), p. 7.
29 Radio and Television Act, 1988 (No. 20 of 1988), s. 18.3.
30 See, e.g. newspaper comment and *Dáil Debates* during the first half of June 1990.
31 Quoted in *Sunday Tribune*, 10 June 1990.
32 *Change and Challenge: the Future for Broadcasting in Ireland*, issued by the RTE Authority (Dublin, 1989), p. 28.
33 *Éire Inniu, an MRBI Perspective on Irish Society Today* (Dublin, 1987), pp. 15–18 and Tables 18.1–3.
34 Rudolf Klein, *Observer*, 7 April 1968.

CHAPTER 5

Patterns of Participation and Representation

I

Modern politics is mass politics. In principle at least, people are entitled, and even expected, to be involved, though the nature, quantity, and quality of that involvement vary considerably. Democracies might appropriately be judged by the amount of popular participation in politics, the ease with which people can become candidates for office or get access to those who hold office, and the extent to which the devices of competitive election and representation are used.

In seeking to measure the extent of participation and representation, it is necessary to pay attention not only to formal procedures and to the holders of formal offices, but also to informal activities and to people who, though they do not hold an official public position, nevertheless play some part in political decision-making and perhaps have some influence on outcomes. For when it comes to making a political decision, the spokesman of a powerful group with an interest in the particular issue might well play a much larger part than an elected parliamentary representative. Nor must we forget those activities that are 'outside the system', or at least outside the normal channels and perhaps even outside constitutional or legal limits. Those who engage in such activities are also participating in politics, albeit by other means.

II

Bunreacht na hÉireann in Article 6 refers to the right of the people 'to designate the rulers of the state and, in final appeal, to decide all questions of national policy'. This sums up people's legal rights, but it exaggerates their actual role. The only active part in governing for most people is by way of voting at elections for public offices and at referenda on questions of public policy that legally require the approval of the electorate. It is curious, therefore, when one considers the importance given to consulting the people in democratic theory, how little attention is paid to the question of the number of occasions that are in practice afforded to the people to vote. In fact, the opportunities to exercise such 'sovereign' power are fewer in Ireland than they are, for example, in the United States.

The Constitution provides for referenda in two circumstances. Firstly, if a majority of the Seanad and not less than one-third of the Dáil petition the President to decline to sign a bill on the grounds that it contains 'a proposal of such national importance that the will of the people thereon ought to be ascertained', the President may accede to such a request and precipitate a referendum or a dissolution of the Dáil and a general election. Because governments are able to command majorities in the Seanad, this procedure has never been invoked. Secondly, and of more practical importance, any proposal to amend the Constitution, having been approved by both houses of the Oireachtas, must be 'submitted by referendum to the decision of the people'. There were thirteen such instances between 1937, when the present Constitution came into force, and 1992. The importance and value of this procedure as a means by which the people are enabled to check their governments and representatives are amply demonstrated by the fact that four of the propositions passed by the Oireachtas were rejected by the electorate. These included proposals to change the electoral system (in 1959 and 1968) and to remove the absolute ban on divorce in Article 41 (in 1986).

Irish electors have three opportunities to take part in the selection of public officials. Elections for members of Dáil Éireann are by law required to be held at least once every five years. In practice, on average, they occur about once every three years. Indirectly, this process produces a government as well as a popular assembly, for the party or group of parties that wins a majority of seats thereby acquires the right to form a government. Thus Irish electors do not directly elect their government as, for example, the American electorate choose their President. Elections for members of local authorities are provided for by law every five years, but they can be, and have in the past been, postponed by ministerial order to suit the government's convenience. The President, who, to use Walter Bagehot's terms when referring to the British monarchy,[1] has a largely 'dignified' rather than an 'efficient' role, is also subject to election every seven years; but, here too, the politicians can connive to produce an agreed-upon candidate. This they did on five out of ten occasions between 1937 and 1990, thus depriving the people of the right to choose. If the opportunities for Irish citizens to elect representatives to speak and act for them are few enough, the part citizens play in the selection process is greater than that played by the citizens of many democratic countries by reason of the scope offered by the election system that is used, the single transferable vote system. However, it is still not as great as that played by American citizens, for not only are a considerable number of congressional, administrative, and judicial offices subject to election in the United States, but the practice of having primary elections (that is, direct popular participation in nominating the party candidates to go forward for election) gives voters a bigger say than they have in Ireland.

Elections in Ireland, as in many other countries, give voters the opportunity to choose between the candidates who are presented to them. The choice of the great majority of these candidates, as of most political office-holders, is made by officials and other active members of political parties. In the same way, the choice of most leaders and spokesmen of interest groups is similarly limited. Thus, most of the more important political office-holders and the politically influential are chosen or put up for final popular choice by quite small 'selectorates' – the government itself, which has enormous patronage; party executives, national and local; selection committees at all levels in parties; and bodies such as trade unions and farmers' organizations, which operate in the political arena. To a very large extent, small groups in bodies such as these choose or sponsor the personnel of politics. These active members form a middle group between the electorate and the very small number of people who hold the most important political offices.

Selection of a different kind, on criteria of merit and often by way of competition, provides another small but vital group of participants – senior public servants in the departments of state and other public authorities. Finally, there is a miscellaneous handful of people such as journalists, advisers, and consultants whose influence arises from the positions they hold or the confidence they inspire in policy-makers.

III

The pattern of participation has well-marked characteristics. For the vast majority, voting at elections and referenda is the limit of their active participation. Many, perhaps most, regard themselves as supporters of a political party, although they are not party members and are not much if at all involved in party politics or any kind of politics. The politically active, even on the least onerous definitions of 'active', are a small minority. The political leadership, including those who directly influence the national decision-makers, is minute. In Table 5.1 an attempt is made to quantify participation. (Some of the figures can only be very approximate.) The resultant profile of participation is similar to that which has been observed elsewhere.

When it comes to voting, the record of the Irish electorate at general elections is not among the best in the European Communities, as Table 5.2 shows. In looking at it, it is necessary to remember that there is a considerable variety of laws and practices in respect of who can vote, voting age, registration, and the obligation to vote. Voting in Ireland is not compulsory as it is in some democratic countries, and only registered voters may participate. The proportion of these who

Table 5.1 **Participation in politics in the 1980s and 1990**

Group	Numbers of participants	Per cent of electorate
Electorate (1989)	2,448,810	100
Voters (general election, June 1989)	1,677,592	68.5
Voters (local elections, 1985)	1,643,020	60.[a]
Interested but not active (1981)	–	51[b]
'Close' to a party (1981)	–	20[b]
Party members (1990)	138,120	5.6[c]
Voluntary workers for party (1981)	–	2[b]
Party 'activists' (1990)	30,000	1[d]
Candidates at local elections (1985)	3,348	0.14
Members of local authorities (1985)	1,618	0.07
Dáil candidates (1989)	368	0.02
Members of the Oireachtas (1989)	226	0.01
Members of boards and chief executives of state sponsored bodies & leaders of major pressure groups	about 1,500	0.07[d]
Senior public servants	about 2,600	0.10[d]

Notes: [a] In 1991, elections were held to the County and County Borough Councils only. The turnout was 56 per cent.
[b] M. Fogarty *et al.*, *Irish Values and Attitudes: the Irish Report of the European Value Systems Study* (Dublin, 1984), p. 243.
[c] *Irish Political Studies*, 5 (Dublin, 1990), p. 160 (compiled from information supplied by party head offices).
[d] Author's estimate.

Source: Compiled by the author.

Table 5.2 **Voting at general elections in Ireland and other countries of the European Communities (per cent)**

	Year	Turnout
Belgium	1987	93.3[1]
Denmark	1988	75.8
France	1988	65.7
Germany	1987	84.3
Greece	1990	84.4
Ireland	*1989*	*68.5*
Italy	1987	90.5[1]
Luxembourg	1990	92.1
Netherlands	1990	80.2
Portugal	1987	72.6
Spain	1990	69.7
United Kingdom	1987	75.4

Note: In Belgium and Italy voting is compulsory. In both cases the proportion of spoiled votes, at 6%, was higher than the other countries.
Sources: 1 T. T. Mackie, 'General elections in western Nations', in volumes of *European Journal of Political Research*.
2 Author's enquiries.

turned out to vote at the fourteen elections between the end of the Second World War and 1990 varied between 77 per-cent and 68.5 per cent (in the 1989 election). Turnout at local elections was lower: in 1985 it was 60 per cent and in 1991, 56 per cent. In more than half a century since 1937, there have been only thirteen references to the people by way of referenda, almost all of them in the last twenty years. The referendum on joining the European Communities attracted a 71 per cent turnout, but those of the 1980s brought out lower proportions of the electorate. The highly contentious issues of abortion (1983) and divorce (1986) evoked turnouts of 53.7 per cent and 60.5 per cent respectively. Voting rights for non-citizens (1984) attracted 47 per cent, and the question of confirmation of the Single European Act (1987), 43.9 per cent. Turnout at elections to the European Parliament held every four years has been considerably affected by whether they are conducted on the same day as domestic elections. The 1989 turnout at 68 per cent was 10 percentage points above the Community average: by contrast the 47 per-cent turnout at the 1984 election was below the Community average.

The propensity to vote is not uniform throughout the Irish community. Notably, a smaller proportion of the electorate in Dublin, the only large city, vote than elsewhere, for the urban population is more mobile and more volatile in its voting habits. More people in the big city than elsewhere fail to register and more are rootless, apathetic, or alienated. Although there is not much difference between the proportion of men and women who vote, there are some differences according to age. As is commonly the case in many countries, a few per cent more of the young voters, especially those who are getting their first opportunity to vote, and of the very old abstain. The reasons for people not voting are, however, more complex than this. Michael Marsh has suggested that it is useful to think of non-voters as falling into two categories, 'short-term' and 'long-term'. 'The former do not vote for reasons which are essentially accidental, the latter abstain for more fundamental reasons.'[2] Data from two post-election surveys in 1989, the general election and the European elections held on the same day, suggest that rather over a half of the non-voters fell into the 'short-term' category – too busy, ill, not on the register, on holiday, and so on – and rather under one half into the 'long–term' category – essentially the apathetic and alienated (see Table 5.3).

Furthermore, while short-term non-voters appeared as 'better educated, more wealthy and more middle class than voters as a whole', though they resembled them in respect of political interest and satisfaction, long-term non-voters were 'substantially more working class, worse off and less well educated'.[3]

Although it is difficult to measure active participation in politics, it is quite certain that the proportion of the population who are in any way active, even by way of an occasional intervention, is very small. Raven and Whelan found that, although about half of Irish adults in

Table 5.3 **Reported reasons for not voting at the general election and the European Parliament elections, 15 June 1989 (per cent)**

Lansdowne Market Research		Eurobarometer	
Short term:	*54*	*Short term:*	*56*
Too busy	16	Sickness, holiday,	
Illness, disabled	11	business reasons	34
Recently moved	10	Not on register	24
No voting card, not reg.	14		
Other short term	4		
Long term:	*44*	*Long term:*	*44*
Not interested	20	No interest in elections	25
No party had solutions	7	No interest in Europe	6
Never registered	9	No party to support	5
Could not decide	7	No info. on Europe	3
Not convinced by		Didn't realize election on	2
any party	4	Result foregone conclusion	1
Don't know	1		
N unweighted	123		125

Source: Michael Marsh, 'Accident or design: non-voting in the Irish general election of 1989', Paper presented to the European Science Foundation/Economic and Social Research Council Conference on Political Participation in Europe, Manchester, Jan. 1990

the early seventies believed that they could do something about a harmful regulation, in fact only 11 per cent had ever acted with the intention of influencing a decision at the local level and only 3 per cent at the national level.[4] Figures for party membership in Table 5.1 were supplied by the parties themselves and at 138,000 (nearly 6 per cent of the electorate) are perhaps optimistic: in the early 1980s the European Values Systems Study reported 4 per cent, a figure slightly lower than the European average.[5] Anyway, membership is in the majority of cases more an indication of commitment than a proof of activity.

In general, party branches, of which there were some five thousand nine hundred in 1990 according to the parties themselves, each have about five officers, who can be assumed to be active to some extent, and there might be a few others also.[6] Thus, about 30,000 people might be active at the branch level. A few branches, particularly in the cities, evoke considerable participation but the vast majority do not. Only at election time is there a flurry of branch activity, with many times this number active for a few days or a week or two. Even the largest parties employ minute full-time staffs. In 1990, they numbered only fifty.[7]

It is not possible to be precise about the number of those whose jobs or membership in organizations involve them in making political decisions or in seeking to influence those who do. If the chief executives and members of the boards or governing bodies of about 100 state-sponsored bodies are included, together with the executives and chief officials of a score of organizations that engage in pressure-group activities regularly or frequently, plus a handful of others, we might reach a total of about 1,500 people, with certainly no more than 200 or so of these occupied full-time in these posts.

When it comes to candidates for elected authorities and elected members, we are on surer ground. At the 1989 general election there were 368 candidates for the Dáil and 127 for the Seanad. Membership of the Dáil and Seanad is 226. At the 1985 local elections there were 3,348 candidates for 1,618 seats. Only a small proportion of all these candidates and representatives are anything like full-time politicians. Almost all of them are in the Dáil. Of the members of the 1989 Dáil, four-fifths were in that category.[8] Even with the fifty full-time employees of the political parties, the total of full-time politicians seems to be only about 200. They are certainly greatly outnumbered by the senior civil servants who advise ministers and manage the departments, and the few senior officers in other public authorities who might be said to exercise political influence, if only occasionally. If we include in this group all civil servants of the rank of higher executive officer and above – and this is to cast the net quite widely – they number about 2,600. Thus, in all, perhaps 2,800 people at most (0.11 per cent of the electorate) are full-time at politics; about 30,000 (a little over 1 per cent) are 'active' in politics; and another 4 to 6 per cent are committed enough to be formally associated with party politics. Politics is certainly only for the few.

So far, we have considered politics within the system. An examination of the incidence of direct action such as demonstrations, marches, and political strikes and the numbers involved in them only confirms this picture. In the past, crowds ranging from a few score to a few hundred and very occasionally more could be assembled by radical groups, particularly nationalist organizations evoking traditional and symbolic causes. A larger, though still small, minority continue to support these causes in a casual way with small contributions collected in pubs and on the streets. Such support does not extend to membership, let alone to active membership in radical or extreme organizations, which is tiny. Today, it is more likely to be tax protesters, farmers, together with anti-American, peace and environmental groups and, occasionally, exasperated local community organizations who take to the streets. Farmers' organizations have sometimes held mass protests, and one such, in 1980, attracted 40,000 participants; but attempts to take more militant action such as commodity strikes have not so far had much success. Withholding taxes or other legal charges or levies has become more frequent and perhaps more effective. In recent years, conservation issues have been among those most likely to arouse interest. In August 1979, 12,000 people went to Carnsore Point to protest about the proposal to build a nuclear power plant there. It was in 1979, too, that independent Ireland experienced its first political strike, a one-day strike and marches to protest about the income-tax code, and there have been others since. Such events perhaps serve to remind politicians that Irish citizens are potentially active if politicians fail them. However, if such activities are regarded as signalling the failure of 'system' politics, it is evident that the 'reach' of the Irish political system has so far usually been sufficient to encompass most political aspirations. Only the numerically tiny extreme republican groups continue to operate outside the system, as they have for well over half a century.

In the area of voluntary and community activity, which is not conventionally regarded as 'political', there is much evidence of vastly greater participation than that evoked by 'politics'. There exists a surprisingly large number of voluntary and community organizations. An increasing number of voluntary bodies is involved in local community welfare services, in the provision of amenities, and in protection activities. Although local authorities can and do cooperate with them, and officially recognize one community association in each area as the official body with whom they do business, the worlds of politics and community action tend to be separate and unlinked. The problem of how to integrate them is a difficult one.[9]

IV

The extent to which people participate in politics differs according to the opportunities, institutionalized and informal, that are available, and these in turn are governed by the social norms and the political culture of the community. Everyone in the community has some 'political resources' – that is, the ability to exert some influence on politics – but these vary enormously according to a person's education, occupation, wealth, status in the community, social involvement, and charisma. Whether these resources remain latent or are used depends upon an individual's interests, the stimuli he or she experiences, the organizations available, and personal psychological needs and drives.

The information available hardly starts to provide an adequate answer to the question: who are the politically active in Ireland? To start with, 'there is little systematic theory relating social, psychological and political variables to participation in politics.'[10] As is the case for other countries also, it is the data relating to characteristics such as sex, education, occupation, residence, and family connections that are most readily available, but these do not go much further than explaining inequalities in *opportunity* to be active.

What leads people to take their opportunities is a vastly more complicated subject, about which we know little.

One thing is immediately clear from the information we do have. The politically active are by no means a microcosm of the community. Notably, the disparity between the proportion of men and women active in politics is enormous. Whereas women have had the vote in Ireland from the very foundation of the state and their propensity to use it differs little from that of men, active participation and particularly candidature is a different matter. The paucity of women in politics reflects cultural norms that are only even now slowly changing. Only in 1978 was a woman first appointed a full minister and member of the government.[11] Since then there have been two others and two women ministers of state. The proportion of women candidates for the Dáil at local and general elections has always been tiny. It took the intervention of party leaders and central executives in 1977 to bring the total of women candidates up to twenty-five (7 per cent). Their experience suggested that this was not a popular move and certainly not a vote winner. The number of women in the Dáil rose to a high point of fourteen (8 per cent) in November 1982: in 1989, thirteen (7 per cent) were elected. Some of these few might owe their election to another reason – family connections – for women Deputies are more likely to be related to a former Deputy than are their male counterparts.[12]

With a record like this, Ireland is in the lower half of the European Community league table, as Table 5.4 indicates. The position is little different at other electoral levels. Both at Seanad and at local authority elections, the record shows percentages in single figures and very small increases with time. Out of the sixty senators who took their seats in 1969, five (8.3 per cent) were women: in 1989 also there were five. At the 1979 local elections, out of a total of 806 elected councillors 55 (6.8 per cent) were women: at the 1985 local elections there were 76 out of 868 (8.4 per cent) and in 1991 there were 99 out of 883 (11.2 per cent).[13] Perhaps a change in this apparently consistent pattern was heralded in 1990 when the country elected its first woman President. She owed her election to many factors, but at least she

Table 5.4 **Percentage of women in the parliaments of the member states of the European Communities (most recent election)**

Belgium	8.5	Italy	12.9
Denmark	33.7	Luxembourg	11.7
France	5.7	Netherlands	24.0
Germany	20.5	Portugal	7.6
Greece	4.7	Spain	12.6
Ireland	7.8	United Kingdom	6.5

Source: M. Gallagher, M. Laver and P. Mair, Representative Government in Western Europe (New York, 1992), p. 163.

showed that a woman with the right qualities can do well in a modernizing Ireland.

In Ireland as in other Western countries active politics is to a great extent a middle-class pursuit dominated by members of certain professions and occupations. There is a notable absence of manual workers and, more generally, working-class people as a whole. The nearer the centre – that is, national level politics and office at national level – the more marked are these features, in particular the dominance of professional people. What is notable about Ireland is the large proportion of teachers and small businessmen – shopkeepers, publicans, traders and proprietors of family businesses of various kinds. The reason for this is, quite simply, that they have particularly valuable 'political resources' at their disposal. Although they might not have the advantages which a professional person can derive from his occupation and social connections, they share with them the facility, if they wish, to take time to engage in political activity, a facility not usually available to employees or business executives. Also, many in these occupations come into daily contact with a much larger number of people in their communities than do office workers, labourers, or executives. In a country where personal and local contacts are important such people are well placed.

Among those active at the rank-and-file level in the parties and in local government, there are few manual workers or small farmers. In rural areas, it is the better-off farmers, shopkeepers, publicans, and family business people, together with teachers and a few professional people, who predominate. Although working-class people can win seats on the smaller authorities, the working class is greatly under-represented. In urban areas there are more professional people and non-manual working-class and lower-middle-class people than in the countryside, but here too the shopkeepers and family business people are prominent. Coming to the capital city, Table 5.5 shows the position after the 1985 local elections. Nearly half the council was in the 'intermediate' group composed of teachers, executives, clerical workers, technicians, shopkeepers, and trade-union officials, but almost four out of ten were professional people or managers and only 5 per cent were manual workers.

At the national level, it is even more obvious that politics is for a special few. Over the years ministerial office and parliamentary seats have increasingly come to be held by people of higher socio-economic status. Although the proportion of parliamentary representatives with third-level education is still low compared with many other Western countries, it has increased steadily. Sixty-six per cent of those elected to Dáil Éireann in 1989 had third-level education. Likewise, the professional element had increased. Table 5.6 shows the occupations of Deputies elected at that election. The professional element loomed large. At 46 per cent it continued the inexorable increase of the last quarter of a century: in 1965 professionals comprised less than 20 per

Table 5.5 **Occupational background of Dublin Corporation and City Council members, 1985**

	Professional & managerial[1]	Intermediate[2]	Manual[3]	Unemployed	Housewife
No	49	60	7	2	12
%	38	46	2	1.5	9

Notes: [1] Company directors, senior managers and businessmen, lawyers, auctioneers, doctors, accountants.
[2] Teachers, executive and clerical workers, technicians, shopkeepers, sales workers, trade-union officials.
[3] Postmen, bus conductors, tailors, printers.

Source: P. Smyth, 'Who runs Dublin?' *Irish Times*, 4 September 1985.

Table 5.6 **Occupations[1] of Deputies elected in June 1989**

		FF	FG	Lab	PDs	WP	Others	Total
Manual	No.	2	0	2	0	1	2	7
employee	%	2.6	0	13.3	0	14.3	33.3	4.2
Non-manual	No.	8	6	6	1	3	0	24
employee	%	10.4	10.9	40.0	16.7	42.9	0	14.5
Commercial	No.	21	13	1	2	1	2	40
	%	27.3	23.6	6.7	33.3	14.3	33.3	24.1
Farmer	No.	11	7	0	0	0	0	18
	%	14.3	12.7	0	0	0	0	10.8
Lower	No.	14	17	2	2	0	1	36
professional	%	18.2	30.9	13.3	33.3	0	16.7	21.7
Higher	No.	21	12	4	1	2	1	41
professional	%	27.3	21.8	26.7	16.7	28.6	16.7	24.7
Total	No.	77	55	15	6	7	6	166
	%	100.0	100.0	100.0	100.0	100.0	100.0	100.0

Note: [1] Full-time politicians are classified according to their previous occupation, and Deputies with more than one job are classified according to their main one. The classification scheme used is as follows. Under 'commercial' are included business people, mainly small businessmen such as shopkeepers, publicans, auctioneers, contractors, and so on. 'Lower professionals' are mainly school-teachers, while 'higher professionals' include doctors, lawyers, lecturers, architects, accountants, and economists.

Source: M. Gallagher, in *How Ireland Voted 1989*, M. Gallagher and R. Sinnott (Galway, 1990), pp. 85 and 93.

cent; in 1977, 32 per cent. On the other haand, the farming and commerical elements declined. The falling proportion of farmers – 1965, 23 per cent; 1977, 15 per cent; 1989, 11 per cent – reflected the decline of farming as an occupation. The commercial element also declined at national level despite its preponderance locally. 'Commercial deputies have dropped from 34 per cent in 1965 to their present [1989] 24 per cent.'[14] Nevertheless, the presence of small business people of many varieties is still comparatively 'the distinctive feature' of the Dáil.[15]

At the top, (that is, at ministerial level), Irish experience has still further confirmed what we have already observed, a 'law of increasing disproportion', as Robert Putnam called it, namely, 'the tendency for the representation of higher status social groups to increase as the level of political activity rises'.[16] As Table 5.7 shows, in the sixty years from the beginning of the state to 1982 the majority of ministers have been professional people (a group that has comprised much less than 10 per cent of the working population). Lawyers and teachers have always been predominant. Twelve of the fifteen in Charles Haughey's 1989 cabinet had been in a profession – four were former teachers; three accountants; three lawyers; a medical doctor and a scientist in a managerial position in the public sector. As Table 5.7 shows also, junior ministerial rank has been less monopolized by the third-level-education professionals, but the tendency over time at this level, too, is in the same direction.

Table 5.7 *Social characteristics of Irish ministers, 1922–82 (per cent)*

	Government ministers (N=94)	Junior ministers (N=80)
Occupational group		
Professional	61.5	38.1
Other non-manual	30.2	31.7
Manual	1.2	2.5
Farmers	7.0	27.8
Selected occupations		
Lawyers	26.7	11.4
Teachers	23.3	11.4
Education		
Third level	75.9	41.9
Secondary	20.3	50.0
Primary	3.8	8.1

Source: Derived from J. Coakley and B. Farrell in *Pathways to Power: Selecting Rulers in Pluralist Democracies*, M. Dogan (ed) (Boulder, San Francisco and London, 1989), p. 204.

In Ireland, membership of a profession or having business interests does not imply a middle-class origin: most such people, however, will not have come from the poorest sections of society, and their occupations will have led to their living in a middle-class style. The same is true of most top civil servants and executives in the state boards and companies. There is, though, no semblance of an exclusive upper-class 'establishment' based on birth, school, university, and social intercourse, despite some talk during the Garret FitzGerald governments of the eighties of the domination of 'the Donnybrook set' (Donnybrook is a suburb of Dublin inhabited largely by middle- and upper-middle-class people).

In the past there was a political elite of a different kind. The surviving leaders of the independence movement, men with what came to be known as 'a national record', and their families, for long dominated Irish politics. This first generation of leaders, who were 'politicians by accident', and their relatives and cronies filled the top positions from the 1920s to the 1950s (most of them were very young in the early 1920s). Some of this generation were able to found political dynasties, for one of the features of Irish political life has been the family tradition. In Ted Nealon's *Guide to the 21st Dáil and Seanad* (elected in 1977) there is a section entitled 'Family seats', which begins with the following sentence: 'Of the 148 deputies in the 21st Dáil, 24 are sons and one a daughter of former deputies.' There were also ten other close relatives of former Deputies. Not much had changed by 1989, for Nealon's *Guide to the 26th Dáil and Seanad* (elected in 1989) records relationships with former Deputies as follows: sons, twenty-five; daughters, four; nephews, five; a niece; and a son-in-law.[17]

Apart from those who got a head start as a result of a family connection, most political leaders until recently have achieved their positions by seniority and service, perhaps allied with ability. By 1972, Cohan was able to observe that 'what distinguishes the contemporary elite pattern from the revolutionary pattern is the greater localism that exists today and the very clearly defined stepping stone pattern'.[18] Although party leaders have made conscious efforts to give accelerated promotion to able young men – and, very occasionally, women – there are still well-marked pathways to power. Attributes such as a family name, proficiency at Gaelic games, and a local political bailiwick are all well proven. Certainly, too, as we have seen, some occupations – lawyer, owner of a small business, shopkeeper, auctioneer, publican – help a political career, whereas the farm labourer, the poor farmer, and people in working-class occupations are unable to make a start, let alone get to the top. The only exceptions are trade-union officials who acquire political skills and other 'political resources' that permit them to enter and advance in politics. The 1989 Dáil included four of them and the Seanad, one.

This analysis, it has to be confessed, does not take us very far. In particular, 'it is not easy to establish clear and reliable connections between personality and political behaviour',[19] although it is certain that the influence of personality and the psychological drives that impel some people to seek fulfilment and satisfaction in politics are among the most potent of all the governing factors.

V

The pattern of political participation that has emerged is by no means unusual for a Western democratic country. On the contrary, studies in many countries suggest that, as in Ireland, active participation in political affairs is not only for the few but for a special few. Equality of opportunity to engage in politics does not exist. However, as Hans Daalder pointed out, we must be careful not to fall into 'the determinist fallacy which sees too direct a link between the social origins of politicians and class bias in their politics'. As he says:

Politics is an autonomous process that certainly is affected by class factors but is not causally dependent on them. Theoretically a political elite (and above all competing elites) composed almost exclusively of a large number of upper class persons can still be fully responsive to pressures from below.[20]

Whether they are or not must be ascertained by studying their behaviour and the working of the political institutions and procedures that can promote or impede the transmission of the wishes and attitudes of the community to the policy-makers.

Notes

1   W. Bagehot, *The English Constitution* (London, 1963), p.61. This work was first published in 1867.
2   M. Marsh, 'Accident or design: non-voting in the Irish general election of 1989', Paper presented to the European Science Foundation/Economic and Social Research Council Conference on Political Participation in Europe, Manchester (Jan. 1990), p. 1.
3   *Ibid.*, p.10.
4   J. Raven and C. T. Whelan, 'Irish adults' perceptions of their civic institutions and their own role in relation to them', in *Political Culture in Ireland: the Views of Two Generations*, in J. Raven, C. T. Whelan, P. A. Pfretzschner and D. M. Borock, (Dublin, 1976), pp. 26 and 30.
5   See M. Fogarty, L. Ryan and J. Lee, *Irish Values and Attitudes: the Irish Report of the European Value Systems Study* (Dublin, 1984), p. 243.
6   See *Irish Political Studies*, 5 (1990), p. 160.
7   *Ibid.*
8   T. Nealon, *Nealon's Guide to the 26th Dáil and Seanad* (Dublin, 1989), p. 161.

9   On this subject, see *More Local Government: a Programme for Development,* a report prepared by the Institute of Public Administration (Dublin, 1971), pp. 16–21.

10 R. E. Dowse and J. Hughes, *Political Sociology*, 2nd edn (Chichester, 1986), p. 288.

11 Countess Markievicz was 'Minister for Labour' in 'governments' appointed by the first Dáil, in April 1919, and the second Dáil, in August 1921, during the period of struggle for independence.

12 See M. Gallagher, in *How Ireland Voted 1989*, M. Gallagher and R. Sinnott (eds), (Galway 1990), pp. 86–7.

13 See F. Gardiner, 'Women in local government', in *Women's Political Association Journal,* 23 (1987), p. 14. The 1991 figure was supplied by Ms Gardiner.

14 M. Gallagher, in *How Ireland Voted 1989*, M. Gallagher and R. Sinnott (eds), (Galway, 1990), p. 85.

15 M. Gallagher, 'Social backgrounds and local orientations of members of the Irish Dáil', in *Legislative Studies Quarterly,* X (1985), p. 376.

16 Quoted by J. Coakley and B. Farrell in *Pathways to Power: Selecting Rulers in Pluralist Democracies,* M. Dougan (ed.) (Boulder, San Francisco, and London, 1989), pp. 204–5.

17 See T. Nealon, (1) *Guide to the 21st Dáil and Seanad* (Blackrock, 1977), p. 134; (2) *Nealon's Guide to the 26th Dáil and Seanad* (Dublin, 1989), p. 161.

18 A. S. Cohan, *The Irish Political Elite* (Dublin, 1972), p. 57.

19 L. W. Milbrath and M. L. Goel, *Political Participation, How and Why do People Get Involved in Politics?* (Chicago, 1977), p. 74.

20 H. Daalder in *Political Parties and Political Development*, J. LaPalombara and M. Weiner (eds), (Princeton, 1966), pp. 70–1.

CHAPTER 6

Political Parties

I

The main political divisions in Ireland after 1921 arose out of disagreements in the independence movement on nationalist isues: Commonwealth status or republic, the extent of the state, and constitutional symbols and forms. The mass parties that developed in Great Britain from the 1860s onwards, reflecting as they did the social and political divisions of a metropolitan society, never had much relevance for the majority in Ireland. Whereas Great Britain became increasingly industrialized, urbanized, and class polarized, Ireland remained largely rural and agricultural and, as a consequence of land reform, increasingly dominated by smallholders. With the successful intervention of a nationalist movement comprising rebel political as well as military organizations, there was little continuity in the party system before and after independence, the less so because, as so often happens in the evolution of a nation to statehood, the parties of the early stages of struggle were superseded or could not take the strains of momentous change and broke up.

Consequently, the party system that emerged in the 1920s bore little resemblance to the system before independence. The Irish Parliamentary Party – the party of the middle-class, moderate nationalists – disappeared, overwhelmed by the tide of events. The split of Sinn Féin and the resulting civil war opened up a cleavage that changed that movement entirely. Only the Labour Party, founded in 1912, continued in existence; but it, too, was greatly changed, like so much else, by the events of 1916 and after.

Nevertheless, although the bases of partisanship and the party system in the new state were to a great extent new and different from what had gone before, it must not be supposed that there was no continuity. As Tom Garvin has pointed out, the 'politicians by accident' who dominated the new scene did not create their movements out of nothing. The organizations that waged the struggles of 1916–22 were the successors of, and were built upon, a number of nationalist, populist, and agrarian mass movements and secret societies of the late nineteenth and early twentieth centuries.[1] The two biggest parties, Cumann na nGaedheal (later Fine Gael) and Fianna Fáil, were formed and developed by rival groups of leaders of the independence movement out of the substantial remains of the existing political and politico-military organizations. In the case of Fianna Fáil, the success of its first organizers in contacting and reviving local units of the former Irish Volunteers in many parts of the country partly explains both the character of the party and its rapid rise to a dominating position in Irish politics.

II

The split of Sinn Féin polarized Irish politics. At first, it almost prevented constitutional politics from developing at all, for it led to civil war; but quite quickly a party system emerged that was essentially bipolar. The dichotomy on which it was based was less the reflection of divisions in the community than the cause of them. Rival groups of leaders created a cleavage in Irish society based upon a division of their own making. As Garvin has pointed out, when the Irish electorate were first consulted – in the 1922 general election – they were far from unanimous that the Treaty issue was the most important one. Nor was the country split into two groups on that issue, for 40 per cent of the voters cast their first preferences for candidates other than the pro-Treaty and anti-Treaty factions of Sinn Féin.[2] However, this rapidly did become *the* issue, particularly after Fianna Fáil's entry into the Dáil in 1927, and the great majority of people were divided upon it above all else. Other parties, in particular the Labour Party, and other politicians 'found their politics to be increasingly peripheral to the concerns of the vast majority of the electorate'.[3]

The two major parties produced by the split helped to perpetuate it. One, Cumann na nGaedheal, was formed by supporters of the Treaty in 1923 and became Fine Gael in 1933; the other, Fianna Fáil, was founded by the opponents of the Treaty, or rather by those of them who turned to parliamentary politics in 1926 with the expectation of soon winning power. These parties and the leaders who personified them were the poles around which the majority of the community gathered in groups large enough to allow first the one and then the other to form governments composed exclusively of their own supporters. Until 1948 at least, there was little crossing the great divide between them, though by then the issues that had split Sinn Féin were either resolved or increasingly irrelevant. Yet the parties continued – their names evoking distinctive images in the public mind; their leaders and aspirant leaders irreconcilable; their traditions (including family traditions) hardened; and their interests vested. Although since then these parties have necessarily altered their strategies and programmes from time to time as they waged party warfare, they have about them the same air of permanence as do the Conservative and Labour parties in Great Britain and the Democratic and Republican parties in the United States.

Other parties and politicians also tended to be committed one way or the other on the Treaty issue. Hence they were orientated to one or the other of the major parties. Because of the particular proportional representation election system that was adopted and the strength of local and personal factors in Irish politics, small parties were always likely to appear. Some explicitly presented variations on the constitutional theme, reflecting merely the dissatisfaction of politicians at the handling of this issue. Such were the National League and Clann Éireann in the 1920s and the Centre Party in the 1930s. Others, ostensibly based on some other community interest, such as farming, were inevitably irreconcilable opponents of one major party and hence, willy-nilly, camp followers of the other. The pre-eminence of this issue inhibited the development of parties based on other community interests or cleavages, and at times of stress, as in the middle 1930s, those that had existed disappeared as ranks closed and tightened. Only two groups did not fit into this pattern: radical republicans, because they cared too much about the issue; and the Labour Party, because it said it cared very little.

From the earliest days of the state there have always been intransigent republicans, some of radical disposition, who have not accepted the regime. De Valera and those who joined with him in eventually founding Fianna Fáil were the first of a long line. From the mid-1920s onwards, after the major part of the anti-Treaty party entered constitutional politics, the die-hards grouped and regrouped in a succession of extreme, fissiparous, and often short-lived organizations. They and their successors have always been able to recruit a tiny and shrinking minority of each succeeding generation. Some of these organizations have been on the verge of constitutional politics. Others, notably the Irish Republican Army, have been committed to force, though from time to time they have had political wings or fronts. Some have sought a republic, or more accurately 'the Republic,' which, they have said, the leaders within the system had subverted or betrayed. Others, the heirs and successors of James Connolly or radicals of the left, have hoped for a socialist republic.

Some have moved unequivocally into the arena of constitutional politics as de Valera did. The temporary success for a few years from 1948 of Clann na Poblachta, led by Seán MacBride, the radical republican and former IRA leader, was due to successful draw-offs into parliamentary politics from both republican streams and their combination with radical elements of the left of both Fianna Fáil and the Labour Party. It was an unstable mixture that could not long survive. The Workers' Party had a similar pedigree. When Sinn Féin split (yet again) in 1970, the majority faction which stood for a socialist republic called itself 'Official Sinn Féin' (the minority became 'Provisional Sinn Féin'; hence 'the Provos'). As it abandoned extreme tactics and shed extreme personnel in favour of socialism of a Euro-communist kind, it changed its name, first, to 'Sinn Féin, the

Workers' Party' (1977) and, then, to 'The Workers' Party' (1982). A further shift led it to change its name yet again in 1992, this time to 'Democratic Left'.

The Labour Party never quite fitted into the dominant pattern imposed upon Irish politics by the two major parties. Established before independence by trade-union leaders as an alliance of trade unionism and socialism, it was deprived by partition of an important source of strength – the industrialized area of Belfast and environs. It soon found itself to a great extent irrelevant in a predominantly rural country, much of whose farming was dominated by smallholders. In default, due to the refusal of anti-Treaty TDs to take their Dáil seats, it established itself as the major opposition party in the new Dáil and played an important part in the establishment of constitutional and parliamentary politics. However, the entry of Fianna Fáil to the Dáil in 1927 finally confirmed the polarization of party and electoral politics, leaving the Labour Party as a third party without a basis for mass support, the less so since it argued – wrongly, in the eyes of most people – that the Treaty was not the most important issue and advocated social and economic policies that 'were essentially welfarist with a minimal attraction to the major economic sectors of the community'.[4] It has remained in that position ever since.

The dominance of national and constitutional issues, as we have seen, inhibited the development of parties based on other community interests or divisions. Perhaps most surprising was the failure of farmers' parties to emerge as permanent features of the system. Because agriculture varied considerably in Ireland, agrarian parties, when they did appear, tended to be regional. The Farmers' Party of the 1920s was predominantly a party of farmers of some substance based on a Farmers' Association with headquarters in Dublin. Although it won fifteen seats and 12 per cent of the valid poll in 1923, it was absorbed within the decade, mostly into Cumann na nGaedheal with which the majority of its prominent members quite obviously belonged. In the 1940s, Clann na Talmhan (the Party of the Land), a loose-knit organization of conservative small farmers of the west who had previously supported the major parties, emerged briefly to represent a very different kind of farmer. Later, in the 1980s, with the increasing strength and professionalism of the main agricultural interest groups, there were signs of the development not of a farmers' party but a farming vote, a political phenomenon of great potential significance.

With the Irish single transferable vote system of proportional representation, it is easier than in most electoral systems for small parties and even people going forward as individuals to win seats. For example, the 1989 Dáil included a representative from the Green Party. In particular, a small breakaway group or persons being expelled or seceding from their parent party might, if they are well-established Deputies, retain their seats as a tiny party or as 'Independents'. Three out of the four 'Independents' elected to the

1977 Dáil were in this category. More significantly, the formation of the Progressive Democrats in 1986 was occasioned by the ousting or withdrawal of dissident Deputies from Fianna Fáil: all of them held their seats at the next election. Without such a firmly based core group of Deputies, the Progressive Democrats would not have survived to assume the pivotal role that they held in the late eighties and early nineties.

III

Since the late twenties, party politics have always been dominated by the same three parties. Other parties have come and gone, usually within a decade. The extent of that domination is clearly evident from the data in Table 6.1. Twice, the 'reach' of the major parties has faltered, firstly in the forties after which the traditional dominance of the established parties was reasserted and, secondly, from the middle eighties. This time perhaps the former pattern might not recur (see below, p. 98). So far, however, this has been a major fact of Irish party politics.

Table 6.1 Combined strength of Fianna Fáil, Fine Gael, and the Labour Party, 1932–89

Election	First-preference votes %	Seats %	Election	First preference votes %	Seats %
1932	88	89	1961	88	92
1933	86	87	1965	97	98
1937	90	94	1969	97	99
1938	95	95	1973	95	99
1943	81	84	1977	93	97
1944	78	83	1981	92	93
1948	70	77	1982 (Feb.)	94	96
1951	84	85	1982 (Nov.)	94	97
1954	88	91	1987	78	87
1957	84	88	1989	83	89

Source: Calculated from election returns by the author.

The second major fact of Irish party politics is that for more than half a century, after Fianna Fáil first realized its full potential as a constitutional party, it has always been able to attract the support of four to five out of ten of the electorate (see Table 6.2).

A party with a volume of support of this order is a classic example of a *parti à vocation majoritaire*, a party that has a parliamentary majority or thinks and acts as though it is likely to be able to command one. Such a party is unlikely to contemplate entering a

Table 6.2 **Maximum and minimum strengths of each of the major parties, 1932–89**

Party	First-preference votes %		Seats in Dáil %	
	Min.	Max.	Min.	Max.
Fianna Fáil	42	52	44	57
Fine Gael	20	39	21	42
Labour	6	17	5	15

Source: Calculated from election returns by the author.

coalition government. It will be the less likely to if, as in the case of Fianna Fáil, it sees itself as more than a party, rather a national movement, and has had as its first leader in its formative years a messianic character like de Valera, 'the Chief'. What is more, for thirty-seven out of the forty-one years from 1932 to 1973, it did hold power and the Irish party system could most accurately be described in Giovanni Sartori's term as a 'predominant party system', that is, 'a type of party pluralism in which – even though no alternative in office actually occurs – alternation is not ruled out and the political system provides ample opportunities for open and effective dissent, that is, for opposing the predominance of the governing party'.[5] Such alternation did in fact occur (in 1948–51 and 1954–57) in the only way it could occur, by the formation of an anti-Fianna Fáil 'rainbow' coalition and from 1973 by Fine Gael–Labour coalitions (in 1973–77, 1981 to March 1982, December 1982–87). By the late eighties, though, it was evident that Fianna Fáil's position was less dominant than it had been.

Until then, however, the continuity imposed by the logic of the electoral arithmetic outlined above was the third major fact of Irish party politics. The triad of parties that emerged after independence continued as the major vehicles for partisan politics long after the issues that threw them up had either been resolved or had ceased to have great importance in the minds of the public. It was not until well into the second half of the twentieth century that attempts were made to pour new wine into the old bottles and even then not without disagreements over the wisdom of the procedure. In all three the process of modernization led to factional strife.

In the fashion of the time the two largest parties, Fianna Fáil and Fine Gael, tended to present themselves as 'catch-all' parties, pragmatic in temper and given to the incremental approach often exhibited after the Second World War by the large established parties of relatively satisfied Western countries. For Fianna Fáil this involved a further consolidation of the pro-business policies with which it had sought in office in the thirties and forties to attract sections of the community hitherto hostile, while retaining the loyalty of its core supporters. Conversely, for Fine Gael it involved moving cautiously towards the welfare state while not antagonizing its core right-wing constituency. Even the Labour Party sometimes seemed to be wooing the social democratic end of the middle ground. It was as if all parties believed that public opinion was assuming a single-peaked profile with, consequently, a centripetal pull towards a moderate centre.

The extent to which the major parties provided clear alternatives on issues of substance from the sixties to the eighties has been a matter of controversy among students of Irish politics. Some have contended that they adopted pragmatic, even opportunistic, strategies; were often not very programmatic at all; and, in any event, by European standards were quite close to one another.[6] On the basis of an analysis of party programmes, Peter Mair, on the other hand, has contended that there was 'more of a policy divide in the Irish party system than is normally acknowledged . . .. If election programmes . . . or the speeches which are based on them do offer a genuine guide to electoral choice, then these data imply the existence of meaningful policy options.'[7] (The 'if' is perhaps important.) Mair's conclusions were that there was conflict over substantive issues and that there were ideological differences. 'The basic ideological division underlying the competition between Irish parties in this period [1960 onwards] and which separated Fianna Fáil from Fine Gael and Labour, was that of corporatist ideology versus social democracy.'[8] This was, to be sure, 'an essentially moderate and loosely defined version' of corporatism encompassing a 'combination of appeals to the national interest and social solidarity . . . towards the enduring goal of economic growth and development . . . under the directive hand of a strong and effective administration.'[9] The National Understandings of 1979 and 1980, the Programme for National Recovery of 1987 and the Programme for Economic and Social Progress of 1991 (see below, pp. 126–28) were clearly products of such a policy, but, Mair argues, there was much more to it than that and over a longer period of time.

Fine Gael and Labour, on the other hand, Mair found, pursued social democratic policies with a stress on social justice and pluralism, and a controlled economy. Their leaders approached these objectives from different directions, but to take up such a stance did allow them both to challenge for the middle ground and to provide a credible and viable alternative to a Fianna Fáil government: indeed, given that party's 'no coalition' strategy, this was the *only* alternative.[10]

Fine Gael's *Just Society* proposals of the sixties and the period of Dr Garret FitzGerald's leadership marked the attempt to turn the party from its traditional conservative stance. This attempt was clearly antipathetic to some in the party and ran into difficulties on the economic front in the recession of the early and middle eighties, and on the social justice and pluralist front with the referendum debates of 1983 and 1986. For the Labour Party, it might seem that rapid industrialization and urbanization from 1960, with a consequent increase in the number of urban working-class people, would offer the opportunity to become the socialist alternative that many European electorates had available at that time. Some in the party thought so, though it would have involved a long haul. If there was then a chance of developing a socialist alternative to the 'right-wing' parties, Labour's equivocal stance as it veered between a social democratic coalition strategy (with Fine Gael) and a go-it-alone policy with a more radical, though still moderate, socialist programme, led to its being outflanked on the left by the Workers' Party, a party that, in spite of its origins, was thoroughly domesticated by the early eighties.

'By 1986, the party system was in flux', according to Mair.[11] There now existed what he called an 'available electorate', i.e., an increasing proportion of the voters were not strongly attached to their parties but could be persuaded to shift their allegiance if what was on offer appealed to them. This volatile pragmatic element in the electorate demonstrated its existence in no uncertain fashion at the 1987 election: 'at least one in every six voters altered their voting behaviour'.[12] Apart from the changes induced by party competition, doubtless growing industrialization, urbanization, and modernization generally had contributed to this. The same factors had created at least the potential for a working-class vote, though the left parties had not as yet mobilized it to the extent that might have been expected. Although it was not likely in the immediate future to be of itself anywhere like large enough to envisage the production of a left-wing government, it was already ensuring the continued growth of the Workers' Party which had attracted it more effectively than Labour.

It was, however, the split in Fianna Fáil that led to the creation of the Progressive Democrats at the end of 1985 which was the catalyst of change at this particular time. Partly due to recession, the PDs' combination of right-wing economic policies, liberal-pluralist social policies, and explicit dedication to 'mould-breaking' appealed to enough people both in Fianna Fáil and Fine Gael to put it into a pivotal position in making and maintaining governments. The failure of Fianna Fáil to win a majority in 1987 led to a tenuous period of minority government followed by the unsuccessful attempt in 1989 to mend the situation. These failures finally induced its leaders to abandon a half-century-old policy of going it alone and to enter into coalition with the Progressive Democrats. 'At last, this key distinguishing feature of the Irish party system may have become a matter of historical record rather than a feature of contemporary reality.'[13] If so, Irish experience in the future might fit more easily into the theory and practice of coalition government than it has hitherto. However, it will need a lot to get the loyal traditionalists in Fianna Fáil to give up what they call a 'core value' and go further down this road: they will certainly have to have proved to them beyond doubt that the party cannot win that elusive 5 per cent of votes that would give them a single party majority government.

IV

Studies of the patterns of support for Irish parties have tended to conclude that, although partisanship is not entirely without social bases, these are comparatively weak. An examination of 1969 data led Mair to conclude that 'political preferences seem remarkably unstructured by social class', and data covering almost the next twenty years suggested, he thought, that 'the Irish party system is characterised by a politics which is even more free of social bases than was the case in 1969'.[14] Michael Gallagher concurs: 'social structure does have less impact upon partisanship in the Republic of Ireland than in almost every other country . . .. What is unusual about the Irish case is that while class has only a small impact on partisanship, everything else has even less impact'.[15]

Perhaps the reason for this phenomenon is that the original basis of the main division in politics was the quarrel over national issues, was political, and was the creation of leaders who succeeded in mobilizing the great majority of the electorate behind them and, subsequently, in continuing to hold them and recruit new support across the board – very successfully in the case of Fianna Fáil. Partisanship was handed down from generation to generation and remained stable. Parties had large 'core' support. It was not until the seventies that this kind of partisanship weakened markedly and Irish voters increasingly became an 'available electorate', and not until the eighties that big changes actually occurred.[16]

Notwithstanding this change and all the vicissitudes consequent upon factional disputes within the party, Fianna Fáil has continued to hold its position, as Table 6.3 shows. It is truly a national party. In 1989, it had more support than other parties, not only in all classes, save the large farmers, but in all regions, and in both urban and rural areas. This was not always so. In its earliest days, its support came mainly from rural areas and from among the small farmers, together with many of the more recent arrivals in the cities, mostly urban working-class, but also middle-class, people with small-farmer backgrounds. This was the 'periphery' which by dominating Fianna Fáil dominated political life.[17] The moderation of Fianna Fáil's leaders that became conservatism in office and its pro-business policies both attracted the support of sections of the community hitherto hostile and conversely lost it some of its support in its former rural strongholds that were in any case suffering continuous population losses. From the forties it became a 'catch-all' party. Its long and continued domination of Irish politics is due to its success in effecting this transformation.

Table 6.3 **Social bases of party support, July 1989 (per cent)**[1]

Category	Fianna Fáil	Fine Gael	Labour	Progressive Democrats	Workers' Party	Others	DK/ REF
All	38	27	10	3	5	4	13
Occupational category[2]							
ABC1	33	32	10	4	2	5	12
C2DE	41	22	12	4	8	4	11
F1	37	41	4	2	0	1	14
F2	40	25	7	0	4	1	21
Area type							
Urban	36	24	12	4	7	5	11
Rural	40	33	7	2	2	2	13
Region							
Dublin	33	22	11	3	10	8	12
Rest of Leinster	40	28	13	2	2	3	12
Munster	38	30	11	5	3	1	12
Connacht and Ulster	43	32	3	3	3	3	14

Notes: [1] This poll was undertaken three weeks after the 1989 general election.
[2] Social group ABC1 (middle class) is composed of people in professional, managerial, and clerical occupations. Social group C2DE (working class) is composed of manual workers. Category F1 are farmers with more than 50 acres, and F2 are small farmers or farm workers.

Source: Irish Times/MRBI Poll, July 1989, prepared by Market Research Bureau of Ireland Ltd (Dublin, 1989), Table 8.

The price it paid was the emergence of factions exacerbated by personal rivalries. It weathered these, even the split that produced the Progressive Democrats in the mid-eighties.

Whereas Fianna Fáil was originally the party of the countrymen and republicans, Cumann na nGaedheal (from 1933 Fine Gael) was at first the party of the Treaty, law and order, and Commonwealth status. As such it was more attractive than Fianna Fáil to the business world, to many shopkeepers and professional people, and to the more prosperous farmers. It looked and behaved like a conservative party and attracted those who desired stable government, those who thought that the Treaty, the Irish Free State, and the Commonwealth connection were the best guarantees of these, and those who could not abide de Valera. As Fianna Fáil established itself and showed in office that it could govern responsibly and was aiming at a conservative, Catholic republic, support for Fine Gael, which had little positive to offer, flagged. Like Fianna Fáil, it attempted from the forties to appear as a national 'catch-all' party. Although it had some success in retrieving its position – its first preference votes climbed to 39 per cent in 1982 – its chances of becoming the majority party were always poor, though many in the party continued to cherish that hope, as once again in the early nineties it found itself, as it did in 1948, at a low point in its fortunes. Nevertheless, it too is a national party, though its support is both more class-based and very much thinner than that of Fianna Fáil (see Table 6.3).

In contrast to Fianna Fáil and Fine Gael, support for the Labour Party is markedly class-based and does not derive from the whole country. The party does have patchy, rural support except in Connacht and Ulster, but it is stronger in urban areas. It derives its main support from urban working-class people. So, too, does the Workers' Party. It is important to notice, however, that Labour and the Workers' Party are not the parties of the working class. Both Fianna Fáil and Fine Gael have consistently attracted more of that class than Labour: in the case of Fianna Fáil many more – in 1989 it had the support of twice as many as Labour and the Workers' Party combined (see Table 6.3).

V

Parties perform three main functions in the political process; from a democratic standpoint we might almost say that they render three services. Firstly, they mobilize the electorate. Their primary aim is to win votes in order to have their nominees elected to political office. From their point of view, this above all is what matters. At all levels the main activity of party structures is directed to this end: at local level almost exclusively so. To do so involves them in communicating opinions and demands to the policy-makers in their own organizations and party policies to the public. It also involves their leaders in processing demands by combining them into coherent courses of action or policies which, they hope, they and their party colleagues will be able to 'sell' to the public. Secondly, parties select candidates for political posts, especially those that are to be filled by election; they are thus important agencies for recruiting political leaders at all levels. Since the spoils system does not operate to any great extent in Ireland, there are not many non-elected public offices to which the parties nominate choices of their own. Thirdly, party leaders take on responsibility for conducting central and local government and for operating the representative and parliamentary processes of discussion, scrutiny, and criticism of government policy and administration. In the performance of this function, opposition leaders are as important as the government.

The organization and procedures that parties adopt to carry out these functions differ according to the nature of the political system and the size of the party. In considering Irish party organization, two distinctions must be made. Firstly, there is a distinction between the three major parties on the one hand, and the smaller parties that have existed from time to time and the independents on the other. In the past, minor parties with pretensions usually tried to model themselves on the major parties, with a similar pattern of organization; but lack of resources, both human and material, was against them. Inevitably they tended to be essentially electoral alliances of Deputies who closely resembled the formally independent members in that each had some sort of organization in his own area, often consisting mainly of personal contacts. Significantly, the two most recently formed minor parties, the Workers' Party (now Democratic Left) and the Progressive Democrats, are more centre-biased than those of the past, reflecting the trend towards more centralization in parties generally.

Secondly, there is a distinction between Fianna Fáil and the rest. Irish parties are poor compared with those of many advanced countries and especially large, rich countries. Until the seventies they exhibited a haphazard, even amateurish approach to the tasks of building membership and getting votes. However, Fianna Fáil was always incomparably the best of them, not because it was firmly controlled from the centre but, quite the reverse, because it was a populist movement rooted in the rural areas where it was strongest in a large number of small local branches. The party, it could be said, permeated local society, and this feature fed its own self-image of being more than a party, rather a national movement. This party 'style', if it may be called such, served it well at least until recently. Certainly, the party always out-performed Fine Gael, traditionally 'a much more cadre-style party . . . mobilised primarily through the influence of local notables'.[18]

The main institutions of the parties are the local clubs or branches (called *cumainn* in the case of Fianna Fáil), each linked to some sort of electoral constituency organization; an annual delegate meeting or convention (called Árd Fhéis in the case of both Fine Gael and Fianna Fáil); the National Executive Committee; the 'parliamentary party', that is, the members of the party who have seats in the Oireachtas; the party leader; and the Central Office. In the rural areas branches are based on the parish, the ecclesiastical unit which is the natural community division: in towns and cities, on urban areas or wards, the local government units. Both Fianna Fáil and Fine Gael have branches almost throughout the country. Labour has a lesser and more patchy coverage; strongest in the east and the south, almost non-existent in rural Connacht. (For details of the number of branches, see Table 6.4.)

Because of the parochialism of politics and the importance attached by the local population to the role of their representatives as intermediaries, national leaders and the Central Offices have traditionally had only limited control over the local branches. What suits an individual representative, his henchmen, and the local party

Table 6.4 **Party branches, 1989**

Fianna Fáil	3009	Progressive Democrats	205
Fine Gael	1865	Sinn Féin	296
Labour	467	Green Party	40
Workers' Party	235 (1988)		

Source: Irish Political Studies, 5 (1990), p. 160.

organizations in his bailiwick is not always to the advantage of the party. No matter: those at the centre can only do their best to inspire, advise, and occasionally cajole the branches into following what they consider appropriate courses of action. To the local leaders and active participants, the ideal role of the centre is essentially as an aid to their local efforts. They resent its interference, particularly when it comes to nominations for office. Rows over the imposition of candidates by the centre occur at every general election.

Although central control over the branches is still limited, it has without doubt increased since the early seventies, when all the major parties began modernizing. At that time they all reformed their Central Offices and put more resources into them. At that time also they began to make use of public relations and marketing techniques and personnel, and to commission market research surveys in order to plan their campaigns nationally. They tried to subordinate local priorities and local interests to national needs when panels of candidates were being chosen. They sought for the first time to exploit the possibilities that the single transferable vote system offers to engage in vote management. As they shifted the emphasis increasingly towards national campaigns with national strategies, targeting marginal seats, and so on, general elections became less a collection of separate constituency campaigns waged locally with central aid and encouragement than they used to be. In Mair's view, to the extent that candidates see the national campaign as important for their chances, 'it is likely that the head offices will gradually gain the upper hand in this enduring conflict between organizational centre and organizational periphery'.[19]

During the organizational reforms of the 1970s, the leaders of the major parties saw the need to recruit their increment, or more if possible, of the burgeoning number of young people, and youth organizations were established. However, efforts at national and regional levels – with highly publicized youth conferences where the elders of the party spend their weekends being told what they are doing wrong by the young – have not been matched at local level. Just as local deputies and local branches find the intervention of the centre unwelcome, so, too, many established elders and long-serving local workers are often less than enthusiastic about the rapid promotion in their vicinity of young people with high potential. Seniority and long service have always been, and continue to be, the major criteria for the advancement of all but the few who are favoured by their family connections. The introduction of even these needs to be handled with care.

The most important functions of the branches are to nominate candidates and to fight elections. For some branches these are almost the only functions, though the officers of many serve as 'contact men' and are important links in the 'service' activities of public representatives for their constituents. The concomitant functions of political education and recruitment of members to the party, that one might think are continuing activities on which successful elections are based, are not pursued actively by most branches. In a few, mainly in the cities and to a greater extent in the Labour Party than in the others, policy is debated, particularly in preparation for the annual convention, where resolutions submitted by the branches are considered. Even fund-raising tends to be confined to the annual collection and to the period immediately prior to a general election.

Evidently branches are not organs of popular participation. Rather they conform to what Richard Rose called the 'top-down' model of party organization. 'From this perspective, the most important activity of party members on the ground is winning elections' and branches are not seen as centres for local popular participation or for the political education of the masses.[20] In so far as they act as channels of information and opinion in the other direction – that is, to the centre – it is often through the local public representatives, who are in any case very closely in touch with their constituents or at least the most important of them. Representatives might well feel that they understand and interpret local opinion better than the active members of the branches, and many would prefer to have a communications system of which they personally rather than party branches were the focal point.

Clearly, it would be dangerous to view local branches purely as instruments of the party. In some, power is in the hands of a small group of the henchmen of a local representative. He and they see the branch, and indeed as many branches as they can control, as part of the representative's 'machine'. It is for this reason that there exist 'phantom' or 'paper' branches which are inactive and exist only for the purposes of influencing nominations.

Since branches are not primarily recruiting agents for the party, it is no wonder that the numbers of party members are low. Party rules require only that a person seeking to become a member must declare his or her acceptance of the party's aims and regulations, must be elected by a branch, and having been elected, must pay and maintain a subscription (except in the case of Fianna Fáil, where no fee is specified). The minimum number of members in a branch is small –

ten in the case of Fianna Fáil; nine in the case of Fine Gael; ten in the case of Labour's urban branches and five in its rural branches. In practice, all that is required is a team of officers and the payment of a very low, minimum registration fee. It is not surprising either that the exact number of party members is hard to ascertain. Fianna Fáil does not know precisely how many members it has: it leaves to the constituency organizations the job of monitoring the general membership. The other major parties have maintained central registers since the early seventies. Details of party membership as claimed by the parties in 1989 are set out in Table 6.5. Almost certainly this is an overestimate.

Table 6.5 **Party membership, 1989**

Fianna Fáil	89,000	Workers' Party	3,450 (1988)
Fine Gael	32,000[1]	Sinn Féin	3,200
Labour	6,720	Green Party	1,200
Progressive Democrats	6,000[2]		

Notes: [1] There were also 3,000 members in Young Fine Gael.
[2] 'The figure for membership represents a core of active members rather than numbers on a mailing list.'

Sources: Irish Political Studies, 5 (1990), p. 160, and 3 (1988), p. 143. The table was compiled from 'information supplied by party head offices'.

In the case of Labour, following the British practice, trade unions and similar organizations may affiliate as corporate members, thus greatly increasing the nominal membership. In 1990, out of a total of fifty-six unions, thirteen were so affiliated in respect of 170,000 members (37 per cent of the Irish Congress of Trade Unions membership).

It is the right and duty of branches to send delegates to the party's annual convention or Árd Fhéis. According to the rule books, the annual convention is the supreme authority in the party. In practice, despite some lip service to the proposition, it is nothing of the sort. Its very size – the Fianna Fáil Árd Fhéis in 1979 numbered about 7,000 delegates; in 1990, a bad year for the party, about 4,000 – and the nature of the gathering make it unsuitable for the effective consideration of policy and demand that it be stage-managed to some extent. It is, rather, an occasion for a demonstration of party loyalty and for the rank-and-file workers to meet their national leaders. Very occasionally, the delegates get a policy devised by their leaders reversed, but for the most part the resolutions that are passed are no more than guides to party opinion. More often, the mood of the party faithful is indicated by their reactions from the body of the hall; these are no doubt noted by the leadership on the platform. The real decision-makers are the party leader and his colleagues who head the

Oireachtas party together with other members of the National
Executive Committee not in the Oireachtas. With these people above
all rests the initiative in proposing party policy and strategy.

The National Executive Committee (in the Labour Party called the
Administrative Council) is elected annually. In each case it consists of
the national officers together with representatives of the Oireachtas
party, of the branches and of ancillary organizations. Although this
body, which numbers eighty-six in the case of Fianna Fáil, forty-four
in the case of Fine Gael, and thirty-six in the case of Labour, is the
organ that runs the party's affairs, it is doubtful whether the policies
that the party will adopt publicly are actually made by it. For when it
comes to policy and to parliamentary tactics and strategy, the leaders
of the Oireachtas party (who in the case of the party in power are, of
course, the government) are expected to take the initiative, and they
are given a free hand to do so. Prominent, and often predominant,
among them will be the leader of the Oireachtas party, who is chosen
by them and who is the party leader. In the case of the party in power,
he will of course be Taoiseach, an office that almost inevitably puts its
holder in a position above his colleagues. There exist from time to
time 'think-tank' committees usually of professional people, not all of
them by any means holding an elected office, which advise on policy.
In general, though, neither the rank-and-file parliamentary representatives nor the active workers in the constituencies have much to do
with initiating or formulating policy. They have other tasks – the
former to support their leaders in parliament and to attend to the
affairs of their constituents, the latter to get out the vote when the
occasion demands.

The small amount of inter-election activity and the comparatively
meagre services given by party headquarters to the branches are
reflected in low levels of income and expenditure. Irish parties as such
do not receive any public funds, as do parties in some European
countries where party political activity is recognized as being properly
chargeable to public funds as an expense essential to democracy. The
only public moneys that go to the parties in Ireland are the allowances
paid to the leaders of the main opposition parties in the Oireachtas to
help support their parliamentary activities, and a small proportion of
members' salaries, which parties levy for expenses. Party finances are,
therefore, the private affairs of the parties: in the case of Fianna Fáil
and Fine Gael they are very private indeed.

However, the broad pattern is clear enough. The most important
single source of income for Fianna Fáil and one of two major sources
for Labour is an annual collection made by each branch, part of which
must be handed over by the branch for the use of the centre, mainly to
fight elections. The proceeds of the annual collection – in the case of
Fianna Fáil in the middle eighties coming close to half a million
pounds – though highly publicized, give little idea of the true income
of any of the parties. Individual party members pay small subscriptions,

which go towards financing branch activities. In the case of the Labour Party, Oireachtas party members contribute a proportion of their parliamentary salaries, and affiliated unions pay small annual subscriptions based on the number of affiliated members, a source which in 1985 contributed about 15 per cent of the party's income. In the case of Fianna Fáil and Fine Gael, a large part of their income comes from industrial and commercial firms and businessmen. Of course, at election time, parties and individual candidates for public office make special efforts to solicit financial help, and collections and appeals, both public and private, are made. It is well known that Fianna Fáil and Fine Gael accumulate election funds, though their size and how they are used are kept secret. The Labour Party receives help from individual unions, but this is usually given by way of subsidies to union candidates individually.

VI

Political parties seem not to be in themselves particularly democratic organizations, though they are essential engines of democracy. Nor are they very effective channels for public participation in politics. However, they are far from being the only channels for public participation. All sorts of associations and organizations in the community engage in political activities, some of them continuously and with great effect. Many, indeed most, of them, choose not to associate themselves too closely with any political party, their main political business being with ministers and civil servants, as the following chapter shows.

Notes

1 See T. Garvin, 'The prehistory of a party system: Irish secret societies and mass political mobilisation', Paper presented at the European Consortium for Political Research Workshop on Nationalism and Territorial Identity, Strathclyde, January 1978.
2 T. Garvin, 'Nationalist elites, Irish voters and Irish political development: a comparative perspective', in *Economic and Social Review*, 8 (April 1977), p. 169.
3 P. Mair, 'Labour and the Irish party system revisited: party competition in the 1920s', in *Economic and Social Review*, 9 (Oct. 1977), p. 62.
4 Mair, *ibid.*, p. 64.
5 G. Sartori, *Parties and Party Systems: a Framework for Analysis*, 1 (Cambridge, 1976), p. 179.
6 For example, see M. Gallagher, 'Social change and party adaptation in the Republic of Ireland', *European Journal of Political Research*, 9 (1981), pp. 279 ff.
7 P. Mair, *The Changing Irish Party System: Organization, Ideology and*

Electoral Competition (London, 1987), p. 169. This analysis is the subject of chapter 4 of his book.

8   *Ibid.*, p. 140.
9   *Ibid.*, pp. 177 and 183.
10 *Ibid.*, pp. 184 ff.
11 *Ibid.*, p. 217.
12 M. Gallagher in *How Ireland Voted: the Irish General Election 1987*, M. Laver, P. Mair and R. Sinnott (eds), (Swords, 1987), p. 64.
13 P. Mair in *How Ireland Voted 1989*, M. Gallagher and R. Sinnott (eds), (Galway, 1990), p. 213.
14 Mair, *The Changing Irish Party System*, pp. 40 and 43.
15 M. Gallagher, *Political Parties in the Republic of Ireland* (Dublin, 1985), pp. 135–6.
16 See M. Marsh in *Electoral Change in Western Democracies: Patterns and Sources of Electoral Volatility*, I. Crewe and D. Denver (eds) (London, 1985), pp. 173–201. See also Gallagher in *How Ireland Voted* M. Laver, P. Mair and R. Sinnott (eds), pp. 64–5.
17 See T. Garvin, 'Political cleavages, party politics and urbanisation in Ireland: the case of the periphery-dominated centre', in *European Journal of Political Research*, 2 (1974), p. 310.
18 Mair, *The Changing Irish Party System*, p. 114.
19 *Ibid.* p. 134.
20 R. Rose, *The Problem of Party Government* (Harmondsworth, 1976), p. 144.

CHAPTER 7

Pressure Groups

I

Political parties are far from being the only channels between the community and the formal institutions of government. There exists as well a very large number and wide variety of organizations which, when the occasion calls for it, press the demands of their members upon those who make public policy or other decisions that have the backing of the authorities, and upon those who might influence the decision-makers. Many organizations, such as trade unions and farmers' associations, exist specifically to protect the interests and further the aims of their members; and, in the course of doing so, they attempt to influence public authorities.

Such organizations are usually referred to as 'pressure groups', but that term will not be confined to organizations set up explicitly to represent the interests of a particular group. When they think it is necessary or useful to do so, the leaders and spokesmen of important institutions in the community, such as churches or ethnic groups, act in the same way; so, for example, do the managers of firms and the governing bodies of universities; so, too, in the public sector itself do the spokesmen of subordinate public authorities, and bodies such as staff associations press their interests upon the central government. In fact, in the modern welfare state, which attempts to direct the economy and regulate the social and physical environment, almost any organization or group in the community, however remote from politics it ostensibly appears to be, might find occasion to press a case upon a public authority, national or local. Nor need a group have a continuous existence or a formal organization: the 700,000 people who took time off work on 22 January 1980 to march the streets of Dublin and other cities and towns demanding changes in the pay-as-you-earn tax system were participating in politics as a pressure group.

Pressure groups can usually be distinguished from political parties. In the words of Richard Rose:

pressure groups do not themselves seek to win control of government by presenting a slate of candidates to the electorate. Parties differ from pressure groups particularly in the degree of their inclusiveness . . .. Furthermore, pressure groups can have extensive non-political activities.[1]

It has to be admitted, however, that the distinction is not entirely clear cut. 'The colonization of groups by parties and the reverse phenomenon of domination of parties by groups',[2] which is such a feature of some countries, is not present to any great extent in Ireland today. However, some trade unions are affiliated to the Labour Party, and, for example, in the 1920s the Farmers' Party was the political arm of a farmers' association. Also, an extreme republican organization like Sinn Féin is hard to categorize. Although, as seems most appropriate, it is regarded as a political party, there has often been considerable interpenetration between it and its consort, the IRA.

The difficulties of categorization are perhaps best illustrated by the experience of environmental organizations. Many Green parties have developed from pressure groups advocating environmental reforms. The Green Party in Ireland is one such; it was formerly the Green Alliance. Once an organization like this steps into the election arena with a candidate, it crosses a rubicon, almost willy-nilly has to take a stand on all sorts of issues, and loses its exclusive concern with its basic objective: it has become a party. In general however, the distinction between pressure groups and political parties is clear enough in the Republic of Ireland. Here, contrary to the situation in some European countries and in Northern Ireland where the Unionist Party and the Orange Order were for long closely identified with each other, pressure groups and parties tend to be autonomous in respect of one another.

Also absent from the Republic is the phenomenon of 'segmented pluralism' – that is, competing complexes of interrelated social, educational, occupational, and political organizations each serving distinct cultural groups or communities based on religion, ideology, nationality, or some combination of these, such as occur, for example, in Switzerland, the Netherlands, and Belgium. In only one or two areas of social activity are the cultural differences between Catholics and Protestants in the Republic reflected in the existence of separate organizations. Because first-level and second-level education is largely denominational, there exist a Catholic Headmasters' Association and other Catholic teachers' associations as well as an Irish Schoolmasters' Association and other Protestant associations. In scouting, too, there are the Catholic Boy Scouts of Ireland on the one hand and the Boy Scouts of Ireland (and a similar organization, the Boys Brigade) on the other, but they do have an umbrella organization, the Federation of Irish Scout Associations.

II

For purposes of classifying and discussing Irish pressure groups, it is convenient to use two simple sets of distinctions as proposed by Maria Maguire.[3] These are, firstly, between 'sectional' and 'attitude' groups;

and secondly, between 'associational' and 'institutional' groups. 'Sectional' groups 'exist to protect and promote the sectional interest of their members, and membership is, by definition, limited to those who share that particular interest'.[4] SIPTU, the Services, Industrial, Professional and Technical Union, Ireland's largest trade union, is an example; so too are the Irish Farmers' Association, the Irish Medical Organization, and the Consumers' Association of Ireland Ltd. By contrast, 'attitude' groups exist to promote a cause, and membership is usually open to anyone willing to support the issue in question.[5] Such are the Irish Association for Civil Liberties and An Taisce (the National Trust for Ireland). Sectional groups far outnumber attitude groups. Their activities, particularly those of the established economic protection groups, are part and parcel of everyday political life, and they 'tend to play a more consistent role in the political process than many other types of group'.[6]

The best-organized of the sectional groups are in industry and commerce and in agriculture, despite the fact that the basic units in these sectors – firms, unions, farms – are mostly very small. Many individual trade associations have a small membership and are comparatively weak. However, in the last twenty years, umbrella organizations have grown rapidly as firms came to recognize the need to be adequately represented at the national level. A few of these organizations are well staffed and efficiently organized. In 1990, the Confederation of Irish Industry, which is the national organization representing industry in matters of trade, economics, taxation, and development, had about 2,500 member firms in over fifty affiliated and sector groups. In the same year, the membership of the Federation of Irish Employers, the major organization on the employers' side in all matters relating to industrial relations and labour matters, had about 3,200 members covering 60 per cent of all economic activity in the private sector, other than the construction industry, which was catered for separately. This membership also included a number of public authorities. The Federation had a staff of ninety and regional offices covering the whole country. The Construction Industry Federation, the representative organization of firms in the building industry, with over 1,300 members, also had regional offices throughout the country.

Like management, labour also is characterized by a large number of small units. In 1990 there were no less than fifty-six unions with members in the Republic, over half of them with less than 2,500 members (see Table 7.1). However, one of them, SIPTU, with 205,000 members, represented over two-fifths of total trade-union membership. Together, these fifty-six unions represented almost half a million employees. The proportion of employees unionized in 1990–51 per cent – was the fourth highest of the countries of the European Communities. Like the employers, trade unions, too, have their umbrella organizations, notably the Irish Congress of Trade Unions (ICTU), which comprises fifty-one of the fifty-six unions and represents 96 per cent of union membership. Professional associations have functions similar to those of trade unions, and a few of them are affiliated to ICTU. Some of them have the added responsibility of safeguarding the standards of their profession, and they are endowed by law with appropriate powers to make rules governing entry and practice and to discipline or exclude members. This sector, like industry and commerce, is composed mainly of small associations because, in a country of three and a half million people, the number practising in any profession is low. Professions, however, tend to be close-knit, and though only small numbers of people are engaged in particular callings, often most if not all of them are members of professional associations. In 1990, for example, 93 per cent of all national (that is, primary) teachers, lay and religious, were members of the Irish National Teachers' Organization. In a few cases, membership is a precondition of being recognized as belonging to a profession.

Table 7.1 **Membership of trade unions in the Republic of Ireland, 1989–90**

Size of union (members)	No. of unions	No. of members	% of all members
Under 500	7	1,900	0.4
500–1,000	7	5,300	1.1
1,000–1,500	5	5,800	1.2
1,500–2,500	13	27,300	5.7
2,500–3,500	4	12,000	2.5
3,500–5,000	2	9,200	1.9
5,000–7,000	3	18,400	3.9
7,000–10,000	3	25,100	5.3
10,000–15,000	5	61,500	12.9
15,000–20,000	6	105,500	22.1
Over 20,000	1	205,000	43.0
Total	56	477,100	100
Affiliated to ICTU	51	458,400	96

Source: Statutory returns made to Department of Labour as at 31 December 1990 under Trade Union Act, 1941. Figures have been rounded to the nearest hundred.

By Western European standards, the proportion of Ireland's labour force employed in agriculture and fishing (about 15 per cent in 1990) is high. Consequently, one would expect agricultural and rural life organizations to be deep-rooted and powerful. Because of the structure of the industry and the diversity of interests among farmers, however, this was not the case until the sixties. No agrarian parties ever established themselves on any permanent basis. Nor did cooperatives develop to any great extent except in areas where milk was produced on a scale big enough to justify a collection service. Because of the diversity of agriculture, there have always been a large number of organizations representing particular interests. In 1991, the list of 'client organizations' of the Department of Agriculture and Food (that is, bodies with whom the Department did or might do business from time to time) numbered 209 (see Table 7.2); in the mid-1960s, there were about 100 names on the list.

Table 7.2 **Department of Agriculture and Food: list of agricultural, etc.**
organizations, 1991

General[1]	55		
Cattle	29	Pigs	6
Cereals & feeding stuffs	9	Potatoes	8
Goats	4	Poultry	5
Horses	23	Sheep & wool	38
Horticulture & bee-keeping	11	Tobacco	1
Milk and dairy products	18	Wine	2
	Total 209		

Note:[1] 'General' includes farmers' associations, trade associations, trade unions and professional associations, educational bodies and public authorities other than government departments.

Source: List made available by the Department of Agriculture and Food giving information about all organizations except other government departments with which officers of the Department might do business at some time or another.

Organizational and personal rivalries have inhibited the development of a single body to speak for all agricultural interests, though there is no lack of sectoral and specific interest associations. From the mid-1960s, the National Farmers' Association, which had been founded in 1955, emerged as the major umbrella organization. In 1990, the Association (which had changed its name in 1973 to the Irish Farmers' Association) had a membership of 80,000, a staff of fifty-five, and an annual budget of over IR£3 million. It owned an influential weekly newspaper, the *Farmers Journal* (circulation, 75,000), provided accountancy and taxation services, had a subsidiary company, Farm Business Development, and engaged in other business activities such as insurance. It also had a Brussels office, and a large headquarters and conference centre, the Irish Farm Centre. It is without doubt among the country's most effective pressure groups: it is also among the most vociferous. Although the Irish Creamery Milk Suppliers' Association, founded in 1950, is not as large as the IFA – in 1990 it had 53,000 members, a staff of over twenty and a budget of IR£350,000 – it rivals its sister organization in the noisy application of pressure, both in Dublin and Brussels.

Ireland's accession to the European Communities brought farmers the considerable financial benefits of the Common Agricultural Policy (CAP) and boosted Irish agriculture as never before. The major farming organizations, in particular the Irish Farmers' Association, seized the opportunity with both hands. Representation in Brussels, established well before Ireland's formal accession, soon became highly expert and efficient and at first more than matched the official presence. Agricultural pressure groups became more Brussels-orientated than the pressure groups of any other sector of the economy and have remained so ever since.

Producers of goods and services are far better organized and equipped for the promotion of their interests than are non-industrial and household consumers. Apart from the users of some particular goods or services such as motor cars which have specific protection organizations, consumers, being a dispersed and amorphous category, are not well organized. The only general consumer organizations are the Consumers' Association of Ireland Ltd, with almost 10,000 members (four times that of a decade ago) and the small but active Irish Housewives Association. Membership in these, as in other more specific consumer groups, tends to be strongest among the middle class in Dublin. In rural areas, the Irish Countrywoman's Association to some extent acts as a consumer protection group.

Consumer groups have always been handicapped by lack of resources. It is only in recent years that some European governments and the European Commission have begun to subsidize them, recognizing – surely rightly? – that they perform a public service. The Irish government has been slow to go down this road. The recent improvements in consumer protection legislation have been largely induced by the obligations of membership of the Community rather than domestic pressure. In 1990, the Consumers' Association of Ireland had an income of almost IR£430,000, of which only one-fifth came from 'grant income', and that mostly from the European Commission and not the state.[7] It is clear that although consumers' interests are slowly coming to be better looked after, protection organizations still 'face an uphill battle in which they lack an influence comparable to the larger economic protection groups to which their interests are often opposed'.[8]

It might be argued that the more general institutions of representation – the public representatives at national and local levels – speak for consumers, since all people consume. There is some force in this, but at the point where many political decisions are made, policies formulated, and business decided, the spokesmen of the producers are present but the public representatives – members of the Oireachtas and the local councillors – often are not. Thus the developing practices of interest consultation have important implications for democracy.

Attitude groups, those based on a shared cause or making a

particular demand, present something of a contrast with sectional groups. Many of the latter are 'insider' groups, and are on close and intimate terms with the public authorities with whom they do business. Many of the former, on the contrary, are 'outsider' groups, often literally: they are kept at arms' length by public officials, political and bureaucratic alike, who regard them at best as goodhearted busybodies and at worst as unreasonable and sometimes fanatical nuisances. This arises because many attitude groups advocate reforms for which there is no great public demand. They are as often concerned to mobilize public support in order to demonstrate political strength as they are to pursue the more forlorn hope of getting changes in policy agreed to directly by decision-makers.

There is a contrast also in respect of numbers. There are comparatively few attitude groups, though in recent years there has been a rush of associations with names like CARE (Campaign for the Care of Deprived Children) and NITRO (National Income Tax Reform Organization). There are even fewer making major demands involving big changes. Only the small republican groups that do not recognize the regime and the tiny collections of extreme Marxists are not comprehended 'within the system', but they are better thought of as political movements than as pressure groups, though they and the 'front' organizations that some of them use often behave like pressure groups.

Groups devoted to the revival of Irish are of long standing and, unlike most attitude groups, have a favoured position. Since their aim is officially government policy, though mostly only lip service is paid to it, these groups receive public moneys from the National Lottery. Among the most important are Conradh na Gaeilge (the Gaelic League), which is the oldest of them, founded in 1893 as part of the nationalist revival; and Gael Linn, an organization that exploits the mass media to promote the language. Coordinating the activities of many of the language organizations is an umbrella body, Comhdháil Náisiúnta na Gaeilge (National Convention of the Irish Language).

The largest attitude group is certainly the Pioneer Total Abstinence Association, which in 1990 claimed an estimated 200,000 to 250,000 adult members plus an unspecified number of juvenile and adolescent members. Reflecting the changed times has been the great growth in the number of, and support for, groups promoting the cause of women, and advocating the protection of the environment, the conservation of natural resources, and the care of the underprivileged such as itinerants, single-parent families, and the homeless. Likewise, in 1990, there were Irish branches of international pressure groups such as the Anti-Apartheid Movement, Amnesty International, and Greenpeace. Family planning, abortion, and divorce, which became major political issues in the seventies and eighties, spawned associations on both sides. Just as such developments mirror the changing culture of the community, the continuing lack of success of associations concerned with abolishing blood sports or cruelty to animals in general reflects a more enduring characteristic of the Irish.

III

The great majority of both sectional and attitude groups are, following Maria Maguire's typology, 'associational' groups – that is, specialized structures of interest articulation formed for the explicit representation of the interests of a particular group. We can draw a broad distinction between these and institutions in society such as churches, the army, the Civil Service, that on occasion act as pressure groups. In some countries, institutional groups of this type wield great political power. This is not the case in Ireland. Just as Ireland is characteristically modern in possessing a large number of specialized associational groups, so, too, it is thoroughly civilian: the army is not a factor in politics, and the Civil Service is at the disposal of any properly elected government. In fact, the only great corporate institution in the community that might seem to rival the institutions of the political system is the Catholic church. As a pressure group it has had, and to an extent continues to have, a unique position.

Writing in 1966, Tim Pat Coogan thought it necessary to point out to his readers that, 'strictly speaking, the Church has no special legal status'.[9] With the removal, in 1972, of the 'special position' clause (itself only declaratory) from Article 44 of Bunreacht na hÉireann, Coogan's observation became literally true. The church is legally not an 'established church'. It does not need to be, for the Irish are a devout people and traditionally they respected and obeyed their clergy, particularly in rural areas. As recently as thirty years ago, Jean Blanchard remarked on the power of the Irish clergy:

The Bishops of Ireland appear to have more power, in practice, than those of any other country in the world. As the natural outcome of a long historical tradition which has created exceptionally strong bonds between the nation and its clergy, their authority is great over the Faithful . . . a member of the congregation listens more readily to his Bishop than he does, for instance, to his deputy (député). The social importance of the head of the diocese is unrivalled.[10]

Although the deference of the laity at the time and the triumphalist demeanour of the clergy have disappeared and priests are not as influential today as they were then (particularly in the cities and among young people), Blanchard's judgement still has some validity, particularly in rural areas and in respect of some matters.

It could hardly be otherwise, if only for the fact that most school education up to the third level is denominational and, hence, overwhelmingly Catholic. The following tabulation shows the position in 1990.

Percentage of schools under Catholic management	
National schools	93.2
Post-primary schools (secondary, comprehensive, community)	
Lay	4.8
Religious	90.0

From the 1960s, the Department of Education with the bishops' consent began to take a more active part in developing the educational system. This, together with the increased representation and role of the teaching organizations and – belatedly – parents' associations, all operating in an environment of decreasing deference, reduced the authority of the clergy and the teaching orders. It does not follow that the Catholic ethos of Catholic schools was diluted, though it was almost universally modernized, shedding in the process its harsher elements. The system still produces a strongly religious community by European standards.

Members of the clergy, then, cannot but have a considerable influence in public affairs if and when they choose to exert it. To what extent do they do so in practice? In Chapter 2, we saw that, when issues central to church teaching arose in the middle eighties, they did intervene with great effect.[11] Here we take a more general look.

Members of the clergy play no overt part and, in the case of the overwhelming majority of them, little if any part at all in party politics. This contrasts markedly with the past, when the clergy, especially parish clergy, were sometimes prominent in nationalist and agrarian agitation. Priests do not stand for political office, though no law of either church or state prohibits them from doing so. Indeed, they rarely *compete* for offices of any sort: in respect of appropriate social activities some like, and a few expect, to be *invited*. As local notables, they are particularly active in rural community projects, rural social organizations, and sporting associations. To the extent that such bodies act as pressure groups, the clergy plays its part like other members. A decree of the Synod of Maynooth (the Council of the Irish Hierarchy) forbids the use of the pulpit for political purposes, by which is meant *party* political controversy. For, of course, many matters that the church considers within its sphere might be 'political' – that is, matters for the attention of public authorities – notably, policy in respect of education, social welfare, health services, marriage, contraception and abortion. Individual priests and bishops engage in political activities as advocates for changes in, for example, health and hospital services and local amenities. In recent years, the clergy, both senior and junior, have increasingly become critics, in some cases radical critics, of the social services, particularly for disadvantaged categories. There have been in the past, and today there are still, individual bishops who are prone to comment publicly and to engage in controversy on political issues. In the past, Dr Cornelius Lucey, former Bishop of Cork, described by T. P. Coogan as 'the archetype of the commentating Irish bishop'[12] and Dr Michael Browne, former Bishop of Galway, were in this mould. More recent examples are Dr Jeremiah Newman, Bishop of Limerick, and Dr Eamonn Casey, Bishop of Galway – the one a conservative, the other a radical, voice.

Many people believe that the church is inclined to give directions to politicians and that it gets its way. To some extent, the view that interference is, or at least was, common arises from a widespread tendency in the past to dub every view expressed by a cleric as the view of 'the church'. In a country where the clergy individually and collectively expected in the past to have all their statements treated as authoritative, the church had only itself to blame if it was sometimes misunderstood. In principle, the position is quite clear. If a major issue arises on which the Catholic church in Ireland wishes to take a stand, it is the bishops collectively as 'the Hierarchy' who speak authoritatively.

Until the changes enunciated by the Second Vatican Council began to permeate, Irish bishops tended to take an 'integralist' view of church–state relations, that is, the church should, to the extent it needed to do so, permeate and if possible control other institutions in society including the state. It was for the church to define the area of its jurisdiction and, in that area, for politicians and public servants to do as the church bade them. Had this principle been pursued vigorously Ireland would have been a 'theocratic' state – namely, one in which the state is unwilling or unable to enact a law which is contrary to the moral law as defined by the church. However, surveying church–state contacts between 1932 and 1979, John Whyte came to the surprising conclusion that in practice the bishops intervened only rarely:

It does not seem likely that contact between government and bishops at the level of policy is at all frequent. To put it in quantitative terms, one might guess that since 1923, there have been three or four dozen items of legislation or other questions of policy on which government and bishops have been in consultation.[13]

Nor did they always get their own way. He concluded that a theocratic model which he defined as 'a state in which the hierarchy has the final say on any matter in which it wishes to intervene', had to be rejected.[14]

By the seventies the church was changing its position. The

enunciation in 1973 of a new principle to guide church–state relations in Ireland reflected the modified stance of the Catholic church after the Second Vatican Council when it was no longer seeking from the state either special recognition or special privileges.[15] It appeared that when it came to public policy-making, the bishops were claiming that the church is in effect a pressure group seeking to have its views taken into consideration by the policy-makers like those of other interests. The passage into law of the Family Planning (Amendment) Act 1985, against the advice of a number of bishops and, perhaps, with scant if any consultation with the hierarchy, suggested that times were indeed changing.

Nevertheless, to conclude that the church is just another pressure group would be mistaken as the experience of the referenda on abortion and divorce in the middle eighties demonstrated:

The analogy between the hierarchy and other interest groups breaks down because, in a mainly Catholic country, the Catholic hierarchy has a weapon which no other interest group possesses: its authority over men's consciences. Most politicians on all sides of the house are committed Catholics, and accept the hierarchy's right to speak on matters of faith and morals. Even politicians who are personally indifferent on religious matters will recognize that the majority of the electorate are believers, and will act accordingly.[16]

Truly, as John Whyte observed: 'the Catholic hierarchy is in a position matched by no other interest group in Ireland'.[17]

IV

The strategies and tactics of those who seek to influence public authorities tend to be governed by a simple and obvious principle: apply pressure where the impact will be greatest. The choice of points of contact and methods of operation is governed by a number of constraints, principally cultural factors, the group's resources, and the political context.

In Ireland, as in other Western democracies, the legitimacy of pressure-group activity is fully accepted, and its great development is recognized as adding another dimension to representation. However, all pressure groups do not have equal access to policy-makers. The tendency is for public authorities 'to accept the role, place, or power, of those interest groups that have "earned" a close relationship with the government' and 'to accommodate the lobby that works closely with government, because there is mutual benefit in the relationship'.[18] Clearly, well-established conventions govern who is to be accorded the status of an 'insider' with regular access to ministers and public servants and the right to be consulted. 'Outsiders' will at most be permitted to hand in a protest to a public office, to send in a deputation of a few leaders to a minister or other politician, and to march and demonstrate.

The institutionalization of this process led to the development of codes of practice well understood by the participants, and to a fairly clear agreement on what constitutes illegitimate activity. Bribery, undue entertainment, and secret bargains (clandestine operations generally) are neither accepted nor, apparently, much practised. By the late eighties, efficient investigative journalism and effective parliamentary opposition by leaders of the left parties were likely to uncover such activities when they did occur.

As elsewhere in the Western world, direct, and even militant, action is more practised than it used to be. Verbal truculence, demonstrations, sit-ins, the withholding of taxes, and the non-payment of bills to public authorities are accepted. In 1979, Ireland had its first political strike, a one-day strike and march by trade unionists to protest against the pay-as-you-earn tax system: there have been others since. By the late eighties, it was commonplace for farmers to be bused to Dublin for a 'demo' and a day in the city; even more commonplace for third-level, and sometimes second-level, students to march and chant.

It is impossible to say exactly where the line between acceptable and unacceptable behaviour is drawn. Two things seem clear. First, illegal activity is generally more condoned than it was; but, second, acceptability depends to some extent on who is involved and what they are advocating. During the eighties the illegal activities of fishermen, including the use of firearms against naval and fishery protection personnel, were never dealt with firmly by successive governments and, indeed, were all but condoned by a few politicians. In 1990, public authorities were very hesitant in their response to illegal activities by settled citizens on behalf of itinerants (called travellers or travelling people by the middle class). The same kind of activities carried out by itinerants themselves often in the past evoked very different responses.

Most sectional organizations are 'insider' groups: the status of attitude groups, in contrast, varies enormously. In a community in which self-conscious nationalism has remained at a high level, organizations that identify their objects with 'the nation' expect, and have sometimes been accorded, special recognition, whether they are sporting organizations like the Gaelic Athletic Association, or the Irish-language organizations, which, under the guidance of Comhdháil Náisiúnta na Gaelige, dispose of public moneys. On the other hand, groups advocating family planning or rights for 'gays' have struggled in an unfavourable climate of opinion. Likewise, until the recent development of a climate of opinion in favour of environmental protection, groups of householders attempting to preserve amenities in the face of industrial development projects offering the carrot of new jobs were as often as not obstructed by public officials.

The resources, human and material, that a group has at its disposal necessarily govern its strategy and tactics. The principal resources are money to mount campaigns and provide the necessary intelligence and representational services, and members who are potential voters on election day. The strongest economic pressure groups, the major agricultural and employer organizations, have very efficient intelligence and representational services. Trade unions, and in particular the Irish Congress of Trade Unions, are less well equipped because they are less affluent. However, they, like the farmers' organizations, have large membership – a valuable political resource, one would think. In the past, though, they experienced an important phenomenon of Irish politics when they tried to mobilize it. At elections, citizens tended to remain loyal to the party they previously supported even when they held views and had interests that were not those being advocated by their party. At first, it was the overwhelming salience of national issues that inspired this loyalty and, later, socialization in early life, largely under family influence, into identification with a party image. In these circumstances, pressure groups had only limited success in mobilizing voters. The experience of recent elections, however, suggests, as we have already noted, the emergence of an 'available electorate'.[19] No doubt many, perhaps most, people are, and will remain, strongly orientated to the political party with which they identify. But even a modest increase in the volatility of voters as more people vote in their immediate material interest will have an important effect upon election outcomes and thus upon politics generally. Increasingly in Ireland, as in many democracies, 'the making of governmental decisions is not a majestic march of great majorities united upon certain matters of basic policy. It is the steady appeasement of relatively small groups.'[20]

The political context within which pressure groups operate has as its major feature in Ireland the fact that, over most areas of public policy and a wide range of policy issues, the government has a virtual monopoly in proposing policy and legislation and an almost complete control of the activities and output of the Oireachtas because it usually enjoys the stable and assured support of its parliamentary party supporters. Until recently, this monopoly extended to all areas of public policy. Today, because of Irish membership in the European Communities, the position is different. In some areas – notably agriculture and fishing – and on an increasing number of industrial, commercial, and fiscal matters, the authorities of the European Communities make the decisions, and this fact is duly reflected in the pattern of pressure-group activities.

In most policy areas, however, it is still Irish ministers and their professional advisers, mostly senior civil servants in the departments, who are the initiators and formulators of policy and administrative action. It is on them, therefore, that pressure groups tend to concentrate their main efforts, if they have access to them. This is not possible for some groups, particularly attitude groups that are proposing sweeping reforms or demanding major changes in sensitive areas, that defy the state itself, or that for one reason or another are not on speaking terms with ministers. These must stay out in the streets and attempt to attract the support of the public by interesting journalists in their cause, by advertising, or by attempting to lobby parliamentary representatives – courses of action that are not likely to get them immediate satisfaction.

The range of contacts between pressure groups and ministers and their advisers is wide and their number enormous. In total, they are an important part of the ordinary day-to-day business of all ministers and many senior civil servants. They include formal deputations to make representations to the minister or to his officials on behalf of their members or to exchange information on reactions to recent events; periodic reviews to fix rates or prices or to consider the progress of an industry; and routine contacts about specific cases or detailed points of administration between the professional servants of the interest groups and appropriate civil servants. In addition, there is a considerable and growing exchange of information and, where the more widely representative bodies are concerned, an increasing amount of positive involvement in government through membership of consultative bodies such as the National Economic and Social Council and of state boards such as FÁS (the Training and Employment Authority), and by involvement in 'tripartite' discussions on economic policy.

The practice of appointing advisory and consultative bodies on which interests have representation has been developed over many years; so, too, has the habit of ministers consulting major relevant interests before appointing the members of regulatory and administrative bodies such as, for example, Comhairle na nOspidéal (the Hospital Council) or quasi-judicial bodies like the Labour Court. Membership in public authorities of this sort and in advisory bodies is desired and sometimes demanded by sectional groups, for it not only signifies official recognition of the standing of an organization but affords a receptive access point to policy-making and policy-makers. Some umbrella associations, such as the Irish Congress of Trade Unions, the Federation of Irish Employers and the Confederation of Irish Industry, have places on a large number of such bodies. In 1990, the Federated Union of Employers had representatives on forty-one public bodies at the regional or national level and eleven at the international level. In the same year, the Irish Congress of Trade Unions, which is accepted by the state as representing the interests of labour generally, had representatives on, or made nominations to, at least two dozen bodies in the domestic public sector (and many more than that in Northern Ireland) and fifteen international bodies.

The fact that pressure groups focus their main efforts on ministers and senior public servants, if they can, by no means implies that 'lobbying' – the attempt to influence the members of the Oireachtas –

does not occur. Pressure groups circularize members, contact personally those whom they think might be sympathetic, and *faute de mieux*, try to impress them by marches and demonstrations. Attempts to promote legislation directly by means of a 'private member's bill' – that is, a bill introduced by a member of the Oireachtas other than a minister – are occasionally made, but few are successful. They are, rather, a device for securing publicity or goading the government into action. An increased number have been introduced in recent years for these purposes.

Some members of the Oireachtas have close connections with pressure groups. Part of the election and parliamentary expenses of some trade unionists are met from union funds, and some members of the Oireachtas can be identified to some degree with occupational interest groups. Nevertheless, except for a handful of independent Senators, public representatives, however closely they are identified with specific interests in the community, are primarily loyal to their parties (if not always in speech, certainly in voting behaviour) and are insulated to some extent from group pressures by the party. When it comes to influencing policy, they are not such useful marks as ministers, though they are often included in pressure-group deputations to add weight. If the matter to be discussed is of local interest, they will themselves seek to be included in order to demonstrate their concern to their constituents.

Because of its composition, Seanad Éireann (the Senate) might appear to be a chamber of interest-group representatives. Legally and formally it has such a basis, for Bunreacht na hÉireann provides that forty-three of the sixty members be chosen from panels of candidates 'having knowledge and practical experience' of certain 'interests and services' – namely, the national language and culture, agriculture, labour, industry and commerce, and public administration and the social services. Furthermore, a proportion of the candidates for seats are nominated by appropriate voluntary associations. In practice, however, it is well known that because the electoral college is itself composed of elected representatives chosen on a party basis, party political rather than vocational considerations predominate. Hence, the Senators so chosen are not markedly more representative of vocations or interests in the community than are members of legislative bodies elected in more orthodox fashion.[21]

The impact of Ireland's accession to the European Communities, in particular to the EEC, has been nowhere more obvious than in agriculture, and it is the effects of this membership upon pressure-group activity in this policy area that we shall examine by way of example. Because the EEC makes agricultural policy (the CAP), the EEC policy-makers, the Commission and the Council of Ministers, are the focus of pressure groups. From the early 1970s, it was no longer sufficient for the Irish Farmers' Association (IFA) and other groups to make representations to Irish ministers or consult with

Irish civil servants. At the end of the decade, Brian Trench reported that 'the direct lobbying of the minister has become increasingly irrelevant, as the big battles leading to a slow-down in the rise in farm prices, or changes in commodity policies are played out at European level'.[22]

The IFA was prompt to recognize the significance of accession and established an office in Brussels well before the event. It also became a member of COPA (Comité des Organisations Professionnelles Agricoles de la CEE), the influential umbrella body for EEC farming organizations, which is regularly and continuously consulted by the Commission before policies are proposed to the Council of Ministers. By 1990, the IFA had had twenty years experience of lobbying on two fronts.

The fact that much agricultural policy is made in Brussels and is binding upon member states has added a new dimension to the relationship of the Minister for Agriculture and Food and his Department with the agricultural pressure groups. At Brussels they are both in some respects pressure groups. It is true that the Minister has a voice in making final decisions, but it is only one voice among twelve: he has not got, as he has in Dublin, the final say. His civil servants no less than the pressure-group spokesmen find themselves attempting to influence the European 'minister', the Commissioner for Agriculture and his 'civil servants', the senior officers of Directorate General VI of the Commission. Thus, new roles and relationships have had to be developed. As the journal *Magill* put it in October 1979, 'Ministers for Agriculture have since Ireland's entry into the EEC become Ministers for Farmers.'[23]

The role of the IFA also was changed. Mark Clinton, a former Minister for Agriculture, explained the change in this way:

The way in which I think the IFA's role has changed is this . . .. For a long time its whole purpose was to fight whatever Government was in power . . . for the best possible prices for farmers because all decisions on these matters were taken by Irish central government. Now it's a different ball game. Aids to agriculture come so much from Brussels . . . that they now have to be regarding themselves as in a kind of partnership with the Government.[24]

In 1991, when the Commission was revising the CAP, the Association was simultaneously putting pressure upon the Irish government to oppose the Commission's proposals and to promise financial aid from the domestic budget if cuts in subsidies were made; lobbying – haranguing, might be a more appropriate word – the Commissioner for Agriculture; and engaging in a spate of committee work and representations at official level in Brussels and in COPA.

The same pattern of activity has developed in other areas of economic policy and in the fields of industrial relations and social affairs. In all of them, ministers no longer have the final say about many matters that they formerly controlled or could have controlled if they had wished. In all of them, also, cooperation between the state and pressure groups in dealings with Brussels seems to be desirable, even essential. Symbolically, on the morning flight from Dublin to Brussels, the civil servants and the pressure-group spokesmen sit side-by-side and not on opposite sides of a table.

V

The enormous scale of pressure-group activity, which is a feature of government and administration today, is a comparatively recent phenomenon. Half a century ago, the pressure-group representatives who gave evidence to the Commission on Vocational Organization established by the Irish government in 1939 were full of complaints about lack of consultation. Today, many interest organizations are regularly consulted, and some do almost daily business with public servants. The most representative of them have more positive governmental functions. Yet it is important not to create an impression of uniformly cosy relationships. In the past, two major interest organizations – the National Farmers' Association and the Irish Medical Association – had for long periods the worst possible relationships with the ministers and departments most closely concerned with them, bad relations that resulted in the ministers' refusal to meet representatives and in the associations' boycott of the ministers.

In spite of the great increase in the volume of consultation, some of those who come into contact with civil servants get the impression that not all of them want genuine consultation, let alone negotiation. They think that some civil servants tend to regard those contacts as a way of getting information and compliance or as a public relations device and they do not see policy-making as a genuinely cooperative activity. There could be a number of reasons for such Civil Service reservations. In the view of many senior officers:

Government is a mediating all-inclusive agency holding the interests of various potential and actual, strong and weak, implicit and explicit, organized and unorganized groups in balance. And this of course has implications for the role of the public service as the particular group, within this network of groups, which has the strongest advisory role in the decision-making of government.'[25]

It is notorious also that some senior civil servants would prefer their minister to get advice only from them or through them. In the past at least, some civil servants had a paternalistic attitude towards citizens and felt that, being professionals (of a sort), they knew best. Today, these are outmoded attitudes in a world in which regular and genuine consultation and perhaps more is an essential feature of successful government. 'Interventionist policies require the cooperation, if not collaboration, of functional groups.'[26]

Increasingly in Western European countries, the peak economic umbrella organizations come to understandings with governments that involve commitments on both sides. Terms such as 'tripartism', 'concertation', 'corporatism', and 'neo-corporatism' have come to be used in a liberal democratic context to describe these procedures. Alan Cawson has defined corporatism as 'a specific socio-political process in which organizations representing monopolistic functional interests engage in political exchange in a role that combines interest representation and policy implementation through delegated self-enforcement'.[27] Such organizations go further than making representations to the government: they negotiate agreements which are held to bind all parties, including the government. It is for each party to seek to get such agreements put in place and enforced in its own bailiwick.

The salient feature of this system is that governments give up their position as unique national policy-makers and seek 'social partners' with whom they make 'social contracts'. When and where this occurs, in Ghita Ionescu's words: 'the centre of decision making is no longer to be found in the centre of national representation . . . it has been displaced to somewhere between the world of political representation and the world of the corporate forces'.[28]

The origins of this system in Ireland are to be seen from the middle of the century onwards in the area of industrial development, price and wage fixing, and, more generally, economic and social planning. The characteristic feature of bodies set up to deal with these matters was their 'tripartite' membership. Characteristically, it was Seàn Lemass who 'presided over the establishment of new procedures for economic and social decision making . . .. Under his aegis, Ireland began to shuffle towards a version of the corporate state.'[29] The National Industrial Economic Council, first appointed in 1963 and 'charged with the task of preparing reports from time to time on the principles which should be applied for the development of the national economy',[30] was essentially an advisory body, as was its enlarged successor, the National Economic and Social Council. Its members comprised the spokesmen of the major economic interests and the appropriate government departments. In their deliberations they informed, educated, and influenced one another and, though they were not bound by the contents of the reports which they produced, they both educated and exhorted decision-makers generally. Thus they influenced policy.

With the work of these bodies there began 'a subtle shift in the nature of public decision-making. They began the integration of management and trade unions into the formulation of public policy.'[31] Nowhere was this more obvious than in the work of the Employer–Labour Conference. Although it was a voluntary body with no statutory basis, composed of the nominees of employer organizations (including the state as an employer) and the Irish Congress of Trade Unions, the Employer–Labour Conference was able throughout the 1970s to make successive National Wages Agreements that were subscribed to by employers and unions and adopted as state policy and therefore were binding on the public sector. Indeed, though voluntary, these agreements came to 'have something of the character of public law'.[32] In addition, it was impossible to restrict these agreements to wage-fixing. As the Federated Union of Employers (now the Federation of Irish Employers) continually pointed out in the early seventies, wages policy could not be considered in isolation from decisions affecting taxation or social welfare benefits and contributions and, thus, budgetary and economic policy generally. Understandings on these matters between the government, unions, and employers began to be sought and obtained. In 1976 a tripartite conference considered a government proposal for a package of tax and other measures in return for a wages agreement permitting more modest pay rises than would otherwise have had to be granted. From 1977, annual budgets contained such packages in return for moderate pay settlements. By 1979, the National Wages Agreement was incorporated as part of a formal 'National Understanding for Economic and Social Development' negotiated directly between the government, the Irish Congress of Trade Unions, and employer organizations, each of which undertook commitments.

With the 'National Understanding', the government had formally acknowledged a new positive role for the major pressure groups in an important sector of economic policy-making and had incurred commitments to them; they in turn had incurred reciprocal obligations involving the conduct of their members. All parties were obliged to do their best to 'deliver' (the term colloquially used). The social partners had evidently travelled some distance down the road towards the corporate state: after a hiatus for much of the eighties, they were to travel it further.

Disillusioned by their experiences, particularly as recession set in in the early eighties, and with an unsympathetic government in power until 1987, the parties abandoned this system only to revert to it in a yet more developed form from 1987 after the return of a Fianna Fáil government. That party, as we have already noted, was more inclined to adopt corporatist policies than its opponents. Both the 'Programme for National Recovery' (1987–90) and its more extensive successor, the 'Programme for Economic and Social Progress' (1991–93) comprised a wages agreement, a set of mutual undertakings and a monitoring device, the Central Review Committee, chaired by the Secretary of the Department of the Taoiseach. The 'Programme for Economic and Social Progress' in particular is wide- ranging and ambitious. It is intended to be the first phase of a 'strategic framework' for the nineties. In the words of the 'Programme', 'the

Government have accepted the Irish Congress of Trade Unions' proposal to adopt a long-term strategy for the development of this country over the next decade. The employer and farming organizations have agreed to this approach.'[33] Besides a pay agreement and a commitment to industrial peace, it covers undertakings by the government on, *inter alia*, tax reform, social welfare, health, education, employment and training, agriculture, and the maintenance of a state commercial sector.

The making and implementing (including monitoring) of agreements such as these show how closely employers and unions have become involved not only in public policy-making but also in its administration. We shall return to the impact of these developments on policy making below (see pp. 155–58). They have considerable implications for the umbrella organizations most closely involved. These include a widening and modification of the role of both employer bodies and unions. Traditionally, these have provided representation of an 'adversarial' character *vis-à-vis* each other, and in the case of unions *vis-à-vis* the state as well. Their members have expected this of them – and to an extent still do. To play the role demanded of them in this system, leaders on both sides have not only to tackle the problems of securing 'delivery' of what has been agreed, but to face the massive task of modifying their respective ideological traditions.

VI

From a democratic point of view, the importance of widespread and systematic exchange of information, consultation, and accommodation between the government and specific interests, particularly representative associations, is clear. S.E. Finer summarizes it admirably in his *Anonymous Empire*. The process, he says,

embodies two basic democratic procedures: the right to participate in policy-making and the right to demand redress of grievances. They are best appreciated by considering . . . government without them. Suppose parties and civil servants simply refused to have any contact with the Lobby [pressure groups]? Suppose the party simply claimed that it was 'the will of the people' with a mandate for doing all it had proposed? Its rule would be a rigid and ignorant tyranny. And if civil servants likewise claimed to be merely the servants of the government in power, with no mandate to cooperate with the Lobby, its rule, in its turn, would be a rigid and stupid bureaucracy. In the age of bigness and technology, the Lobby tempers the system.[34]

On the other hand, as Finer points out, although this process adds a further dimension to democracy, it is 'a very "lumpy" kind of self government'. Close relationships between government and pressure groups are handy and are becoming more and more essential; but 'to put the matter crudely, a close relationship tends to become a *closed one*'. Moreover, many of the processes and persons traditionally and commonly associated in the public mind with democratic government and the representation of public opinion – elections, parties, the Oireachtas itself – in truth play a comparatively small part in shaping policy. Much of the activity of policy-making and administration is carried on far from electoral politics and the Oireachtas. Because this is so, much interest group activity, including that which is most effective, is concentrated where the Oireachtas and the public do not and cannot see it. The increase in the volume and importance of such activity and in particular the development of 'concertation' in corporate structures and processes contribute to a growing isolation of electoral and parliamentary politics from public policy decision-making. In Finer's words, 'by the same process as it brings the "interested" publics into consultation, it shuts the general public out of it'.[35]

Notes

1 Richard Rose, *Politics in England*, (London, 1965), p. 130.
2 F. G. Castles, 'Towards a theoretical analysis of pressure politics', in *Political Studies*, 14 (1966), p. 347.
3 See M. Maguire, 'Pressure groups in Ireland', in *Administration*, 25 (1977), pp. 349–64.
4 *Ibid.*, p. 349.
5 *Ibid.*, pp. 349–50.
6 *Ibid.*, p. 352.
7 *Choice*, Magazine of the Consumers' Association of Ireland, Oct. 1990, p. 304.
8 Maguire, 'Pressure groups in Ireland', p. 354.
9 T. P. Coogan, *Ireland Since the Rising* (London, 1966), p. 211.
10 J. Blanchard, *The Church in Contemporary Ireland* (Dublin, 1963), pp. 18–19. This book is a translation of Blanchard's *Le droit ecclésiastique contemporain d'Irlande* (Paris, 1958).
11 See above p. 31.
12 Coogan, *Ireland Since the Rising*, p. 239.
13 John Whyte, *Church and State in Modern Ireland, 1923–1979*, 2nd edn (Dublin, 1980), p. 365.
14 *Ibid.*, p. 368.
15 See above, p. 31.
16 Whyte, *Church and State in Modern Ireland, 1923–1979*, p. 368.
17 *Ibid.*, p. 369.
18 T. McNamara, 'Pressure groups and the public service', in *Administration*, 25 (1977), pp. 368–69.
19 See above, p. 98.
20 R. A. Dahl, *Preface to Democratic Theory* (Chicago, 1956), p. 146.
21 See below, p. 197.
22 B. Trench, 'Stormy weather and divided ranks', in *Magill*, Oct. 1979, p. 26.

23   *Ibid.*
24   Quoted in *Irish Times*, 10 Feb. 1977.
25   McNamara, 'Pressure groups and the public service' p. 369.
26   A. Cawson in *Democratic Theory and Practice,* G. Duncan (ed.) (Cambridge, 1983), p. 181.
27   A. Cawson in *Organized Interests and the State, Studies in Meso-Corporatism,* A. Cawson (ed.) (London, 1985), p.8.
28   G. Ionescu, *Centripetal Politics: Government and the New Centres of Power* (London, 1975), p. 4.
29   J. J. Lee in *Ireland, 1945–70*, J.J. Lee (ed.) (Dublin, 1979), p. 20.
30   S. Lemass, statement made at the inaugural meeting of the National Industrial Economic Council, 9 Oct. 1963.
31   Lee, *Ireland, 1945–70*, p. 20.
32   C. McCarthy, *Decade of Upheaval: Irish Trade Unions in the Sixties* (Dublin, 1973), p. 197.
33   *Programme for Economic and Social Progress* (Stationery Office, Dublin, Jan. 1991), p. 7.
34   S. E. Finer, *Anonymous Empire*, 2nd edn (London, 1966), p. 113.
35   *Ibid.*, p. 114.

CHAPTER 8
Elections

I

A democracy might be – perhaps ought to be – judged by, *inter alia*, the extent of popular participation in the making of political decisions. Elections, and in Ireland referenda also, are the opportunities for participation offered by the system to the people as a whole. One may appropriately ask how extensive are the opportunities offered by the electoral arrangements, how much use is made of them and how are they used in practice.

In Ireland, people have the opportunity to take part by casting a vote in four domestic decision-making procedures and one European Community electoral process, the election of fifteen Irish members of the Community Parliament open to all Community citizens resident in the country. The domestic occasions are: (1) the election of the President every seven years (but see p. 77 above), at which the vote is confined to citizens of Ireland; (2) referenda on proposed constitutional amendments, also confined to Irish citizens (up to the end of 1991 there had been thirteen such referenda); (3) elections to local authorities, at which residents no matter what their nationality may vote (supposedly, every five years, but in the past sometimes postponed); (4) elections to Dáil Éireann, one of the two houses of the Oireachtas, at which Irish citizens may vote and also citizens of European Community countries on a reciprocal basis. Under this provision, British people were the only Community citizens entitled to vote in 1991.[1]

The term of office of a Dáil is not fixed, though by law the maximum length is five years. The Taoiseach, however, may at any time advise the President to dissolve the Dáil and thus precipitate a general election. The President must normally comply. Only if the Taoiseach no longer commands the confidence of the Dáil has the President himself discretion to grant a dissolution, but in those circumstances it is almost certain that he would. Only one of the twenty-five Dála between September 1922 and June 1989 lasted the maximum period of five years; six others lasted more than four years. The average length of life was about three years.

The extent to which the popular vote is used in Ireland is much the same as in most other democratic countries, though the opportunities for Irish voters might seem to be rather few compared with those of US voters, who participate in the selection of many more officials and in some cases have far more chances to record their views on policy proposals. However, in fact though not in form, Irish voters, like Americans, do have the opportunity to choose their government, for that is what, above all, a Dáil election, called a 'general election', is for. It is for this reason that general elections are the most important sites on which party encounters take place. It is there that the battle is fought over who shall rule the country: victory or defeat on this site is decisive.

Formally, Bunreacht na hÉireann assigns to the Dáil the function of choosing a Taoiseach and approving a government. In practice, until the eighties, general elections usually determined which party or group of parties would form the government; the Dáil merely ratified a decision already made. For a party or coalition of parties to win a majority of seats in the Dáil was in practice to be able to form a government and, as we shall see, acquire an almost exclusive power to change state policies. When an election does not produce a party or declared coalition of parties known to be able to command a majority, it falls to the incoming Dáil members, actually and not merely formally, to decide by their votes who shall form a government. As happens in many other democratic countries, government formation is then by way of post-election party negotiations or bargaining with independents, culminating in a subsequent Dáil vote. In the past this was rare, but between 1980 and 1990 it happened on three out of five occasions.

II

The electoral system used in general elections to the Dáil is, in the words of Bunreacht na hÉireann, 'the system of proportional representation by means of the single transferable vote' in multi-member constituencies. In Ireland the system is almost universally known simply as 'PR', as though there were no other proportional representation systems. It is used, also, for the election of forty-nine of the sixty Senators, who are elected by electoral colleges, and of members of local authorities. It is the most frequently used system for elections to membership in public bodies of all sorts as well as by private associations and clubs. Although the Constitution (in Article 12) requires the President also to be elected 'on the system of proportional representation', the arrangement is in fact the alternative vote system, a single transferable vote in a single-member constituency; likewise, the procedure for filling casual vacancies in the Dáil at by-elections.

It might seem strange that a state whose political institutions and procedures derived largely from British practice should have adopted any proportional representation system, let alone one that, for all its theoretical and academic interest, has never been much used. As it happened, however, when the Treaty was being made, the leaders of both the independence movement and the British government were committed to it. Owing to the activities of the Proportional Representation Society (now called the Electoral Reform Society), the single transferable vote system was well known in political circles in the United Kingdom in the early part of this century. On the Irish side, it was espoused by Arthur Griffith, who was a founder member of the Proportional Representation Society of Ireland, and was adopted as Sinn Féin policy. On the British side, it was included in the Home Rule Bill of 1914 and in subsequent legislation applying to Ireland as a device to secure full representation for the Protestant and Unionist minority in future parliaments. In the negotiations leading up to the Treaty of December 1921, Arthur Griffith, then leader of the Irish plenipotentiaries, promised that the single transferable vote system would be used in the future independent state as one of the safeguards sought by the British for the Southern Unionists. The Irish Free State Constitution made provision for it. The system then established has been retained virtually unchanged. Attempts by Fianna Fáil governments in 1959 and 1968 to have it replaced by the single non-transferable vote in single member constituencies, the so-called 'first-past-the-post' system, were rejected by the electorate at referenda.

Under the single transferable vote system, the elector has the opportunity to indicate a range of preferences by placing numbers opposite candidates' names on the ballot paper. If the voter so indicates, a vote can be transferred from one candidate to another if it is not required by the prior choice to make up that candidate's 'quota' (the number of votes necessary to secure election) or if, owing to the poor support given to the prior choice, that candidate is eliminated from the contest. Voters need not vote for all the candidates, but those who do vote for more than one must number their preferences continuously – 1, 2 3, and so on. To ascertain who has been elected, votes are initially sorted according to first preferences, and any candidate who obtains a quota or more is declared elected. The quota used in Irish elections is the Droop quota, so called because it was proposed by H. R. Droop in 1869. It is the smallest number of votes that suffices to elect enough candidates to fill all the seats being contested while being just big enough to prevent any more from being elected.

If the number elected at the first count is less than the number of places to be filled, as it usually is, a process of transferring votes takes place in subsequent counts until all the seats are filled. First, the 'excess' votes of any candidate who has won a seat – that is, votes in excess of the quota – are distributed proportionally to the second or next available choice of the winner's supporters. If, when no surpluses remain to be distributed, there are still seats to be filled, the candidate with the fewest votes is eliminated and his or her votes are redistributed according to the next available preferences indicated. The transfer of the excess votes of elected candidates and of the votes of eliminated candidates continues until all the seats are filled. (A fuller description of the system and procedures is given in Appendix 1.)

In order to achieve proportional representation, the single transferable vote system operates, as we have seen, in multi-member constituencies. Bunreacht na hÉireann provides that 'no law shall be enacted whereby the number of members to be returned for any constituency shall be less than three'. It also provides that 'the total number of members of Dáil Éireann shall not be fixed at less than one for each 30,000 of the population, or at more than one member for each 20,000 of the population', and that the ratio between the number of members for each constituency and its population 'shall, as far as it is practicable, be the same throughout the country'. The Oireachtas is required to revise constituencies 'at least once in every twelve years', and it is now generally accepted that this process ought to be carried out after each national census. Indeed, in 1989, Mr Justice Hamilton in the High Court found the Oireachtas to have failed in its constitutional duty in not having revised the constituencies in line with the findings of the previous (1986) census.[2]

Successive Electoral Amendment Acts have altered the number of members and constituencies (see Table 8.1). Consequent upon an important High Court decision in 1961, the tolerance permitted in a constituency revision scheme – that is, the difference between the maximum and minimum number of persons who are to be represented

Table 8.1 **Dáil constituencies and members, 1923–91**

Year of Electoral Act	No. of constitu- encies	No. of members per constituency 9 8 7 6 5 4 3	Total no. of members	Average no. of constituents per member
1923	30	1 3 5 – 9 4 8	153	21,358
1935	34	– – 3 – 8 8 15	138	21,536
1947	40	– – – – 9 9 22	147	20,103
1959[1]	39	– – – – 9 9 21	144	20,127
1961	38	– – – – 9 12 17	144	20,127
1969	42	– – – – 2 14 26	144	20,028
1974	42	– – – – 6 10 26	148	20,123
1980	41	– – – – 15 13 13	166	20,290
1983	41	– – – – 15 13 13	166	20,743
1991	41	– – – – 14 15 12	166	21,329

Note:[1] Some sections of this Act were held to be repugnant to the Constitution (*O'Donovan v. Attorney General*, [1961] IR 114) and it never operated. The scheme it envisaged was replaced by that provided for in the 1961 Act.

Source: Compiled by the author.

by one member – is very small, but because of rapid population changes it has not been possible to maintain anything like an equality of ratios at all times.[3]

III

Legally and formally, a general election consists of a number of constituency contests to elect Deputies to Dáil Éireann. In practice, it is also, and indeed primarily, a competition between political parties for the right to form a government and govern the country. This being so, it might be argued that the electoral system should be judged by its propensity to offer the elector a clear choice of governments and to produce governments with enough consistent parliamentary support to enable them to govern. In the eyes of Irish politicians this has always meant a stable majority, or as near it as possible, of their own party. Coalition government has traditionally been seen as at best an uneasy situation and at worst a necessary evil; and for most in Fianna Fáil, at least until recently, unthinkable.

Governments with stable majorities are not, of course, the product of elections alone, still less of electoral systems, but it is a fact that the application of one set of electoral laws might create a majority where another would not. In practice, as Douglas Rae pointed out, 'in most cases, electoral systems function to the advantage of large established parties and to the disadvantage of small established parties and insurgents [i.e., parties new into the field]'. Although, as Rae said, 'it is clearly silly to conclude that PR causes the multiplication of parties', it is often argued that it contributes to such an outcome.[4] Irish experience in this respect is of particular importance because Ireland offers one of the very few examples of the use of the single transferable vote system (in 1990, it was in use in only one other state, Malta, for general elections). The major issue of Irish general elections is for most of those involved, whether actively or otherwise, who is to form the next government. Clear alternatives, however, have not been offered to the electorate on every occasion. For a decade or so from the late 1930s, in the late 1950s and 1960s, and again at the end of the 1980s, no viable alternative to Fianna Fáil was unequivocally on offer by the opposition parties. For such an alternative to exist, electoral alliances would have been required, but these were not made. On three occasions, a coalition was effected after election results were known: once, in 1948, when the results were seen to offer the possibility of ousting Fianna Fáil after sixteen years in office; a second time in November 1982, when Fine Gael and Labour put together an agreed *Programme for Government*; and again in 1989, when Fianna Fáil for the first time entered a coalition in order to stay in government.

From the the early 1930s, one alternative has regularly been on offer – a Fianna Fáil government. A combination of two circumstances has caused this. The first is the consistent size of electoral support for Fianna Fáil. Once its initial build-up was completed, a process that took from 1927 to 1932, it has always been able to win the first-preference votes of almost a majority – and on two occasions of an actual majority – of the electorate. The second circumstance favourable to Fianna Fáil is the electoral system's translating of votes into seats. This has operated to boost Fianna Fáil's support by providing a 'bonus' sufficient to enable the party to win a majority of seats, or sometimes, when it did not achieve this, to come close enough to enable it to assume power as though it had (see Table 8.2. for details). In these circumstances, Fianna Fáil tended to adopt strictly competitive electoral and parliamentary strategies and to eschew coalition. Consequently, Irish politics for more than half a century was locked into a rigid framework of strict competition between Fianna Fáil and the rest. This resulted in an 'ins-and-outs' pattern of parliamentary government. By the end of the eighties, however, it seemed possible that this pattern would change provided Fianna Fáil was willing to continue to make electoral or parliamentary alliances and enter coalition, as it did in 1989 (see above, p. 98).

Table 8.2 *Percentage of first-preference votes and seats won by Fianna Fáil, 1932–89*

Election	First preference votes	Seats won	Position after election
1932	44.5	47.1	Government
1933	49.7	50.3	Government
1937	45.2	50.0	Government
1938	51.9	55.8	Government
1943	41.9	48.6	Government
1944	48.9	55.1	Government
1948	41.9	46.3	Opposition
1951	46.3	46.9	Government
1954	43.4	44.2	Opposition
1957	48.3	53.1	Government
1961	43.8	48.9	Government
1965	47.8	50.0	Government
1969	45.7	52.0	Government
1973	46.2	47.9	Opposition
1977	50.6	56.8	Government
1981	45.3	47.0	Opposition
1982 (Feb.)	47.3	48.8	Government
1982 (Nov.)	45.2	45.2	Opposition
1987	44.1	48.8	Government
1989	44.1	46.4	Government (in coalition with PDs)

Source: For 1932–44, compiled by the author from unofficial figures published in Flynn's *Parliamentary Handbooks* and elsewhere. For 1948 onwards compiled by the author from *Election Results and Transfer of Votes* (Stationery Office, Dublin), published after each election.

If coalition strategies were for so long inappropriate for Fianna Fáil, they might seem to be natural, even necessary, for the other permanent parties, Fine Gael and the Labour Party. In view of the pattern of popular support, electoral pacts involving the transfer of lower preference votes between the two would have led to a one-party versus two-party type of bipolarism and the possibility of more frequent alternation in office than actually occurred. In the 1930s and 1940s, the ideological differences between Fine Gael and Labour were too great to make coalition palatable. In 1948, however, after a sixteen-year unbroken spell of Fianna Fáil government, an agreement between the leaders of all parties except Fianna Fáil, hastily arranged after the election results were known, brought about the defeat of that party and the formation of a coalition. After two three-year periods of coalition, the major partners, disillusioned with their experience, resumed strict competition. Another sixteen-year period of Fianna Fáil government ensued.

By 1973, ideological differences between Fine Gael and Labour seemed to have lessened; programmes overlapped, and some of the leaders were power-hungry. In any case, they were faced with the need to present a viable alternative to Fianna Fáil in order to retain credibility with the electorate. A coalition platform was agreed to, and a cooperative campaign was waged successfully. Disciplined transfer of lower preferences played a large part in effecting a coalition victory. The defeat of that coalition in 1977, however, led once again to the Labour Party in particular voicing doubts about partnership. Although Fine Gael–Labour coalitions followed on and off for a few years in the eighties (June 1981 to February 1982 and December 1982 to February 1987), the partnership broke up in 1987, not to be renewed at least in the short term. There can be little doubt that Irish political leaders generally – and not only those in Fianna Fáil – have regarded adversary politics and competitive strategies as the norm, and consensus politics and coalition as at best a tiresome necessity in order to get and hold power. Many, perhaps most, of the rank-and-file activists in the parties have held this view even more strongly than their leaders. However, by the late eighties this was becoming an untenable attitude, for the pattern of electoral support for the parties would probably make coalitions of one sort or another almost inevitable.

Although Irish politics has exhibited some of the typical features of a bipolar system, single-party governments with a majority of their own supporters was not always one of them. Between 1922 and 1989, nine single-party governments had a majority composed of their own party and nine did not: there were, in addition, five coalition governments. Experience does not suggest, however, that this has been accompanied by instability. Parliamentary defeats or threats of defeat leading to dissolution have been infrequent. Up to 1981, no government had ever been put out of office by a Dáil vote and on only three occasions had governments gone to the country rather than suffer defeat. Though parliamentary majorities have been small and usually to be counted on the fingers of one hand, the history of almost seventy years up to 1990 included two unbroken periods of office of sixteen years each (1932–48) and 1957–73) and one of ten years (1922–32). This is a record of great stability, but it came to an end – at least for a while – in the eighties. That decade saw five general elections – Ireland is 'one of the few democracies ever to experience five general elections within one decade'.[5] It saw also two parliamentary defeats on matters of confidence, and one cabinet break up and resignation, each leading to dissolution and a general election. As a consequence, at the end of the decade some politicians were beginning, however unwillingly, to reappraise electoral strategies, and a few to cast a cold eye again upon the electoral system.

Just as Irish experience lends no support to the view that the single transferable vote system leads to instability, neither does it contribute much evidence to support a widely held view that PR encourages the multiplication of parties. The same three parties have always dominated the scene (see Table 6.1, p. 95 above). Although minor parties have come on the scene, none established itself for much more than a decade or so except the Workers' Party (founded in 1977 and still in existence, albeit under another name, in 1991). The number of parties contesting elections and gaining representation in the Dáil has gone through a number of cycles, rising to seven (in the 1920s and again in the 1940s, 1950s, and the end of the 1980s) and falling to three (in the early 1930s, 1960s, and 1970s) in a way that might best be explained by the ability of the major parties to hold their supporters or to attract radicals. Often, new parties have originated out of discontent with the original and permanent three. In these circumstances, independents and small groups have been able to win considerable support and even seats. Nevertheless, throughout the seventies and eighties more parties contested elections and won seats in British general elections under the 'first-past-the-post' system than in Irish general elections under the single transferable vote system.

Exploring the impact of election systems upon the number of parties, Michael Gallagher used the concept of 'fractionalization', a measure for comparing the number and size of parties in a political system. This measure, applied to twenty-two countries, showed Ireland – in eighth place – to have a 'relatively low' level of fractionalization by international standards. He concluded that 'the electoral system has not caused a fragmented party system'.[6] A survey of the experience of ninteen European states in and around 1990 showed Ireland falling between the average of those countries with PR systems and that for non-PR systems (see Table 8.3).

All-in-all, Irish experience, as Cornelius O'Leary concluded from his survey of general elections, has, or should have, 'helped to modify dogmatism' about the effect of the system on the number of parties and on the chances of stable government.[7]

Table 8.3 **The 'effective number of parties'[1] in parliament in nineteen West European** **countries after their most recent elections**

Non-PR systems	Ireland	All PR systems
2.6	3.0	4.0

Note:[1] The concept of the effective number of parties was devised by M. Laakso and R. Taagepera (see *Comparative Political Studies*, 12, pp. 3–27). Gallagher describes it as 'essentially a measure of fragmentation: the higher the figure, the more fragmented the parliament' (Gallagher, *Irish Political Studies*, Vol. 2 (1987), p. 46).

Source: Derived from M. Gallagher, M. Laver and P. Mair, *Representative Government in Western Europe* (New York, 1992), pp, 163–4.

IV

Since elections are occasions of mass involvement in politics, the quantity and quality of participation can rightly be deemed to be important criteria for judging electoral systems. The opportunities for Irish citizens to select representatives to speak and act for them, though as numerous as in most democratic countries, are few enough. Under the single transferable vote system, however, the part the citizen can play in the election process is greater than in most systems. This arises because of the opportunities the system offers, opportunities that are used.

When considering elections as a democratic procedure, it is necessary to notice that 'it is the selection of candidates which is often the most decisive stage in the process of recruitment'.[8] At this stage, the involvement of the mass of Irish citizens is low when compared to a country like the United States where 'primaries' (that is, elections to choose candidates) are part of the electoral process. In Ireland 'it is the parties and the party system that structure the opportunities for participation by aspiring politicians, and for choice by voters'.[9] Most election candidates are party nominees selected at constituency conventions attended by representatives of each branch in the constituency. These conventions, which in the case of Fianna Fáil rural constituencies might number up to 400 or 500 people, but are usually only half that number, are presided over by one of the party's national leaders. The job of the presiding leader is to persuade or cajole the locals to nominate an appropriate number of suitable candidates selected to cover the whole constituency. A study of nomination practices at the end of the eighties led Michael Gallagher to conclude that 'there seems to be fairly wide involvement of party *members* in the selection process, even though the great majority of party *voters* is excluded'.[10] (author's italics). Because parties are unable to be precise

about the number of members they have, his figures (see Table 8.4)
are necessarily estimates.

Table 8.4 Involvement of party members and voters in candidate selection in Ireland

	Average attendance at selection conference	As % of party members	As % of party voters
Fianna Fáil	220	23	1.2
Fine Gael	320	44	2.0
Progressive Democrats	58	10	0.9
Labour	50	34	1.3

Source: M. Gallagher, in *Candidate Selection in Comparative Perspective; the Secret
Garden of Politics*, M. Gallagher and M. Marsh (eds) (London, 1988), p. 126.

To a great extent, candidate selection is a local matter, with the
local sitting Deputy or Deputies usually having a major say.
Nominations have to be ratified by the National Executive Committees
of the parties, and sometimes names are added to the slate by party
headquarters. Interference, however, is usually resented at local level,
sometimes with disastrous consequences for the party's subsequent
election campaign in the constituency or even longer-term
repercussions such as breakaway movements. National leaders and
professionals at party headquarters admit the need to influence
candidate selection more than they do at present in order to get
sufficient candidates of good quality into the field. In the case of
minor parties, except the Workers' Party which in the past was highly
centralized and disciplined, nomination is usually a wholly local and
often personal matter. Independents are almost by definition self-
propelled.

Voting in Ireland is not compulsory, but only registered voters may
cast a vote. The percentage of electors who vote (the turnout) has
varied from the low 60s at the first elections (1922 and 1923), when
unsettled conditions obtained, to 81 per cent at the 1933 election,
when there was great excitement and tension. The turnout at the
fourteen elections from the end of the Second World War up to 1989
varied between 68 per cent and 77 per cent, which is low by European
Community standards (see Table 5.2, p. 79, for European comparisons).
Turnout is not uniform over the country. It is lowest in the Dublin area
and in one or two of the mountainous and least-developed western
seaboard constituencies. (For further information on voting and not
voting, see pp. 80–81 above.) Evidently, electors do not find it
difficult to do what the law requires of them, for invalid votes are
usually less than 1 per cent (0.8 per cent in 1989). The positive
response of many voters to their party's exhortations about how to

allot lower preference votes or to refrain from allotting them suggests that most people understand the significance of indicating preferences and how the counting system works.

It is a feature of the single transferable vote system that most voters give more information about their wishes than they can in other systems. They have the opportunity to indicate support for more than one candidate if they rank candidates in order of preference. In Rae's terminology, the Irish voter has an 'ordinal' choice, as opposed to the 'categorical' choice facing the electors under the single non- transferable vote system – the so-called 'straight vote' of the 'first-past-the-post' system – and some of the party-list systems.[11] When it comes to counting, more information is available about most Irish voters' wishes than about the wishes of voters under categorical ballot systems, and the rules are designed to give effect to voters' intentions.

Most Irish electors get the satisfaction of seeing their wishes fulfilled. The proportion of electors who see their first choices elected is about 70 per cent. As important, between 75 and 80 per cent of votes cast help elect someone. Compared with party-list systems, the proportion of non-effective votes in Irish elections (between 20 and 25 per cent) is high, though not all of these are 'wasted' votes, since perhaps up to 5 per cent of them become non-transferable during the count by the deliberate choice of voters to abstain if their first choices are not used. The results achieved under party-list systems are due to narrowing the voters' choice to parties and having constituencies return very large numbers of members. The contrast that Irish people themselves are more likely to make is with British voters with their categorical choice and the possibility overall of considerable disproportionality between votes and seats.

Almost all Irish voters vote for more than one candidate, ranking at least some of the candidates in an order of preference. There is much evidence to suggest that in doing so they are above all party-orientated and take notice of their party's advice to 'vote X, Y and Z in order of [their] choice'. Estimates of such 'solidarity' on the part of supporters of the three main parties in the four elections from 1977 to November 1982, made by Richard Sinnott, reveal figures of between 75 and 80 per cent for Fianna Fail, in the seventies for Fine Gael, and (except at one election) in the sixties for Labour (see Table 8.5).

Further evidence of the party orientation of many Irish voters can be seen in their propensity to comply with their party's suggestions about what to do with lower preferences when no more candidates of the party are available. Such patterns of transfers are often vital for winning or losing seats and power. The National Coalition victory in 1973 was largely due to the disciplined preferential voting of the supporters of the two parties involved, which was critical in a number of marginal constituencies. This pattern continued throughout the period of the alliance and, as Michael Gallagher pointed out, had important consequences: 'At the five elections of 1973–82 . . . Fine

142   *The Government and Politics of Ireland*

Table 8.5 **Party solidarity, 1977 to November 1982**

Election	Fianna Fáil	Fine Gael	Labour
1977	75.9	72.1	66.7
1981	78.3	77.5	61.1
Feb. 1982	80.4	79.5	58.7
Nov. 1982	80.2	79.7	64.3

Note: The entries in the table are estimates of the proportion of a party's vote that are transferable to a candidate of the same party when at least one such candidate remains in contention.

Source: R. Sinnott, in *Ireland at the Polls, 1981, 1982 and 1987: a Study of Four General Elections*, H. R. Penniman and B. Farrell (eds) (Durham NC, 1987), p. 90.

Gael and Labour voters generally transferred their votes to each other and this cooperation was crucial in depriving Fianna Fáil of an overall majority at each election except 1977.'[12] On the other side, Fianna Fáil 'invariably gave few transfers and received few, and in 1987 was deprived of 13 seats by transfer among the other parties'.[13]

Such loyalty to party and compliance with party wishes offer opportunities for 'vote management' – that is, 'the art of trying to ensure that the votes are distributed in such a way as to maximise the seats won'.[14] According to Gallagher, the technique 'has been practised in Ireland since the 1930s at least'.[15] It involves devising a strategy in a constituency and requiring electors to follow party suggestions as to how to order their preferences. Vote management is, however, a tricky business. It can play a part in deciding the result in only a minority of constituencies and these need to be identified. It necessitates an intimate knowledge of the party's vote in a constituency – in these days often acquired by parties through private polls in selected marginal constituencies; and it is liable to encounter resistance from either candidates or voters or both. Gallagher considered it was 'a factor' in eighteen constituencies at the 1987 election and that, at the 1989 election, 'there were at least six constituencies, and possibly nine, where parties forfeited seats through inadequate vote management'.[16]

The opportunities offered to parties when voters are loyal are clearly considerable, but there are, as we have already noted, some signs that less of the electorate than in the past identify unequivocally with a party. There is, on the contrary, evidence of volatility. Marsh and Sinnott found that at the 1989 election, 'some 21 per cent of voters reported that they changed their minds during the campaign' and, for the same election, Gallagher calculated that the average volatility per constituency was 12.4 per cent, highest in Dublin and lowest in Connacht and Ulster.[17] Consequently, the number of seats changing hands at elections is rising. At each of the 1982 elections, seats changed hands in fourteen constituencies; in 1987, in twenty-six constituencies (thirty seats); in 1989, eighteen constituencies (nineteen seats). Traditionally, loyalty to one's party was widespread and strong: it governed the character of party politics to a considerable extent. If and as it dissipates, Irish politics will alter – perhaps is altering – considerably.

Party preference, however, is not of itself sufficient to enable eight out of ten voters to cast a vote, for in all constituencies Fianna Fáil and Fine Gael, and in a few constituencies Labour also, offer more than one candidate. Choices have to be made between them or they have to be rank-ordered. Many voters and most local activists have local and personal loyalties to particular candidates. Candidates, especially, in rural constituencies, are identified with particular areas in their constituency where they hope to win the greater part of their first-preference support. Each has carefully nurtured the party supporters of a particular area and hopes to garner the first preferences of enough of them to get elected, or, if not, to remain in the contest in the hope of receiving lower preference votes later in the count. Each is as much in competition with fellow party candidates as with candidates of other parties for the relatively fixed number of votes the party expects to get.

In rank-ordering their party's candidates, voters might be influenced by any of a number of factors. Most people give their first preference to the senior and best-known member of their party's team or to the candidate from their own district, whom, in rural areas at least, they are likely to know. The strong localism of rural voters finds full expression through the election system. Because of this, what is formally a multi-member constituency system is in places something rather different. In John Whyte's view some constituencies are no more than 'a federation of single member seats', and terms like 'fiefs' and 'bailiwicks' have been used to describe them.[18]

Personality and personal factors also influence rank-ordering. Increasingly over the years, prominence in Gaelic football and hurling replaced 'a national record' – that is, active participation in the struggle for independence – as a prime qualification for candidature and office. Well known in Irish politics, too, is the sympathy vote that serves to put a widow or a son into a dead man's seat, which can be retained at subsequent elections if son or widow works hard. Indeed, the dynastic element generally remains strong.

Perhaps most important of all for most candidates is their record of 'service' to their local constituents and to their area – the attention paid by them to requests for help over applications to, or difficulties with, public authorities, local and national, in connection with matters such as housing, social welfare, health benefits and facilities, land redistribution, drainage grants and the siting of factories. Surveys have consistently shown 'service' to be the most important criterion of choice (see Table 8.6).

Table 8.6 *Voters' perceptions of the most important criterion determining their vote, 1977-89*

Criterion	1977	1981	Feb. 1982	Nov. 1982	1987	1989
Choosing a Taoiseach	8	16	20	19	15	14
Choosing ministers who will form a government	18	16	17	15	18	9
Choosing between the policies of parties	21	24	27	25	29	15
Choosing a TD who will look after the local needs of the constituency	46	42	35	41	38	40
Choosing a TD who will perform well on national issues in the Dáil[1]	n.a.	n.a.	n.a.	n.a.	n.a.	16

Note:[1] This option was not included until 1989.

Source: M. Marsh and R. Sinnott, in *How Ireland Voted 1989* M. Gallagher and R. Sinnott (Galway, 1990), p. 121.

Because many of these matters are handled at local government level, most TDs think it is essential for them to be members of their local authorities: 70 per cent of the Deputies elected in 1989 were local councillors. Candidates who are the most preferred of their party at one election might easily slip at the next if they have not assiduously attended to their constituents' requests for help. Such changes in popularity can and do lead to defeat.

The considerations mentioned in preceding paragraphs not only influence the order of choice of party-orientated voters, who are the vast majority, but also lead some voters to give lower preferences to candidates of other parties after they have exhausted their own party's choices. A few voters might also cross party lines in ordering their preferences, perhaps even to the extent of placing a candidate of a party other than their own first on the ballot paper.

The practice of voters ranking candidates and in doing so taking into account any factors that they regard as important has considerable consequences for the whole political system. It has an important effect upon the composition of the Dáil, and it greatly influences the behaviour of deputies. To a great extent, it governs their relationships with their constituents and their perceptions of their role as parliamentarians. By making it possible for electors to combine in groups that do not coincide with party divisions and to support candidates who are not party choices, the system has permitted the existence of independents and the survival of party rebels and outcasts. An outstanding example for two decades is Neil Blaney. A Deputy and former minister representing a rural north-western constituency where he had a virtual fiefdom, he was expelled from Fianna Fáil in 1971 but retained his seat in subsequent general elections.

The effects upon the conduct of elections of the way the electoral system is exploited by the electors are very obvious. The selection of candidates is particularly affected. Although the law does not require it, candidates are predominantly local people in the sense that they live and belong in their constituencies. Except in Dublin, almost all live in or are identified with a particular part of the constituency they are contesting, where they have a following and which they regard as their area. Consequently, most candidates for rural constituencies are country people; there are very few urban 'carpetbaggers'. This virtual requirement of local residence has a marked effect upon the composition of the Dáil.

The campaigns waged by these locally selected and usually local candidates tend to be self-contained and self-sufficient; the central organizations of the parties play a supporting, though increasing, role. National issues, activities, and materials designed to influence electors at large – television and radio programmes, party manifestos and pledges, campaign tours by party leaders, T-shirts, and party songs – are, though of growing importance, still a backdrop against which a candidate seeks the support of his or her locality.

As we have seen, the candidate's best asset by far is a record of service in the home district. Here, naturally, sitting Deputies have a great advantage, for they can offer, and in many cases have already given, service as a contact and advocate at the central government level as well as at city or county hall. A good record of service is an asset to any candidate and is the foundation of the position of Deputies of small parties and independents. The candidates of the main parties use it chiefly not against political opponents of other parties, but against their fellow candidates of the same party. Candidates cannot fight their fellow party candidates on policy or party record; they try, instead, to present an image of more assiduous and more successful service to constituents. Politicians know this well and act accordingly.

Concentration on the personal and local is more evident in the rural areas than in the big cities. This can be seen particularly in canvassing activities. All candidates and all party officials believe that canvassing is the most effective method of electioneering. In the city it does not matter much who the canvassers are, but in small towns and villages and in the countryside the candidate must personally approach all supporters of consequence in his or her area and as many others as possible. In turn, prominent supporters seek the votes of their neighbours. Thus links in a chain of personal approach are forged, a matter of necessity in dealing with a rural population that still values face-to-face contacts, regards personal influence as an important factor in the conduct of any business of importance, and likes to feel that a potentially influential person has asked a favour and incurred an obligation.

No doubt the increasing tendency in the television age for the parties to present elections as gladiatorial contests between national leaders and to offer tax and other inducements to an electorate that is becoming more volatile and susceptible to material offers has changed Irish elections. Nevertheless, the editors of the 1989 election study sounded a note of caution on this. They summarized the personal accounts of six candidates which they included in their volume as follows:

What they write does not bear out the view that candidates are merely cogs in a machine run from party headquarters. On the contrary the picture to emerge is that candidates have to fight their own fight in their own constituencies, often with little or no contact with head office throughout the campaign. The whole perspective at local level is sometimes very different from that of the national strategists.[19]

V

When a country has an election system that is said to be a proportional representation system, much attention is naturally paid to the degree of correspondence in practice between votes cast and seats won. It is customary to measure proportionality in terms of first-preference votes cast for each party and seats won by the party. Measured thus, the degree of proportionality achieved by the Irish system is quite high. Rae concluded from his comparative study that the Irish system 'in general behaves like any other sort of proportional representation. It operates quite proportionally.'[20] 'Quite'; but not quite. As generally happens elsewhere, the largest parties have tended to win a more than proportionate share of seats and, in particular, Fianna Fáil has always won a bonus (see Table 8.7). Because of the critical size of its electoral support, that bonus has often been vital for its chances of winning power as the data in Table 8.2 (p. 136, above) show.

The number of Deputies per constituency is often considered to have an important impact upon proportionality, but Irish experience tends to contradict this. The Irish system, as we have seen, delivers a high degree of proportionality and it does so 'in the face of a severe obstacle, namely an exceptionally small district magnitude (the number of deputies elected from each constituency). . . . With such a small district magnitude, no electoral system could be expected to have delivered more proportionality than STV has in Ireland.'[21] Moreover, variations in proportionality cannot be attributed to

Table 8.7 **Disproportionality at general elections, 1948–89**

	Average % votes	Average % seats	Average bonus	Highest bonus	Lowest bonus
Fianna Fáil	45.7	48.8	+3.1	+6.5	+0.3
Fine Gael	31.4	33.0	+1.6	+4.0	-1.2
Labour	11.1	10.5	-0.6	+0.9	-4.4
Others	11.8	7.7	-4.1	-0.8	-9.1

Source: Data supplied by M. Gallagher, Department of Political Science, Trinity College, Dublin.

constituency size.[22] Nevertheless, politicians have always thought it important, and when in power have sometimes tried to adjust both constituency boundaries and the number of members in constituencies to their own party advantage. Constituency revision was carried out by the government in office until 1979 when the practice of appointing constituency commissions was instituted. Revision schemes were, until then, prepared by the Minister for Local Government (renamed Environment in 1977) directly and frankly with an eye to maximizing party advantage within the rules. In the 1930s and 1940s, spokesmen for governments revising constituencies openly justified their proposals to break up big constituencies and to increase the number of three-seat and four-seat constituencies on the grounds that 'it is made easier for a party which may be called upon to shoulder the responsibility of government to get sufficient seats to enable them to undertake that task with adequate parliamentary support'.[23] For the same reason some leaders of the two largest parties have always wanted to abandon the system altogether, as we shall see (see below, p. 148–9).

If proportionality is the aim of an electoral system, chance or extraneous elements that might distort the picture of the electors' wishes ought to be eliminated so far as possible. Two such elements in the Irish system should be noted. The first arises during the count when surpluses are transferred. The proportion of ballot papers of an elected candidate that is to go to each continuing candidate is calculated as a ratio of the surplus to the number of transferable papers. Each candidate receives this proportion of the appropriate bundle of votes that show next preferences for him or her. It is when this transfer is actually made that an element of chance arises, for a physical transfer of votes is made, the appropriate number from the top of the elected candidate's pile being taken and placed with the other votes of the transferee. In a tight marginal situation at the end of the count where very few votes divide the last two candidates, it is possible that if different sets of papers had been taken earlier in the count, the pattern of next preference shown on these papers might be different and the difference might alter the end result.[24]

More important, perhaps, is the influence of printing candidates' names on the ballot paper in alphabetical order. Irish politicians have for long recognized that a candidate whose name is high up on the printed list has an advantage. Robson and Walsh, using statistical techniques, have demonstrated not only 'the distinct advantage enjoyed by candidates, and non-incumbent candidates in particular, if they are alphabetically first among their party's candidates', but also the cumulative impact this has had on the outcome of elections. They found that 'TDs' surnames are now markedly different in alphabetical distribution from the Irish population as a whole'.[25]

VI

The single transferable vote system in multi-member constituencies has been retained without any major changes throughout the whole life of the state. When, in the mid-1930s, de Valera was preparing a new constitution for the country, the system was not called in question, and Bunreacht na hÉireann provided for its continuation. It was, perhaps, too soon after the events and circumstances that had dictated its inclusion in the first place to be looking for a change. Nevertheless, faced with the tantalizing situation of permanently being the largest party and of regularly winning very nearly a majority of the votes cast, it is not surprising that de Valera and Fianna Fáil should have contemplated changing the system.

Not until the late 1950s, however, at the very end of de Valera's long reign, did he broach the question of electoral reform. In 1959, the Fianna Fáil government initiated a constitutional referendum providing for the replacement of the forty multi-seat constituencies with between 100 and 150 single-seat constituencies and the substitution of the single non-transferable vote for the transferable vote. If the reform was approved, the candidate getting the most votes would win the seat, as in the system used in the United Kingdom. De Valera's main arguments and those of his colleagues centred on the malignant effects of the single transferable vote system. De Valera himself put it thus:

PR has not, in my opinion, in recent times worked out well . . . it worked very well for a time because there were issues so large in the public eye that they dominated all other issues, and, therefore, the people voted on one side or the other. . . . Some of this stability was acquired rather in spite of the system. . . . The whole effect of the present system of PR has been to cause multiplicity of parties. . . . Under the system of straight voting they will have to unite beforehand, not after. . . . Those countries which have most successfully built up democratic institutions are the countries in which there is a single nontransferable vote.[26]

In the event, the proposal was narrowly defeated.

Nine years later, when Fianna Fáil for the second time attempted to get approval for the 'straight vote' system, they were once again beaten, this time decisively. On this occasion, too, Fianna Fáil leaders used the same arguments. The *Irish Times* reported that Charles Haughey, then Minister for Finance, warned his audience in Sligo that:

proportional representation was a divisive force. Unlike the straight vote which compelled electors to make a direct choice between candidates and policies, proportional representation relieved the voters of the task of political decision. In our case because of special circumstances it had not yet – and he emphasised the word yet – brought the multitude of small parties and the instability of government that had followed in its wake as inevitably as night follows day in every country where it existed. . . . He hoped that they would bear in mind also that in modern times democracy had never died in a country which had the straight vote, but the instances were many where it died under proportional representation and gave way to totalitarianism of one kind or another.[27]

Clearly, at that time there existed a considerable and settled public opinion in favour of the single transferable vote. Probably, there still is, based upon experience with the system and the contrast offered by British experience with the so-called 'straight vote'. However, some politicians, and particularly leaders of the largest parties, have always hankered after a change. When in the early eighties three general elections were held in the space of seventeen months, the issue was once again canvassed in the name of 'stability'; and yet again in the late eighties as Fianna Fáil strove vainly to win that elusive majority. If politics in the nineties are as unsettled as in the eighties, it might well be raised again.

Notes

1   Bunreacht na hÉireann provides another possible opportunity for citizen participation. Article 27 provides that

a majority of the members of Seanad Éireann and not less than one-third of the members of Dáil Éireann may by a joint petition . . . request the President to decline to sign and promulgate as a law any Bill to which this Article applies on the ground that the Bill contains a proposal of such national importance that the will of the people thereon ought to be ascertained.

The President has it in his discretion to grant such a request and, if he does, he delays signing the bill 'until the proposal shall have been approved either (i) by the people at a referendum . . . or (ii) by a resolution of Dáil Éireann passed . . . after the dissolution and reassembly'. This provision has never been operated

2   *O'Malley* v. *An Taoiseach and the Attorney General* [1990] ILRM 461.

3   *O'Donovan* v. *Attorney General* [1961] IR 114.

4   D. W. Rae, *The Political Consequences of Electoral Laws* (New Haven and London, 1971), pp. 169 and 167.

5 M. Gallagher and R. Sinnott, in *How Ireland Voted 1989*, M. Gallagher and R. Sinnott (eds) (Galway, 1990), p. 1.
6 M. Gallagher, 'Does Ireland need a new electoral system?' in *Irish Political Studies*, 2 (1987), p. 30.
7 C. O'Leary, *Irish Elections, 1918–77: Parties, Voters and Proportional Representation* (Dublin, 1979), p. 112.
8 M. Marsh, 'Transformation with a small "t": candidates for the Dáil, 1948–82', in *Irish Political Studies*, 4 (1989), p. 60.
9 *Ibid.*
10 M. Gallagher, in *Candidate Selection in Comparative Perspective: the Secret Garden of Politics* M. Gallagher and M. Marsh (eds) (London, 1988), p. 125.
11 Rae, *The Political Consequences of Electoral Laws* pp. 42–3.
12 M. Gallagher, in *How Ireland Voted 1989*, M. Gallagher and R. Sinnott (eds), p. 78.
13 *Ibid.*
14 M. Gallagher, in M. Laver, P. Mair and R. Sinnott (eds), *How Ireland Voted: the Irish General Election 1987* (Swords, 1987), pp. 83–4.
15 *Ibid.*
16 Gallagher, *How Ireland Voted: the Irish General Election 1987*, p. 85, and *How Ireland Voted 1989*, p. 82. See also the personal accounts of two (successful) candidates in *How Ireland Voted 1989*, p. 46 (Charlie McCreevy) and pp. 49 ff. (Ivan Yates).
17 *How Ireland Voted 1989*, p. 121 (Marsh and Sinnott) and p. 68 (Gallagher).
18 J. Whyte in R. Rose (ed.), *Electoral Behavior* (New York and London, 1974), pp. 629–30.
19 M. Gallagher and R. Sinnott, in *How Ireland Voted 1989*, pp. 2–3.
20 Rae, *The Political Consequences of Electoral Laws* p. 111.
21 M. Gallagher, 'Does Ireland need a new electoral system?' in *Irish Political Studies*, 2 (1987), p. 29.
22 See M. Gallagher, 'Disproportionality in a proportional representation system: the Irish system', in *Political Studies*, 23 (1975), p. 503.
23 *Dáil Debates,* Vol. 108, col. 924 (23 Oct. 1947). See also *ibid.*, Vol. 51, col. 1283 (13 March 1934).
24 For a possible example, see J. Knight and N. Baxter-Moore, *Republic of Ireland: the General Elections of 1969 and 1973* (London, 1973), p. 45.
25 C. Robson and B. Walsh, 'The importance of positional voting bias in the Irish general election of 1973', in *Political Studies*, 22 (1974), p. 203.
26 *Dáil Debates*, Vol. 171, cols. 993–8.
27 Reported in the *Irish Times*, 28 Aug. 1968.

CHAPTER 9

The Policy-makers

I

General elections in Ireland produce governments and parliaments, the two institutions that are at the very centre of government, whether making or applying policy and laws. Legal authority to make policy and laws gives the government and the Oireachtas their central roles. They are surrounded, however, by other persons and groups who also have a part to play in policy- and law-making because they too have power or influence of one sort or another. In *The Policy-making Process*, Charles E. Lindblom explained policy-making in terms of power: 'Power is always held by a number of persons rather than by one; hence policy is made through the complex processes by which those persons exert power or influence over each other.' He characterized these processes as a 'play of power'.[1]

To quote Lindblom again: 'The play of power proceeds, for the most part, according to rule; it is gamelike'.[2] However, neither in Bunreacht na hÉireann nor in ordinary law are all the rules of the game stated. To begin with, the Constitution gives an incomplete enunciation of the functions performed by governments and the Oireachtas, and it spells out a division of governmental powers that is incomplete and does not obtain in reality. Furthermore, it does not mention, though by implication it allows for, the existence and activities of parties and pressure groups.

That is not to say that the Irish Constitution is a fraud or that it is flouted in the practice of politics. Rather, being a legal document, it expresses legal relationships and is written in conventional, even traditional, legal language. Conventionally, also, it embodies the *concepts* of Western, liberal constitutional theory largely in the form in which it developed in late-nineteenth-century Britain. The *practice* of cabinet government as it evolved in the United Kingdom up to the First World War was different in important respects, and it was this model that was adopted by Irish governments and is still in use.

The main features of this early-twentieth-century Westminster model, as it might appropriately be called, are as follows:

(1) Governments usually emerge as a direct result of general elections. The electorate chooses leaders to govern them from rival groups of politicians, each consisting of a party leader and his or her

most important colleagues. Almost all candidates are identified with one of these groups. The winners in this electoral contest acquire the right to assume government office and power. If the election results do not produce a winner, post-election bargaining between parties instead of electoral choice produces a majority coalition government. The leader, or, in the case of coalition, the leaders of the constituent parties, form a cabinet – in Ireland called 'the government' – composed of ministers, each in charge of one or more departments. The government meets as a committee to decide the major issues of public policy and the measures its members intend to present to the Oireachtas for approval, to coordinate the work of the departments they control, and generally to manage central government business.

(2) The government governs the country. It makes, or at least endorses, all the decisions that have to be made at the very highest political level. Its members in their various roles – as party and Oireachtas leaders and as ministers – are expected by their supporters and by the country generally to identify issues and problems of public importance, to propound effective solutions, to gain acceptance for their solutions in the Oireachtas and the country in so far as this may be necessary, and to put them into operation. In performing these functions, they have the aid and advice of senior civil servants, and they take account not only of parliamentary and party opinion but of the views of the spokesmen of relevant pressure groups (with whom they may deal directly) and of electoral opinion generally.

(3) The Taoiseach is, as the Constitution puts it, the 'head of the Government'. He is pre-eminent among his colleagues, for he is the leader of the party or coalition that has won the election and, as such, personifies the government. He chooses his colleagues and can dismiss them, though his freedom to choose and to dismiss in some circumstances (notably in a coalition situation) might be restricted. When he resigns, they go out of office too; and, while he has the support of a majority of the Dáil, he it is who decides when to call a general election. The precise degree of his pre-eminence, however, might well vary from Taoiseach to Taoiseach. Personalities and political situations make for differences between one and another.

(4) The government leads and is maintained by its supporters in the Dáil (they being a majority of that body) and in the Seanad. The Dáil majority is, normally, a stable one, held together by party loyalty. Although the members of the majority group look to their leaders to take the initiative in formulating measures to be adopted, to manage the business of the houses of the Oireachtas, and generally to govern, they expect the leaders to consult with them and pay attention to their wishes and comments. Their views, however, are only some of the opinions that a government takes into account.

(5) The government is opposed in the Oireachtas by one or more rival groups of leaders and their parliamentary supporters. These form 'the opposition'. The principle which governs the content and style of

the challenge which oppositio...
they will be offering themselv...
government whenever the opportu...

(6) The members of the gove...
both collectively and individually,...
collective and individual responsibil...
system but are not precise. In general,...
each minister has special responsibility...
activity and conducts the affairs of his own...
answering for it in the government, in the...
community), the government as a whole is held...
a general way for the manner in which public...
Constitutionally, the Dáil has the power to effec...   the
Taoiseach and his government if a majority of ...   ...ires. In
practice, given the party composition of the Dáil and ... ...able support
for leaders, individual ministers and governments are rarely dismissed
by the actions of the Dáil. Nevertheless, expressions of dissatisfaction
or signs of unrest in the majority group will have some effect, perhaps
even leading to a dissolution.

(7) The houses of the Oireachtas have two major functions. First,
they discuss in public the proposals put before them by the
government. Because the government commands the support of the
majority in the Dáil and because the Seanad has only a subsidiary role
in the parliamentary process, the government controls the timetable
and the conduct of business. It can expect to get almost all its
proposals passed, though concessions to parliamentary opinion might
be deemed expedient for reasons of party or election strategy. Second,
the Oireachtas appraises and comments on the conduct of
administration by the government and elicits information on matters
big and small. In performing these functions, both sides, government
and opposition, have an eye to the electorate. In this public forum they
make bids for electoral support.

Within the context of this model, it is possible to characterize the
policy-making process in a general way and to identify the roles of
various participants. A system such as this tends to produce rather
strong government and a pattern of relationships a long way removed
from the traditional liberal model with its notion of a representative
assembly reflecting the will of the people in legislation and policy
declarations that are put into effect by 'the executive' and the public
service.

II

The term 'public policy' was defined by William Jenkins as 'a set of
interrelated decisions taken by a political actor or group of actors
concerning the selection of goals and the means of achieving them

...on where these decisions should, in principle, ... of these actors to achieve'.[3] Making public policy ...ng what matters are to be taken up and considered by ... (in this case at national level); what is to be done about the ...ms, issues, or opportunities that are involved in these matters; ...hat steps are to be taken to achieve the objectives that are decided upon; how motions or draft legislation to be put before the Oireachtas are to be formulated; how motions and bills are to be processed through the Dáil and the Seanad; and, when they are passed, how these policies are to be further developed in an 'implementation' stage to produce 'outputs', a stage which might well involve the implementers, mostly civil servants and other public servants, contributing to the content of policies, thus qualifying as 'policy makers'. 'Public policy' suggests broad rather than narrow, and general rather than detailed, decisions. It is nevertheless necessary to notice that governments and parliaments also make decisions that are very specific, simply because some issues, however narrow, are of great political importance and must be taken at the top. Such issues, like those of wider scope, are equally subject to the play of power.

It is important to realize that the processes we are about to analyze are not the only ones by which policy is made. General courses of action sometimes emerge from many individual and specific decisions that in their totality can be seen to fall into patterns which might appropriately be called 'policies'. The courts, too, sometimes make decisions, the contents and consequences of which lead public authorities to modify state action; thus, courts make policy. For example, when the Irish courts in a series of judgements in the 1960s whittled away some of the privileges the state had enjoyed in its dealings with the citizen (privileges that had been inherited as part of the British constitutional legacy), they only did what the Oireachtas might have done and what the British prliament had actually done in the Crown Proceedings Act 1947. It is not appropriate, however, to deal with this particular form of policy-making here, for it is carefully and deliberately insulated from politics and from the pressure of participants in the political process, which is to be analyzed in this chapter.

Finally, we must notice that the word 'policy' is also used to describe the general decisions and conduct of subordinate public authorities which have power delegated to them by the government and the Oireachtas to make rules that have the force of law. Some of these rules can appropriately be called 'policies'. It is quite legitimate to speak of the Wicklow County Council's policy on housing itinerants or Comhairle na nOspidéal's policy on the staffing of hospital maternity units. However, the policy-making activities of these bodies and those like them are not included in this analysis, since these bodies are essentially subordinate authorities. They derive their functions and powers from government and parliament, and their policy-making is constrained within the policies of the superior bodies.

III

In classifying the contributors to public policy-making, Lindblom identified a core group of what he called 'proximate policy makers'. He defined them as 'those who share immediate legal authority to decide on specific policies, together with other immediate participants in policy decisions'.[4] He distinguished these from other participants who influence them. He viewed both categories as involved in a 'play of power' that constitutes an important element of democracy of the 'pluralist' variety.[5] In this analysis of public policy-making, we shall adopt Lindblom's useful categories.

In the making of much of Irish public policy, the proximate policy-makers are (1) the members of the government (that is, the cabinet) and ministers of state (who are not in the cabinet); (2) the members of the Dáil and Seanad; and (3) some senior civil servants, including temporary 'advisers' and, possibly, a few other public servants. The main influences upon them are political parties, pressure groups, the public service (that is, the Civil Service, the local government service, and the executives of the state-sponsored bodies), the mass media, and public opinion. In addition, there is a growing external influence, the European Communities or, more precisely, the obligations imposed upon the Irish government by reason of Ireland's membership in the Communities. These influences interact upon one another. In particular, the mass media are important in informing, and perhaps influencing, those who in turn influence policy, as well as those who make it. Finally, it is necessary to notice that policies formulated by the proximate policy makers might have their content modified by those whose job it is to 'implement' them. Most of these so–called 'administrators' would not think of themselves, or be regarded by others, as proximate policy makers, but they might and do have an effect upon the final output (see below, p. 165). This arrangement is presented diagrammatically in Figure 9.1.

Although this categorization seems to suit the facts of policy-making as it takes place much of the time in many areas, it has to be modified when it comes to others. In Chapter 7 (on pressure groups), attention was drawn to the practice in Ireland from time to time recently of associating the major economic umbrella bodies (the Irish Congress of Trade Unions, employer bodies and farming organizations) more closely with the state in structures and procedures for devising socio-economic policies which might appropriately be termed 'corporatist' (see pp.126–28 above). These arrangements draw the pressure groups concerned so closely into the policy-making process as to make them proximate policy makers in respect of the social and economic policies embodied in the resultant 'agreements', 'understandings', and 'programmes'.

With the government negotiating agreements binding itself, and the Oireachtas reduced to a rubber-stamping role, some see corporatism as

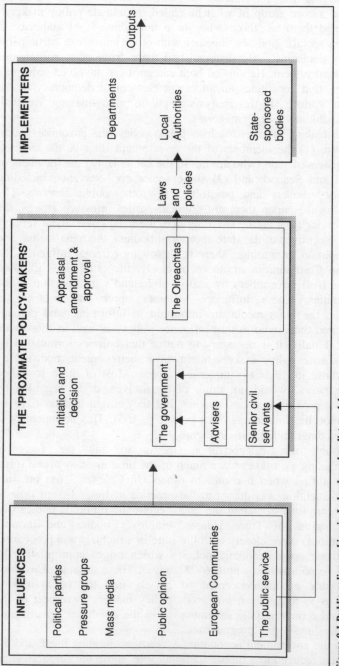

Figure 9.1 Public policy-making in Ireland: a pluralist model

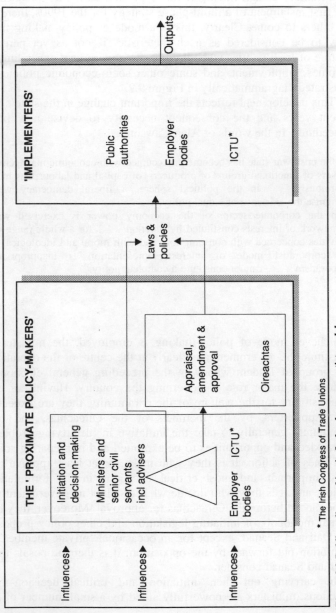

Figure 9.2 Public policy-making in Ireland: a corporatist model

THE 'PROXIMATE POLICY-MAKERS'

Initiation and decision-making

Ministers and senior civil servants incl advisers

Employer bodies   ICTU*

Appraisal, amendment & approval

Oireachtas

Influences
Influences
Influences

Laws & policies

'IMPLEMENTERS'

Public authorities

Employer bodies

ICTU*

Outputs

* The Irish Congress of Trade Unions

attenuating democracy. We should beware, however, of seeing the state as just another organization in a corporate world. In the end, the government must govern, and the legitimacy which comes from having won the preceding election endows it with the authority to do so. It is this that distinguishes the government from other participants.

The *Programme for Economic and Social Progress* (1991) was one of a number of agreements of this type and, as it was intended to be the first instalment of a multi-phase strategy for the 1990s, there might be others to come. Clearly, this is a mode of policy-making that has now to be considered as a characteristic, if not as yet permanent, feature of Irish politics when it comes to government expenditure, tax, incomes, employment, and some other socio-economic policies. It is illustrated diagrammatically in Figure 9.2.

This development reflects the important change in the state's role in recent years and the consequent necessity to devise new political procedures. In the words of Alan Cawson:

As the post–war state has become preoccupied with economic management the powers of functional groups of producers, of capital and labour, has increased enormously. . . . in the political sphere of liberal democracy we must recognise the existence of a dual polity. . . .

In the corporate sector of the economy power is exercised within a framework of interests constituted by function . . . for a whole range of state activities concerned with consumption, and with moral and ideological issues, the corporatist mode of interest representation is inappropriate . . . corporatism . . . cannot constitute a complete polity.[6]

IV

Whichever mode of policy-making is employed, the ministers who constitute the government are clearly at the centre of the operation. As the group of leaders who won the preceding general election, they assume the major role in governing the country. Having an overall responsibility for the welfare of the community, they are expected by their supporters, by the members of the Oireachtas, and by the community generally to take the initiative in identifying problems to be tackled and opportunities to be exploited and in preparing solutions and lines of action. It is they who make, or at least approve of, the most important and most critical decisions in the formulation of policy; and it is they who decide what to adopt as government policy to be placed before the Oireachtas for approval. Moreover, they have a virtual monopoly of initiating legislation and other policy proposals in the Dáil and Seanad; except for an occasional 'private member's bill' or motion put forward by the opposition, it is their proposals that the Dáil and Seanad consider.

In carrying out their initiation and critical decision–making functions, ministers are powerfully aided by a small number of senior civil servants. These are professional managers of the state's business and advisers to their ministers with whom they have contacts of a kind that might give them the opportunity to influence ministerial decisions. Besides the senior administrators, ministers might also consult professional officers in their departments – scientists, medical doctors, veterinarians, economists. The views of a few public servants such as chairmen or chief executives of state-sponsored bodies might also be sought from time to time on matters within their own areas.

Besides these career public servants, there are now a few 'advisers'. From the late 1960s, some ministers began to appoint one or two aides – either civil servants transferred from other duties and perhaps other departments, or outsiders employed as temporary civil servants. These aides are people whose counsel ministers wish to have because they are politically in tune with them or knowledgeable or both. In the words of a former Secretary of the Labour Party, Brendan Halligan, they 'are nothing more than the political extension of the minister – they are the extension of his political personality. Their role ends when his political life ends'.[7] At the end of 1990 there were less than a dozen of them, and it could not by any means yet be said that the continental European system of the *cabinet du ministre* was a feature of Irish government. If the permanent civil servants have their way, it never will be, for on the whole they resent these outsiders. However, an increasing number of ministers are coming to recognize the need for the kind of advice and support that they cannot get from career civil servants.

It is difficult to describe in general terms the part that civil servants play in policy-making or to distinguish the respective contributions of ministers and civil servants. In making such an attempt in the British context, Peter Self drew a distinction between what he called 'climate setting' and the identification of major objectives and priorities, on the one hand, and decisions on specific policies (such as what steps are to be taken to achieve major objectives) on the other. The first are, without doubt, jobs for politicians:

The most obvious and universal contribution of politicians to policy–making occurs through the formulation of general attitudes, opinions and ideologies. 'Climate setting' influences the way in which particular issues are approached and the kind of measures which are favourably regarded, but is too generalised an activity to produce specific policies.[8]

The accession to office of a new government is particularly an occasion for climate setting. At such a time, civil servants wait for ministers to indicate what policies they will be pursuing and what their priorities will be. They have also to 'size up' their new ministers and to assess their 'form' and 'style'. Who can doubt that there was a distinct change in the climate in, for example, March 1932, when Fianna Fáil first took office; or in February 1948, when, after sixteen years of unbroken Fianna Fáil rule, the Inter-Party Government succeeded to office; or in March 1973, when the National Coalition took over after another sixteen years of Fianna Fáil government; or in 1981 when Charles Haughey gave way to Dr Garret FitzGerald leading a two–party coalition?

Although climate-setting and the identification of major objectives are clearly ministerial functions, in some circumstances civil servants might contribute very positively. The part played in the late 1950s by T. K. Whitaker, then Secretary of the Department of Finance, and his colleagues in launching the Irish government into the era of state planning has long been recognized.[9] So, too, from time to time, there has been known to exist among officers of some departments fixed views about their departments' roles and general lines of policy. Ruth Barrington provides a good example in one policy area in *Health, Medicine and Politics* (Dublin, 1987). Even if this is not the case, departments might well have schemes long-prepared and ready, awaiting only a minister to give the go-ahead. Séamus Ó Buachalla, a former officer of the Department of Education, put it thus: 'A policy is guaranteed adoption if the minister favours it; however, it is not abandoned if he/she does not, but joins the considerable body of long-running department policy lines, awaiting another time, or more likely one of his/her successors'.[10] Again, incoming governments with election pledges to be redeemed have sometimes to be forced to face harsh financial realities by civil servants.

Setting the climate, identifying major objectives, and indicating priorities provide the framework within which policy is made. Measures still have to be formulated and choices made to produce an operational policy that a department or other public authority can implement. There are two distinct phases in producing such a policy. The first entails collecting and appraising data, analyzing problems, defining issues, and identifying and evaluating possible courses of action. Much of this is work for civil servants who also do some of the negotiating with the spokesmen of the interests whose views have to be taken into account and with the other departments of state that must be consulted. The second phase involves making policy decisions. The minister makes the critical rulings. It could not be otherwise, for the process is governed by the fact that under Bunreacht na hÉireann the minister is responsible. In making his decisions, he must satisfy his ministerial colleagues, the Oireachtas, and the public; it is his career that is at risk. For his part, the official 'knows that the policies he proposes will have political consequences for Ministers. He accepts, therefore, that decisions on significant issues of policy should be taken by Ministers: they must in some sense be able to say that the policies they defend are "their own".'[11]

Ministers have the last and authoritative say, but how far are the decisions they make 'their own'? Those who prepare the memoranda, put up the papers, and explain the issues to the minister might in some circumstances have an important, even decisive, influence upon the outcome. In some cases, a minister reading a file will see only one possible course of action, but this might be due to the way in which the matter is presented. In other cases, ministers, by temperament or habit, might be disposed to accept what is put before them. Nevertheless, interventions by the ministers are decisive, as Ronan Fanning was able to show again and again in his study of Irish administrative history, *The Irish Department of Finance, 1922–1958* (Dublin, 1978). In this book he demonstrated clearly that the ability of the Department of Finance to get its way and do its job as it conceived it, waxed and waned as a result of political changes.

The constitutional authority to legislate, which is to invest proposals with the force of law, resides with the houses of the Oireachtas. The Oireachtas is, therefore, by definition a proximate policy-maker. However, the part it plays as an institution in formulating or influencing the content of the measures it considers and passes is meagre. A Fine Gael policy document on the reform of the Dáil published in 1980 put it thus: 'Under the Constitution the Oireachtas has the "sole and exclusive power of making laws for the state". Nonetheless in practice it plays practically no effective part in either making the laws or even the expert criticism of them.'[12] A decade later, with the institution of a committee system and some improvements in the quality of information made available to members, the position is a little better. Nevertheless, while the system itself remains unchanged, the potential of the Oireachtas as a formative influence on policy will remain very limited.

The contrast between the Oireachtas and the parliaments of some other democracies is striking. Members of the US Congress, for example, initiate bills; and Congress, through its powerful committees, really makes law. Bills, whatever their source, are not only subject to scrutiny and criticism but are freely altered and added to in committee by members who regard themselves in fact as legislators with an actual power to make the laws. In Ireland, by contrast, to quote the Fine Gael document again, 'one of the most disciplined party systems in Europe has ensured that it is the Government, not the Oireachtas, that exercises the power'.[13] The government has an almost exclusive initiative in proposing measures. With the assured, stable support of the party majority in the Dáil, and almost always in the Seanad too, the government controls the passage of business through the two houses. Its proposals are usually endorsed by the Oireachtas with few changes. As a result of criticism in debate or criticism expressed privately by government supporters after a bill is published, some revisions in wording might be made, but these rarely involve matters of principle or major policy changes. Very occasionally, a government misjudges the temper of its own parliamentary supporters and has to withdraw or extensively revise a bill.

The Irish system, therefore, like the British is, in K. C. Wheare's words, ' a system where you can say that the Government makes the laws with the advice and consent of the representative assembly'.[14] Nevertheless, the role of the Oireachtas must not be underestimated. In addition to the fact that it is the forum for public debate, its advice is authoritative and its consent essential. To get that consent, governments are obliged to pay attention to the opinions of the members, particularly their own supporters, when they formulate policy. The process of doing so takes place at the pre-parliamentary stage and largely in private.

This examination of proximate policy-makers has shown, first, that the three groups involved play different parts in the process. The necessary coordination of their activities is effected by the government, which manages the other two groups. The rules and conditions that govern its relationships with the one are of course very different from those governing the other. Civil servants are servants of the government of the day. The Dáil and Seanad are managed by the government while it retains the support of a majority, which means in effect that it must satisfy its own parliamentary supporters, who are the majority. The relationships between governments and their parliamentary supporters are usually such that governments enjoy stable and assured support.

This examination has also shown that the proximate policy-makers are by no means all elected politicians. On the contrary, much policy is formulated and made by the interaction of a few top-level politicians

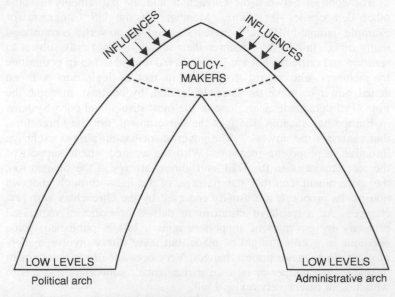

Figure 9.3 The political–administrative arch

and a few top-level public servants. In *Administrative Theories and Politics*, Peter Self wrote of a 'political–administrative arch'. He described it in this way:

The junction at the top represents the critical point at which political will flows into and energises the administrative system: and it is also the point at which influences that have been generated *within* the administrative process flow back into the higher levels of the political process. There is, thus, at the apex of the arch, a fusion of political and administrative influences which have been generated lower down the two arcs.[15]

Figure 9.3 perhaps illustrates Self's concept in respect of policy making.

A third – and striking – feature about the proximate policy-makers is how few they are, a fact already revealed in a general way in the profile of political participation in Chapter 5. At the apex of national government, the number of people with immediate legal or actual power or both is tiny, as the following tabulation shows:

Members of the government, ministers of state, and the Attorney General	31
Civil servants including 'advisers' and other public servants	at most 400
Members of the houses of the Oireachtas other than members of the government and ministers of state (omitting the Ceann Comhairle)	195
Total (in 1991)	approx. 626

V

The proximate policy-makers are subject to a number of constraints arising from both the cultural and the political contexts within which they work. First, public policy-makers accept in a general way the political traditions of the country, which include quite well-defined concepts of the roles and responsibilities of ministers, the Oireachtas, and the public service. For the most part they respect the rules of the game: the behaviour of politicians and administrators alike is governed by their perceptions of how people like themselves *ought* to behave. They are also constrained by the limitations both of their decision-making procedures and of the resources available to them. To a considerable extent, politicians take these limitations for granted. With few exceptions they pay little attention to improving the decision-making processes or to ensuring that they have access to the kinds of professional expertise that almost certainly would improve their performance of their jobs. Without political backing for such reforms, public servants cannot get very far, even if they wholeheartedly desire to, which some do not. Yet there can be little doubt that there is considerable scope for legislative and administrative reform.

The constraints that the proximate policy-makers themselves are likely to be most conscious of are external, arising from the demands and pressures of persons and groups in the community who seek to influence the making and content of policy and, in recent years, from the obligations of membership in the European Communities. Some of these – political parties, pressure groups, and the European Communities – are very positive influences; another – public opinion – is more negative; yet another – the media – is more problematical as an influence.

As our analysis both in Chapter 6 and in this chapter has shown, a continuous concern with policy is limited to a few in the political parties – namely, the party leaders and to a lesser extent the rank-and-file members of the parliamentary parties. However, a few others in the parties – some of the activists in the branches and at the annual conventions – press their leaders to adopt new policies or modify existing ones. They also act as channels of information and opinion between leaders and the 'grass-roots' of the parties and as sounding boxes of public opinion.

Pressure-group spokesmen, too, deal directly with proximate policy-makers, particularly with ministers and senior civil servants, if they can gain access to them. If they cannot, they will try to make their voices heard from outside. Their activities were the subject of Chapter 7. Earlier in this chapter, we showed that the part played by some pressure-group spokesmen, particularly those of the major producer organizations, in formulating policy in some areas is such that they too must be regarded as proximate policy-makers.

The 400 public servants, almost all senior civil servants (Principal Officers and above), who have been identified as among the proximate policy-makers, might not be as sensitive to party and public opinion as their politician masters, but they are certainly aware of it. They will also know very well the views of at least the major pressure groups with whom they deal. Almost inevitably they will be greatly (perhaps overwhelmingly) influenced by the traditions and attitudes of their own small and intimate professional world, especially the departments they work in and perhaps have always worked in. They will also know the views of the state-sponsored bodies for which their ministers are responsible. It is they who use the resources of the departments to gather, process, and present the material that they think is relevant to any problem under review. In the course of this information-gathering and appraisal, the civil servants involved will, as they must, frame generalizations and draw conclusions, many of which their senior colleagues and politician masters are not likely to question. Critical centres of what March and Simon called 'uncertainty absorption' are inevitably deep inside departments, and some are way down in the departmental hierarchy.[16] They are almost certainly coloured by service and department perceptions and attitudes. The civil-servant advisers of ministers are at the confluence of a great flow of information and conclusions from which they distil the essence for transmission to their masters. All of it is expert, but some of it may well be service – and department – flavoured. In any case, most of it will have to be accepted.

It is civil servants, too, together with other public servants who 'implement' policy. Implementation is often thought of as turning policy into action. However, as Christopher Ham and Charles Hill have pointed out: 'it is dangerous to regard it as self evident that implementers are working with a recognisable entity that may be called a policy.' In fact, policy 'may really only emerge through an elaborate process that can include those stages which are conventionally described as implementation'.[17] If we define policy as an output, administrators – civil servants and others, of both high and low ranks – might well contribute to its content in what might be called the concretization stage. To refer again, by way of example, to the Wicklow County Council and the problem of itinerants, what the Council, their officers and servants actually do – their policy, one might say – might well be very different from that which the government thought it was willing, if indeed it was at all clear what that was. The performance of implementers is governed by a number of factors: their understanding of the intentions of the authorities whose wishes they are turning into action; their own values and attitudes; their motivation and training; the resources, both personal and institutional, which they bring to bear; and many organizational factors as well. At this stage their influence is not upon policy-makers as conventionally defined: rather, it is upon an emerging policy.

Although party activists and interest-group spokesmen represent important bodies of opinion, political leaders are well aware that they do not necessarily reflect public opinion – that is to say, popular opinions widely held. By using the press, radio, and television, political leaders are easily able to communicate with the general public directly, and to some extent these media aid the reverse flow of information and demands. In addition , political leaders increasingly resort to the use of opinion polls to measure public reactions to persons, situations, and policies as an aid to political decision-making. In general, public opinion is a negative influence. To pay attention to it is 'a way of estimating what the public will stand for rather than an expression of what the public wants'.[18] Governments often see public opinion as placing limits upon what they can do and how they can do it. Between general elections they pay some attention to it, though the clamour from minority interests, including their own party activists, to some extent blots it out. The nearer to a general election, however, the more leaders seek to gauge public opinion.

All involved, whether proximate policy-makers or those who influence them, are consumers of the products of the mass media. For all in the community, including the few who participate in policy-making, the media are important sources of information; for some, almost their only sources. For some, too, the media might well be important sources of opinion, not least for the proximate policy-makers and those who influence them directly, for many of these communicate with one another not only in person but by means of the media. These form a small elite where information and ideas are concerned, and horizontal political communication at this high level might constitute more of a closed system than the parties concerned realize. However, the exact effect of consuming the products of the media, particularly upon the formation and changing of opinions and attitudes, is problematical.

Besides the domestic influences upon the proximate policy-makers, there is an external influence of increasing importance – the law and the policies of the European Communities. Of course, this is not the only external influence upon Irish policy-makers. They have always had to bear in mind the state's treaty obligations, the policies of neighbouring states, and all sorts of pressures and opportunities whose origins lie outside the state. The influence exerted by the European Communities, however, is of a different kind. Community legal instruments that are directly applicable (regulations and decisions) become in effect part of the law of the land as do the rulings of the Court of Justice. Directives, on the other hand, which are the normal instruments used to harmonize the laws of the members, do not themselves become part of the national law but they do place on the member states an obligation to put directives into effect in their own way. Thus they oblige national policy-makers to formulate policies and legislation with only a small amount of elbow room for choice. In addition, the policies adopted and administered by Community organs, not least schemes involving money, influence the content of policy in the member states.

The impact of the law and activities of the European Communities is widespread. It extends not only to policy areas stipulated in the Treaties such as agriculture and fishing, production, trade and commerce, currency and banking, transport, health, workers' rights, consumer protection, and, increasingly, social policy; but also those added by the Single European Act (1987) such as the health and safety of workers, problems of the environment, technological development, foreign policy, and security. Furthermore, the legal competence of the Communities is constantly and, it seems, inexorably, expanding. (The impact of the Communities upon Irish government is the subject of Chapter 17.)

VI

Public policy-making in Ireland emerges as a complex process, but it involves comparatively few people, who operate against a background of comment, criticism, and advice in the media, and within the parameters of public opinion. Although the most authoritative decision-makers – the government and the Oireachtas – are elected officials and the process involves consultation and negotiation with spokesmen who are in some sense representative of the groups for whom they speak, the way of doing things is far from being very open or democratic. On the contrary, the critical phases are conducted largely in private. What goes on between ministers and their civil service advisers is confidential, no doubt of necessity; so, too, is much of what passes between pressure–group spokesmen and the civil servants and ministers to whom they make representations; so, too, are the meetings of the Oireachtas parties and other contacts between party leaders and their parliamentary followers. The public procedures – that is, the parliamentary stages – usually begin only after the government has evolved a policy that it hopes is a finished product. For all the virtues of the parliamentary process in ensuring a public statement and restatement of the pros and cons of proposed measures, 'what the procedure does not permit', as J. P. Mackintosh pointed out, 'is an exploration of alternative approaches, an understanding of the views of outside groups (unless they think it worth briefing MPs) and there is no scope for public opinion to form and react before the Government has committed itself to a definite approach to the problem'.[19] Mackintosh was here talking of the British parliament, but what he said is true also of the Oireachtas. In this respect, public policy-making is not as open a process as it is in some other democratic countries whose parliaments have a more positive role.

Notes

1   C. E. Lindblom, *The Policy–making Process* (Englewood Cliffs, New Jersey, 1968), p. 29.
2   *Ibid.*, p. 30.
3   W. I. Jenkins, *Policy Analysis: Political and Organizational Perspective* (London, 1978), p. 15.
4   Lindblom, *The Policy-making Process*, p. 30.
5   On pluralism, see D. Held, *Models of Democracy* (Oxford, 1987), ch. 6, and P. Self, *Political Theories of Modern Government, its Role and Reform* (London, 1985), ch. 4.
6   A. Cawson, in *Democratic Theory and Practice* (Cambridge, 1983), G. Duncan (ed.) pp. 180–2. For a brief discussion of corporatist policy-making, see *A Strategy for the Nineties: Economic Stability and Structural Change,* National Economic and Social Council (Dublin, 1990), pp. 455–60.
7   *Seanad Debates*, Vol. 75, col. 486 (11 July 1983).
8   P. Self, *Administrative Theories and Politics*, 2nd edn. (London, 1977), p. 153.
9   See J. J. Lee, *Ireland 1912–1985, Politics and Society* (Cambridge, 1989), pp. 342–7. For a longer appraisal, see J. F. McCarthy (ed.), *Planning*

Ireland's Future: the Legacy of T. K. Whitaker (Sandycove, Co. Dublin, 1990).

10   S. Ó Buachalla, *Education Policy in Twentieth Century Ireland,* (Dublin, 1988), p. 328.

11   N. Johnson, 'Who are the policy makers?' in *Public Administration,* 43 (1965), p. 283.

12   *Reform of the Dáil: Fine Gael Policy on Reform of the Dáil,* Jan. 1980 (Dublin, 1980), p. 3.

13   *Ibid.*

14   K. C. Wheare, *Legislatures* (London, 1963), p. 163.

15   Self, *Administrative Theories and Politics,* p. 68.

16   J. G. March and H. A. Simon, *Organizations* (New York, 1958), pp. 165–66.

17   C. Ham and M. Hill, *The Policy Process in the Modern Capitalist State* (Brighton, 1984), p. 101.

18   Lord Windelsham, 'Can public opinion influence government?', the *Listener,* 22 Aug. 1963.

19   J. P. Mackintosh, *The Government and Politics of Britain* (London, 1970), p. 123.

CHAPTER 10

The Government and the Dáil

I

The analysis of public policy-making in Chapter 9 demonstrated the dominant role of the government and the modest part played by the Oireachtas. Even so, confined as it was to policy-making, that analysis did not reveal the full extent of the part ministers play in politics. They hold a number of positions in the system. In their corporate capacity as a cabinet, as heads of departments of state, and as party leaders both within the Oireachtas and outside, they dominate a large part of the whole process of government. They do so while they have the support of a majority in Dáil Éireann. Such support is the necessary and sufficient condition for them to carry out their extensive functions subject to the statutory maximum term of the Dáil, which is five years.

In Irish conditions, this all-important support is ordinarily accorded to ministers regularly and continuously, for the parliamentary parties are unified and their members vote consistently as they are bidden by their leaders. The members of the government who are the leaders of the party or group of parties thus have an almost assured majority on any issue. Occasionally, governments have assumed office without an actual majority behind them, their support boosted by the votes of Deputies who, though they called themselves 'Independents', were rather camp followers, or by members of small parties, or both. Although the Seanad has a part to play in the performance of parliamentary functions, the support of a majority of that house is usually not vital to governments, for they can override Seanad decisions with their Dáil majority. In any case, they usually command majority support in the Seanad too.

To understand cabinet government in Ireland necessitates investigating the nature and terms of this consistent parliamentary support. It involves examining not only the formal rules governing the appointment, functions, and tenure of office of the government but, more important, who and what the ministers are, the pathways to ministerial office, the ministers' pluralist role in the political system, and their relations with their parties and, in particular, with their parliamentary supporters. These relationships account for what Walter Bagehot in 1867 termed the 'singular approximation' of cabinet and parliament, which he rightly identified as the 'efficient secret' of British-style cabinet government.[1]

II

Rules governing the government are to be found in the constitutions of all countries. In countries with a constitutionalist tradition, these basic rules provide a framework within which the organs of government do in practice function. This is the case in Ireland, although the provisions of Bunreacht na hÉireann relating to the government reflect reality inadequately. Nevertheless, these provisions, together with a number of constitutional conventions and practices, define the tenure of office and operations of the government and provide a framework within which the politicians operate.

Article 13 provides that the President of Ireland, the formal head of the state, shall appoint the Taoiseach on the nomination of the Dáil and that he shall appoint the other members of the government 'on the nomination of the Taoiseach with the previous approval' of the Dáil. Up to the legal limit of the life of the Oireachtas, the Taoiseach holds office either until he chooses to resign, in which case the other members of the government are deemed also to have resigned, or until he 'has ceased to retain the support of a majority in Dáil Eireann'. In this case, he must resign, unless on his advice the President chooses to dissolve the Dáil and thus precipitate a general election. Except in the case of loss of majority support, the Taoiseach may at any time secure a dissolution of the Dáil – and thus a general election – on request to the President, a request with which the President must comply.

In the past, the Dáil's constitutional job of appointing the Taoiseach and the government was usually purely formal, the preceding general election having settled the issue. Once, in 1948, a parliamentary coalition of all parties other than Fianna Fáil, with the support of a number of independents, was formed by the leaders of the newly elected representatives after the results were known and before the Dáil met. In the less stable eighties, however, experience was different. Election after election threw up results that necessitated post-election politicking by leaders and key persons and groups. By 1987, Brian Farrell was able to say: 'government formation is no longer a neat ceremonial function following on in some clear-cut and predictable liturgical sequence from the declaration of the election results'.[2] Nevertheless, by 1990, political leaders had not yet learned to handle these situations with assurance: an air of crisis regularly marked the post-election periods, further evidence, if it were needed, of the unwillingness of some to adopt the practices of coalition politics as the norm, as they are in many democratic countries.

The nomination of the members of the government is made by the Taoiseach. The new Dáil, having nominated the leader of the majority party or group to be Taoiseach, adjourns for a few hours while the leader calls upon the President and is formally appointed to that office. He then returns to the Dáil and puts forward the names of the members of his government. These are approved *en bloc* by the Dáil, though in the early days of the state there was some attempt to have them discussed and approved individually. They are then appointed by the President and assigned their departments by the Taoiseach. Appointment to the government and appointment as head of a department are quite distinct. The Taoiseach has the right to assign departments to the members of his government. He informs the Dáil, but the Dáil is not required specifically to approve the assignments.

Article 28 of Bunreacht na hÉireann requires that the government shall consist of no fewer than seven and no more than fifteen members. The Taoiseach, the Tánaiste (Deputy Prime Minister), and the Minister for Finance must be members of the Dáil. The other members must be members of the Dáil or Seanad, but not more than two may be members of the Seanad. (In practice, in the history of the state up to 1991 there were only three senator ministers.[3]) Every member of the government has the right to attend and speak in each house of the Oireachtas. Although there is a legal distinction between being a member of the government and head of a department, the positions are in fact virtually identical. There is, it is true, provision in the Ministers and Secretaries (Amendment) Act 1939 for the appointment of members of the government without departmental responsibilities: such a person 'shall be known as a Minister without Portfolio'. The government, however, may 'assign to any particular minister without portfolio a specific style or title'. One such equivocal 'minister without portfolio' was appointed – a Minister for the Coordination of Defensive Measures, who held office from 1939 to 1945.

Until recently, the general practice was for each minister to head a single department, although occasionally as a matter of convenience a minister was put in charge of more than one. However, as the number of departments increased after the Second World War – in 1924, there were eleven; by 1950, there were fifteen; by 1977, there were eighteen; and in 1990, sixteen – it became necessary for all governments to have some ministers managing more than one.

Since all ministers are members of the government and the government is composed exclusively of ministers, the structure is simple. In fact, in the past there was only a handful of other politician office-holders of any sort in the administration. By 1980, however, the number of under-ministers, called 'parliamentary secretaries' until 1977, when they were renamed 'ministers of state', had grown from ten to fifteen. The increase was said to be in order to cope with the larger number of departments and to relieve the strain on ministers occasioned by the need to travel on European Community business. No doubt also there were party political reasons. 'Technically the appointments are a function of the government as a whole; in practice they are part of the parliamentary patronage at the disposal of the Taoiseach', which is now considerable, for the proportion of office-holders in the parliamentary party in power could be 35 per cent or more.[4]

In addition, there is a law officer, the Attorney General, with a small department. The Attorney General is the government's adviser in matters of law and represents the state in important legal proceedings. According to Bunreacht na hÉireann, he is precluded from being a member of the government, but he does attend cabinet meetings. He is not required to be a member of the Oireachtas, though Declan Costello, who held the office between 1973 and 1977, was a Deputy. If the Attorney General is a TD or a Senator, he may be heard in either house. He may engage in private practice in addition to his state duties, and some have done so. The only other regular attenders at cabinet meetings are the government 'Chief Whip', that is, a parliamentary party manager who is appointed to a minister-of-state post, and a civil servant, the Secretary to the Government.

III

If a government consists of members of a single party, the incoming Taoiseach as party leader will probably have had considerable freedom of choice as to who the members will be, the more so because there are no ethnic, religious, or other divisions in the country to be taken account of, although the Minister for the Gaeltacht (the Irish-speaking areas) needs to have fluent Irish, which many Deputies do not have. What limitations there are upon him arise from the expectations of powerful colleagues and the parliamentary party. These have no doubt imposed constraints on some Taoisigh in the past. An extreme example occurred in 1979 when Charles Haughey was obliged not only to appoint his defeated rival for the leadership, George Colley, and to designate him Tánaiste (Deputy Prime Minister), but also to allow him 'a virtual veto on nominations of the two key security ministers, Justice and Defence'. He had also to swallow Colley's openly expressed qualifications about his loyalty. As Brian Farrell observed: 'in earlier times it would have been inconceivable'.[5] By this time, though, the traditionally loyal, even monolithic, Fianna Fáil party was faction-ridden.

A decade later Haughey again had to accept considerable constraints upon his choice of cabinet colleagues, but that was in a coalition situation. In 1991, the Progressive Democrats, the minor partner in a coalition with Fianna Fáil, vetoed the Taoiseach's nomination to a ministerial post. Obviously, the position of leaders of coalitions is different when it comes to selecting colleagues, as is the method of appointment. Coalition governments are – and must inevitably be – formed following formal agreements by the participating parties covering policies and posts. When the posts to be allocated to each party are identified, the respective party leaders nominate their appointees. In their first ventures into government, in 1948 and 1954, the Labour Party's appointees were chosen by ballot, but the party has not used this procedure since.

For almost half a century from the foundation of the state, cabinets once installed changed little. Resignations, retirements, and dismissals were infrequent. In the twenty- five years between 1922 and 1948 only thirty persons held ministerial office, and this long reign of the venerated 'revolutionary generation' continued until the late fifties when a veritable generational change took place. The average age of members of the January 1922 government was thirty-three years: members of Cosgrave's 1927 government averaged forty-one years, and so did de Valera's Government of 1932. De Valera's 1951 government, however, had an average age of fifty-seven years. By the late 1950s, however, a process of regeneration had begun and the average age of cabinets dropped to below fifty by 1965. Haughey's 1979 government averaged a little over forty-seven years of age, and his 1989 government fifty-two years.

The criteria for selection have changed also. The 'revolutionary generation' were veterans and heroes of an independence struggle. Seniority and a desire to span the party were important criteria of choice. Seán Lemass, de Valera's successor, tended to replace the fading older generation with comparatively young professional men picked for their potential ability, and all leaders since then have paid attention to the quality of their teams by advancing people of this sort to office. Lately, as parties have more and more exhibited factional tendencies, 'personal loyalty has become an increasingly important criterion'. Both Haughey and FitzGerald were disposed 'to select within their party colleagues who share their own distinctive philosophies'.[6] In 1992, when Albert Reynolds succeeded in ousting Haughey, he was ruthless in rewarding his supporters and getting rid if Haughey's.

The combination of localism and clientelism that has traditionally marked Irish politics would lead, one might think, to regional considerations being of considerable importance. In Brian Farrell's view, surprisingly, 'the evidence on this point in regard to cabinet positions is not persuasive'.[7] The early leaders paid little attention to geographical considerations. Later Taoisigh have followed different practices. Coakley and Farrell concluded from their analysis of government formation that 'Fianna Fáil governments tend to be less Dublin centred than Fine Gael – Labour coalitions': their leaders 'are careful to give symbolic recognition to traditional sources of party support in the West and South'.[8] From his first accession to office in 1979, Haughey displayed 'an evident concern to achieve some even geographical spread and a sensitivity to constituency reactions'.[9] By contrast, FitzGerald did not, and was much criticized in his party on that account. Whatever their leaders think, it is very obvious that Deputies from outside Dublin and – very important – party activists do attach great importance to having a cabinet member from their own area, and some have carried this to the extent of publicly importuning their leader. In 1991 some Cork businessmen who supported Fianna Fáil were said to be dissatisfied because there was no Cork-based minister in the cabinet and were 'grooming' a local Deputy for a place.[10] Where a marginal seat is at issue the potential pay-off for the presence of a ministerial car in the constituency has proved irresistible because of the supposed superiority of ministerial patronage. The existence of fifteen posts of minister of state (the so-called 'half-car') has much eased both regional pressures and the need to reward loyalty.

IV

The first leaders of the state were, as we have already observed, 'politicians by accident', men who had survived the independence struggle and the subsequent civil war. They included a number of journalists, teachers, and lawyers; from the beginning Irish governments were dominated by professional men. As Table 5.7 (p. 87, above) shows, six out of ten of all ministers in the sixty years from 1922 to 1982 were professional men or had been trained for a profession before they became full-time politicians. Further, as Table 10.1 seems to suggest, most, if not all, governments in the past have contained a majority of such. As is the case in most Western countries, this tiny occupational group dominates the top levels of politics. Likewise, as in the West, lawyers have always figured prominently: less usual is the number of teachers who have featured particularly in recent years.

Just as some occupations have always been strongly represented in government, others have not and yet others have been strikingly absent. Although Ireland has always had a comparatively large agricultural sector and well into the second half of the century a quarter of all TDs were farmers, the proportion of farmers who have attained cabinet rank has been tiny. Almost no working-class people, whether urban or rural, have reached the top in politics. Evidently they have lacked the resources that create the potential for office – time, money, 'centrality' (certain occupations are very 'central'), social prestige, useful relations, a record. Women too, have been strikingly absent. If we except the remarkable Countess Markiewicz who was 'Minister for Labour' in 'governments' appointed by the First and Second Dála (1919–21) during the period of struggle for independence, the first woman cabinet minister was appointed as recently as 1978.[11] Up to 1990, there were only two more, and two have held posts of minister of state.

Table 10.1 **Professional people in government, 1922–89**

Profession	Certain governments, 1922–89								
	Aug. 1922	Mar. 1932	Feb. 1948	Mar. 1957	Apr. 1965	Jul. 1977	Dec. 1979	Nov. 1982	June 1989
Accountant	–	–	–	–	1	1	1	–	3
Barrister	1	1	3	1	2	3	2	1	2
Solicitor	1	1	–	–	2	2	2	1	1
Engineer	–	1	–	2	2	–	–	–	–
Journalist	2	1	–	–	–	–	–	–	–
Medical doctor	–	1	2	1	1	–	–	–	1
Teacher	2	2	–	1	–	5	5	4	4
Other professions	–	–	–	–	–	–	1	1	1
Total	6	7	5	5	8	11	11	7	12
Total membership of government	10	10	13	11	14	15	15	15	15

Note: Ministers are classified according to the profession they followed or for which they were trained before they became full-time politicians.

Source: Flynn's Oireachtas Companions (various dates); T. Nealon, Ireland: a Parliamentary Directory, 1973–74 (Dublin, 1974); Nealon's Guides to the Dáil and Seanad (various dates); newspapers and other published sources.

V

The domination of the political scene by ministers arises as much or more from the roles they fill in office as from who they are or what they have done in the past. Whatever they were before, on being appointed members of the government they become leading figures in their party, more particularly in the Oireachtas party and, therefore, in the Oireachtas itself, and heads of departments of state – all positions of considerable power and influence. In their persons they combine leadership of the majority party, management of the Oireachtas, and the control of the central administration. It is this combination of positions that gives members of the government their pre-eminence, whatever their antecedents, and this applies even to those few who become members of the government on their first day in the Dáil.[12] Such pre-eminence in turn gives them social prestige, for they are at the very centre of affairs, 'in the know', and better able than most to do a favour.

Their position is the stronger since they, together with their rivals – the leaders of the opposition parties, among whom there is a potential alternative government – have a virtual monopoly of political leadership. There are few, if any, other party leaders outside the Oireachtas, though it is possible that one or two trade-union leaders might sometimes exercise political power and the National Executive Committees of the parties might as bodies exert some influence. There is no one to challenge party leaders in the Oireachtas, for the only officials there besides themselves are the ministers of state, the whips (party managers), and the party leaders in the Seanad, none of whom have the status, power, or influence of ministers on the government side or party spokesmen ('shadow ministers') on the opposition side. The Oireachtas does not have a strong committee system that might spawn powerful chairmen and influential *rapporteurs* in positions to challenge ministers, nor do the parliamentary parties as such make much use of committees. Furthermore, the members as a whole lack any strong sense of the dignity of the Oireachtas as the national parliament; they have a modest view of its functions and powers. Finally, there are no rival leaders in the departments, for the members of the government are themselves heads of departments and, as such, are both constitutionally and politically responsible for the actions of civil servants and theoretically the sole source of decisions and information.

The picture that emerges – of ministers with a triple role that gives them a virtual monopoly of the centre of the political stage – is by no means reflected in Bunreacht na hÉireann. That document states that the executive power of the state is to be exercised by or on behalf of the government. It makes the government responsible for the work of the departments. It requires the government to prepare estimates of expenditure and present them to the Dáil, and it gives the government exclusive initiative to make proposals for public expenditure. This is clearly an inadequate statement of the essentials of cabinet government in the British style, the more so because it is couched in terms of the separation-of-powers theory. Also, necessarily perhaps, Bunreacht na hÉireann makes no mention of the party role of the members of the government, though their position in the party is bound up with their other roles. Nor, finally, does it convey the overall responsibility of this group for the general welfare of the community and, consequently, the initiative that the community expects them to take in identifying and solving public problems.

VI

Members of the government depend for their continuance in office on maintaining an adequate level of satisfaction in their party or parties and also, if they are to win the next election, in the community. They hold their positions on certain conditions. To understand the government of the country, it is necessary to ascertain what those conditions are.

There are, first, some constitutional requirements to be observed, but these do not take us very far. Once appointed, the government is 'responsible to Dáil Éireann', and its leader, the Taoiseach, must retain the support of a majority in the Dáil. If he does not, he must resign unless the President grants him a dissolution and, thus, an appeal to the electorate. When the Taoiseach resigns, all the members of the government are deemed to have resigned also, as are the ministers of state and the Attorney General. By mentioning the Dáil specifically, the Constitution emphasizes the minor role and secondary importance of the Seanad.

The government's responsibility to the Dáil is collective, for the government is required 'to meet and act as a collective authority'. Collective responsibility is, however, an elusive concept. It suggests that ministers are a team – but how united a team? It suggests that they must answer for their performance and might be removed from office – but in what circumstances will they be obliged to go?

In *The Government of Great Britain*, Graeme Moodie described the principles of collective responsibility as they were understood in the United Kingdom. It was these principles that almost certainly were intended to be covered by the wording of Article 28.4.2° of the Constitution.

All members of the administration are expected publicly to support its policies and its actions, regardless of their private feelings on the matter. Should they for any reason no longer be prepared to do so, they must resign their office (although not, usually, their seats in Parliament). Constitutionally, they cannot acquiesce in a decision and then, at some later stage when for example, it becomes unpopular, claim that they were opposed to it and thus seek personally to escape the political penalties. . . . By the same token, it is impossible for the House of Commons to vote for the removal of a particular member of the Government, unless it is clear that the Government is prepared to sacrifice that individual either as a scapegoat or because no collective responsibility is involved.[13]

The rules do not require each member of the government personally to favour a particular proposal. What they do require, as Moodie goes on to point out, is 'that the argument be conducted in private' (hence the necessary corollary of cabinet secrecy, which has traditionally been quite strictly observed in Ireland), resolved in private, and the decision treated as the decision of each and every member.

Constitutional theory, however, is one thing; practice might be, and occasionally has been, quite another. It is important to notice that the principles enunciated by Moodie had evolved for, were suited to, and perhaps presupposed, single party governments. The Cumann na nGaedheal governments from the beginning had reliable followers and were able to operate in general according to the rigid conventions that operated in the United Kingdom at that time. Although they were broad-based governments, the essential and sufficient binding element was the pro-Treaty stance of its members and their recognition of the primacy of security and border issues. The three resignations that occurred between 1922 and 1932 were all the result of disagreements over such issues, and it is clear that the principles outlined by Moodie were accepted by both the government and its parliamentary supporters.

With the coming of Fianna Fáil governments, de Valera's dominating position and preference for firm cabinet government and definite leadership resulted in cabinets with even more monolithic public faces. In his time, there were no resignations over policy and no overt disagreements. His successor, Seán Lemass, inherited a party long schooled in this tradition, and being so clearly an unrivalled master of the economic policy issues that had come to dominate politics, Lemass seemed also to dominate his government. The resignation in 1964 of Patrick Smith, Minister for Agriculture, a senior and respected member of the party, indicates that in the Lemass era, too, the principle that ministers must resign if they cannot publicly support government policy was the rule then. Later, from Lynch's time, 1966–73 and 1977–79 onwards, when faction bedevilled the party, necessity led to looser practices. During his first years in office a significant formula, 'the minister was speaking as an individual', had occasionally to be used. If the 'arms scandal' crisis leading to the dismissals and resignations of May 1970 seemed to show that collective responsibility was still at least the norm, the behaviour of Haughey during Lynch's last months in office when he signalled his dissent from some aspects of government policy, and after his accession in 1979 when he disassociated himself even more clearly, showed how far deviations from the norm could go when winning and holding power were the prizes. Neither Haughey nor his colleagues, nor indeed the members of the Oireachtas party, gave any indication that they thought this behaviour deviated from what the Constitution envisages and perhaps requires.

During periods of coalition government, necessity almost inevitably demanded looser practices. The first so-called 'Inter-Party' government (1948–51) was a coalition not only of all the other parties but also of some independents who, for the sake of convenience, were regarded as a coherent group with the right to a ministerial post in the parcelling out of offices. The basic coalition agreement was confined to specified points: 'Any points on which we have not agreed have been left in abeyance,' John Costello, its leader, told the Dáil.[14] Although it and its successor (1954–57) were comparatively effective, their members could not always avoid explicit disagreement in public. Sometimes ministerial statements, both in the Dáil and outside, revealed differences of view on policy matters. The government maintained in public, and some of its members perhaps even believed, that a minister could properly speak 'as an individual' on current policy issues. Referring to differences between himself and the Minister for External Affairs, Deputy Patrick McGilligan, then Minister for Finance, said in the Dáil:

Deputies on the other side of the House have anguished themselves with talk about the public embarrassment which there is over the fact that the Minister for External Affairs does not talk the same financial language as myself. I have yet to meet anybody outside the ranks of the professional politicians who is worried about that. Nobody is worried. Have we got to the stage in this country, when on a matter which may be an important point of policy when it is decided, we cannot have freedom of speech? Have we got to the stage when men, just because they join the Government circle, must all, as one Deputy said, when they go out of the council chambers speak the same language?[15]

In the latter stages of the first Inter-Party government, disagreement and poor communications between members led in some cases to a state of uncoordinated independence. In the Dáil itself, it was necessary on a few occasions to resort to a 'free vote' when the Inter-Party group was divided, and even some members of the government itself voted against the government.

During the Fine Gael-Labour coalitions of the seventies and eighties many policy differences were settled by the party leaders meeting to hammer out solutions which their cabinet colleagues were then expected to endorse. Thus policies in some areas were sometimes heavy with compromises that were well publicized. By this time better investigative journalism and the growing practice of 'leaking' resulted in disagreements in the cabinet being ever more frequently identified. Eventually major differences over budgetary policy brought the resignation of Labour ministers and the end of the government – as per the Constitution, one might say. The first Fine Gael-Labour coalition, however, did witness the spectacle of the Taoiseach himself, Liam Cosgrave (together with one of his Fine Gael ministerial colleagues), voting with the Opposition against the Control of Importation, Sale, and Manufacture of Contraceptives Bill – a government measure that the cabinet had agreed to introduce. Because of unease in the parliamentary parties, the government had agreed to a free vote in the Dáil, but Cosgrave voted against the government measure without even giving his cabinet any indication of his intention to do so. At least one distinguished constitutional lawyer, Senator Mary Robinson (later President of Ireland) contended that he and his government acted unconstitutionally. Conscience or no: 'A Government Bill is one upon which the Government must act with collective authority and *Government Ministers are not entitled under the Constitution to vote against such measures*'[16] (Mary Robinson's italics).

Irish experience suggests that, although the constitutional principles of collective responsibility as enunciated by Moodie and envisaged in the Constitution have been the norms, deviations from them have occurred with impunity when necessity or convenience dictated. As Mary Robinson ruefully commented:

The constitutional imperative requiring the Government to act as a collective authority – with collective responsibility for its actions – can only be enforced by political pressures. There is no legal procedure to ensure that the Government in office discharged this constitutional obligation.[17]

However, it is unlikely to be politically enforceable, for those who breach it are probably going to have a parliamentary majority and are thus able to pay scant regard to it when it suits them.

Collective responsibility requires the government to present a united front to the public and to be accountable to the Dáil which has the power to remove it *en bloc*. In practice, until the eighties, Irish governments were rarely defeated. It happened on only six occasions in sixty years; at least one of these was an accident; and in no case at all was it obvious that the Taoiseach had in any general way ceased to retain the support of the majority in Dáil Éireann. On only two occasions during this period was defeat followed by a dissolution, and in both cases the defeat had been welcomed by the governments concerned as an opportunity to improve their position at the general election that followed. It was rather the threat of defeat that had more often led to dissolution, but even this occurred on only three occasions.

Experience in the eighties, however, was different. Governments were defeated on two occasions in 1982 and the country had three general elections in less than eighteen months. It was at this time, too, that an attempt was made to persuade the President to exercise for the first time his constitutional power under Article 13, on his own discretion to refuse a dissolution to a Taoiseach who had ceased to retain the support of a majority, and thus to force him to resign and give the opportunity to the Dáil to nominate a successor.[18] Later, in 1987, the break-up of the Fine Gael–Labour coalition and the certainty of an imminent defeat of the government precipitated a dissolution and a general election. It may be said, then, that the Dáil can, but only very occasionally does, force governments to submit to the electorate and that this is most likely to occur in periods of coalition government. As Table 10.2 shows, the Dáil has much more often been dissolved at a tactically favourable time as it was coming to the end of its term of office or for other tactical reasons.

This record is due to the all-important fact of parliamentary party solidarity, a phenomenon that is by no means universal in Western democracies. It is the more surprising when one considers that in the end a government depends on its parliamentary supporters. This is clear when one asks how a government can be defeated between general elections. It can happen only if a critical number of its own

Table 10.2 **Reasons for the dissolution of Dáil Éireann, 1923–89**

Reason	No. of occasions
Taoiseach chooses opportune moment as government approaches the end of its term of office	12
Taoiseach chooses to dissolve	3
Taoiseach welcomes a defeat to get a general election	2
Danger of Dáil defeat and loss of confidence	4
Dáil defeat on a matter of confidence	2

supporters defect. In Ireland, because of the volume of electoral support for the various parties and the use of the single transferable vote system, that number is usually small. What is more, it is quite possible, if the circumstances are right, for individual deputies to defy their party, break with it, or even be excluded from it, and still retain their seats. Yet this seldom occurs and the record suggests, as we have seen, that Irish governments are unlikely to suffer defeat. This is because for historical reasons – the experience of the home rule movement, the independence struggle, and the civil war and their aftermath – loyalty became and remained the great political virtue. Changing sides, like 'going over' (that is, changing one's religion), was unthinkable in oneself and treacherous in others. A strong tradition of allegiance to leaders was established and it has persisted.

Loyalty inhibits Deputies from endangering their leaders and their party's position, but they need not accept all that their leaders propose or confine themselves to passive support, though in the past they did so to a considerable extent and most still do. There has always been a considerable willingness on the part of ordinary TDs to leave policy to party leaders and to expect them to get on with it. For many Deputies, the formulation of policy and its articulation and, when their party is in power, the conduct of administration have been seen as the leaders' business. Ordinary Deputies' business is to tend to the personal and local problems of their constituents and, by paying attention to their home base, nurture this all- important source of electoral support. However, TDs do expect that any misgivings they express – often at the local impact of general policy – will be heeded.

This traditional willingness to give the government considerable initiative and control over policy and administration is partly attributable also to the fact that Ireland adopted the British system at a period of parliamentary decline. By the early years of the twentieth century, the British parliament had signally failed to develop effective procedures to counter the emergence of strong rule by party leaders brought about by the advent of mass parties in the late nineteenth century. British efforts since then to build a parliamentary committee system have not altered the position radically, and the same is true of Ireland. In fact it was not until the early eighties that any attempt at all was made to establish a system of parliamentary committees (see below, p. 202–204). In 1990 it was still the fact that Irish leaders had more elbow room for manoeuvre in many policy matters than those in most democracies. Irish governments were more likely to be halted in their tracks by pressure-group activities than by parliamentary dissent.

Constitutionally, ministers are not only collectively responsible; they are also individually responsible for their own activities and those of the departments they control. Both in the Oireachtas and outside, the minister speaks for his department, explaining and defending government policy on matters within its purview, his own decisions, and those of his officials. Because he has the right to the last say, he is held to have had that say and all departmental decisions are regarded as his. However, although he will be held responsible in law for matters within his competence, on the political front it is he who in practice decides what he will and will not answer for. That this is the case arises from a considerable failure on the part of the Oireachtas to devise and operate efficient machinery for eliciting information, assessing it, and holding ministers accountable.

It is very unlikely that the Dáil will force a minister to resign. Up to the end of 1991 there had been only ten cases of individual resignation and they were mostly caused by disagreements with their cabinet colleagues over policy: perhaps three or four were for health or technical reasons.[19] Five ministers have been dismissed by Taoisigh with the acquiescence of the Dáil – reluctant acquiescence on the part of the majority of Deputies.[20] In addition, five junior ministers have been got rid of in the same way, one forced to resign and the others dismissed.[21] This amounts to only ten individual sackings in nearly seventy years (and of these five in the aftermath of an unsuccessful attempt to get Haughey to retire): can there have been so few foolish or unacceptable decisions, so little incompetence or personal misbehaviour? It would be remarkable if that were the case.

The truth is that a minister can be forced to resign by the Dáil only if the government or the Taoiseach with government support decides to abandon him. This is a question of their deciding which course of action would harm the government more – a forced resignation with its attendant publicity, or casting the mantle of collective responsibility over a colleague in trouble and making the matter one of confidence in the government as a whole and brazening it out. It is the latter course of action that Taoisigh and governments have almost always adopted. Thus, the enforcement of individual responsibility by the Dáil has been largely thwarted by the practice of collective responsibility. It cannot be said that a minister will be punished by loss of office for his shortcomings or those of his civil servants. In practice, in the past, the failures and the liabilities survived until the next general reshuffle; and such has been the pull of loyalty that some survived even beyond that.

VII

So far, we have talked of the government as a collective body. However, the head of the government has a special position. It is necessary, therefore, to give separate consideration to the functions and role of the Taoiseach; but, first, we must distinguish the head of the government from the head of state.

The President of Ireland is the formal head of state. He or she is both the symbol of the state and the centre of ceremonial. He or she performs many acts of government at the request of those who have the real power – namely, the Taoiseach and the government. The British constitutional myth that the government is the government of the head of state – His Majesty's or her Majesty's government – which had been embodied in the Irish Free State Constitution, was not perpetuated in the republican Bunreacht na hÉireann. On the contrary, the Taoiseach is specifically designated as 'the head of the government', and is required only to keep the President 'generally informed on matters of domestic and international policy'. The President does not see cabinet papers. In the past, he was kept 'generally informed' by means of a regular visit from the Taoiseach. By the mid-1970s, however, the visits were far from regular: Liam Cosgrave visited President Ó Dálaigh on only four occasions during his two years as President.[22] In 1980, Charles Haughey refused to answer a parliamentary question asking for details of visits.[23]

The office of President as conceived by de Valera, however, was something more than a purely formal head of state. The President is linked with the people by virtue of being directly elected; in the words of his creator, 'he is there to guard the people's rights and mainly to guard the Constitution'.[24] He is endowed with certain real powers to this end. Bunreacht na hÉireann gives him power to act in four circumstances. In the exercise of the first three, he is obliged to consult, though not necessarily to follow the advice of, the Council of State, a body consisting of named office-holders (such as the Chief Justice and the chairmen of the Dáil and Seanad), former office-holders (such as the President and Taoiseach), and not more than seven others appointed by the President himself. First, he may refer any bill to the Supreme Court to be tested for unconstitutionality (up to 1991, eight bills had been so referred). Second, if a majority of the Seanad and not less than one-third of the Dáil request him to decline to sign a bill on the ground that it 'contains a proposal of such national importance that the will of the people thereon ought to be ascertained', the President may, if he or she so decides, accede to the request and precipitate a referendum on the measure. Third, he may at any time convene a meeting of either or both houses of the Oireachtas, a power obviously intended to be used in an emergency. Up to 1991, the second and third provisions had never been used. Finally, the President has it 'in his absolute discretion' to refuse a dissolution to a Taoiseach who has ceased to retain the support of a majority in the Dáil (which has happened twice) or who, welcoming a defeat in a Dáil vote, chooses to interpret it as a loss of confidence and seeks a dissolution (as de Valera did on two occasions, in 1938 and 1944). On all four occasions, a dissolution was granted: except in case of emergency, it is difficult to see a President doing anything else.

Without doubt the exercise of these powers might involve the President in political controversy, the more so since they are intended to be used precisely at moments of crisis or considerable political disagreement by a President who will have been chosen at an election fought on party lines. It was largely the continuous existence of stable majorities in Dáil Éireann and the absence of crises that prevented the office from becoming a focus of controversy for nearly forty years. The first Presidents helped too: they were elderly, inert, and scrupulous in keeping themselves outside and above political argument. The reaction of most politicians, not least those in his own party, to the concept of a more active President put forward by Erskine Childers on taking office in 1973, was unfavourable. They were uneasy at Childers' suggestion that the President should publicly back good causes that were undeniably in the public interest and on which the parties were agreed. Fortunately, perhaps, Childers did not go far in practising what he had advocated.

His successor, Cearbhall Ó Dálaigh, a former President of the Supreme Court and subsequently member of the European Court of Justice, was subjected to public criticism that led directly to a constitutional crisis and his resignation when he showed signs of active interest in another aspect of the office. In September 1976, Ó Dálaigh referred the Emergency Powers Bill 1976 to the Supreme Court to test its constitutionality. In doing so, he was clearly acting within his constitutional powers, but the National Coalition government, or at least some members of it, were privately critical of his action. One member, Patrick Donegan, Minister for Defence, attacked him publicly and in a clearly improper manner. The failure of the Taoiseach to disown Donegan unequivocally for his *bêtise* led to Ó Dálaigh's resignation.

The affair, farcical though the Donegan episode was in some respects, showed that it is not possible in Irish circumstances for the President, who is regarded primarily as an apolitical symbol of the state, exercising mostly formal powers, to act with unquestionable authority in the name of the people in an emergency or crisis. There are bound to be some who will question any discretionary action and thus expose the President to criticism, very likely of a partisan nature.

Rightly so, too: as John Kelly put it, the President 'must be prepared for the wind of criticism to which everybody else in public life who makes a decision is also subject'.[25] Perhaps, as has been suggested, 'the Office of President as envisaged by de Valera and laid down by the Constitution is an inherently unsatisfactory one'.[26] But what is 'laid down' by the Constitution?

Mary Robinson, elected to the office after a unique campaign in 1990, challenged the traditionally accepted role of the President. She maintained that the concept of the office held by former Presidents and politicians generally and the bounds within which they conventionally worked were too restrictive. She saw herself as an active player in public life. In the words of one of her campaign leaders: 'An office is a place of work, not retirement.'[27] Direct election, the President argued, gave her a mandate to speak for the people in season and, if she thought appropriate, out of season: 'Áras an Uachtaráin will, to the best of my ability, become a home as well as a house – a home for all those aspirations of equality and excellence which have no other home in public life.'[28] This went further than Erskine Childers and his 'good causes' and 'issues on which all parties are agreed'. She explicitly espoused change not only in the office but in Irish society: 'I have a mandate for a changed approach within our Constitution. I spoke openly of change and I was elected on a platform of change.'[29] 'Within our Constitution': these are important words. As a constitutional lawyer, she was careful to point out that she could not intervene in on-going policy issues. There will be a difficult line to be drawn here, and Childers' experience is not encouraging. Even if she and her supporters are right and she does epitomize a desire for change, it will be difficult to intrude another active player on to the political scene.

VIII

The model for the office of Taoiseach (the earlier title, used in the Irish Free State Constitution, was President of the Executive Council) was the British Prime Minister. However, to compare the Taoiseach with the Prime Minister is not to say very much. It does suggest that he is the central figure, to a great extent the centrepiece and symbol of the government. His pre-eminence among his colleagues stems from four facts. Firstly, he is usually the party leader. Secondly, elections have often taken the form of gladiatorial contests between designated party leaders, thus emphasizing the personal leadership of the victor, and television and modern campaign practices have increased the propensity to focus on the leader. He personifies the government, and, from the time of Lemass onwards, the practice of building up the personal image of leaders by assiduous public relations activities has increased their potential to dominate. Thirdly, except in the case of coalition governments, he chooses his colleagues. Fourthly, by the nature of his position he has a special responsibility to take the lead or speak when an authoritative intervention is needed.

The functions of the Taoiseach have been described in this way:

He is the central coordinating figure, who takes an interest in the work of all Departments, the figure to whom ministers naturally turn for advice and guidance when faced with problems involving large questions of policy or otherwise of special difficulty and whose leadership is essential to the successful working of the Government as a collective authority, collectively responsible to Dáil Éireann, but acting through members each of whom is charged with specific Departmental tasks. He may often have to inform himself in considerable detail of particular matters with which other members of the Government are primarily concerned. He may have to make public statements on such matters, as well as on general matters of broad policy, internal and external. He answers Dáil questions where the attitude of the Government towards important matters of policy is involved. He may occasionally sponsor Bills which represent important new developments of policy, even when the legislation, when enacted, will be the particular concern of the Minister in charge of some other Department of State. . . . he secures the coordination, in a comprehensive Parliamentary programme, of the proposals of the various Ministers for legislative and other measures in the Houses of the Oireachtas.[30]

Seán Lemass, a former Taoiseach, also put the emphasis on the coordinating role that was becoming more necessary and important in his day:

The Taoiseach's primary task, apart from acting as spokesman for the Government on major issues of policy, is to ensure that governmental plans are fully coordinated, that the inevitable conflicts between Departments are resolved, that Cabinet decisions are facilitated and that the implications of Government policy are fully understood by all his Cabinet colleagues and influence the shaping of their departmental plans.[31]

Beyond this, as Byrum E. Carter wrote of the British Prime Minister, 'the Office cannot be defined, it can only be described in terms of the use to which it was put by different individuals of varying abilities, who faced different problems and dealt with different colleagues'.[32]

Perhaps one general trend can be discerned: both constitutionally and in practice the role and power of the Taoiseach have increased since 1922. Some provisions and wording of the Irish Free State Constitution revealed the intention to reduce the status and role of the President of the Executive Council below those of a British Prime Minister. W. T. Cosgrave, who held the office from 1922 to 1932, sometimes went out of his way to belittle his own position and stress that of the Council as a whole. In 1937, speaking of the dismissal and resignation of ministers in his time, he said he had not had the power to compel the resignation of his ministers, and he thought this a good thing: 'Ministers in my view ought to possess security and a measure of independence.'[33] In fact, he seems to have acted more like a British Prime Minister than either the words of the Constitution or his own utterances suggest.

Under the same constitutional rules, de Valera from the beginning had much greater status and power because he led a much more united party accustomed to his strong style of leadership. In Bunreacht na hÉireann, his own Constitution, he was able to embody his view of the proper position and powers of a Prime Minister. The very title he chose, Taoiseach, though it is far from connoting an absolute ruler, suggests that the Irish Prime Minister is the essential pivot on which the government rests. Whereas the Irish Free State Constitution gave powers and duties to the Executive Council as a whole, Bunreacht na hÉireann gives them to the Taoiseach in most vital and many purely formal matters. In practice, too, de Valera towered above his colleagues as Cosgrave never did. Revered as 'the Chief' by ministerial colleagues and party followers alike, he could and did dominate when he cared to, and in cases of difficulty he dealt individually with his ministers and not through cabinet procedures.

Although Seán Lemass (1959–66) had not the charisma of de Valera, he was of the 'revolutionary generation' and had long been the heir apparent and the most active and able of all de Valera's ministers. After he took over, the role and range of activities of Taoiseach increased. This was the beginning of a new era in Irish politics: the first of the new post-revolutionary generation of ministers had recently been appointed, and the state's role in planning the development of the economy was coming to be recognized. The extension of state activity and the need for more coordinated policy-making and administration that this entailed called for stronger management than hitherto. Moreover, Lemass was by temperament a manager; he believed in crisp decision-making and in following up progress after decisions were made. He was prepared to interfere with colleagues in matters in which he was interested. He held firmly that when a minister disagreed on a policy issue, the minister had to go. Furthermore, he told an interviewer that in the event of being unable to carry a majority of his colleagues on a major issue, he would say to them: 'Do as I do or get another Taoiseach.'[34]

In their different ways, de Valera and Lemass were, to employ Brian Farrell's typology ('chairman', or 'chief'), the very epitome of chiefs.[35] The Fianna Fáil leaders who followed them, Lynch and Haughey, no doubt looked to the revered godfathers as role models but they operated in different circumstances and in a different climate. Jack Lynch (1966–73 and 1977–79) was the first Taoiseach from the 'post-revolutionary' group of leaders. He was also the first Fianna Fáil leader to attain office as the result of a contested election in the parliamentary party. To the outsider at least, Lynch appeared to adopt a quiet, even passive, approach to leadership. After the 1969 general election, in which he proved conclusively that he was the party's greatest electoral asset, his position *vis-à-vis* his ambitious cabinet colleagues was stronger. His style always remained 'low-key', and he was prepared, if there was disagreement in the cabinet, to talk matters out or put them back for reconsideration rather than take a vote, the very hallmarks of the chairman, one might think. Nevertheless, he could and did act decisively, even ruthlessly, as during the arms for Northern Ireland crisis in spring 1970. Lynch's experience suggests two things. Once in office, a Taoiseach who heads a single-party government and is a proven election winner is probably impregnable; but once he begins to slip he is open to a palace revolution led by a determined opponent. Haughey, his successor, showed that a leader who is as determined to hold on to power as he had been to seize it is very hard to displace: he survived a number of attempts by his colleagues to oust him, but in the end he, too, was displaced by his colleagues in 1992 when it was clear that he had become a liability. By then he was in a coalition situation however.

The leaders of coalition governments are very differently placed. To begin with, they are bound by coalition pacts and understandings. They have not the power of appointment, allocation to departments, or dismissal in the case of those posts allotted to parties other than their own. Even if they want to, they cannot exert the kind of forceful leadership and management open to the leader of a single-party government. If necessary, they have to be prepared to tolerate public expression of disagreement with government policy by cabinet colleagues, and they are more likely to have to use cabinet committees, direct negotiations with the leaders of other coalition parties or similar devices to resolve policy differences. They are, then, inevitably, in Farrell's terminology, chairmen rather than chiefs. In the context of coalition after the 1989 election, even Haughey, undoubtedly a chief by temperament, seemed rather to be a chairman masquerading as a chief, at least when he faced his own tribe. His successor, Albert Reynolds, was in a similar situation. Coalition leaders might have some leverage by reason of the fact that their cabinet colleagues know that the government not only has to survive intact as a group, but also needs to appear united if they are to win a second consecutive term of office. Up to 1992, no coalition had ever achieved this.

The variations in the power, performance, and style of the successive holders of the post of Taoiseach have arisen from differences of character and from the circumstances in which they have found themselves. Perhaps the increase in the volume of state business, the greater need to coordinate social and economic policies and summitry have created a greater need and given increased scope for strong leadership. Summitry in particular has focused attention upon the top man and has served to personalize and dramatize his comings and goings, especially if he himself chooses to exploit them. Farrell is no doubt right when he says: 'there is constant pressure to play the role of chief'.[36] If, however, Ireland is likely to have coalition governments rather than single-party governments, future Taoisigh might perforce find themselves chairmen rather than chiefs.

IX

In this chapter and in Chapter 9 we have attempted to show that the government and the Oireachtas are at the centre of the political system and that the relationships between them are perhaps the key linkages in the system. The main features of these relationships are, firstly, the domination of the government over the Oireachtas (which is made possible by the loyal support of backbenchers, support that is consistent and dependable but is not wholly without conditions), and, secondly, the view that politicians have of the respective roles of ministers and Deputies. In the chapter that follows, it will be seen that the corollary of a powerful government with a monopoly of initiative and great powers to manage is a puny parliament peopled by members who have a modest view of their functions and a poor capacity to carry them out.

Notes

1 W. Bagehot, *The English Constitution* (London, 1963), pp. 65–6.
2 B. Farrell, in *How Ireland Voted: the Irish General Election of 1987*, M. Laver *et al*. (eds) (Swords, 1987), p. 141.
3 Joseph Connolly combined a ministerial post with the party leadership of the Seanad from 1932 to 1936. Seán Moylan, a senior minister and an old comrade of de Valera, was defeated at the 1957 general election. He was nominated to the Seanad by the Taoiseach to enable him to continue in office. In 1981, FitzGerald appointed an adviser and confidant, Professor James Dooge, as Minister for Foreign Affairs. He was simultaneously appointed (not elected) to the Seanad as one of the Taoiseach's nominees.
4 Brian Farrell, in *Ireland at the Polls 1981, 1982, and 1987: a Study of Four General Elections* H. R. Penniman and B. Farrell (eds) (Durham, NC, 1987), p. 150.
5 *Ibid.*, p. 136.
6 *Ibid.*, p. 137.
7 *Ibid.*, p. 149.
8 J. Coakley and B. Farrell, in *Pathways to Power: Selecting Rulers in Pluralist Democracies*, M. Dogan (ed.) (Boulder, San Francisco, and London, 1989), p. 209.
9 Farrell, in *Ireland at the Polls*, p. 149.
10 See *Irish Times*, 10 May 1991.
11 Máire Geoghegan-Quinn. She was a teacher. She succeeded to her father's Dáil seat in 1975 at the age of 25.
12 There have only been four – Noel Browne, appointed Minister for Health in 1948; Kevin Boland, appointed Minister for Defence in 1957 when his father, Gerard Boland, was retired from office by his old comrade, de

Valera (see B. Farrell, Chairman or Chief? The Role of the Taoiseach in Irish Government (Dublin, 1971), pp. 38–49); Martin O'Donoghue, appointed Minister for Economic Planning and Development in 1977 (he had been economic adviser in the Department of the Taoiseach from 1970 to 1973); Alan Dukes, appointed Minister for Agriculture in FitzGerald's first government in 1982; he succeeded FitzGerald as leader of the party in 1987.

13 G. M. Moodie, *The Government of Great Britain* (London, 1964), p. 88.

14 *Dáil Debates*, Vol. 110, col. 77 (18 Feb. 1948).

15 *Dáil Debates*, Vol. 119, col. 2521 (23 March 1950).

16 *Irish Times*, 24 July 1974, quoted in B. Chubb (ed.), *A Source Book of Irish Government* revised edn. (Dublin, 1983), p. 63.

17 *Ibid.*

18 The events of the night of 27 January 1982 are still not completely clear. Conflicting accounts of the episode given by Brian Lenihan, Tánaiste and Minister for Defence, during the Presidential election in 1990 led to his dismissal from office by the Taoiseach, Charles Haughey. See *Irish Times*, 29–31 Oct. and 1 Nov. 1990. See also Lenihan's own account in B. Lenihan, *For the Record* (Dublin, 1991).

19 In 1936, Senator Connolly resigned on the abolition of the Senate of which he was the majority leader.

20 In May 1970, Jack Lynch dismissed Charles Haughey and Neil Blaney because of their alleged complicity in a conspiracy to import arms and ammunition into the state for transmission to Northern Ireland. In October 1990, Charles Haughey dismissed Brian Lenihan after he had refused to resign over apparently inconsistent statements about alleged attempts to persuade President Hillery to refuse a dissolution request by Garret FitzGerald in January 1982 (see note 18 above). In November 1991, Haughey dismissed Albert Reynolds and Padraig Flynn in the aftermath of an attempt by some party members to force his resignation as Taoiseach.

21 A Parliamentary Secretary was forced to resign in 1946 after a judicial inquiry into the affairs of a firm with which he was connected. In September 1986, a Minister of State was dismissed by Garret FitzGerald on the grounds that he had misled the Taoiseach about his involvement in a business deal. Charles Haughey dismissed three ministers of state who had voted for his removal from office in November 1991.

22 See *Dáil Debates*, Vol. 294, cols. 429–31 (23 Nov. 1976).

23 See *ibid.*, Vol. 325, cols. 563–5 (9 Dec. 1980).

24 *Ibid.*, Vol. 67, col. 51 (11 May 1937).

25 *Dáil Debates*, Vol. 293, col. 188 (21 Oct. 1976).

26 M. Gallagher, 'The Presidency of the Republic of Ireland. Implications of the "Donegan Affair" ', in *Parliamentary Affairs*, 30 (1977), p. 382.

27 Catherine Donnelly, quoted in F. Finlay, *Mary Robinson: a President with a Purpose* (Dublin, 1990), p. 53.

28 Speech made after she was declared elected on 9 Nov. 1990, quoted in Finlay, *Mary Robinson*, pp. 8–9.

29 *Ibid.*

30 M. Ó Muimhneachain, 'The functions of the Department of the Taoiseach', in *Administration,* 7 (1959–60), p. 293.

31 'Lemass on government', interview quoted in *Léargas,* 12 (Jan.–Feb. 1968), p. 3.

32   B. E. Carter, *The Office of Prime Minister* (London, 1956), p. 200.
33   *Dáil Debates,* Vol. 68, col. 348 (14 June 1937).
34   *Irish Press,* 3 Feb. 1969.
35   See B. Farrell, *Chairman or Chief? the Role of Taoiseach in Irish Government* (Dublin, 1971).
36   In J. Blondel and F. Müller–Rommel, (eds.), *Cabinets in Western Europe* (Basingstoke, 1988), p. 45.

Chapter 11

The Oireachtas

I

In Chapter 9, we identified the members of the Oireachtas as 'proximate policy-makers', for they are among 'those who have immediate legal authority to decide on specific policies'. Paradoxically, however, analysis in that chapter and in Chapter 10 of the role of the Oireachtas showed that it is comparatively minor and passive. The Oireachtas as an institution is not an important, positive contributor to policy. This is due to the domination that the government has over it, a domination that is both accepted by almost all those involved and made the more effective by the habit of party loyalty and strict adherence to the party line in the voting lobbies.

Such a division of functions and powers is by no means universal in democratic countries. In some, parliaments won and have jealously maintained an important role in policy-making and considerable powers to check and restrain governments. Where this has occurred, they tend to be very self-conscious about their autonomy and their ability to control their own business and procedures. The members of such parliaments have a high opinion of their position and carefully guard it. Such representatives contribute positively to policy and are genuine 'legislators'; at the same time, they exert considerable control over the administration of policy.

In Ireland, following the UK tradition, constitutional development has been very different, although a widespread acceptance of the legal fictions of the constitutional lawyers has tended to obscure the facts of the situation. The generally accepted propositions about the functions and role of the Oireachtas do not reflect the facts, although the behaviour of those actually engaged in politics shows that they recognize them at the level of action. From the early seventies, however, there was a growing recognition by Irish politicians of the weakness of the Oireachtas *vis-à-vis* the government, and demands began to be made – as always by those out of power – for reform. By the early nineties, however, the position had not radically altered.

In this chapter, we shall examine the functions which the Oireachtas actually performs, paying particular attention to its part in making policy; to the procedures it adopts and the resources that members have available to them; and to the members themselves, especially to how they see themselves. Before doing so, it is necessary to define exactly what the Oireachtas is. Strictly, following the British conception that parliament consists of the monarch, the House of Lords, and the House of Commons, the Oireachtas must be defined, as it is in the Constitution, as consisting not only of two houses, Dáil Éireann and Seanad Éireann, but of the President also. In practice, however, the term is used to refer to the two houses alone. Ireland has, then, a bicameral legislature, though the Seanad, like many senates, plays a minor and subordinate role.

II

In his study of parliaments, K. C. Wheare discusses their functions under the following headings: (1) making (and breaking) the government, (2) making the government behave, (3) making the laws, and (4) making peace and war (that is, the conduct of foreign relations and defence.)[f] Although the Oireachtas constitutionally and formally has an authoritative say about all these matters, the part it plays in practice is very much less than one might suppose from reading the rules.

In the choice of government, the function of the Dáil (for in this case the Seanad has no part at all to play) has been examined in Chapter 10. Usually the Dáil registers a result – that of the general election by which it was itself elected. However, this need not necessarily be so. Given the presence of more than two parties and independents, it is possible in some circumstances that post-election bargains might be struck and coalitions put together or narrow minorities turned into majorities: then, the members of the Dáil are indeed the government-makers. Until the eighties this had only happened once, in 1948. In the more turbulent eighties, however, it occurred after three of the five general elections of that decade. In Chapter 10 we saw too that the choice of the members of a government is made by the incoming Taoiseach and approved *en bloc* by the Dáil, though the freedom of choice a Taoiseach has and the extent of the influence upon him of members of the Oireachtas (parliamentary) party may vary considerably with the party and the circumstances. In coalition situations he will at most choose an agreed number of colleagues from his own party and allocate them to the posts he has at his disposal. The leader or leaders of the other party or parties in the coalition will do likewise.

When it comes to dismissing the government – that is, passing an adverse vote that would necessitate either the government's resignation and replacement by another or a general election – the record is similar. In nearly sixty years (from 1923 to 1982) no government was actually dismissed by a vote of the Dáil, though the threat of defeat drove the leaders of three of them to resign and seek a dissolution.

However, in the eighties, two governments were dismissed and a third was forced to resign and seek a dissolution. (see Table 10.2, p. 181 above). We may say, then, that the Dáil might appoint and dismiss governments and, recently, has had occasion to do both.

'Making the government behave' is recognized as a major function of parliament in all democratic countries. John Stuart Mill in his classic *Representative Government* (1861) maintained that this, rather than legislating, is its 'proper office', and many would regard the adequate performance of this function as an important test of democracy. Ministers are constitutionally responsible for their conduct of affairs but, as we have seen, cabinet responsibility is a very blunt instrument. It is a notorious fact that Ireland's model, the British parliament, failed to develop adequate procedures to make effective its scrutiny of the growing range of state activity since it fell under government domination in the late nineteenth century. That situation, transposed to Ireland at independence, has never been remedied.

Many of the weaknesses from which the Oireachtas suffers in attempting to scrutinize the conduct of the government are equally evident when it comes to 'making the laws' and even more so in 'making peace and war'. To begin with, as we have seen, the government has a virtual monopoly of new legislation and policy changes; and, by its control (by means of its majority) of the timetable and of divisions, it governs the processing of bills into law in large measure unaltered, at least in essentials. This perhaps more than any other is the distinguishing characteristic of the Oireachtas and parliaments like it such as the British. They are not 'legislatures' in the sense in which the US Congress is a legislature, nor do the members consider themselves 'legislators' as congressional representatives do. These facts are reflected in turn in the legislative procedure, the leadership, and the general conduct of business both in the Dáil and in the Seanad.

Almost all bills are proposed by the government; the legislative programme is decided at government meetings. Each bill is prepared by the appropriate department and is subject to overall cabinet approval after such consultation as it deems necessary. It is at this stage that the effective pressures are brought to bear and the important interests are considered. The minister thus introduces a bill, a government measure, that the government considers has already taken major interests and views sufficiently into account and that the parliamentary party will be expected to support. Nearly all bills are introduced and passed in the Dáil first and then are submitted to the Seanad: occasionally, non-controversial bills have been introduced and processed by the Seanad before going to the Dáil.

There is provision in each house for 'private member's bills' (bills introduced by members who are not ministers), but in practice these are not a significant source of law. In the whole history of the state fewer than twenty of these bills have been passed. Governments usually oppose such bills and they fail; or they take them over. There is, in the words of Ruairi Quinn, a former minister, a convention (which he deplored) of 'not accepting legislative initiatives from the other side, irrespective of their merits or demerits', a manifestation no doubt of the strictly adversarial style of Irish parliamentary behaviour.[2] The private member's bill is in fact often used as a device to get publicity, to jump in ahead of a government already contemplating legislation on a topic, or to try to force the government itself to take action. This was the case, for example, with Senator Mary Robinson's bills on contraception in the seventies and Deputy Jim Mitchell's bill in 1989 to ensure privacy to people doing business in public offices.

The procedure for dealing with proposals for legislation follows the characteristic pattern of the Westminster model. After a formal introduction (first stage), there is a general debate on the principles of the measure proposed (second stage), after which the bill is regarded as having been approved in principle and not subject to serious alteration. This is followed by an examination of the bill section by section, at which time amendments may be proposed that do not negate the bill as a whole (third stage). This stage is usually conducted by the Dáil in full session. Although the rules permit the use of a 'special committee' consisting largely of members with an interest or knowledge, this procedure is rarely used. The bill as amended is then considered once again before being passed on to the other house, usually the Seanad.

The principles governing legislative procedure seem to be four. Firstly, the house considers proposals in an advanced stage of preparation. The idea that governs the legislative procedures of many parliaments – namely, that a bill is only a proposal to be investigated by a committee that will interrogate its authors and hear interested parties before preparing its own version to present to the full house – is alien to Irish parliamentary tradition. Secondly, the principles of a bill are debated first and in full house and, having been agreed upon, are not thereafter open to amendment. Thirdly, it is ordinarily the job of ministers to bring in bills and to sponsor them; the Oireachtas expects this and is organized accordingly. Fourthly, business is so arranged and rules so framed that the government can get its bills passed without too much delay, while at the same time the Opposition has opportunities to deploy its case against them. In doing so, the Opposition will sometimes be as much concerned to persuade the public outside the house that the running of the country would be better placed in their hands at the next election as to influence the government to alter its proposals (though at the third stage particularly, much hard, detailed work is done – albeit by a small minority of members – to amend details of bills and to improve them technically). The orderly and timely passage of business is assured by the government's majority and by the activities of the party whips, who manage their respective parties, arrange the timetable in consultation with each other, and make sure that members are present to vote. As the system operates in practice, it is hard to resist A. J. Ward's conclusion that 'the parliamentary procedures of the Dáil are designed to maximize the power of the government and to minimize the power of the deputies and the Dáil itself as an institution'.[3]

The same principles and similar procedures obtain when the Oireachtas is considering policy proposals in the form of motions and proposals for spending public money. In the case of expenditure, the government is required by Article 28 of Bunreacht na hÉireann to prepare and present annually to the Dáil estimates of receipts and expenditure. Annual estimates for public services are formulated into motions that are introduced in the Dáil, but only some of them ever get debated. Proposals for raising funds are also introduced as motions and, when passed, are incorporated in the annual Finance Bill. Financial resolutions in connection with legislation that would necessitate the expenditure of public funds are introduced and dealt with when the relevant bill is under consideration in the Dáil. The importance of finance and of the need to control it are reflected in the fact that, in dealing with money matters, power is formally allocated somewhat differently than it is in the case of policy generally. Firstly, the authority of the Dáil as the popularly elected house is greater *vis-à-vis* the Seanad than it is in respect of other matters; secondly, the government has the exclusive power under the Constitution to propose the expenditure of public money.

III

In considering the functions and role of the Oireachtas, attention tends to focus upon the Dáil rather than the Seanad. The Seanad plays a smaller part than the Dáil and has a subordinate position. The relative inferiority of the second house is a common, though not universal, phenomenon of modern democratic states. In the case of Seanad Éireann, it is the sequel to a troubled past.

The first Irish parliament in 1919 consisted of a single house, for the independence movement neither needed nor wanted more. When the Treaty was being negotiated, however, promises were sought and given that the new state would have a senate in which the unionist minority would be strongly represented, and provision was made for this in the Irish Free State Constitution. That senate had a chequered career. No satisfactory formula for its composition could be found. When it exercised its right to hold up legislation that had been passed in the Dáil, it was immediately open to the charge not only of thwarting the real representatives of the people but of being un-Irish as well. It was especially anathema to de Valera and Fianna Fáil, and it did not long survive their accession to office, being abolished in 1936 after acrimonious debates during which de Valera declared himself unconvinced of the value of any senate but open to persuasion. However, a general belief in the usefulness of second houses prevailed, and the 1937 Constitution made provision for a new senate, Seanad Éireann.

Seanad Éireann is both singular in its composition and circumscribed in its powers. In considering a new senate, de Valera was attracted by one of the proposals of a commission set up to advise on the composition of a new house, a proposal for a body selected on a vocational basis and obviously inspired by the principles enunciated in the encyclical *Quadragesimo Anno* of Pope Pius XI. However, he recognized that the country was not in fact sufficiently organized on vocational lines to allow direct choice by vocational bodies, and he was also concerned not to have a body that would be likely to oppose the government of the day. The scheme he evolved, which has survived with only minor changes, provided for a body comprising three groups. Six senators are elected by the Irish graduates of the National University of Ireland and Dublin University (Trinity College), the two universities which existed when the Constitution was enacted, three from each.[4] Forty-three are elected by an electoral college of nearly 1,000, which is composed of the members of the Oireachtas and the county and county borough councillors. They are chosen from five panels of candidates nominated in part by bodies representing five groups of interests (education and culture, agriculture, industry and commerce, labour, and public administration and social services) and in part by members of the Oireachtas. The remaining eleven senators are nominated by the Taoiseach himself after all the others have been chosen. Thus the Taoiseach has an opportunity to give representation to any group that he thinks needs it, to bring in persons of eminence, and – de Valera frankly admitted when proposing it – to ensure a government majority.

The scheme for the election of the forty-three was admitted to be only a step towards vocational representation. Yet in itself it was defective, for not only did the structure of the community not correspond to vocational principles, but the composition of the panels, with labour separated from management, seemed actually to go contrary to those very principles. More serious for genuine vocational representation, the dilution of direct representation of vocational organizations in order to make the system more democratic permitted party domination, which has in fact been complete. The parties have controlled the elections to the exclusion of almost all the truly vocational elements. Since most of the Taoiseach's nominees tend also to be identified with a party – usually of course his party – the Seanad is composed largely of party politicians not very different from their colleagues in the Dáil and, in the case of many of them, with only tenuous connections with the interests they affect to represent. Usually between one-quarter and one-third of them have been TDs, defeated or retired, and many of the rest are party men who have earned a reward or consolation prize. In recent years, a few have been aspirant deputies, younger people using the Seanad as a stepping-stone to the Dáil. In 1989, no less than twenty-five of the incoming senators were unsuccessful candidates in the Dáil general election.

Because so many of them are rising, falling, or resting politicians, it is not surprising that many Senators (unlike Deputies) are not front-rank party men. A very few are not real politicians at all: the university representatives, included to compensate the universities for having lost their representation in the Dáil in 1936, tended in the past to approximate the vocational type, representing professions such as law and medicine and the professional classes generally. Naturally, the prestige of the Seanad suffers from the fact that, by and large, it is merely another selection of party politicians chosen in an unnecessarily complicated and not particularly democratic manner.

The Seanad suffers also from its evident inferiority and subordination to the Dáil. In Bunreacht na hÉireann, it is deliberately placed to one side of the political stage. The Dáil nominates the Taoiseach and approves his government. The government is constitutionally responsible to the Dáil and must maintain a majority there. The Dáil is required by the Constitution to consider the estimates of public expenditure, to ratify international agreements, and to approve any declaration of war. Almost all legislation is introduced in the Dáil, and all major policy statements are made there. The Seanad's meagre powers to amend or delay emphasize the point that it is primarily a revising body with the power to draw public attention to a proposal by compelling the Dáil to reconsider it. Even this it has done on only a few occasions.

The subordinate status of the Seanad in law and in practice and its lack of prestige are emphasized by three facts. Firstly, there are usually no senator ministers. The Constitution permits up to two members of the government to be senators, but from 1938 to 1990 there had been only two ministers in the Seanad.[5] The majority side of the house is led and business is controlled by a majority leader, who, though he is always senior, does not have ministerial rank. Secondly, the Seanad's business is subordinated to that of the Dáil. In the ten-year period between 1969 and 1978, according to Smyth, 'approximately 90–95 per cent of the work consisted of the consideration of legislation sent to the second chamber by the Dáil'.[6] Very few bills are initiated in the Seanad. There was a marked increase in government legislation initiated there for a few years during the FitzGerald government (1982–87) – a part of that government's attempts to reform the Oireachtas – but the number fell off again with the return of Fianna Fáil. What is more, 'the sittings of the Seanad are largely dependent on the volume of business sent to the House from the Dáil. While the Dáil is discussing the estimates, very little legislation is passed by it and the Seanad has no occasion to meet.'[7] Later in the parliamentary year, it has sometimes been forced into an unseemly rush, processing without proper consideration a number of bills that the government wishes to have passed before the recess. Thirdly, sometimes its consideration of items on its agenda has been delayed, interrupted, or impaired by the failure of ministers to attend as arranged.

There is a vicious circle here. Lacking prestige and being government-controlled, the Seanad cannot insist on a more active role or on more consideration for its dignity or convenience. Because it does not do so, it is condemned to hold an undignified position and to underuse what potential it does have. It does some useful work, however. Its debates on current issues are sometimes important; bills are improved, some considerably, as a result of its efforts; a few of its members serve on Oireachtas joint committees (and much more use could be made of them in this way). However, the air of leisure that pervades its debates, its light programme (in the decade 1969 to 1978, it met on average thirty-five times a year: in 1989, on forty-two occasions), the absence of any feeling of urgency or of momentous political cut and thrust, and the comparatively poor publicity it gets, all emphasize its lack of importance and contribute to its low prestige. If it were more important, its composition would undoubtedly evoke more than the half-hearted criticism that is now heard from time to time, but to government and to community alike, this does not seem to be a matter of much moment.

IV

In carrying out its functions of making the laws, as also in making the government behave, the Oireachtas is sadly ineffective, a fact that has been increasingly acknowledged by politicians themselves over the last twenty years or more. Barry Desmond, a former Labour Party minister, summed up the situation in the middle seventies thus: 'Our present parliamentary malaise is that we have allowed our parliamentary institutions to atrophy so much that many deputies and senators are, in the parliamentary sense, politically uninvolved.'[8] Likewise, in 1980, a Fine Gael policy document entitled *Reform of the Dáil:* 'In practice it [the Dáil] plays practically no effective part in either making the laws or even the expert criticism of them.'[9] Criticisms of this kind continue to be made by members and outside commentators alike.

The Oireachtas is deficient on three counts. Firstly, its procedures and techniques are archaic and ineffective. Secondly, the staff and facilities available to members are meagre. Thirdly, the education and experience of many members and, more important, the view that they have of their job, ill equip them to make the kinds of enquiries that are necessary or to appreciate the kinds of data that could be made available – and are now to some extent coming to be made available – in order to judge performance. Neither the methods employed nor the personnel involved, whether representative or professional, are adequate to appraise large programmes of public expenditure for an ever-increasing range of economic and social objectives, including long-term capital programmes and extensive subsidies. Even if they were, the style and demeanour of much opposition – and it is the Opposition on which the performance of this function to a great extent depends – and the conception members generally have of their functions do not favour really effective, let alone constructive, criticism.

The methods used by the Oireachtas to deal with the policy proposals of governments are those evolved by the British parliament in the nineteenth century. Parliaments are basically debating assemblies. In the Dáil and Seanad, as in the houses of the British parliament, ministers explain and make the case for their proposals, the Opposition opposes, and members generally comment, using a variety of debating-body techniques as procedural pegs on which to hang their discussions. These same pegs are used for the surveillance of the conduct of public business – that is, making the government behave. They are of three kinds – debates, questions, and committees.

Both houses of the Oireachtas debate the proposals that the government puts before them, often more than once, within the framework of procedures for dealing with various types of bills; in debates on estimates; and in debates on motions of various kinds, including motions of censure and 'no confidence' and 'adjournment motions'. In both quantity and quality, the performance of both houses leaves much to be desired. Between 1969 and 1978, the Dáil met on average only eighty-seven days per year; in 1989 it was no better: it sat on seventy-nine days. Likewise, the Seanad, as we have noted. It is hard to measure the quality of debate in any objective fashion. Debates are no doubt valuable as a device to deploy the pros and cons of a proposed course of action and are important for the publicity they give to it and to the case for and against. However, in Ireland – no doubt as elsewhere – debates are often discursive, uninformed, and sometimes, except perhaps to the speaker concerned, irrelevant to the major issues of the topic under discussion. In any case, the quality of debate depends inevitably upon the quality of the information available. Too often in the past, ministers briefed by their civil servants were the only well-informed participants. The Opposition and ordinary members generally had no comparable resources for acquiring and appraising information.

During the eighties, and particularly in the period of the Fine Gael–Labour coalition (1982–87), there were considerable improvements in the quantity and quality of information becoming available. They owed much to the energy and persistence of a Fine Gael Deputy, John Bruton, who was Minister for Finance at various times during the eighties and 'leader of the House' from 1982–86. (In 1990 he became leader of the Fine Gael Party.)[10] Firstly, a new method of presentation of government expenditure proposals was devised and initiated, the Comprehensive Public Expenditure Programmes. 'In these Programmes expenditure is categorised according to the programme on which it is spent, rather than by department, and there is a multi-annual focus.'[11] Secondly, a number of select committees were set up and given resources to enable them to employ professional assistance. They generated material about their subject area, for those who cared to use it, of a higher quality and more immediate relevance to matters in debate than had hitherto been available to parliamentary representatives.

Important as it is, good information is not the only requirement for improving the effectiveness of debates. Oireachtas debates are the less efficient as a method for dealing with policy proposals because of the fact that they are usually gladiatorial set pieces conducted on party lines by politicians who are wedded to the concept of strictly competitive or 'adversary' politics. Counter-proposals and amendments, even good ones, made by the Opposition are liable to be rejected by the government because of their source rather than their intrinsic value, except perhaps on minor matters when there is little or no publicity. The inevitable reaction to this is that Opposition Deputies are more concerned to score points and to use this high-visibility forum to demonstrate the ineffectiveness of the government and its unfitness to govern, which is their major objective in any case. This does not conduce to constructive debate and a rational consideration of the merits and demerits of governmental proposals and Opposition amendments, let alone to consensus politics.

Again, because of the nature of the political system, in particular the localism of Irish politics and the tendency to clientelism, some participants in debates, rank-and-file members in particular, use the opportunity to raise matters of local interest in order to get publicity in their local newspapers in their home territories. This is entirely rational behaviour on their part, given their constituents' and their own concept of their functions and role. Such contributions, however, do not usually illuminate the major principles and aspects of public policy initiatives.

The main burden of debating government proposals falls upon a fraction of Oireachtas members – the members of the government and the ministers of state, the Opposition shadow ministers called 'spokesmen', and a few others who by temperament or training or for reasons of ambition have a greater interest than most in general policy issues. Recently, the number of such people seems to have grown with the election of more young and ambitious professional and business people. All three parliamentary parties have regular meetings, usually weekly, when the houses are sitting. None of them makes much positive contribution to legislation or policy: the Opposition committees because they are in a minority situation in a process of strictly adversary politics; the government party Deputies because the government, already committed to its proposals, regards its backbenchers as at best a negative sounding board that will occasionally force ministers to think again.

Parliamentary questions are not of much importance in policy-making. The Dáil has a question time on the well-known Westminster model and, as in the United Kingdom also, parliamentary questions are 'a simple, convenient and speedy routine . . . available to deputies for getting information from the Government'.[12] The principal use of question time, however, is to seek information about, and to question, administrative action or inaction; it is thus mostly concerned with 'making the government behave', to use Wheare's terminology. Many rank-and-file Deputies use it extensively to enquire about, or draw attention to, constituency matters in pursuance of their duty, as they see it, to 'service' their constituents and thereby – given the election system – to safeguard their seats.

In many parliaments, the most important work on policy is done in committees. For each area of policy and administration there will be a powerful committee with its own staff to process both government-sponsored and other proposals for new legislation on policy and to make its own proposals. In addition, such committees supervise the administration of policy in a particular subject area. With experience, their members and staffs acquire considerable knowledge and expertise and, to some extent at least, can challenge ministers and civil servants on not-too-unequal terms. The UK parliament, however, never developed a strong committee system of this sort, contenting itself until recently with 'select committees' to enquire into the conduct of administration. Their rather restricted terms of reference usually precluded the questioning of government policy. The most effective of these, the Public Accounts Committee, worked (and still works) well within its restricted remit. That approach and that type of committee was adopted by the Oireachtas, including a Public Accounts Committee. Until the mid-seventies, there was no development beyond that point. Even then, a new committee necessitated by Ireland's accession to the European Communities, the Joint Committee (that is, of the Dáil and Seanad) on the Secondary Legislation of the European Communities, was clearly hampered in its work by inadequate staffing and services.

With the appointment in 1978 of a Joint Committee on State-Sponsored Bodies to 'examine the Reports and Accounts and overall operational results of State-Sponsored Bodies engaged in trading or commercial activities', the Oireachtas achieved something of a breakthrough against the reluctance of governments and civil servants to countenance an efficient parliamentary committee. Not only were professional staff appointed to assist the Joint Committee, but the Committee itself soon found that judging the performance of public enterprises involved enquiring into their policy briefs. This it proceeded to do. It was but a short step thence to commenting on policy issues, and by 1980 the Joint Committee was doing so. Its reports provided information on the bodies it investigated in quantity and quality never before achieved by Irish parliamentarians. A second major advance was made in 1983 when the Fine Gael–Labour government set up no fewer than eight new select committees. Although the move owed much to the initiative of John Bruton, the number and remits were the result of both inter-party and intra-party pressures. A glance at the topics – public expenditure; legislation; women's rights; marriage breakdown; small businesses; cooperation with developing countries; crime, lawlessness, and vandalism; the Irish language – is sufficient to show how far such pressures had compromised the concept of a systematic coverage of all state activity. 'What should have begun as a modest investigative experiment blossomed into an uncoordinated mish-mash of committees.'[13] Some languished; others reported and disappeared; one, the Public Expenditure Committee, made a considerable impact not least because its terms of reference specifically directed it to enquire into 'the justification for and effectiveness of on-going expenditure'. However, 'its very prominence may have been its downfall'.[14] Its excursions into policy and its wholesale criticism generated hostility among ministers and senior civil servants alike.

The return of a Fianna Fáil government in 1987 saw a marked reduction in parliamentary committees. Only three were constituted: Women's Rights, the Irish Language and Commercial State-Sponsored bodies. A combination of Fianna Fáil's traditional lack of enthusiasm for intrusive committees; the failure of the Dáil to debate more than a few of the reports that they produced; the reluctance of all but a few of their members to put much effort into them; and the equivocal attitude of Deputies generally, all combined to spell the end of the first – flawed – attempt at grafting a comprehensive committee system on to the procedures of the Oireachtas. Although these committees did publish information of a kind and in quantities hitherto unavailable, it is clear that the average Deputy considers that the personal and political costs of participation outweigh the benefits: 'their work earns little or no electoral premium, except where a chairperson can develop a media profile. Even this is not without danger, considering the risks inherent in being associated with controversial investigations.'[15] As Fine Gael's document *Reform of the Dáil* rightly observed: 'Politicians can only survive if they receive public recognition for their work.'[16] The kind of work that gets recognition – and pays dividends – is what they will concentrate on.

Perhaps there is another fundamental problem. A. J. Ward put it succinctly: 'A committee has the effect of creating within the same legislature an alternative centre of information, expertise, prestige and power which necessarily inhibits the government's freedom of action.'[17] The fear of such an 'alternative centre' causes governments to be slow to countenance the development of powerful committees. Without doubt, 'well-developed committee systems are not easily blended with parliamentary democracy on the Westminster model'.[18]

The major part in examining and criticizing the government's proposals falls to the members of the party or parties in opposition. The concept of 'the Opposition' as an essential complement to 'the government' is basic to the Irish system. It is symbolized by the allowance paid to the leader of the opposition party or, if there is more than one opposition party, to the leaders of the two biggest, to enable them and their colleagues to carry out their functions of opposing the government. The style of the Opposition resembles that which Wheare described as typical of the British system: 'The leading idea upon which it is organized is that it offers itself before the country as an alternative government. It criticizes upon the understanding that, given the opportunity, it could do better itself.'[19] The Oireachtas and particularly the Dáil is a platform upon which the Opposition makes a continuous appeal to the electorate. This style of opposition is the consequence of the tradition of bipolar and strictly adversarial politics and of governments with a monopoly of initiative, particularly since there are few opportunities for constructive committee work. The Opposition either does not want to play a constructive role or, if it does, it is not permitted to do so. Proposals emanating from Opposition sources are all too often not considered on their merits, for no public credit can be allowed to accrue to them: equally, the job of the Opposition is to criticize the government and all its works.

Together, the government's monopoly of policy initiatives and the views of members on the roles of the government and the Opposition and the appropriate style of conducting them have combined to inhibit the development of the Oireachtas as a legislature and to prevent the members from seeing themselves as legislators. For the same reasons, Deputies and Senators do not see themselves as constituting a corporate institution with powers to check the government on behalf of the people.

V

The poor performance of the Oireachtas arises partly because it is badly organized and equipped and poorly informed. But, more fundamentally, poor performance results from, firstly, a general acceptance by members of the dominant role of the government as policy-maker, and, secondly, the preoccupation of many members with their own local positions. These considerations have led them to see themselves as having another function to perform, the function of 'servicing' their constituents. In so doing, members of the Oireachtas generally, and TDs in particular, constitute themselves more a factor in the *administration* of state policy – particularly in detailed administration

– than as *legislators*. They adopt this role both by inclination and by force of circumstances, a fact best explained by considering who and what they are and how they attain and hold office.

In Tom Garvin's words, 'the classic duty' of an Irish parliamentary representative is

to be a local man, well entrenched in the local social system, resident in or near the constituency and concerned more with being an ambassador for his community to the central government than with the task of making national policy or law.[20]

Early in the history of the state, the national heroes or, for a while, members of a dynasty founded on one such were exempt from this obligation; the rest had to conform to this pattern. In time, all have had to.

In 1922, seven out of ten Deputies were resident in the constituencies they represented: today eight or nine out of ten were born in and live in, or in close proximity to, their constituencies. In fact, identification with an area has always been even more specific. Many, perhaps most, TDs, except those living Dublin, have been identified with the particular part of the constituency in which they live or are reckoned specially to represent. Multi-member constituencies notwithstanding, there is a marked tendency for Deputies to have 'bailiwicks'. Senators, except those representing the universities, do not have constituencies. Nevertheless, in recent years most of the two-thirds of them who live outside Dublin are identified with their home areas in much the same way as Deputies, and in practice they perform the same services for their localities as Deputies.

The localism of parliamentary representatives is the greater since, for most of them, the route to membership in the Oireachtas is by way of local government and the basis of their electoral support lies in the help they can give their constituents in respect of local services such as housing and health. Most Deputies and Senators are members of the principal local authorities, the county and county borough councils: in 1989, 86 per cent were members (see Table 11.1) and so too were 62 per cent of Senators.

Many, perhaps most, of these were also serving on one or more of a variety of other local public bodies such as town councils, county committees of agriculture, vocational educational committees, harbour boards, and health boards. All these offer opportunities for influence and service that enhance a politician's local reputation and help secure a quota of first-preference votes. Nor is this to be thought of as a phenomenon of the countryside: thirty-nine of the forty-three Dublin-area Deputies elected in 1989 were or had been councillors. In addition, members of the Oireachtas are to be found in all kinds of voluntary bodies, particularly trade unions, trade associations, farmers' organizations, and other occupational bodies. Yet, strangely, they are

Table 11.1 **Local government background of deputies**

	Before entering Dáil		After entering Dáil		Never a member		Total	
	N	%	N	%	N	%	N	%
Fianna Fáil	51	66.2	16	20.8	10	13.0	77	100.0
Fine Gael	40	72.7	3	5.5	12	21.8	55	100.0
Labour	13	86.7	2	13.3	0	0	15	100.0
PD	4	66.7	2	33.3	0	0	6	100.0
Workers' Party	6	85.7	1	14.3	0	0	7	100.0
Others	4	66.7	0	0	2	33.3	6	100.0
Total	118	71.1	24	14.5	24	14.5	166	100.0

When did Deputy become member of the local authority?[a]

Note:[a] The term local authority here covers county councils and county borough councils only.

Source: M. Gallagher in How Ireland Voted 1989 M. Gallagher and R. Sinnott, (Galway, 1990), p. 87.

not to be found in great numbers in social, cultural, or religious organizations with the notable exception of the Gaelic Athletic Association, membership in which is generally reckoned to be particularly useful.

As the luminaries of the revolutionary generation disappeared, they were not replaced by others of their kind. Their personal followings evaporated and the parties took over. By the seventies, only Neil Blaney exemplified something of the *personalismo* of the earlier generation of semi-independent Deputies; but, significantly, he is an example of another marked feature of the composition of the Oireachtas and of Irish politics generally to which attention has already been drawn – namely, the dynastic element. The Blaneys, father and son, have represented their part of Donegal for well over sixty years since Neil Blaney entered the Dáil with de Valera and Fianna Fáil n 1927. 'Family seats' became quite common and they still remain so. The 1989 Dáil, as we have already noted, contained twenty-five sons, four daughters, five nephews, a niece, and a son-in-law of former Deputies. In the past, to inherit a 'family seat' was almost without exception the only way a woman could become a parliamentary representative. Of the twelve women who sat in the Dáil between 1922 and 1948, three were widows and three sisters of prominent leaders of the independence movement, and five others were widows of former Deputies. Thirty years later the position had not changed: of the six women Deputies elected in 1977, only one was not in this category. By the early eighties however, it *was* changing, and by 1989 only four of the thirteen women Deputies were daughters (and another, Sile de Valera, was a granddaughter): a class of more professional women politicians seemed to be emerging.

Since almost all Deputies belong in their localities and since Ireland is overwhelmingly a Catholic country, there are few Protestants in the Oireachtas. In the past, Protestants represented constituencies where the people of their faith could muster a quota of votes – for example, in Donegal until the late 1960s or in some Dublin constituencies. Where there are pockets of Protestants, the major parties sometimes find it politic to have a senator of that faith. But the Protestant population declined in numbers over the years and became more assimilated into the mainstream of politics. Accordingly, where, as in the Dála of the 1920s, there were a dozen or so, in 1965 there were four, and in 1989 there was one Protestant (and three Jews) in the Dáil.

Generational changes are also evident in the age distribution of parliamentary representatives. The revolutionary Dáil of 1919 contained a large proportion of young men, and over half of the 1922 Dáil were under 40. Once elected, members were able to retain their seats comparatively easily and the turnover was low. Moreover, new entrants tended to be over 40, reflecting the conservatism and respect for seniority that marked Irish politics. Consequently, as Table 11.2 shows, the Dáil was a steadily ageing body until the 1950s, when, inevitably, the first generation began to be replaced quite quickly. The pattern seems to have stabilized over the last quarter of a century. According to Gallagher, it suggests that Ireland has 'a fairly young parliament by international standards'.[21]

Table 11.2 Age distribution of members of certain Dála between 1922 and 1989 (per cent)

	Dáil						
Age group	1922	1932	1944	1965	1977[a]	Nov. 1982[a]	1989[a]
20–29	14	1	2	6	4	5	6
30–39	38	27	12	20	24	27	24
40–49	24	39	31	31	36	37	33
50–59	18	26	37	24	24	25	29
60–69	4	5	17	14	9	5	8
70 and over	2	2	1	5	1		

Note:[a] For the Dála of 1977, 1982 and 1989, the age groupings are shifted up one year: 21–30, 31–40, etc.

Source: For 1919–44, derived from J. L. McCracken, *Representative Government in Ireland* (London, 1957), pp. 31–91. For 1965, derived from J. Whyte, *Dáil Deputies*, Tuairim Pamphlet No. 15 (Dublin, 1966), p. 33. For 1977, T. Nealon, *Guide to the 21st Dáil and Seanad* (Blackrock, 1977), p. 135. For 1982, M. Gallagher, in *Legislative Studies Quarterly*, X, p. 384. For 1989, *Nealon's Guide 26th Dáil and Seanad* (Dublin, 1989), p. 162.

Likewise, changes brought about by the eventual disappearance of the old guard no doubt go some way to explain the big changes in the educational qualifications of Deputies that began after the Second World War. However, the dramatic changes revealed in Table 11.3 reflect, rather, the improved educational opportunities that were part of the industrialization and modernization of the community and the growing realization of party leaders that a better educated population wants better-qualified candidates. As Table 11.3 shows, two-thirds of the 1989 Dáil had had third-level education or professional training.

Table 11.3 *Education of members of certain Dála between 1922 and 1989 (per cent)*

Year	Level attained		
	First	*Second*	*Third*
1922	40	34	26
1932	44	32	24
1944	48	29	22
1965	20	50	30
1977	7	56	37
1989	4	31	67

Source: As for Table 11.2.

Higher educational standards have been reflected in a changing occupational structure. Writing in 1972, Garvin concluded that 'studies of biographical information on Dáil Deputies have established clear-cut trends towards professionalisation of the House in recent decades'.[22] As we noted in Chapter 5, the professional element grew rapidly as the country modernized from the sixties, and by 1989 it comprised about half of the House (see pp. 85–87 and Table 5.6. above). Teachers and lawyers predominated. The halving of the proportion of farmers during the same period mirrored the decline in the number of people in that occupation. However, many more than appear from the figures have an immediate interest in farming either because they combine their principal profession or business with farming or because one way or another they depend on farming. This is particularly true of the small business people whose presence in the Dáil is a marked and, compared to many countries, distinctive feature.

This pattern of occupations means that the membership of the Dáil, as also the Seanad, by no means reflects the occupational structure of Irish society. Working-class Deputies and Senators are, and always have been, few and far between. Likewise, there are very few small farmers. Evidently, here as elsewhere in politics, the occupations that are 'central' or permit time for politics tend to be over-represented, and, conversely, others are under-represented.

These data provide a clear enough picture of the membership of the

Oireachtas as measured by objective data. But how do the members see themselves? There can be little doubt of what the answer is. For most of them, a public representative is, as Léo Hamon said of the French deputy, ' a man at the beck and call of his electors', though the Deputies and Senators themselves would prefer to use words such as 'service' and 'available' instead.[23] This applies as much to the increasing number of Deputies who have wider horizons and are policy-orientated as to the majority. Ministers are not exempt either: indeed, more is expected of them in this line because of their positions; and, judging by the numbers of staff in their 'private offices' working on constituency matters, they give this high priority. As we shall see, the service given by parliamentary representatives – for the same applies to Senators as to Deputies – covers a wide range of minor administrative matters at both the local and central government levels. The public expect this: 'There is a fixed notion that cannot be got out of people's heads that Deputies can get you something that you cannot get from anybody else.'[24] The election system puts a premium on it: 'Of course you must canvass in another form from the day on which the election is over till the date of the next election.'[25] Those comments, made thirty years ago, are as true today as they were then.

For a good many, the path to office may well be through service at the local government level, and the maintenance of one's position certainly requires continuing to provide it. Service of this kind is thus an integral part of the web of personal contact and influence that is the foundation of the position of the public person, certainly in rural areas and to some extent in urban areas also. Moreover, this type of activity is not declining. On the contrary, it is if anything increasing, and members certainly work at it as assiduously as in the past and perhaps more ruthlessly. Most accept such work without resentment: on the contrary, there is evidence that many give it priority and some exploit it. Some members of the European Parliament pursue parochial matters there too. On 11 October 1979, Seán Flanagan asked the Commission to state 'whether it has agreed to grant aid to the Spaddagh-Ballyhaunis water scheme and, if so, when payment will occur'.[26] There are officials who will say that some Deputies deliberately create the impression among their constituents that their intervention is necessary or helpful.

VI

The Irish parliamentary representative, as we have argued, is more a factor in administration and a 'consumer representative' than a legislator. However, it is important to note that the Constitution as interpreted by those brought up upon traditional constitutional theory does not recognize this. Mr Justice Budd in the *O'Donovan* case declared:

Most important duties are positively assigned to Deputies by the Constitution, the paramount duty being that of making laws for the country. . . . It will be found again, however, that the Constitution does not anywhere in the Articles relating to the functions of Deputies recognize or sanction their intervention in administrative affairs.[27]

The welfare state creates the opportunities and the need for this type of activity. What might be doubted is whether the parliamentary representative should perform it, or at least the more routine elements in it. Yet, rightly or wrongly, it might well be that, as the citizen sees it, the representative engaged in these activities is performing 'an indispensable function which no other political unit or device can perform so well'.[28]

Nor does it follow that representatives would give it up if they were no longer forced by the election system to do it. This kind of activity by public persons and this kind of relationship between them and their clients are deeply rooted in Irish experience. For generations, Irish people saw that to get the benefits that public authorities bestow, the help of a man with connections and influence was necessary. All that democracy has meant is that such a person has been laid on officially, as it were, and is now no longer a master but a servant.

What does not follow is that to perform service functions for constituents necessarily precludes representatives from playing a more active part in the formation and scrutiny of policy. Adequately paid representatives with access to appropriate facilities in a properly organized Oireachtas ought to be able to do both, as many parliamentary representatives in other democratic countries do. The three factors that most inhibit the development of the potential of the Oireachtas are, as we have argued, the view of all political leaders when in government that they must have a monopoly of initiative, the practice of strictly competitive politics in dealing with parliamentary business, and the acceptance by most members of the present meagre role of the Oireachtas in the political system.

Notes

1 K. C. Wheare, *Legislatures* (London, 1963).
2 Quoted by J. Carroll in *Irish Times*, 16 Feb. 1990.
3 A. J. Ward, 'Parliamentary procedures and the machinery of government in Ireland', in *Irish University Review*, 4 (1974) , p. 229.
4 The Constitution (Election of Members of Seanad Éireann by Institutions of Higher Education) Bill (1979), approved by referendum in July 1979, amended Bunreacht na hÉireann by providing for the election by universities and other institutions of higher education specified by law of up to six senators as prescribed by law. Up to 1992 no law had been enacted under this provision to alter university representation.
5 See above p. 189.
6 J. McG. Smyth, *The Houses of the Oireachtas*, 4th edn (Dublin, 1979), p. 52.

7   *Ibid.*

8   B. Desmond, *The Houses of the Oireachtas: Plea for Reform, a Memorandum to the Government* (Dublin, 1975), p. 4.

9   *Reform of the Dáil: Fine Gael Policy on Reform of the Dáil*, January, 1980 (Dublin, 1980), p. 3.

10 John Bruton was largely responsible for the Fine Gael policy documents *Reform of the Dáil* (1980) and *A Better Way to Plan the Nation's Finances* (1981).

11 D. Gwyn Morgan, *Constitutional Law of Ireland: the Law of the Executive, Legislature and Judicature,* 2nd edn (Dublin, 1990), p. 121. From 1988 they were entitled *Summary of Public Expenditure Programmes.* For parliamentary reforms generally in the eighties, see Gwyn Morgan, *Constitutional Law of Ireland,* pp. 121–3 and 278–81.

12 T. Troy, 'Some aspects of Parliamentary Questions', in *Administration,* 7 (1959), p. 252.

13 A. Arkins, 'The Committees of the 24th Oireachtas', in *Irish Political Studies,* 3 (1988), p. 94.

14 *Ibid.,* p. 96.

15 *Ibid.,* p. 95.

16 *Reform of the Dáil: Fine Gael Policy on Reform of the Dáil,* Jan. 1980 (Dublin, 1980), p. 4.

17 A. J. Ward, 'Parliamentary procedures and the machinery of government in Ireland', in *Irish University Review,* 4 (1974), pp. 234–5.

18 *Ibid.*

19 K. C. Wheare, *Legislatures* (London, 1963), p. 119.

20 T. Garvin, 'Continuity and change in Irish electoral politics', in *Economic and Social Review,* 3 (1972), p. 361.

21 M. Gallagher, 'Social backgrounds and local orientations of members of the Irish Dáil', in *Legislative Studies Quarterly,* X (1985), p. 383.

22 Garvin, 'Continuity and change in Irish electoral politics', in *Economic and Social Review,* 3 (1972), p. 360.

23 Léo Hamon, 'Members of the French parliament', in *International Social Science Journal,* 13 (1961), p. 557.

24 Senator M. Hayes, *Seanad Debates,* Vol. 55, Col. 1686 (19 Dec. 1962).

25 Deputy M. Hilliard, quoted in D. E. Butler (ed.), *Elections Abroad* (London, 1959), p. 202.

26 *Official Journal of the European Communities,* 11 Feb. 1980 (Office for Official Publications of the European Communities, Luxembourg).

27 *O'Donovan* v. *Attorney General* [1961] IR 114 at p. 136.

28 J. D. B. Miller, *Australian Government and Politics,* 2nd edn (London, 1959), p. 116.

CHAPTER 12

The Pattern of Public Administration

I

By the end of the nineteenth century, the United Kingdom of Great Britain and Ireland had an up-to-date and integrated public administration. The process of constructing it had been one not only of modernization but of democratization as well. It was based upon the principle that there should be two systems of government: central government and local government. The former would be responsible to parliament by means of ministers controlling departments manned by a professional career Civil Service. The latter would be a subordinate system, ultimately controlled by parliament, which governed its structure and gave it its tasks, but administered by locally elected councils. Almost all public business was, in principle, to be subsumed within one or the other of these two systems. The only exceptions were functions of a quasi-judicial nature or activities, such as the recruitment of civil servants, deemed to need insulating from political nepotism. Functions such as these – and they were thought to be quite few – were allocated to independent boards or commissions.

Irish administration as part of the UK system was, as far as possible, moulded into this pattern, although it was always recognized that in some respects the island had perforce to be treated differently. Until the beginning of the nineteenth century, Ireland had been a separate kingdom with its own political, administrative, and judicial institutions. Because of this, because of the security needs of imperial rule, and because British governments tended to be more paternalistic towards Ireland than towards other regions of the United Kingdom, the country was treated to some extent as a special case in terms of both the allocation of government functions and administrative structure and judiciary: a measure of decentralization was deemed both necessary and convenient.

After the Union, when Ireland became an integral part of the United Kingdom, some Irish departments were merged with their British equivalents, but others were not. In the course of the century, some British departments acquired new duties in respect of Ireland; in other cases, purely Irish departments or offices were set up, some headed by ministers, others by appointed boards or commissions. R. B. McDowell summed up the situation:

It is apparent from a cursory glance at Irish administrative history in the nineteenth century that there was a strong tendency to tackle newly-appreciated problems on simple *ad hoc* lines, which often meant the creation of a new department with little regard for the general structure. Though functions were from time to time transferred between departments, no attempt was made to plan systematically the distribution of duties between all the departments, British and Irish, functioning in Ireland, nor were the arrangements for controlling and [coordinating] their activities adequate.[1]

Indeed, by the end of the century, when the state began to intervene on a more massive scale and when, because of the Home Rule movement, there was a desire to associate Irish people more closely with the administration of their own public services, there was a marked increase in the number and variety of organizations administering them. Ireland, it was said at the end of the century, had as many boards as would make her coffin.

The control of the Chief Secretary (a sort of Minister for Irish Affairs) over the various offices varied considerably. Tidy-minded colonial administrators with experience in India, like J. W. Ridgeway, Under-secretary from 1887 to 1893, and Lord McDonnell, who held the same office from 1902 to 1908, fretted at the lack of overall control they were able to exercise, owing to the institution of semi-independent boards, on the one hand, and the interference of the British Treasury, on the other. It should be noted, however, that although the emerging development and welfare services were in a variety of hands, the basic essentials of law and order were very firmly and directly controlled by 'the Castle', which, by and large, was the centre of influence and patronage.[2] Moreover, the scale of the administration was so modest, Dublin so small and compact, and the senior officials so homogeneous and used to meeting one another at their clubs that, as McDowell recalls, George Wyndham, Chief Secretary from 1900 to 1905, found that the government of Ireland was 'conducted only by continuous conversation'.[3]

Even if Ireland qualified for paternal treatment, the local government system was in most respects the same as that evolved in Great Britain itself and was democratized by the same stages. The structure of authorities and the allocation of functions between the central and local governments were almost identical to the British. The basic local government services in Ireland, as in Great Britain, were roads, the environmental health services ('public health' and 'sanitary services', as they were called), and the relief of the poor, including the provision of medical services. But in Ireland, unlike Great Britain, a combination of paternalistic attitudes and a desire to ensure military security resulted in the police being nationalized and education largely so. Furthermore, in Ireland at the end of the nineteenth century, the development of agriculture and the resuscitation of the poorest rural areas were both central services, though administered by or with the advice of boards on which Irishmen sat rather than by standard

departments headed by civil servants answering directly to the Chief
Secretary or some other minister.

Although Ireland was something of a special case in regard to both
administrative structure and functions, the same could not be said of
the public service, at least from the time of the Civil Service reforms
of the third quarter of the nineteenth century onwards. The
development of a Civil Service divided into distinct classes common
to all departments, mostly appointed by a competitive examination set
on ordinary school or university subjects and advanced by bureaucratic
promotion procedures, occurred in both Ireland and Great Britain.
Since Irish educational standards were approximately the same as
British, Irishmen could and did join the Civil Service in large numbers
and served both in Ireland and in Great Britain. Nor were they barred
from the higher posts. True, it was a standing complaint that the
Treasury was niggardly in the number of 'first division' (that is, top
administrative cadre) posts they authorized for Irish departments, but
those that did exist, together with other senior posts, were likely to be
occupied by Irishmen. In an analysis of the forty-eight most senior
civil servants in 1914, McDowell points out that they were
'overwhelmingly Irish', only ten of them having come from across the
Channel. On the other hand, twenty-eight of them were Protestants and
twenty were Catholics, a manifestation of the favourable social and
economic position of the Protestant community and yet at the same
time evidence of the fact that it was far from a monopoly.[4]

It will readily be seen from all this that political independence for
Ireland did not precipitate the problems that later beset many of the
states of Asia and Africa as they emerged to independence. Not only
did there exist a range of public services more or less at British levels,
but the new state took over a complete apparatus of government, both
central and local, with its own public service, which had a sure source
of recruits from well-established secondary schools and universities. In
the formative period of these institutions, during the Union, they were
inevitably closely assimilated into the emerging British system and in
essentials were similar to the British pattern. Independence, though
important politically, did not much affect the well-established and
powerful departments such as those dealing with environmental
services, health, agriculture, and the collection of taxes. Much
administration continued to be conducted as previously. At
independence only the messy pattern of central authorities contrasted
sharply with the position in Great Britain, but the new government
saw to that at once.

II

In a notice dated 19 January 1922, the Provisional Government
announced that the business of the new state would for the moment be

carried on by nine departments, which would incorporate the various existing departments, boards, and other offices of the previous regime. 'It will be obvious', the notice stated, 'that under the altered circumstances certain of the [existing] departments . . . will no longer be required'. This presaged a drastic reduction of the jungle to uniformity, which was accomplished to a large extent by the Ministers and Secretaries Act, 1924, section 1 of which decreed that

There shall be established in Saorstát Éireann the several Departments of State specified and named in the eleven following sub-paragraphs, amongst which the administration and business of the public services in Saorstát Éireann shall be distributed as in the said sub-paragraphs . . . and each of which said Departments and the powers, duties and functions thereof shall be assigned to and administered by the Minister hereinafter named as head thereof.

All at once, it seemed, Irish administration was forced into a neat dichotomy. On the one hand was a central administration subdivided into ministerial departments. On the other was a system of local authorities subordinate and answerable to the Oireachtas through the Minister for Local Government and Public Health and other ministers, but administering their services under the direction and control of locally elected representatives. This was not to last for long, however. Within five years, the first of a collection of boards and commissions had emerged, the prolific growth of which has been a feature of native Irish government.

A Civil Service Commission to examine candidates for the service, insulated from direct ministerial control on the British pattern, was perhaps to be expected: the senior civil servants, themselves products of the British system, certainly thought so. In 1927, four 'state-sponsored bodies', as they later came to be called, were created. As T.J. Barrington pointed out, these four illustrate the 'diverse origins' of this type of public authority.[5] The assigning of the ownership and control of the generation of electricity to a public corporation, the Electricity Supply Board, was not at all strange, for it was universally agreed in the British Isles that, as the Minister for Industry and Commerce put it, 'the Civil Service was not recruited for the purpose of running business undertakings like this'.[6] The Agricultural Credit Corporation was set up to supply capital to farmers who could not get it from the banks. The Dairy Disposal Company was a rescue operation to save a number of creameries. The formation of the Medical Registration Council to control entry to the profession followed a well-established practice in the United Kingdom. These were the first of many such bodies set up to carry out an ever-widening range of activities embracing not only so-called public-enterprise undertakings but also increasingly diverse regulatory, social service, and developmental functions. The generic name 'state-sponsored bodies' gradually became common usage (although the earlier term, 'semi-state bodies', is still sometimes used), but there is

Valera took over. If there were tremors in the army at that time, they were very minor and there was no purge. Because of its composition and because of terrorist activity, members of the Garda Síochána in some areas had all too often found themselves combating subversives, and the 'Special Branch', the unit concerned with state security, was certainly pushed into the role of a political police by IRA activity. With de Valera's accession there were a few dismissals at the top and a few additions. The 'Special Branch' became 'a definite Fianna Fáil presence' in the Gardaí.[8] However, after a period of indecisiveness, the force settled down to serve the new government as efficiently as it had the old. The Rubicon had been crossed.

Thus, neither army nor police became independent forces outside the control of civil authorities or got involved in the struggle for political power. In the British tradition, their officers did not even conceive of themselves as having a right or duty, should the circumstances arise, to protect the state against the politicians. On the contrary, both accepted the legitimacy and were the servants of elected governments. The Garda Síochána, in contrast to its predecessor, the Royal Irish Constabulary, which had 'combined the functions of a rural gendarmerie, a civil police and – outside of the larger towns – a rudimentary civil service',[9] was an unarmed force whose role was very like that of the British police in Britain, though it was a unified national force. By the late 1930s, when the Fianna Fáil government had demonstrated that it was impartial in its administration of services and had shown that it, too, would not tolerate subversives (even former comrades), 'the lot of the Gardaí in rural areas became an infinitely more pleasant one'.[10] The role of the defence forces, apart from acting as a reserve force for internal security, was much less clear, for the state obviously could not go to war against its powerful neighbour and at the same time was protected against external third parties by the British military and naval shield.

Over the years, both forces tended to be ground down by Civil Service parsimony and ministerial indifference, which held up their acquisition of equipment and their ability to make use of new technology. The defence forces enjoyed some expansion during 'the Emergency' (the term used in Ireland to describe the period of the Second World War in which Ireland was neutral) and were rejuvenated by service in UN peacekeeping forces from the mid-1950s onwards. The role of the Garda Síochána from the mid-1940s was so placid and uneventful that few noticed how little the force was permitted to develop and keep abreast of modern police methods. The Northern Ireland troubles from the late 1960s, with their spill-over effects in the Republic and the eventual appearance in Ireland of signs of the urban industrial society syndrome of drugs, violence, and hostility to the forces of law and order, found the Gardaí less well equipped to handle the problems posed than they might have been. For half a century at least, however, there has been no doubt about the position of either force as servants of the elected government of the day, no matter who composes that government.

III

The administrative machinery of the new state did not have to be created: what existed was taken over by nationalist rebels, most of whom were by no means revolutionaries looking to effect great social and political reforms. In any case, they had other, more urgent problems on their minds, and they worked in a pragmatic, common-sense way to construct the machinery of government as quickly and economically as they could. Their senior Civil Service advisers, steeped in the British tradition, saw no need for changes in administrative structures or practices. They looked for and got much friendly cooperation and avuncular advice from the Treasury, the very centre of British bureaucratic traditions. The administrative system established by these busy young national leaders and their conservative Civil Service advisers was not systematically reviewed for almost half a century, and it is only in the last few years that it has begun to undergo considerable reform. Even so, it is still not very different in essentials from what it was in the twenties.

It is hard to discern what, if any, were the principles on which new functions as they were assumed were allocated among departments and between departments, local authorities, and state-sponsored bodies. Growth and change were handled in a decidedly pragmatic way, at least until the 1970s. Many apparent inconsistencies and discrepancies can be explained only by history, contemporary reasons of political or administrative convenience, and an *ad hoc* approach by ministers whose manner was as pragmatic as that of Irish administrators in the nineteenth century. Until the late 1950s at least, there seemed to be no need to review the administration systematically. A Commission of Enquiry into the Civil Service in the 1930s heard little or no complaint and found no major faults. Certainly senior Civil Servants, from whom any initiative for change would necessarily have had to come, saw no need to pay much if any attention to organization. Over a century ago, Walter Bagehot observed that public servants as a profession tended to see the organization as 'a grand and achieved result, not a working and changeable instrument'. So, too, in 1969, the Public Services Organization Review Group remarked that resistance to change is found in all organizations, and noted that proposals in the late 1950s to reform the Civil Service had been successfully resisted by senior officers in various departments. The Review Group warned: 'This could happen again but it must not';[11] but it did.

This is not to say that there were no changes or that general tendencies are not, in hindsight, discernible. It is true that the central administration grew only modestly, by the subdivision of existing departments for immediate political or administrative convenience when developments in health, welfare, and environmental services on the one hand, and in state planning and control of the economy on the other, seemed to call for it. The local government system, however, underwent purposeful change in the first twenty years of the regime. It was modified from the late-Victorian tiered system of authorities whose activities were conducted by committees of elected councillors to a system that was predominantly county (including county borough) government, administered bureaucratically and subject to strong central surveillance and control. Increasing pressure on local authorities because of the inexorable demand for expensive services and higher standards that many had not the resources (either funds or skills) to meet hastened this process, and led also to the removal of some services from local government. In particular, in 1980, most of the health services were hived off to health boards, single-purpose statutory bodies more akin in their legal status to state-sponsored bodies than local authorities.

Just as the traditional local government system was found wanting, so too, eventually, was the central administration, though there was little if any overt criticism of it until the late 1950s. Evidently, the two systems, central and local, which in mid-Victorian times were expected to be able to subsume virtually all public administration, could not cope with some of the activities and services being undertaken by the state in the middle of the twentieth century. The result was a proliferation of state-sponsored bodies, a far more supple and adaptable administrative form, to cope with an ever-growing variety of quasi-commercial, regulatory, social service, and developmental activities. Their creation was a haphazard business carried out with little systematic attention to the need to provide them with clear mandates or to spell out the exact extent of ministerial and parliamentary control.

Thus it is possible to see in the first half century of Irish administrative development both centralizing and decentralizing tendencies – the former in local government, the latter in the creation of state-sponsored bodies. However, from 1970, the propensity to centralize was without doubt the major feature of Irish public administration. There were two reasons for this: first, the exigencies of state planning and control of the economy, and, second, the influence of the report of the Public Services Organization Review Group, a major enquiry into public administration carried out between 1966 and 1969.

IV

The origins of the Public Services Organization Review Group lay in a growing volume of dissatisfaction expressed in the early 1960s about the structure of the administration and the quality of administrators, especially those at the centre. A serious economic recession in the late 1950s brought home the size of the gap that had opened up between Ireland and the rest of Western Europe and precipitated change. Following the publication in 1958 of *Economic Development* (a study of national development problems and opportunities) and the first five-year development programme, the 1960s in Ireland was a decade of unparalleled growth and rapid change. Events rapidly overtook an administration that was hardly adapted to cope with tasks now suddenly demanded of it. The assumption by the government of responsibility for developing and directing the economy necessitated efficient policy-making units in departments, and these were evidently lacking.

More was needed than a reform of the Civil Service, however. A planned economy necessitated coordinated action between the various public authorities involved, yet not only did some central departments operate without much regard for others, but some of the bigger and more powerful state-sponsored bodies pursued very independent policies. The National Industrial Economic Council in its *Report on Economic Planning* in 1965 said that one of the main obstacles to effective planning lay in the public sector itself:

The need for steps to ensure that all departments of the public service and state enterprises play their full part in implementing the programme is reinforced by the priority given to the attainment of economic growth in the second programme. The implication of this development and the need for a realignment of policies and administrative machinery may not be completely realized as yet in some parts of the public service and in all the state enterprises.[12]

The terms of reference of the Public Services Organisation Review Group were wide:

Having regard to the growing responsibilities of Government, to examine and report on the organization of the Departments of State at the higher levels, including the appropriate distribution of functions as between both Departments themselves and Departments and other bodies.

Although many of its recommendations were not implemented, the impact of the report and particularly the great stress it laid upon the concept of a single public service strongly controlled from the centre has, for better or worse, been considerable.

The Devlin Group, as it came to be called after its chairman, Liam St John Devlin, did not take long to diagnose two major faults in the administration – inadequate emphasis on policy-making, and lack of coordination within the public service as a whole. Among the many reforms proposed, three were fundamental. Firstly, in each department a policy-making 'Aireacht' comprising the minister and top civil servants was to be hived off from 'executive offices' administering the various services for which the department was responsible and controlled by 'directors'. The Aireacht would be the policy-making and review body for all executive units coming within the department's bailiwick, whether executive offices under their directors or 'executive agencies' (that is, the non-commercial state-sponsored bodies) under their boards, and for the commercial state-sponsored bodies, which 'must be effectively integrated in the public sector'.[13] Secondly, the executive offices, though still part of their parent departments, were to have considerable legal authority devolved upon them. Ministers would no longer have direct responsibility for all executive action (or inaction); that responsibility would fall upon the directors. Consequently, the range of parliamentary questions would be much attenuated, for ministers would be answerable to the Dáil for much less than previously. Thirdly, all executive bodies would be controlled in a general way by their responsible ministers by means of four 'coordinating systems' – finance, planning, organization, and personnel. At the departmental level, each Aireacht would include the heads of these 'staff' units. At the level of the central administration as a whole, the Department of Finance would have overall control of finance and planning, and a projected new department, the Department of the Public Service, would be responsible for organization and personnel. 'Through these functions, essential communications can be maintained throughout the public service and overall coordination of the service secured.'[14] Clearly the Irish public administration was to be a tighter ship altogether.

The recommendations of the Devlin Group were wholesale and thorough. Perhaps also they were doctrinaire. By the mid-1970s, intellectual doubts were being expressed by a senior officer of the Public Service Department itself: 'Some of the recommendations of the report . . . while having much managerial logic and combined wisdom as their basis, could perhaps be regarded as too technocratic and neat for their effective and immediate application to the democratic institutions and processes of our State.'[15] Many of them were not implemented and others only partially. A Department of the Public Service, which was intended to be, and in practice became, the engine of Devlinesque change and the heart of the organization and personnel functions, was set up in 1973 (but was absorbed in 1987 into the Department of Finance whence it had come). The Aireacht concept was introduced half-heartedly into a handful of departments in the 1970s but had little visible impact on their working practices or on the attitudes of the officers concerned. In any case, the concomitant creation of executive offices, which would have required changes in legislation to relieve ministers of responsibility and confer it upon the heads of the executive offices, was not carried out. The main impact of Devlin was in the increasing attention paid to recruitment, training, and executive development; in the introduction of modern management practices and techniques; and in the systematic introduction of staff support systems.

The failure to implement the core recommendations of the Devlin Group, despite the lip-service paid to them by successive governments, was due, however, not so much to intellectual doubts about the soundness of their theoretical foundations as to the lack of political will for reform and the resistance of public servants generally to the changes involved, particularly changes involving any loss of departmental autonomy. In the words of C. H. Murray, a former Secretary of the Department of Finance: 'the problem appears as one of how to engage the commitment of a government machine that is both the agent and the object of change'.[16] That was, indeed, and remains the problem. In 1975, the Public Service Advisory Council reported that there was little hope of the major Devlin reforms being implemented 'unless there is a clear lead from the top, from the individual ministers and the government'.[17] Despite further declarations of support for reform by ministers, that was not forthcoming for another decade. When it was, in the mid-eighties, the focus was narrower and the prescriptions somewhat less doctrinaire.

The Fine Gael–Labour coalition government of 1982–87 included in its ranks a number of reformers from both parties, not least the Taoiseach, FitzGerald, himself. Changes in parliamentary procedures and control of expenditure, to which we have already drawn attention (see pp. 202–204 above), were matched by a renewed effort at administrative reform under the aegis of John Boland, then Minister for the Public Service. Much heralded, the proposals were in the form of a 'White Paper', the traditional vehicle for outlining government policy and proposals for action. It looked back to the Public Services Organization Review Group report which, it said, provided 'an overall blue print for change', but it conceded that 'the pace of change in the public service has been regrettably slow'.[18] Now, however, in John Boland's words in his preface, 'for the first time' there was 'a clear expression of Government policy as to the way in which the public service will gear itself to meet the needs of our country in the years ahead'.[19] As in 1969, the major problem was diagnosed as:

no clear or satisfactory separation between the policy advisory functions and the day-to-day management of executive activities. As long as this remains so, there will not be sufficient emphasis either on the managerial concern with getting results, reducing costs and improving the service to the public or on the development of corporate planning and long term policy analysis.[20]

The major theme of the White Paper was the correction of this state of affairs:

at the centre of the Government's plans for tomorrow's public service is a management improvement programme which will involve the introduction in all departments of managerial systems based on corporate planning and emphasising personal responsibility for results, costs and service.[21]

Although the tone of the White Paper was not as dogmatic as the 1969 report and the word 'Aireacht' was not used, the proposals did include in slightly watered-down form the all-important legislation to permit the separation 'where suitable', of the distinct roles of advising on policy and managing operations.

In general, the reforms specified in the White Paper, some of which were already in train, have been pursued, although the enthusiasm that seemed to be generated at its publication was not translated into a sustained momentum at the level of action. Nevertheless, most senior and middle-ranking officers in the Civil Service in the early nineties recognized that the service was changing inexorably: many outside had not, however, taken that in. Much comment and criticism, on the one hand, failed to recognize that there are significant differences between 'managing' in the private sector and 'administering' in the public sector and, on the other, took too little account of the reforms that were in train.

Despite the reference to the Public Service in its title, the White Paper concentrated mostly on the Civil Service: 'The reason for this is that the civil service and, more particularly, the powers of ministers, are central to any process of change or development of the public service. . . . Future White Papers will announce further improvements in the management of the public service.[22] Significantly – characteristically, perhaps, when it comes to administrative reform – they did not appear.

Certainly, there was need for them. The *malaise* in local government that had led governments from time to time from the sixties onwards to suggest the need for, or to propose, reforms seemed to require a more radical approach than those governments and their advisers were prepared even to contemplate, let alone adopt, in the face of the certain political and local pressures that any proposals for change would evoke. It was not until the early nineties that there were signs of anything like radical change being contemplated.

In the state-sponsored body sector, there was growing scepticism and hostility among the top ranks in the commercial bodies from the early seventies over possible 'integration' as envisaged by the Devlin Committee. This was exacerbated by central government attempts to establish 'consistency' between their salaries and those of senior officers in the various branches of the public service by means of another Devlin Committee, the Review Body on Higher Remuneration in the Public Sector, and to control public service salary increases generally by placing them under the surveillance of the Department of the Public Service.

By 1980, attempts to integrate state-sponsored bodies, in particular the public enterprise group, were being strongly resisted and fiercely attacked. A study group with a prestigious membership, appointed by the National Economic and Social Council to examine measures to mobilize more fully enterprise in the public sector, noted that 'the concept of the unity of the public sector has begun to be interpreted more rigidly and narrowly than in the past. There is an increasing emphasis on centralised decision-making within the public sector and a tendency towards greater central control of the activities of state-sponsored bodies.' The group condemned this tendency: 'In our view these efforts to introduce uniformity throughout the whole of the public sector are seriously impeding enterprise in the state-sponsored bodies.' In the study group's opinion, 'changes are urgently required in some official attitudes within Government Departments towards state-sponsored bodies and how they operate. We are concerned about the danger of an inexorable growth of unnecessary administrative control'.[23] Asked to comment on the group's views, a number of government departments returned trenchant replies.[24] The debate was further complicated in the eighties by increasing demands that public-sector enterprises must make profits and stand on their own feet whatever the public service content of their activities, and by the fashionable call for privatization. All in all, the public sector was in an unsettled state in the early nineties, with serious differences of view at the top levels both in politics and public administration.

Notes

1   R. B. McDowell, *The Irish Administration, 1801–1914* (London, 1964), p. 27.
2   Dublin Castle was the centre of the Irish administration. The office of the Chief Secretary was there, and it was the headquarters of the police and of the administration of justice and security.
3   Quoted in McDowell, *The Irish Administration*, p. 31.
4   *Ibid.*, pp. 47–8.
5   T. J. Barrington, *The Irish Administrative System* (Dublin, 1980), p. 59.
6   *Dail Debates*, Vol. 18, col. 1907 (15 March 1927).
7   *Serving the Country Better: a White Paper on the Public Service* (Stationery Office, Dublin, 1985), para. 1.6.
8   C. Brady, *Guardians of the Peace* (Dublin, 1974), p. 197.
9   *Ibid.*, p. 2.
10   *Ibid.*, pp. 224–5.
11   *Report of the Public Services Organization Review Groups*, 1966–69.
12   National Industrial Economic Council, *Report on Economic Planning*, Report No. 8 (Dublin, 1965), p. 14.
13   *Report of the Public Services Organization Review Group, 1966–1969*, p. 163.
14   *Ibid.*, p. 145.
15   N. Whelan, 'Reform (or change) in the Irish public service, 1969–75', in *Administration*, 23 (1975), p. 110.
16   C. H. Murray, *The Civil Service Observed* (Dublin, 1990), p. 24.
17   Public Service Advisory Council, *Report for Year Ended 31 October 1975*, Report No. 2 (Dublin, 1976), p. 23.
18   *Serving the Country Better: a White Paper on the Public Service* (Stationery Office, Dublin, 1985), paras. 1.2 and 1.3.

19 *Ibid.*, p. vi.
20 *Ibid.*, para. 1.13
21 *Ibid.*, para. 1.14.
22 *Ibid.*, para. 1.7.
23 National Economic and Social Council, *Enterprise in the Public Sector*, Report No. 49 (Dublin, 1979), pp. 16–17 and 32.
24 See *ibid.*, pp. 47–67.

CHAPTER 13

The Central Administration and the Civil Service

I

The basic statute governing Irish public administration is the Ministers and Secretaries Act 1924. This act did two important things. Firstly, it provided the legal basis for the structure and organization of the central administration by designating the extent of ministerial authority in respect of the performance of public functions. Secondly, it established the departments of state and allocated public business between them. Subsequent amending acts and orders have made adjustments without seriously altering the fundamentals of the system then established.

The Irish Free State Constitution provided for cabinet government and required ministers to be responsible to Dail Éireann. The Ministers and Secretaries Act followed it up by making precise the nature and extent of that responsibility:

Each of the Ministers, heads of the respective Departments of State mentioned in Section I of this Act, shall be a coporation sole under his style or name aforesaid . . . and shall have perpetual succession and an official seal (which shall be officially and judicially noticed), and may sue and (subject to the fat of the Attorney General having been in each case first granted) be sued under his style or name aforesaid and may acquire, hold and dispose of land for the purposes of the functions, powers or duties of the Department of state of which he is the head or any branch thereof.

In essence, the minister *is* the department, and normally all the department's acts are reckoned to be his. In practice, of course, this is not possible and, although he is not empowered by statute to do so, he must delegate. The legal and political responsibility of the minister is, nevertheless, complete. 'The official knows that the minister will stand over his action *vis-à-vis* public and parliament if this action is in conformity with his general views. The Minister knows that the official in taking any action will always be conscious that the Minister may . . . be challenged.'[1] Both the manner in which public business is conducted and the whole character of the Civil Service are governed by the relationships implied in this act.

This concept of ministerial responsibility with the particular minister–civil servant relationships and the basic characteristics of the Civil Service that flow from it was not new to Ireland by an means. For the former British Civil Service, which was simply taken over, life went on much as before. *The Final Report of the Commission of Enquiry into the Civil Service, 1932–35* describes the impact on the service of the change to independence.

The passing of the State services into the control of a native Government, however revolutionary it may have been as a step in the political development of the nation, entailed, broadly speaking, no immediate disturbance of any fundamental kind in the daily work of the average Civil Servant. Under changed masters the same main tasks of administration continued to be performed by the same staffs on the same general lines of organization and procedure.[2]

Perhaps not everything was the same. According to Eunan O'Halpin: 'when examined in detail British bureaucracy in Ireland appears more politicised than has generally been acknowledged'. Paradoxically, 'Post-independent Ireland saw less of what commentators have termed a continuance of British apolitical values in the Irish civil service than their introduction.'[3]

The Civil Serviced had, in fact, already prepared for the change, for under the abortive Government of Ireland Act, 1920, provision had been made for dividing the personnel of the various Irish offices between Dublin and Belfast, the capital of the new Northern Ireland. In the event, men working in the South who had worried whether they would (or would not) be transferred to Belfast under that arrangement found that they could decide for themselves. Those few (a hundred or so) who wished to go north did so and joined the new Northern Ireland administration. Swiftly, something like an iron curtain came down between the two administrations, partly perhaps because many of the Northern Ireland senior officers were not Irish or had no Dublin connections, but also because at the political level the atmosphere was glacial. There had to be some contacts, of course, but they were mainly confined to technical matters and technical men for many years.

Under the treaty the future tenure and conditions of employment of the officers transferred to the service of the Irish Free State were protected, and generous provision was made for compensation in the event of retirement. It is no wonder, therefore, that the Treaty was welcomed with relief by most civil servants. The number who transferred to the service of the new state was about 21,000 out of a total of 28,000 who were then working in Ireland. Of these 21,000, fewer than 1,000 decided to retire prematurely under favourable conditions in the first few years. To what was thus virtually a complete service were added 131 people who had served in the Dáil administration service and 88 who had formerly been in the Civil

Service but who had resigned or been dismissed because of nationalist sympathies or activities. In addition, 64 officers holding posts in departments in Great Britain were invited to transfer and returned to Ireland in the next year or two.

Naturally, there were unrivalled opportunities for advancement, for each of the new departments had to be provided with a full headquarters organization and top management. In fact, the process was remarkably free from nepotism, and there was no great scramble for place, owing largely to the presence in the Department of Finance, which controlled personnel, of austere senior officers strongly imbued with British Civil Service traditions, among them officials lent to the new Irish government by its erstwhile foes. At the political level also, 'ministers wanted clean and economical administration, not jobs for the boys'.[4]

As analysis of the careers of the thirty-four secretaries and assistant secretaries of their equivalents in the new departments reveals that twenty-six of them were career civil servants, though a few of them suddenly found themselves considerably higher in the hierarchy than they could otherwise have expected to be. Among those who retired, there might well have been a few who were in effect forced to retire, but there was nothing in the nature of a purge. The smoothness of the operation and the overwhelming sense of continuity ked to the central administration's being carried over into a new regime to a great extent unaltered, in working order, and operating according to the strictest British standards. In O'Halpin's words:

The 'British' virtues now ascribed to our civil service were insisted on by key figures in administration in the early years of the state. . . . They were assisted in this by the fact that between 1920 and 1922 the British Treasury had taken a belated interest in the organisation and staffing of Irish departments. The result was that the new state came into being with a civil service which had just been reorganized along the most modern lines.[5]

The value of this legacy was immense.

II

The departments in which civil servants found themselves, though new creations, were in most cases composed of existing units transferred *en bloc* as going concerns. The Ministers and Secretaries Act finalized the *ad hoc* reduction and grouping made in 1922 of the forty-seven departments, boards, or other offices that existed before the Treaty, and created eleven departments including a Department of the President of the Executive Council (Prime Minister). The circumstances of the time precluded any comprehensive survey of the functions of the state and their allocation to administrative organizations, central or local, on some overall scheme based on administrative principles. Introducing the bill, W. T. Cosgrave, President of the Executive Council, told the Dáil: 'As the House well knows, there were during the British administration, quite a multiplicity of Boards and statutory bodies, and during the last two years it has not been possible to survey the whole field and to see how better we may construct the Government machine.[6] With few exceptions, the existing offices as they stood were accepted and were combined into common-sense groupings. To a large extent, the offices of the previous administration fell into natural enough groups by reason of either proximity of purpose or historical connections. In addition, two departments, Finance and External Affairs, had to be created, for under the Union there had been no call for them.

The allocation of functions made in 1924 was not systematically reviewed under the Devlin Group's enquiry in the late 1960s. Over the years, a few new departments were created, and a few transfers of divisions from one department to another were made. In most cases, the creation of new departments resulted from the increase in state functions: firstly, the growth of the social services after the Second World War; secondly, the assumption by the state of responsibility for the planning, development, and control of the economy. (See Table 13.1) The Devlin Group's proposal to reallocate government functions to fourteen departments (there were sixteen at the time) was not followed. The Public Service Advisory Council was right in remarking in its 1979 report that in the matter of distribution of functions to ministers, Ireland is no different from other countries: 'functional logic is not the major determining factor'. Rather, apart from some basic functional requirements, changes of this sort depend 'on political considerations and on the management style of the Prime Minister'.[7]

The assumption of new duties and the creation of new departments as state services expanded inevitably brought an increase in the number of civil servants. In 1980, the size of the Civil Service, (60,500 approximately) was nearly three times what it had been at the inception of the state. During the eighties the giant Department of Posts and Telegraphs and the Forestry Service of the Department of Energy were converted into state-sponsored bodies – An Post (1984); Bord Telecome Éireann (1984), Coillte Teo (the Irish Forestry Board, 1989). If we omit their staffs from our calculations, the Civil Service in 1990 at just over 28,000 was some 6,000 less than it had been at its peak in 1983, the result of vigorous retrenchment from the middle eighties onwards.

The ever-increasing need to coordinate and control an expanding range of functions led not only to the addition of new departments and new divisions in existing departments, but also, and notably, to a big increase in the numbers in the top ranks of the service (secretaries, assistant secretaries and their equivalents). They have quadrupled in the seventy years since the foundation of the state.

Table 13.1 **Major government deparmtents in 1922 and 1991**

1922	1991
Department of – President of the Executive Council	**Deparmtent of** – Taoiseach
– Finance	– Finance
(a) Office of the Revenue Commissioners[1]	(a) Office of the Revenue Commissioners[1]
(b) Office of Public Works[2]	(b) Office of Public Works[2]
– Foreign Affairs (renamed External Affairs, Sept. 1992)	– Foreign Affairs
– Home Affairs (renamed Justice, 1924)	– Justice
– Defence	– Defence
– Local Governemnt (renamed Local Government and Public Health, 1924)	– Environment
	– Health
	– Social Welfare
– Economic Affairs ⎱ became Department of – Trade ⎰ Industry and Commerce, – Labour ⎰ Sept. 1922	– Industry and Commerce – Tourism and Transport – Communciations – Labour – Energy
– Education	– Education
– Agriculture (renamed Lands and Agriculture, 1924)	– Agriculture and Food
	– Marine
– General Post Office (renamed Posts and Telgraphs, 1924)	See note [3]
	– Gaeltacht

Notes: [1] The Revenue Commissioners operate under the general aegis of the Minister for Finance.
[2] The Minister of State at the Department of Finance (before 1977 called the Parliamentary Secretary) acts as a Minister for Public Works.
[3] In 1984, two new state-sponsored bodies (An Post and Bord Telcom Éireann) were established to carry out the postal and telcommunications functions of the Department of Posts and Telegraphs, and the department was wound up.

III

The service that emerged in the 1920s was a British-type Civil Service in miniature, and in many respects it remains so. This continuity over seventy years is clearly to be seen in the structure of the service.

At the top of each department there is a 'Secretary', the Civil

Service head of the department, who 'is answerable to the Minister for every official action of every officer of his department'.[8] He is the minister's chief adviser and, as the Devlin Report delicately put it, 'the apex of the machine through which policy questions are formulated for ministerial consideration'.[9] (As we observed in our analysis of policy-making, the influence of senior civil servants is often likely to be greater than that statement suggests.) The Secretary is also 'responsible for the overall management of the Department'.[10] The Secretary's immediate subordinates are deputy secretaries and assistant secretaries, and below them are principal officers and assistant principals.

These top managers are at the head of what, following British terminology, are known as the general service classes, who are 'recruited to perform the general duties of Departments from the routine clerical operations to the highest policy advisory and managerial work'.[11] They are recruited at appropriate education levels into what is for most of them a life-time career in one or another of the 'classes' – clerical assistant, clerical, executive, and administrative. Figure 13.1 shows the strong resemblance of the Irish structure to that of the British just after the First World War (and for long after).

This class system had its origins in Victorian Britain. In theory, and originally to a great extent in practice also, each class performed work suited to the ability of the people in it; each was recruited directly from school or university; and once in a class an officer progressed up through that class. In Ireland, as in the United Kingdom, the concept of a class system was progressively modified. The Devlin Group reported that

There are still promotion groupings related to class and movement from one group to another involves either a competition conducted by the Civil Service Commissioners or acceptance by the Commissioners that the person concerned is qualified for appointment to the new position. However, in the general service, movement from the clerical to the executive class is now relatively unimpeded and all higher administrative posts are open to members of the Executive grades.[12]

Thus 'it is still possible to speak of the general service classes but, in practice, they are merging into a single class'.[13] More recently, the age limits for entry into the service, which were related to the ages at which people normally left school or university, have been drastically widened to fifty years. This change follows from a government commitment made in the *Programme for Economic and Social Progress:* 'In the context of changing work patterns, the provision of job opportunities for the long-term unemployed, and the desirability of promoting equal access to employment, the Government commit themselves to a policy of substantially raising recruitment age limits throughout the public service.'[14]

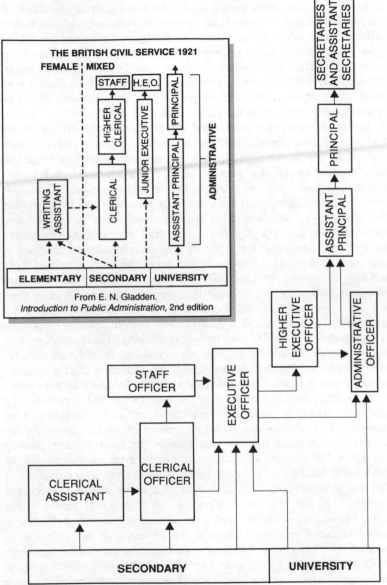

THE BRITISH CIVIL SERVICE 1921
FEMALE | MIXED

From E. N. Gladden.
Introduction to Public Administration, 2nd edition

Normal upper age limit: 50; normal lower age limit: 18.

Candidates for entry as Clerical Assistant or Clerical Officer do not require any specific educational qualification.

Candidates for entry as Executive Officer require a specified minimum standard in the the leaving Certificate or equivalent

Candidates for entry as Administrative Officer require and honours degree or equivalent

Figure 13.1 Structure of the Civil Service in Ireland, general service grades, 1990

It will be seen from Figure 13.1 that the higher posts, those of Assistant Principal and above, are appointed both from administrative officers (who might in turn have come from the executive officer grade) and from higher executive officers, who are the best of the executive officers, promoted after a few years in the grade. Administrative officers and higher executive officers thus form a pool from which higher officers are selected, and they perform the same type of duties, being interchangeable with each other.

In departments with specialized duties such as the Office of the Revenue Commissioners, there are departmental classes, each in turn with many grades. In general, these classes and grades are related to one or another of the general service classes and grades, and promotion from them by competition into the general service is possible. Thus, there exists the possibility for almost all of promotion from grade to grade and class to class, and there is considerable movement of this sort. By 1980, over half of the 2,000 Executive Officers had come into the grade by way of competitions confined to serving civil servants. Likewise, at the top of the service, half of those holding the posts of Secretary, Deputy Secretary, or Assistant Secretary had advanced through the executive grades. Finally, there are other specialist officers recruited to do jobs for which particular professional or technical qualifications are required. These are 'professional', 'scientific', or 'technical' officers. Their numbers, too, doubled in the decade up to 1980. (It is difficult to make meaningful comparisons for the eighties because of the distorting effects of crude retrenchment policies. Overall numbers were reduced by 17 per cent.)

Surveying the Civil Service in the late 1960s, the Devlin Group obviously found its structure complicated and even confusing. One member, T. J. Barrington, had long before dubbed it an 'elaborate contrivance', arguing that 'the variation in the level of work passing through a Government department is not as great as the number of grades that handle it. Thus each grade tends to overlap the other . . . and indefensible lines of demarcation tend to be drawn between the grades.'[15] At the time, there were no less than 1,000 grades in the Civil Service as a whole, and even the comparatively few people above Higher Executive Officer or its professional equivalent were divided into 300 grades. Moreover, although the general classes were in theory available to serve in any department, there was not much mobility at higher levels and each department had tended to be a self-contained unit with most promotions made internally.

Because of this and because of the comparative lack of coordination, notwithstanding financial and personnel controls operated by the Department of Finance and later by its offshoot, the Department of the Public Service, the Devlin Group's 'first impressions of the civil service tended towards the view that there is not one civil service but sixteen, that each department has its own service'. The Group commented on the difficulties in this situation of getting a free flow of talent to where it was most needed. This was made the more difficult by the protective policies of the service unions. 'Barriers between organisations tend to impede the flow of the best talent to where it is most needed. . . . In the civil service, interdepartmental barriers are often as hard to surmount as the barriers between other bodies in the public service.'[16]

Following recommendations by the Devlin Group, the efforts of the Department of the Public Service to institute schemes of service-wide promotion, each of which involved negotiations with the staff associations, gradually facilitated movement between departments. It was, though, a long, hard slog. At what might be termed 'management' levels, the position had, however, altered radically by 1985. Half of the vacancies at Higher Executive Officer level were being filled by interdepartmental competition: likewise at Assistant Principal level, where up to that date four-fifths had been filled internally. At Principal level, where even in the early eighties almost all appointments were made within the department, all new posts and one-third of vacancies were filled by interdepartmental competition.

It was at the very top, however, that the most significant changes were made. At Secretary, Assistant Secretary, and equivalent levels, where hitherto virtually all posts were filled from within the department concerned, appointments were now being made on the recommendation of a 'Top Level Appointments Committee' set up in 1984 and comprising the Secretary to the Government, the Secretary (Public Service Management and Development) in the Department of Finance, two serving departmental Secretaries, the Chairman of the Public Service Advisory Council and, for each appointment at Secretary level, the outgoing Secretary of a department for his successor. All staff at Principal level and upwards are eligible to apply for any post.

The effects of this change have been considerable and even upsetting within departments where expectations have been dashed – so upsetting, in fact, that the procedure for appointing Secretaries was modified in 1987 to provide that the names of three people not ranked in order of merit go to the government which makes the appointment, thus giving the outgoing Secretary and his minister the major say if they want it. C. H. Murray, a former Secretary of the Department of Finance, summed up the impact of this major reform of senior appointments by saying: 'If it is competition that makes Sammy run, the civil service pace has undoubtedly quickened . . . in this respect at least we are abreast of the best practice elsewhere.'[17]

IV

Although the Civil Service retained many of the structural features that it inherited, it was not to be expected that so Irish an organization would remain unaltered in character and *mores* for long. Some basic characteristics were, it is true, retained. Given the great continuity and the acceptance by politicians and public servants alike of the British cabinet system and the minister – civil servant relationships that went with it, and given also the comparatively high level of morality in public affairs in the British Isles, it was only natural that the Civil Service should remain an incorruptible, non-partisan, and usually anonymous corps whose members, secure in their employment, considered themselves the servants of the legitimate government, whoever they might be. It was also natural that they should tend to conservative austerity with regard to the functions of the state and to their role in public business.

This was, in Barrington's words, 'a formidable asset for the state', but, as he pointed out:

certain weaknesses were also inherited, particularly the lack of overall concern for the performance of the system as a whole, as distinct from the day-to-day operation. One of the maxims of the British civil service was 'clear sight over short distances'. This became very much the mark of the Irish civil service. Coupled with this was the tradition, reinforced by the bent of the Irish temperament, of being suspicious of any thinking that claimed to be systematic and concerned with the long-term.

Writing in 1980, after a decade of reform, Barrington maintained that 'these still remain, overall, significant criticisms that can be made of our civil service'.[18]

Although the Irish temperament in this instance underpinned and perpetuated some characteristics of the service inherited from the United Kingdom, in respect of others, it tended to modify the inheritance. Despite the fact that Ireland was to some extent assimilated to Great Britain culturally and enjoyed comparable types and levels of education, the social structure was always different and became more so after the Treaty. It was to be expected that Irish institutions would increasingly reflect Irish rather than British conditions.

To begin with, the British Civil Service, like many European services, had a distinctively upper-class tradition in its higher ranks, and its social tone in the early twentieth century was still rather superior. The tone of the service, especially its gentlemanly 'generalist' tradition, was set by this group and continued to be so until well after the Second World War. Although Irish higher civil servants in Ireland before the Treaty were by no means so uniform in origin and training, they too could be said to be part of a local 'establishment'. This situation could hardly continue in the new Ireland.

Although the independence movement had been inspired and led largely by middle-class people, they were on the whole not people aspiring to higher social psosition, and they led a movement that cut across the class lines of the lower strata of society. The character of the newly independent community reflected this. It was bourgeois and replubican, and although the class lines that developed later are hard to trace, it is clear enough at least that there was no aristocracy and no 'establishment'. This was bound to be reflected in the Civil Service, which soon became peopled at the top levels by officers who, although middle-class, were often lower- rather than upper-middle-class and by no means out of the same mould as their equivalents in the British service. One of the most obvious results of this was that senior officers had (and continue to have) an understanding of, and affinity with, the *administrés*, which comes from close association and personal knowledge. Thus, one of the necessary changes in the character of the bureaucracy to make it suitable for a modern democratic state was quickly and easily effected.

Because university graduates entered the service in only small numbers and because of the arrangement by which top jobs were (and are) open to Higher Executive Officers, the higher Civil Service became increasingly composed of people who had entered the service directly from secondary school. Since secondary education was not free before 1976 and since many country people were not close enough to a school for their children to attend daily, the children of the poorest, especially the poorest country people, tended to have a Civil Service career barred to them. With this important exception, many children of all social classes attended schools run by religious orders, which provided the bulk of Irish secondary education remarkably cheaply, and it is from these that most of the recruits to the service came. Some were the sons of salaried people or of farmers of some substance, albeit far from rich. At the poorer end of the scale, however, were many whose parents could hardly afford even the small expense of sending their children to these very cheap schools. Despite the fact that the situation changed somewhat in the seventies, the service was still heavily peopled with the products of the earlier situation.

It was this Civil Service which was the subject of critical comment by the reformers from the early sixties on and for which the Devlin Group proposed considerable reforms. The reformers were for long a small minority. The majority, on account of their schooling and their socialization within the service, tended to accept 'the system' with little question, though in this they surely did not differ from civil servants almost everywhere. Also, they tended to share with the public servants of many, perhaps most, countries the belief that the outsider probably had little to contribute. Men of this sort were admirable at 'running the machine' and administering the comparatively modest public services that were the feature of the first half of the state's existence, but some thought that they did not measure up to the demands that subsequently were, all of a sudden, made upon them.

Paradoxically, the publication of *Economic Development* in 1958 and the inauguration of the first programme of economic development owed much to the initiative of a handful of civil servants and were the outcome of a fruitful partnership between a few ministers, a few civil servants, and one or two professional economists. However, they did not mark or evoke a change in the attitudes of many higher civil servants, who saw no need for reform, particularly if the Department of Finance was behind it. Consequently, the higher Civil Service was soon being identified as an obstacle to development by the tiny but increasing number of politicians and administrators who were promoting it.

V

In 1961, the Taoiseach, Seàn Lemass, who was by then urging departments to see themselves as 'development corporations', voiced his doubts about the ability of the Civil Service to act in that capacity:

I think it is true to say that in some government departments there is still a tendency to wait for new ideas to walk through the door. It is perhaps the normal attitude of an administrative department of government to be passive rather than active, to await proposals from outside, to react mainly to criticism or to pressure of public demand, to avoid the risks of experimentation and innovation and to confine themselves to vetting and improving proposals brought to them by private interests and individuals rather than to generate new ideas themselves.[19]

Lemass said frankly that doubts about the suitability of the Civil Service to do development and promotional work had led to the widespread use of the state-sponsored body type of organization. He urged the need for departments to think in terms of new opportunities and to provide leadership. The Permanent Secretary of the Department of Finance, who had been the chief inspiration and author of *Economic Development*, echoed him: 'What is needed is a more lively and general appreciation by the Civil Service of the part it can and should play in promoting national development.'[20]

Following Lemass, a small but growing number of senior officers and some politicians began to recognize the need for a thorough reappraisal. That reappraisal was conducted by the Public Service Organization Review Group (the Devlin Group), to which reference has already been made. That Group provided a blueprint for change and, although the basic structural reforms which they proposed were not fully implemented – as much because of lack of political will as of administrative hostility – much of what they proposed became in effect a programme for implementation as and when practicable. It was a formidable programme, covering recruitment, education, training, staff development, mobility, the introduction of modern management techniques, the development of management services and operations research, the exploitation of the computer, and mechanisms for reviewing cost-effectiveness. The public service in general and the Civil Service in particular were to be thoroughly modernized in accordance with modern management theory and precepts.

The period of reform ushered in by Devlin has continued ever since, though often agonizingly slowly. In the middle eighties, the reforming zeal of a few ministers in the Fine Gael–Labour coalitition government gave a boost to the process. A strong White Paper, *Serving the Country Better*, with its forthright declaration of intent, seemed to presage major changes along the lines advocated by the Devlin Group, which it declared frankly still 'provided an overall blueprint for change'.[21]

By this time, too, a marked generational change had occurred in the top ranks of the Civil Service. Although the generation of those whose experience stretched back to the early days of the state was replaced by men only a little if at all elss conservative, *their* successors tended increasingly to be more open to change. The Civil Service was also more outward-looking, more willing to engage expert advice and hire consultants, and to contemplate their prescriptions. Ireland's accession to the European Communities widened horizons and made demands to which the service rose. Face-to-face with Brussels the service could stand comparison.

The major theme of *Serving the Country Better* was the need to install 'management systems based on personal responsibility for results and value for money'.[22] This very much reflected the fashion of the day in Western Europe and particularly Great Britain that stressed the need to evoke personal initiative and to reward it. In the context of economic recession and increasing public and political demands for public expenditure cuts, this inevitably meant that staff numbers, performance indicators, and financial results would be the measuring rods. Changes that could be linked with savings were on, others were not. According to an OECD survey in 1990: 'The approach to public management improvement in Ireland continues to give priority to the policy of reduction of public expenditure'.[23]

Many commentators think that the 1985 White Paper was not followed up. '[It] seems to have been an exercise in deliberation followed by inaction.'[24] Where political iniatives and sensitive political decisions were concerned this is true. For eample, the legislation promised to make possible the most far-reaching reform, involving some ministers divesting themselves of their powers and responsibilities for the administration of services, never materialized. However, where the Civil Service – that is, the Department of Finance – could get on with the job itself (no doubt with ministerial approval of course), there has been progress.

Perhaps the most significant change involving a considerable department from traditional Civil Service procedures has been the introduction of delegated 'administrative budgets'. Administrative (that is, non-programme) expenditure comprises such items as pay, travel and subsistence, training, consultancy, information technology and communications, and cost of office premises; it does not include 'programme' expenditure, such as social welfare benefits and government grants.[25] In 1991, administrative costs were estimated to comprise 10 per cent of total departmental expenditure, and 70 per cent of this amount was represented by salaries. Administrative budgets are agreed for a three-year period and, because of the climate of opinion about the need to reduce public expenditure, those made in 1991 incorporated an annual reduction of 2 per cent in real terms. Departments have freedom to switch resources between items, to carry over unspent funds from one year to another, and to create and fill posts up to middle-management level.

For this system to work a number of the administration's sacred cows will have to be slaughtered. The arrangement involves a considerable loosening of the traditional detailed control by finance and personnel divisions, both in the Department of Finance and in individual departments. Hitherto, senior officers in the Civil Service were not real 'managers' as that term is conventionally understood, for they did not dispose of their funds or their staffs as they saw fit. Now, within the limits of what is subsumed in the administrative budget, to a considerable extent, they do. If this system operates as intended and, for example, hard-pressed governments looking for savings do not mop up end-of-year surpluses and the Department of Finance can adapt itself to genuine system monitoring rather than maintaining a controlling role, it 'will profoundly affect the way the civil service is managed. . . . Administrative budgets constitute one of the most important initiatives taken in the Irish civil service'.[26]

Other reforms mention in *Serving the Country Better* on which action was being taken in the late eighties and early nineties included the following:

1   Performance pay for senior managers – a salary range replaced automatic movement up a salary scale. Successful performers can progress from bottom to top in three annual jumps; the average performer will take six years and the weak performer nine. This is clearly the corollary of responsible management.
2   The institution of an Efficiency Audit Group with outside, including trade-union, representation – it examines the working and practices of departments.
3   The bringing together of the increasing number of information technology specialists in the Department of Finance into a single Central Information Technology Services unit 'to ensure best use of skilled staff, closer alignment between the planning and development processes and a more coordinated, better targeted response to the needs of individual ministers'.[27] A communications network has been developed. An intra- and interdepartmental data network was put in place and a country-wide Government Tele-

communcations Network was being developed from 1988. The outward and visible signs of all this are immediately evident on the desks of all senior staff, and most others also.

4   A review of all statutory and information requirements of all government departments and agencies which affect business and industry was instituted in 1988. Together with the assessment of 'compliance costs', it comprises a considerable agenda for an 'Industrual Costs Monitoring Group composed of senior officials that started work in the middle eighties'.[28]

Equally – perhaps more – important is the development of a deliberate managerial *esprit de corps* by the creation of a network at Assistant Secretary and Principal levels involving contacts, exchange of information, and regular conferences, including residential conferences.

Such changes, which have come about largely at the instigation of senior civil servants themselves, were summed up by the Department of Finance thus: 'The initiatives being taken . . . will, it is expected, result in a sharper management style which will be more flexible and innovative in tackling new tasks and providing higher quality service to the client/taxpayer.'[29] There is still a way to go – for example, in the position and prospects for women in the service, a resource that has yet to be fully exploited. A programme for women in middle management has been running since 1984 but, as Table 13.2 suggests, women are much underrepresented in the higher ranks. As a woman civil servant suggested in 1991: 'the responsibility to recognize and promote policies in line with women's long-term work potential devolves upon the state as one of the foremost recruitment agencies in the country'.[30]

Table 13.2 **Percentage of male–femal in general service grades of the Irish Civil Service, 31 December 1989**

Grade	M	F	Grade	M	F
Secretary	100	0	Higher Executive Officer	72	28
Deputy Secretary	100	0	Executive Officer	57	43
Assistant Secretary	97	3	Staff Officer	40	60
Principal Secretary	92	2	Clerical Officer	32	68
Assistant Principal Officer	79	21	Clerical Assistant	16	84

Source: Eager in *Seirbhís Phoibli* 12(1) (1991), p. 19.

Important as the reforms outlined above, and great as the changes in climate which they have induced, undoubtedly are, really radical restructuring of the administration depends upon the willingness of political leaders to alter their own power and responsibilities along the lines suggested by the Devlin Group. Their aireacht – executive concept involved the separation of policy-making and development from the implementation of policy, a concept repeated in the 1985 White Paper. The role of the minister and his relationship with parliament as envisaged in the Westminster–Whitehall model are, however, basic to the whole structure of government which independent Ireland adopted and, experience suggests, will not easily be modified. In the words of John Dowling of the Association of Higher Civil Servants: 'it has become part of the political culture as it affects the civil service that not only are ministers burdened with the minutiae of the departmental business but that they refuse to shovel it away'.[31]

In *Serving the Country Better*, the government proposed that where departments had a sufficiently large volume of purely executive work, ministers would by law be able to transfer such work to separate 'executive officers' who would have full responsibility for carrying it out. Consequently, the work transferred would not be the responsibility of ministers, and they 'will not be answerable to the Dáil for the day-to-day oprations of the office'.[32] To satisfy the requirements of the Dáil in respect of accountability, 'the Government will propose to the Dáil the establishment of a new Committee of Public Management with the remit of examining and reporting on the adequacy of the system used to ensure the efficient management of departments'.[33]

So far, most ministers in all governments have been unwilling to give up their powers and responsibilities. No doubt, as John Dowling observed: 'Irish politicians, and ministers in particular, must be always conscious of constituency needs and demands and . . . even ministers who ignore their constituency demands are putting their seats in peril.'[34] The increasing numbers of civil servants in their private offices dealing in 'minutiae of departmental business' on their behalf and that of their Dáil colleagues is evidence enough of that, and no doubt this consideration is uppermost in their minds.

There is, however, another consideration. To judge by the experience of Oireachtas committees of inquiry up to the present, it would be optimistic in the extreme to suppose that a Committee of Public Management, or any committee in present circumstances, would satisfy legitimate parliamentary requirements in a devolved system. This doubt was well summed up by Eunan O'Halpin:

There is . . . a chance that structural and legislative changes could undermine the doctrine of ministerial responsibility, the central organising principle of the service. This doctrine has been much criticised, but the alternatives canvassed in the name of effectiveness do not appear properly to address the problem of whether political and ultimately popular control of bureaucracy can be sustained or enhanced by freeing ministers from formal responsibility for much of what the civil service does or fails to do.[35]

Perhaps, then, attempting to turn senior civil servants into full-blooded managers of the private enterprise variety is not after all the desirable reform that many think it is, but, rather, a dangerous delusion.

Notes

1   *Report of the Public Services Organization Review Group, 1966–1969* (Dublin, 1969), p. 61 (hereafter cited as the Devlin Report).
2   *Report of the Commission of Enquiry into the Civil Service, 1932–35* (Dublin, 1935), para. 8.
3   E. O'Halpin, 'The Civil Service and the political system', in *Administration*, 38 (1991), p. 284 and 287.
4   *Ibid.*, p. 288.
5   *Ibid.*, pp. 287–8.
6   *Dáil Debates*, Vol. 5, cols 917–18 (16 Nov. 1923).
7   Public Service Advisory Council, *Report for Year Ended 31 October 1979*, Report No. 6 (Dublin, 1980), p. 13.
8   Devlin Report, p. 63.
9   *Ibid.*
10   *Ibid.*
11   *Ibid.*, p. 65.
12   *Ibid.*
13   *Ibid.*
14   *Programme for Economic and Social Progress* (Dublin, 1991), p. 96.
15   T. J. Barrington, 'Elaborate contrivance', in *Administration*, 3 (1955), p. 97.
16   Devlin Report, p. 52.
17   C. H. Murray, *The Civil Service Observed* (Dublin, 1990), pp. 115 and 116.
18   T. J. Barrington, *The Irish Administrative System* (Dublin, 1980), p. 31.
19   S. Lemass, 'The organization behind the economic programme', in *Administration*, 9 (1961), p. 5.
20   T. K. Whitaker, 'The Civil Service and development', in *Administration*, 9 (1961), p. 84.
21   *Serving the Country Better, a White Paper on the Public Service* (Stationery Office, Dublin, 1985), para. 1.3.
22   *Ibid.*, para. 2.5.
23   *Public Management Development Survey*, OECD (Paris, 1990), p. 63.
24   E. O'Halpin, in *Administration*, 38 (1991), p. 299.
25   See P. J. Moore, 'Administrative budgets, a new era for Civil Service managers,' in *Seirbhís Phoibli*, 12 (1991), pp. 24–8.
26   *Ibid.*, p. 28.
27   Information supplied by the Department of Finance.
28   *Public Management Development Survey*, OECD (Paris, 1990), p. 65, and information supplied by the Department of Industry and Commerce.
29   Information supplied by the Department of Finance.

30   C. Eager, in *Seirbhís Phoibli*, 12 (1991), p. 22.
31   J. Dowling, in *Administration*, 34 (1986), p. 293.
32   *Serving the Country Better*, para. 3.10.
33   *Ibid.*, para. 3.6.
34   J. Dowling, in *Administration*, 34 (1986), p. 293.
35   E. O'Halpin, in *Administration, 38 (1991)*, pp. 299–300.

CHAPTER 14

State-Sponsored Bodies

I

The considerable variety of administrative bodies that was a feature of Irish government before independence was only temporarily reduced to near uniformity when the new state took over. Within a few years, new public authorities in forms other than that of a ministerial department or local authority began to be set up. Since then, with the great growth in the range and volume of state activity, the number and variety of such bodies have increased considerably. They now surround the central administration like satellites, each one to a greater or lesser degree under the surveillance or control of a department. A general term has been coined to refer to most of them, though its connotation is far from precise. They are generally known as 'state-sponsored bodies', a term that has to a large extent superseded 'semi-state bodies', which was once much used.

There seems to be no legal or other authoritative definition of 'state-sponsored body'. In 1976, the Minister for the Public Service told the Dáil that

it is not possible to give a precise definition of the term 'state-sponsored body'. Generally, the term may be taken to include bodies established by or under statute and financed wholly or partly by means of grants or loans made by a Minister of State or the issue of shares taken up by a Minister.[1]

He was quoting from the Ministers and Secretaries (Amendment) Act, 1973, in which, it seems, the first attempt was made to define the term legally, although the term itself is not used in the act. However, he omitted to add the words 'as stand designated for the time being by regulations made by the Minister', which are also in the definition in section 1 of that act.[2]

Inspection of those bodies which are generally reckoned to be state-sponsored bodies suggests the following as a 'good enough' check list of the defining characteristics of these public authorities: they are endowed with duties and powers by statute or by ministerial authority; their staffs are not civil servants (though they are in the public sector); they are financed wholly or in part from public funds; the government or individual ministers appoint some or all of the members of their governing boards or councils; ministers have some measure of authority, both formal and otherwise, over them.

The legal form of many state-sponsored bodies is that of a statutory corporation or of a public or private company incorporated under the Companies Acts with a minister or ministers holding some or all of the shares. Some, however, are 'statutory companies'; others are set up as corporate bodies under general enabling acts; still others are unincorporated. Some state-sponsored bodies are not even wholly publicly owned but are mixed public and private enterprise: one, the Foyle Fisheries Commission, is a 'cross-border' authority set up by statutes of both the Irish and the United Kingdom parliaments.

Each state-sponsored body has a sponsor minister who is ultimately responsible for it. Thus, the overall picture is, as the Devlin Group saw it, of

a central core of departments with their associated fringe of agencies reporting to those departments with which they are functionally connected. . . . In essence, each state-sponsored body . . . consists of a Board with a Chairman reporting to the Minister and an executive and/or operational staff under a chief executive with a more or less informal reporting relationship to the Department.[3]

This type of organization has been used for a wide variety of purposes, including the regulation of certain economic and social activities; the provision of certain social services; the operation of a number of infrastructure industries and a wide range of other enterprises producing goods and services for sale; the provision of finance; and the provision of marketing, promotional, and research and development services. There is no definitive list of state-sponsored bodies, and lists drawn up by authoritative bodies such as the Department of Finance and the Review Body on Higher Remuneration in the Public Sector (in their Report No. 30, 1987) do not tally. The list in Appendix 2 (pp. 324–25) might well omit the names of bodies that are recognized as state-sponsored bodies in some quarters and include others that are not. It numbers ninety-six bodies, a few of which in turn have spawned subsidiary organizations. In 1990, their staffs numbered 79,000 and comprised almost 30 per cent of total public-sector employment.

Clearly, state-sponsored bodies do not constitute a neat or even coherent group of public authorities. On the contrary, a thoroughgoing pragmatism uninfluenced by socialist doctrine or administrative theory was the main feature of their growth and development in Ireland. A general acceptance of the proposition that ministerial departments are suitable for the direct administration of only a comparatively narrow range of state activities was the starting point of a search for the most practicable form of organization when a new problem arose, a new opportunity presented itself, or the need for a new state initiative was realized. However, the search was never a long one and never systematic. Governments and ministers adopted practical solutions *ad hoc*, sometimes paying scant regard to the need on constitutional grounds to provide clear and comprehensive legal instruments or adequate parliamentary control. Individual departments even developed their own particular practices and 'house style' in the forms they adopted and the relationships they prescribed.

The situation is the more complicated and confusing because both inside and outside the central administration's penumbra of state-sponsored bodies are organizations of many kinds. They range from bodies that are to all intents and purposes departments, though they do not have ministerial heads, such as the Civil Service Commission and the Office of the Revenue Commissioners, to bodies like the Economic and Social Research Institute and the Institute of Public Administration, which, though they were not set up by the state, carry out functions in which the state has an interest and for which it pays. These and bodies like them, including the universities, are on the outer edge of the public sector and are being inexorably sucked into it. On the outer edge also are subsidiaries of state-sponsored bodies and private-sector companies in which the state has financial interests, or a so-called 'golden share' – that is, a share which gives its holder power to prevent the board doing certain things, as, for example, selling out to a foreign buyer.

The essential feature of state-sponsored bodies, it might be thought, is that they have some degree of legal and operational independence of the central administration. For the Devlin Group, their appearance on the administrative stage was significant precisely on this score:

It represented, in the first place, an abandonment, in particular areas, of the concept of the Minister as a corporation sole; there was delegation by law to appointed boards of some executive powers of the State. Secondly, it brought together in the area of government, persons with public and private sector experience to guide and assess the performance of management of public enterprises and, thirdly, it introduced new freedoms in the performance of executive functions of government.[4]

Nevertheless, we should be hesitant to use the word 'autonomous' in respect of them, as some writers do. A legal existence separate from their parent departments they do have, and their functions and powers are prescribed in some legal instrument or other; but such endowments by no means ensure operational independence from their sponsor departments. It does not necessarily follow from their having their own boards or their own (non-Civil Service) staffs or from their not being bound to comply with Civil Service rules and procedures that they will be independent of their minister and sponsor department. Nor does independence follow from their being free from detailed Oireachtas scrutiny: as we shall see, ministerial control and Oireachtas surveillance are not always coextensive. In practice, the degree of independence that state-sponsored bodies enjoy varies enormously from one to another and depends in each case on one or more of three main factors: (1) the nature of the function performed and particularly its political significance or sensitivity; (2) the financial position of the body and especially its sources of funds; and (3) the habits of departmental control that have become established and that might perhaps have originated largely in accidents of personality.

II

Although it is not possible to categorize all state-sponsored bodies unequivocally, most of them seem to fall into one or another of three main groups. Firstly, there are those set up to engage in producing goods and services for sale or which, being so engaged, were for one reason or another taken under state control. These are often referred to as 'commercial bodies' or 'public enterprises'. Secondly, there are those established to carry out marketing, promotional, or development (including research) activities connected with industry and commerce. Thirdly, there are bodies that administer or regulate some area of social or economic activity or provide a social service.

Surveying the administrative scene in the late 1960s, the Public Service Organization Review Group found that 'the commercial state-sponsored bodies form a sector of the public service qualitatively different from the non-commercial bodies and there is an instinctive recognition of this fact in the tendency to refer to them as "public enterprises" '.[5] However, even if they are to be thought of as the state in business – and this is certainly the way they have been thought of – they owe their origin to a political decision that the state should go into or acquire some productive enterprise in the national interest and not simply to make profits. Sometimes, too, they find themselves obliged to engage in activities or to pursue policies for social rather than for economic reasons. Governments make such decisions; state-sponsored bodies, however entrepreneurial they might seem to be, are essentially agents of government policy. For example, the rural electrification programme of the Electricity Supply Board and its use of turf (peat) as a fuel to make electricity were both policies dictated by governments and undertaken 'in the national interest'. More recently (in 1991), An Post was required, indeed ordered, to abandon proposed policies devised to bring it into profit (as it had been required to do) in order to preserve rural post offices for social reasons and jobs so as not to exacerbate a politically embarrassing situation.

The 'public-enterprise' sector in Ireland is quite large. By the early sixties it was, in Garret FitzGerald's view: 'relatively highly developed . . . bearing in mind the absence of heavy industrial activity which in some other European countries is partly or even largely under the control of the state'.[6] In the middle eighties its size was 'in the middle range of the developed countries judged both by contribution to GDP and to gross capital formation'.[7] In 1991, it comprised twenty-three organizations employing 72,000 people (27 per cent of public-sector employment) and included the four largest employers in the state. As in most countries, the public-enterprise sector in that year included most of the infrastructure industries: energy (but only a toe-hold in oil); transport; postal services; telecommunications; banking and the provision of capital; and broadcasting. As in other countries, also, it included a miscellaneous collection of other industries and enterprises whose presence in the public sector owed more to particular circumstances than to general policy.

How did this come about? It owed little to socialist theory. After the eclipse of the left wing of the labour movement during the latter part of the First World War, there were few socialists in Ireland, no socialist movement worth the name, and no developing body of socialist doctrine. The very term 'socialism' was anathema to most, and more so because, following the lead of the Catholic church, most people identified it with communism. The Irish Free State was liberal-democratic and conservative. Its governments and those that followed reflected public opinion generally in showing no lack of confidence in private enterprise. Irish opinion was and still is truly reflected in Article 45.3.1 of Bunreacht na hÉireann (one of the 'Directive Principles of Social Policy'), which declares that 'the state shall favour and, where necessary, supplement private initiative in industry and commerce'. This attitude was echoed in 1961 by the then Taoiseach, Seán Lemass, when he stated:

Even the most conservative among us understands why we cannot rely on private enterprise alone, and state enterprise in fields of activity where private enterprise has failed or has shown itself to be disinterested, has not only been accepted but is expected. . . . Nobody thinks of us as doctrinaire socialists.[8]

It was, however, precisely the considerable need to 'supplement private initiative in industry and commerce', and at times to rescue it, together with the inexorable and universal tendency for public utilities to come under public management, that led to the sizeable public-enterprise sector. Thus, there was little nationalization of already existing business enterprises. Only some half-dozen businesses were taken over, in every case either as a rescue operation or in response to the need to ensure an adequate public service. On the other hand, there was considerable state initiative in starting enterprises.

It should be remembered that the Irish state started out with considerable economic handicaps. Ireland remained very much part of a larger economic and financial unit that was London-oriented; and it was, considered as a unit by itself, in some respects relatively underdeveloped and certainly unbalanced, as was the rural western seaboard of the British Isles generally. This situation was exacerbated by the exclusion from the Irish state of the only industrial area in the island, Belfast and its environs. Because of this and because of the more attractive prospects for capital on the London market, which was still open to Irish investors, private capital was not available to the extent necessary for development, and private enterprise was distinctly unenterprising.

Conservative in outlook though it was, the first government of the Irish Free State nevertheless inherited the tradition of Sinn Féin, and followed a definite line of development leading to state enterprises to provide capital and to exploit the natural resources of the country. In transport, although the exact circumstances under which the state started companies or nationalized them differed from case to case, their inclusion in the public sector was in line with developments in many other countries. This was so, also, in radio and television and in the nationalization of central banking. The remaining trading enterprises either owed their origin to rescue operations or had a social service origin. Examples of the first were the Irish Life Assurance Company Ltd and Irish Steel Holdings Ltd. An example of the second was An Bord Iascaigh Mhara (the Irish Sea Fisheries Board) whose origins are well illustrated by the fact that it was originally registered as a 'Friendly Society' – that is, an association registered under the Friendly Societies Act. In the eighties and nineties it was rather the desire to exploit opportunities that led to the setting up of yet more public enterprises – for example, Bord Gáis Éireann to exploit finds of natural gas; and to the hiving off of activities hitherto carried on by departments but thought to have commercial potential – for example, Coillte Teo (the Irish Forestry Board) and the Irish Aviation Authority. Similarly, the desire to get specializsed commercial management led to the creation of the National Treasury Management Agency in 1990.

Most of the bodies in the second group, the marketing, promotional, and research and development organizations, came into existence as the Irish state, again like most other developed states, assumed responsibility for the development of the economy as a whole. They were created to aid and stimulate Irish enterprise by promoting markets for Irish goods and services, as, for example, Bord Fáilte Éireann (the Irish Tourist Board), Córas Tráchtála (the Irish Export Board) and Córas Beostoic agus Feola (Irish Livestock and Meat Board); to encourage and facilitate the setting up of new industries in Ireland, which is the function of the Industrial Development Authority; to carry out training and employment programmes and to maintain an employment and recruitment service, which is the job of FÁS (Feras Áiseanna Saothair – The Training and Employment Authority); to provide advisory, research, education, and training services to the agricultural and food industries, as does Teagasc; similarly An Bord Glas in the case of horticulture.

The use of the state-sponsored body for these purposes arose, it seems, from ministers' perception that the suitability of the Civil Service to engage in development work was limited; in general, the state-sponsored body reflected a lack of confidence in the ability of departments to cope with some of the new tasks of the modern state. Speaking in 1961, the Taoiseach, Seán Lemass, was quite explicit about this:

It is fair to assume that it was the persistence of doubt about the suitability of Government Departments, as now organised, to operate as development corporations and to perform, in the manner desired, particular functions deemed to be necessary for the nation's progress – functions which required exceptional initiative and innovation – which have led to decisions of the Government from time to time to set up by statute or otherwise a number of more or less independent authorities. I am not referring to the administration of state-owned commercial-type undertakings. . . . I have in mind the administration of activities of another kind, where the purpose is to provide services to promote development generally or to help private concerns to make headway – such as aids to industrial development, export trade, tourism and so forth.[9]

There were, he conceded, other reasons also: the need to attract the services of people who were not, and would not become, civil servants; the desire to be free of detailed departmental and Oireachtas control; the hope that the public would cooperate more readily. Over the thirty years since Lemass spoke, these motives have prompted the creation of a growing number of such developmental bodies. By 1991, there were twenty of them.

There can be little doubt about the role and position of the bodies in this group. They do not produce goods for sale and do not, therefore, have enough funds of their own, even if they impose levies or charges on their clients. They must rely to some extent on state grants. As the Devlin Group pointed out, they 'are really agencies with a governmental role . . . more in the nature of service bodies for the producer'.[10] Nevertheless, since the activities of many of this group are designed to promote business, those who work in them are orientated to the world of trade and commerce and would claim to be as 'business-like', even entrepreneurial, as any in the public enterprise sector. The practices, habits, and *mores* of Civil Service-type administrators would not do in their business.

The administrative, regulatory, and social service group, which in 1990 comprised fifty-three bodies, can be divided into three main sub-groups: (1) bodies established for the government of certain professions, (2) bodies set up to control certain economic activities, and (3) bodies set up to provide or administer certain social services, particularly health and environmental services. Little need be said about the first. Although professions are almost by definition self-governing, many need the backing of the state, and in the case of some, the public interest makes it necessary to define the functions and powers of their governing bodies. In the past, they got powers to regulate entry and govern the profession by charters from the British Crown; in modern times, they are governed by statutes that set up governing bodies endowed with duties and powers.

There can be no doubt about the genesis of most of the second and third sub-groups: they were created as executive agencies of government – the term that the Devlin Group in fact proposed should be applied to all the 'non-commercial' organizations – a convenient alternative to administration by the Civil Service. In the view of the Group, this was an easy, even lazy, way out of an organizational problem:

For the 'non-commercial' function, the state-sponsored body type of organisation is an attempt to cure, on an *ad hoc* basis, defects in the traditional organisation of the executive functions of government. Most of the activities of the 'non-commercial' state-sponsored bodies are such as are, were or could be carried out within the civil service . . . every decision to allocate a new function to a state-sponsored body while similar functions are left in the existing civil service structure represents a failure to face the problem of the efficiency of the existing machinery of government, or at least, to think through the roles of the parts of that machinery.[11]

This was, perhaps, a harsh judgement, at least so far as it was aimed at areas of activity in which there was a need to associate interested parties with the administration of their own business, or the users or recipients of a service with the administration of that service. Nevertheless, in many cases the increasing propensity, after the Second World War, to devolve segments of public administration to state-sponsored bodies that were sometimes mere extensions of their sponsor departments did reflect simply administrative convenience. Where a standard pattern was deemed necessary or useful, convenient enabling legislation was enacted. In the case of both the Health (Corporate Bodies) Act 1961 and the Local Government Services (Corporate Bodies) Act 1971, the extensive powers of the sponsor ministers to create and control such bodies are the most notable features of the legislation.

III

The increased use of state-sponsored bodies from the Second World War onwards precipitated major problems of their relationships with ministers and departments, and also problems of the proper extent and appropriate means of Oireachtas control. It is essential to distinguish clearly between the two.

According to the pre-war 'autonomous corporation' theory, at least the trading bodies were to be free of both ministerial and Oireachtas control except in emergencies. Ministers being responsible for very little, it followed that the Oireachtas could hold them accountable for very little. Today, no one doubts that ministers often have considerable powers, sometimes extending from the most general policy to matters of comparative detail. In the past, the Oireachtas had neither the information nor the procedures to effect adequate control. In 1976, a Joint Committee of the Dáil and Seanad on Commercial State-Sponsored Bodies was established and its reports have provided information for that sector in quantity and quality hitherto unavailable. Even so, it is only recently, with the placing of an obligation on state enterprises to prepare and regularly update corporate plans and to get them cleared, that departments themselves have had – or should have had – systematic information on which to base effective ministerial control. In practice, the Oireachtas does not yet seem to be in that position. Ministers might, therefore, exercise power without responsibility.

Ministerial (or governmental) power over state-sponsored bodies is of four kinds. Firstly, the sponsor minister (sometimes with the consent of another interested minister) or the government appoints members of the governing boards. In the case of eleven of the commercial bodies, this power has been modified by the institution of a small proportion of elected worker directors – under the Worker Participation (State Enterprises) Acts 1977 and 1988. In some cases ministers appoint only a proportion of board members. They also have the power to dismiss their appointees as well as the worker directors. This power is a potential source of great patronage. When a party is in power for a long time, as Fianna Fáil has been, the boards tend to become peopled by party supporters and those who deserved well of of it. Certainly, the changes of government from Fianna Fáil to National Coalition and back again in the 1970s were each followed by a spate of appointments very obviously influenced if not governed by considerations of party or patronage. In many and perhaps even most cases, however, the choice of directors, at least until recently, was as explicable in terms of relevant experience, representation of interests, and the preferences of senior civil servants as in terms of party politics or nepotism.

Secondly, in each case, the appropriate minister has the power, stated or implied, to see that the organization's operations are kept in line with government policy. This involves approval for capital projects and other important policy proposals and for matters such as general wage and salary increases. In 1990, the National Economic and Social Council noted that

Each state-sponsored enterprise is now required to prepare a corporate plan covering a five year period on a 'rolling' basis, containing an outline of corporate objectives, the strategies which are being adopted and the detailed programmes to achieve the objectives. There has also been considerable emphasis on approving the appraisal of capital expenditure.[12]

Thirdly, ministers have a general power of surveillance and the right to intervene on behalf of the community since, at the end of the day, they have an overall responsibility for the organizations in the departmental penumbra. The extent and degree of control vary greatly from body to body and perhaps from time to time. Certainly, it is often not possible to rely upon legal instruments to gauge their extent. Ministerial intervention (including under that head the activities of the minister's civil servants) sometimes has no statutory or other basis; a minister might have no explicit legal power to direct a body whose decisions he in fact influences decisively or even dictates.

Finally, the minister has powers to govern the presentation and form of reports and accounts and to provide for audit, and he also has the right to be given whatever information he requires. These matters, unlike those mentioned previously, are usually specifically provided for in statutes, orders, or articles of association. Here, too, the National Economic and Social Council recorded improvements recently: 'A number of measures have also been introduced to increase the clarity and comprehensiveness of the reports and accounts and improve financial control of the state-sponsored companies'.[13]

Ministerial supervision and control require not only that ministers should know what boards are up to or have in mind but also that each organization ought at all times to know what the policy of its sponsor department is. In fact, it is not uncommon for boards and state-sponsored bodies not to know what a minister's policy is and to be unable to find out. Clearly, also, below policy level, departments have to have an intimate knowledge of the activities of the bodies within their orbit. The contacts necessary to effect this are made at all levels. They are by no means confined to the boards and senior executives on the one side and the minister and his senior civil servants on the other. Civil servants at all levels have frequent routine contact with officials of state-sponsored bodies of appropriate management and supervisory ranks. These 'second level' contacts, many of them of a very informal nature, are an essential part of a satisfactory relationship. They can also be the means by which departments exercise considerable detailed control, often far beyond the reach of parliamentary scrutiny.

Supervision and control might also be effected by the device of appointing civil servants to boards. This practice is quite common except in the public-enterprise group. Obviously, the work of many of these bodies needs to be coordinated with that of their sponsor departments, and the presence of civil servants on boards is a handy coordinating device. Nevertheless, there are some objections to the practice. C.S. Andrews, a former chairman of Córas Iompair Éireann, the state transport authority, cogently condemned the practice when he said, 'I cannot see how a civil servant functions properly if he is wearing two hats and if, having participated in the councils of a board, he returns to his Department and sits in judgement on the decisions reached'.[14] Obviously, also, the practice could (but should not) be used as a means of effecting departmental control while avoiding detailed parliamentary control. It is equally undesirable for ministers to tell Civil Service members of boards how they are to vote on issues, for to do so might make it impossible for them properly to discharge their obligations as board members.

It is only comparatively recently that problems of ministerial control have come to be recognized. They hardly arose in the first twenty or thirty years of the state's existence when there were comparatively few state-sponsored bodies. After the Second World War, the number of state-sponsored bodies increased enormously, and by the late 1960s there were over seventy of them. The growing propensity to use this form of organization for developmental, regulatory, and social service purposes brought into existence many bodies that were simply executive agencies, but 'no serious attempt was made . . . to work out a comprehensive system of communication and control within a unified public service'.[15] On the contrary, Lemass took the opposite view: 'We do not work on the basis of theory. We work always on the basis of the best method of getting a particular job done.'[16] As a result, by the 1960s, the area was an administrative jungle made the worse by the casual way in which some bodies were created and the cavalier failure in some cases to draw up adequate legal instruments governing functions and powers.

Once it was recognized that the government's job was to steer the national economy, the policies of at least the major public enterprises had to conform to overall government programmes. Surprisingly, the need for compliance was not at first always accepted. Lemass drew attention to this in 1959: 'There develops a tendency in some boards to think of themselves rather as sovereign independent authorities than as integral parts of a larger organisation and they are sometimes disposed to resent pressures to keep them in line.'[17] In 1965, the *Report on Economic Planning* by the National Industrial Economic Council made a similar complaint.[18] In the next decade, the far-reaching implications of central planning of the economy, as ministers and senior civil servants saw them, were inexorably brought home to the boards and executives of even the most powerful public enterprises, not least in respect of pay policy, including the salaries of their chief executives. By this time, too, many of the more recently spawned administrative agencies were no more than extensions of their parent departments, their activities quietly controlled or guided by civil servants but operating well below the horizon of the Oireachtas.

What was lacking was a set of agreed principles to regulate such bodies, and in particular minister–board relationships. The Devlin Group criticized this deficiency in particular and, in order to remedy it, proposed two systems of uniform relationships and procedures – one for the public enterprises; the other for the remainder, lumped together as 'non-commercial' bodies. In their view, departments should become small policy-making and reviewing bodies coordinating the activities of all the units charged with implementing state policy in their functional areas. In the case of non-commercial, state-sponsored bodies these units would be of two types. Where an executive function was being exercised by a department, the Devlin Group recommended that it be hived off to a unit called an 'executive office'. Where the function was being carried out by a state-sponsored body, the board should continue in existence, and the unit should be known as an 'executive agency'. In both cases, department – unit relationships would be identical.[19]

In the Devlin Group's view, the position of the public enterprises was different, but not all that different: 'While we refer to these bodies as commercial, it must be remembered that they are all instruments of public policy and cannot operate with full commercial freedom.' The Group recommended unequivocally that 'the commercial bodies must be effectively integrated in the public sector . . . the sponsoring Departments should not interfere in viable commercial operations but should actively engage in the definition and review of goals, the appraisal of results and the control of capital expenditure'.[20]

The recommendations of the Devlin Group on this subject were never formally accepted or fully implemented. In fact, they enunciated a view of the position and role of public enterprises that was fiercely resented and resisted by some of the boards and executives of these bodies. Their contrary views were epitomized in the strictures of a study group of the National Economic and Social Council, in its report *Enterprise in the Public Sector*. The study group's report was a fierce attack on the attempt of the central administration to corral public enterprises, to the detriment, they thought, of initiative and dynamism.

It has been recognised from the beginning that the practices and procedures which govern the operation of other public agencies were not the most appropriate to state-sponsored bodies. . . . Yet the acceptance of this distinctive nature of state-sponsored bodies is being eroded. The concept of the unity of the public sector has begun to be interpreted more rigidly and narrowly than in the past. There is an increasing emphasis on centralised decision-making within the public sector and a tendency towards greater central control of the activities of state-sponsored bodies. . . . In our view, these efforts to introduce uniformity throughout the whole of the public sector are seriously impeding enterprise in the state-sponsored bodies.[21]

The exchange of views between the study group and the central departments, which was published in the report, revealed a deep division of opinion between them. The Chairman's accompanying letter is as acidulous and pointed as it is possible to be in published official exchanges:

It is our unanimous view that there is nothing in them [the departmental comments] that causes us to alter our recommendations. . . . Most of the comments from Government Departments exemplify the perspective of the controller as opposed to that of the entrepreneur. These illustrate explicitly the attitudinal problems which we identified as the central crucial issue in our report.[22]

The chairman was right: there was a crucial issue here. It was very clear in 1980 that the problem of the proper relationship between public enterprises and the central administration was unsettled and becoming acute.

During the eighties, it was increasingly contended that the public enterprises were in general not performing well. In an era of recession, over-inflated public expenditure, and a fashionable demand for 'privatization' in the developed world, the criteria employed to reach this conclusion were commercial and economic: 'by the simplest financial criterion the state-sponsored bodies are not performing well. . . . It is . . . clear that, by any of the criteria conventionally applied to commercial companies, the commercial state sponsored bodies are not healthy.'[23] Of course, it could be argued that a wider perspective might be more appropriate. The operation of public enterprises might well be influenced by social and political objectives legitimately imposed upon them by governments.

What is clearly necessary in this sector is that governments should get adequate information to give them the ability to set coherent objectives and to have progress towards realizing such objectives effectively monitored. To this end, the departments, in particular the Departments of Finance and the Public Service (until 1987) seemed to be continuing throughout the eighties to pursue their inexorable campaign, begun in the seventies, to get this sector under control. Taking an increasingly sophisticated approach, they began to identify and put in place the elements of a systematic regulatory framework that would provide them with appropriate kinds of information to set targets, and appraise and monitor performance while leaving elbow room and offering incentives for enterprising commercial behaviour.

It is far from certain that such measures will – or could – impose a regulatory regime that ensures both coherent and coordinated policies and a truly competitive environment for each enterprise. If they do not, privatization might become a live issue. As yet that debate has hardly begun in Ireland.[24] Some public enterprises have been privatized, albeit in the same *ad hoc* kind of way as nationalization had previously taken place. As early as 1972 the strikingly misnamed Dairy Disposal Company, which was set up in 1927, was at last disposed of. Others have followed – Bord Bainne, Nitrigin Éireann, the Irish Sugar Company, the Irish Life Assurance Company: some, perhaps all, were obvious candidates. On the contrary, however, as we have noted, the eighties saw new commercial state-sponsored bodies established. Certainly there has been nothing approaching the crusade for privatization that swept the United Kingdom. In general, it seems to be recognized that privatization does not ensure greater efficiency and that, as P. J. Kelly put it: 'more attention needs to be placed in policy circles on how competition can be encouraged and ensured as a means of improving performance and efficiency without introducing an overregulated environment'.[25] How apt this observation was became very evident in 1991 when revelations of alleged scandals both reflected upon the adequacy of departmental surveillance of some public enterprises and cast doubts upon the desirability of privatization.

IV

Whereas the power of the central administration over state- sponsored bodies increased as their numbers and role grew, the ability of the Oireachtas to scrutinize them for long remained trivial. The result was a constitutional imbalance that was as obvious as it was undesirable.

The requirements of constitutional propriety seem clear enough. Ministers are responsible to the Dáil not only for the duties laid upon them by the Constitution and the statutes, including their failure to act when they should have acted, but also for all their actions as ministers and for those of their departmental officials. There is a political obligation upon them to explain and defend, and the Dáil (with the Seanad as a potentially useful auxiliary) ought to be in a position to make this responsibility a reality. Surprisingly, when it came to state-sponsored bodies, such a view was not universally held.

Seán Lemass, who as Minister for Industry and Commerce was responsible for the creation of a number of these bodies and whose views on them were rightly influential, took a different line: 'There has arisen . . . in recent times, in Dáil Éireann, and perhaps even more suprisingly, in Seanad Éireann, a tendency towards endeavouring to make the decisions of some statutory boards, taken within the powers given to them by law, subject to review and even to veto in the legislature.'[26] Lemass deplored this. Correctly, he saw a danger: 'These bodies were set up with the deliberate intention of avoiding close state control.'[27] However, 'it is probable that when any semi-state board becomes the centre of controversy – as is not unlikely at some period of its existence – its independence is likely to be in serious jeopardy, because Ministers, realising the folly of accepting responsibility without effective power, will be disposed to bring their operations under closer supervision, which could reduce if not eliminate their special utility as an administrative device'.[28]

However, Lemass's contention that 'additional parliamentary control is unnecessary having regard to the wide ministerial powers in relation to state-sponsored bodies' was surely mistaken.[29] It is, indeed, exactly the reverse. Additional parliamentary control is necessary precisely when ministers exercise additional powers. Ministerial control is not sufficient: the Oireachtas must be in a position to scrutinize ministers' exercise of (or their failure to exercise) their powers. Above all, it must be crystal clear what those powers are and what in practice are the relationships between ministers and boards and between departments and executives of state-sponsored bodies. Unfortunately, echoes of the Lemass view can still be heard particularly in Fianna Fáil circles, and more particularly when that party is in government. Nevertheless, consequent upon the less favourable view of public enterprise taken from the middle 1980s, political and public opinion seems to be moving in favour of more effective Oireachtas control.

The problem of Oireachtas control is not just one of principle, however. The Oireachtas suffered from serious practical handicaps that until recently made its control of this sector little more than cursory. Firstly, there was – and still is – the basic handicap that the precise objectives of some state-sponsored bodies are not clearly stated and, more generally, that the statutes and legal instruments constituting and regulating them are sometimes inadequate or anomalous, particularly in defining the respective functions and powers of ministers and the relationship between them. Ministers might, and do, wield considerable powers without specific authority. Secondly, until the late 1970s, there were no adequate procedures and facilities for acquiring information or for the systematic scrutiny of the performance of state-sponsored bodies. The inadequacies of question time and debates as procedures for scrutinizing performance are manifest. Furthermore, in the past, most members of the Oireachtas did not seem to care very much, particularly when, as was the case until the eighties, it was generally believed that the state-sponsored bodies were doing a good job. Debates were both few and far between; those who participated in them, except for the minister, were poorly informed and in many cases concerned only with parochial matters.

From the late 1940s, desultory requests for a select committee, which British and continental European experience had shown was the best device for systematic scrutiny, were made from time to time by members of parties out of power. Lemass himself, when in opposition briefly, had made a motion for a select committee 'akin to the Committee of Public Accounts to which these [state-owned] company accounts and reports would be submitted'[30] only to reject the idea when in power, as we have seen. Eventually, a growing awareness among parliamentarians of the inadequacies of Oireachtas control led in 1976 to the Fine Gael–Labour government's moving to set up a Joint Committee on State-Sponsored Bodies to examine the Reports and Accounts and overall operational results of state-sponsored bodies engaged in trading or commercial activities. Introducing the motion, the Minister for the Public Service justified the decision to confine the committee to twenty-six of the commercial bodies:

There is a significant difference between the commercial and non-commercial state-sponsored bodies. The latter are in many ways similar to the executive branches of Government Departments, except that they have a larger degree of operating freedom. There is a problem in relation to their responsibility to the Oireachtas but, at this stage, it seems that a solution may well be in a redefinition of their relationship to Ministers.[31]

That statement seemed to presage a change in the status of that group following the Devlin Group's recommendations, but this did not occur. In March 1980, with Fianna Fáil in power again, an opposition motion for a Joint Committee on Autonomous Non-Commercial Bodies was rejected by the Dáil, the minister arguing that it was necessary to have more time to evaluate the experience of the existing committee dealing with public enterprises before venturing on another.[32]

From 1978, the Joint Committee on State-Sponsored Bodies, which takes evidence in public and was the first select committee to have professional help made available to it, began to produce reports that immeasurably improved the quantity and quality of information made available to the Oireachtas and published. Unfortunately, these reports have been discussed in the Dáil and Seanad only infrequently. Members tend to make reference to them only when they contain 'revelations' or suggestions of poor performance. On the other hand, their impact on the enterprises which they investigate and on sponsor departments might in some instances have been considerable. Audrey Arkins's study of the committee during the period 1982 to 1987 led her to suggest that:

Quite possibly . . . it was the sheer existence of the SSBC enquiry which prompted government action in relation to Ostlanna Iompair Éireann, Irish Shipping, and Údarás na Gaeltachta. Certainly the situation in each of these companies altered radically within weeks of committee hearings. In each case government action eclipsed SSBC reports and recommendations, nevertheless each enquiry seemed to reveal vital information which might otherwise have remained undisclosed.[33]

Evidently, the means of effective scrutiny and control are to hand: it remains for Oireachtas members to make full use of them.

Notes

1   *Dáil Debates*, Vol. 293. col. 1407 (10 Nov. 1976).
2   Ministers and Secretaries (Amendment) Act 1973 (No. 14), s.1.
3   *Report of the Public Services Organization Review Group, 1966–1969* (the Devlin Report) (Dublin, 1969), p. 30.
4   *Ibid.*, p. 14
5   *Ibid,.* p. 31
6   G. FitzGerald, *State-Sponsored Bodies*, 2nd edn, (Dublin, 1964), p. 1.
7   *A Strategy for the Nineties: Economic Stability and Structural Change*, National Economic and Social Council Report (Dublin, 1990), p. 354.
8   S. Lemass, 'The organisation behind the economic programme', in *Administration*. 9 (1961), p. 3.
9   *Ibid.*, p. 5. See also his statement quoted on p. 238.
10 Devlin Report, p. 31.
11 *Ibid..* pp. 43–4.
12 *A Strategy for the Nineties*, p. 356.

13 *Ibid.*
14 *Administration*, 6 (1958–59), p. 298.
15 Devlin Report, p. 14.
16 *Seanad Debates*, Vol. 33, col. 1583 (16 April 1947).
17 S. Lemass, *The Role of the State-Sponsored Bodies* (Dublin, 1959), p. 9.
18 See National Industrial Economic Council, *Report on Economic Planning.*, (Dublin, 1965), p. 14.
19 Devlin Report, pp. 157–8.
20 *Ibid.*, pp. 163–4.
21 *Enterprise in the Public Sector*, National Econmic and Social Council Report No. 49 (Dublin, 1979), p. 16.
22 *Ibid.*, p. 29.
23 B. Walsh, 'Commercial state-sponsored bodies', in *The Irish Banking Review* (summer 1987), p. 30.
24 But see F. Convery and M. McDowell (eds). *Privatisation: Issues of Principle and Implementation in Ireland* (Dublin, 1990) for some economists' views.
25 P. J. Kelly in Convery and McDowell, *Privatisation*, p. 81.
26 *Administration*, 9 (1961), p. 7.
27 *Ibid.*, p. 11.
28 *Ibid.*, p. 7.
29 *Ibid.*, p. 11.
30 *Dáil Debates*, Vol. 119. col. 367 (21 Feb. 1950).
31 *Dáil Debates*, Vol. 293, col. 1406 (10 Nov. 1976).
32 See *Dáil Debates*, Vol. 319. cols 169–202 (19 March 1980).
33 A. Arkins, 'The Committees of the 24th Oireachtas', in *Irish Political Studies*, 3 (1988), p. 97.

CHAPTER 15

Local Government

I

In all countries, the administration of public services involves not only the central departments, but also some combination of functional and areal dispersion of duties and powers. In Chapter 14, we examined functional devolution to state-sponsored bodies. In this chapter, we turn to areal dispersion.

In Ireland the areal dispersion of government functions and powers has taken two forms: one has its roots deep in history and is bound up with the development of democracy; the other is an *ad hoc* and piecemeal creation of politicians and bureaucrats in recent times for administrative convenience. The first is local government, the devolution of functions and powers to locally elected representative authorities – principally the councils of counties, county boroughs, boroughs, urban districts, and 'towns'. Although subject to the supremacy and supervision of the national government, these local authorities have been endowed with jurisdiction over the provision of certain services subject to the approval of their electors. The second is regional government, a term used imprecisely to cover a number of arrangements for devolving and deconcentrating business to authorities whose jurisdiction embraces areas larger than those of the local authorities.

As it is used at present, the term 'regional government' covers several types of organization. Firstly, there are authorities having the administration of some service devolved upon them, whose governing bodies consist of representatives of local authorities and interested associations or groups in the region – for example, the eight Area Health Boards and the eight Regional Tourism Organizations. Secondly, in the provision of some services, the central authorities concerned have decentralized business to regional organizations or offices for administrative, managerial, or, occasionally, customer convenience. 'These represent the deconcentration of significant powers to the appropriate managers.'[1] For example, state-sponsored bodies like the Electricity Supply Board have regional organizations, and the Industrial Development Authority has 'regional offices'. Likewise, some government departments with branch offices or field services divide the country up into administratively convenient units whose managers have some discretionary powers.

More recently, following the reform of the European Community Structural Fund, the Irish government set up a 'sub-regional' structure to contribute to the preparation of the National Development Plan to be submitted to Brussels – 'sub-regional' because in Community eyes the Irish Republic is itself a single 'region'. The bureaucratic bias of this exercise was evident in, firstly, the regional 'Working Groups' which comprised representatives of government departments and other state agencies together with the city and county managers (it was only on a parallel series of 'Advisory Groups' that chairmen of local authorities and representatives of interest groups appeared); and, secondly, from the fact that the National Development Plan submitted to Brussels in 1989 was based on national programmes rather than regional ones. Evidently, 'the "consultation" mechanism was regarded as simply a cosmetic exercise to pander to the aspirations of Brussels'.[2]

All – the authorities with devolved powers, the organizations set up for deconcentration of administration, and the so-called 'sub-regional' organizations – have boundaries to suit the immediate convenience of their creators. The regional areas thus created do not coincide. Since there is also an underlying network of local authorities, the result is a jungle of administrative areas that is both impenetrable to the ordinary citizen and frequently inconvenient for any kind of business that involves more than one authority or regional organization. Many of these arrangements have come into existence in the last forty years or less. The words of the Institute of Public Administration's study group in 1971 were still true twenty years later: there has been, the group said, 'rapid and uncoordinated growth both of regional authorities and systems of regional administration'.[3] This 'rather haphazard tangle of regional boundaries' badly needs reducing to order.[4]

Evidently, the creation of regional bodies owes nothing to a democratic desire to devolve political power or increase popular participation: on the contrary, they exist for bureaucratic convenience. Notwithstanding the tendency for them to proliferate, the main focus of government and politics at sub-national level is, as it always has been, local government, which is the main subject of this chapter. Despite all that we shall say about the domination of local government by the central authorities, it is another level of genuine government, albeit mostly administrative. Until recently, it was the *only* other level of jurisdictional authority. From the early 1970s, however, a third level has come into place, the European Community system, a system that is concerned largely with policy prescription rather than implementation. It will be the subject of Chapter 16.

II

Viewed as part of a national system of public *administration*, local government can be seen as one of a trio of groups of authorities, the others being the central departments and the state-sponsored bodies. However, local authorities are not to be regarded *simply* as administrative organs allocated functions by the central authorities as convenience dictates, though this is to a large extent what they have become. The system of local government developed in Great Britain and Ireland in the nineteenth century was one of two systems of government (central and local) to cope with virtually all public business. It was intended to be local *self*-government – democracy carried down to the smallest community unit practicable and, by the device of committee administration of all services, to the most intimate details of their application. The great growth of the state-sponsored bodies may be seen simply as the development of devolved or decentralized administration of central government functions, for state-sponsored bodies answer to ministers and the Oireachtas. Local government should not be similarly viewed. To do so is to ignore both its history and its rationale.

It cannot be denied, of course, that local government is subordinate government, since local authorities, having no inherent authority of their own, derive their functions and powers from the Oireachtas. Nevertheless, local authorities are different in kind from state-sponsored bodies, for they are in themselves representative. Local government embodies the concept of local democracy as an integral feature. Services are administered under the supervision of locally elected persons who have some discretion in their conduct of affairs and who can be called to account. No doubt, in the twentieth century, the exigencies of the welfare state pressed inexorably in upon the body of local self-government, crushing it almost to death. Nevertheless, local government will not be understood unless it is remembered that originally the citizens who paid local taxes (for local government has a source of funds of its own, the 'rates' – now much attenuated) were intended to have considerable autonomy in the provision of local services.

In this tradition, there is a generally accepted belief in Ireland in the value of local government as a *democratic* institution, perhaps even as an essential part of democracy. This legacy of Victorian liberalism was expressed in 1971 in a government White Paper on the reform of local government:

The real argument . . . for the provision of local services by local authorities . . . is that a system of local self-government is one of the essential elements of democracy. Under such a system, local affairs can be settled by the local citizens themselves or their representatives, local services can be locally controlled and local communities can participate in the process and responsibilities of government. Local government exists, therefore, for democratic as well as practical reasons.[5]

Paradoxically, Irish local government is, in T. J. Barrington's opinion, 'one of the most centrally controlled of local government systems'.[6] In addition, local authorities are themselves more bureaucratic than they were when the system was inherited from the British. Ireland has a council-manager system of local government, having largely abandoned the British principle of direct committee administration of services in favour of the conduct of all services under the direction of a single individual, the city or county manager, who answers to his council but yet has a statutory position and statutory powers. Since managers are appointed and local government committees in the British tradition consist of elected councillors, there is obviously a greater willingness in Ireland to forfeit participation in order to achieve efficiency. Perhaps, also, Irish people do not feel very strongly about local self-government. When, in the 1960s, the 1970s, and the 1980s, local elections were postponed to suit the convenience of the national political timetable, hardly a voice was raised in protest. When councils were suspended or abolished for non-performance of their duties, they went out of existence with scarcely a whimper or cry of alarm. Even the suspension of the Dublin City Council in 1969 for failure to strike an adequate rate did not arouse much public hostility. If the public does not care all that much, neither do all but a few politicians: indeed, the present national–local relationships and the bureaucratic administration of services suit many of them quite well, as we shall see.

The equivocal attitudes of public and politicians reflect the fact that there is a fundamental problem in local government: how are democratic procedures and local autonomy to survive in the face of the evident trend of modern states towards uniform and ever-rising standards and levels of service that people demand but that seem to require bigger and bigger catchment areas and are increasingly expensive? The importance of the problem can be gauged by noting the nature and range, and measuring the size, of the services provided by local authorities.

Table 15.1 shows the total expenditure of 'local authorities' as officially (but narrowly) defined: namely, authorities that come within the ambit of the local government acts and the city and county management system, and are supervised by the Department of the Environment. In 1991, they comprised county councils (27), county borough corporations (5), borough corporations (6), urban district councils (49), plus a number of other minor bodies.[7] Their expenditure in 1988 amounted to 8 per cent of the public-sector budget. It might be better, however, to add the expenditure of two other groups of authorities that are essentially local both in respect of the services they administer and the nature of their governing bodies. The first are the eight area health boards which were set up in 1971 when the local authorities lost their health functions and which are composed of local authority representatives, persons elected by the medical and para-medical professions in the area, and appointees of the Minister for Health. The second are the Vocational Educational Committees which, though statutory bodies in their own right, are committees of those local councils that provide vocational education. It is obvious that both are very much in the local government sector and are generally so regarded. If their expenditure in 1988 be added to local authority expenditure, the total was over £3,000 million, amounting to about one-fifth of the total public-sector budget and 14 per cent of the gross domestic product in that year. Furthermore, the objects of this considerable expenditure include the provision of the most basic and essential environmental services such as roads, water, sewerage, refuse collection, burial grounds, and fire protection. Although the removal of responsibility for personal health and public assistance services in the 1970s was a major piece of administrative surgery, this was to some extent compensated for by the extension of local authorities' control over physical planning and development and building.

Table 15.1 **Total expenditure of local authorities,** [*] **1988**

Total expenditure of local authorities	IR£m1,217.5
Total public-sector budget	IR£m14,885
Local authorities' expenditure as percentage of total public-sector budget	8.2%

Note: [*] 'Local authorities' are those authorities which come within the ambit of the Local Government Acts. They comprise county councils, county borough corporations, borough corporations, urban district councils, town commissioners, and a number of joint bodies.

Source: derived from official sources.

Table 15.2 **Objects of local authority * expenditure, 1988**

	Expenditure (IR£m)	
Programme group	Current	Capital
Housing and building	222.5	139.9
Road transportation and safety	298.8	12.7
Water supply and sewage	102.4	54.0
Development incentives and controls	23.3	6.0
Environmental protection	110.4	6.7
Recreation and amenity	76.2	8.2
Agriculture, education, health and welfare	56.5	0.9
Miscellaneous services	74.7	24.3
	964.8	252.7

Note: [*] For definition of Local Authority see Table 15.1.

Source: Derived from Returns of Local Taxation, 1988 (Stationery Office, Dublin, 1991), pp.12, 13 and 26.

Local authorities, it seems, have reverted to what they were in the past: the providers of environmental services and the protectors of the environment. This fact is well illustrated by the headings of the 'programme groups' of local authorities' functions listed in official documents: housing and buildings; road transportation and safety; water supply and sewerage; development incentives and controls; environmental protection; recreation and amenity; and two ragbags of residual or peripheral functions, namely, 'agriculture, education, health and welfare' and 'miscellaneous services'. (For a detailed list of local government functions, see Appendix 3.) As Table 15.2 shows, in terms of spending, the big business of local government lies in the first three of the programme groups: housing and building, roads, and water and sewerage. These are the heart of local government and mark its essentially environmental character. This reversion of local authorities to being principally environmental authorities was symbolized in 1977 by the alteration of the title of their principal sponsor minister from Minister for Local Government to Minister for the Environment.

Although Irish local authorities are the providers of important services and, in particular, essential environmental services, it should be noticed that their range of responsibilities is quite restricted. In the other countries of the European Communities, local authorities are involved in police and court functions, in education (at various levels), in the provision and promotion of cultural services to a far greater extent than the meagre library and museum services provided in Ireland, and in a wide range of health and welfare services. Even in respect of physical planning and industrial development, where, with the enactment of the Local Government (Planning and Development) Act 1963, it seemed that local authorities might be expected to play a leading role as developers of their areas, in Barrington's judgement 'the real action was to lie elsewhere'.[8]

In order to understand these limitations and the differences between local government in Ireland and elsewhere (except the United Kingdom), it is necessary to appreciate the contrast between the way in which local government is perceived and its treatment in law. In most European countries local authorities have a constitutional status and a general competence; that is, they may undertake any activity not forbidden by law or assigned to another authority. In Ireland, following the British tradition, local authorities have no constitutional status but are creatures of statute and possess no inherent powers. They may do only what the law assigns to them. (Ireland is one of the few European countries that has not signed the European Charter of Local Self-Government adopted in 1985, which provides that local authorities shall have a general competence.) Because of this and because of the strong centralizing bias of those who control central government, the range of local authority functions is, in T. J. Barrington's words, 'much the most restricted of the European democracies'.[9] In a valuable comparative study, he found that Ireland was at or near the bottom of league tables measuring spending as a percentage of total public-sector expenditure and gross domestic product; employment as a percentage of total public-sector employment; and range of functions discharged.[10]

III

The structure of the local government system derives, on the one hand, from the British tradition of civic autonomy and, on the other, from the British practice of placing the onus for law and order in the countryside on the local gentry, whose representatives were designated 'Grand Juries'. These Grand Juries were also expected to administer on an amateur and unpaid basis such state regulations as applied in their neighbourhood and such public services as were absolutely essential, like the relief of destitution and the provision of roads. From the 1830s, a new and unified system was created in stages to deal with the social problems of the industrial revolution when and as they were perceived in Great Britain. It was completed by the end of the nineteenth century.

The authorities then created were representative and were progressively democratized. The system was extended to Ireland stage by stage in line with developments in Great Britain with as few modifications as were essential, though conditions in Ireland were often different from those 'across the water'. Thus, to understand Irish local government, it is necessary to begin with British experience and British solutions applied in an Irish setting. However, in the twenty years from independence to the Second World War, modifications and additions of such magnitude were made by the first indigenous governments that the resultant pattern was by no means merely a variation of the British model.

The reforms and developments of the nineteenth century centred principally on three units: (1) the counties, (2) the boroughs and other towns, and (3) the poor-law 'unions' created in 1838, each with its 'board of guardians' to administer the relief of destitution. It was to these three groups of authorities that the state turned from the 1830s on for the administration of a growing range of services, particularly public health and other environmental services designed to protect the community and to relieve the worst hardships of its poorest members. In particular, the efficient poor-law guardians were loaded with the administration of public and personal health services and the provision of housing that went far beyond the relief of destitution. These three sets of authorities were reorganized and reformed when rising standards of efficiency and a growing acceptance of the principle of democracy so demanded.

By 1880, two types of representative urban authority had been created. The councils of sizeable towns, including the boroughs – the 'urban district councils', as they came to be called – were developing as major multipurpose authorities. The representative bodies of the smaller towns, called 'town commissioners', were endowed with a narrower range of responsibilities. With the reshaping of county government in Great Britain in 1888 and 1896, the administration of services in the countryside in Ireland was clearly due for reform. Under the Local Government (Ireland) Act 1898, the functions of the grand juries were transferred to democratically elected county councils, Since the franchise was wide, extending as it did to male householders or occupiers, a considerable measure of democracy came to the Irish countryside with dramatic suddenness and was immediately turned to account in the developing national struggle for independence.

Besides providing democratic government at the county level, the 1898 act arranged for the transfer of the public health functions of the poor-law guardians to county district authorities called 'rural district councils', thus setting up a two-tier system in the countryside as in the towns. However, the largest boroughs (Dublin, Cork, Limerick, and Waterford) were created counties (termed 'county boroughs'), as the largest British towns had been in 1888, and were completely divorced for local government purposes from the adjoining county areas. The county borough councils in effect became all-purpose local authorities. Thus, by the end of the century, a more or less coherent pattern of authorities had been established to replace the confusing mass of overlapping bodies that had been created *ad hoc* earlier in the century, and a simplified taxation system in the form of the rates, a tax on housing and other fixed property, provided an autonomous source of funds. On paper at least, this system resembled very closely the British pattern, lacking only the parish councils that in Britain formed a third or bottom tier of local authorities in the rural areas and were the culmination of Victorian grassroots democracy.

Between 1898 and independence, local government was dominated by national political issues and movements. The new franchise brought about a great change in the composition of the councils. The county councils in particular became centres of nationalism, and, as J. J. Horgan put it, 'the Local Government Act of 1898, although indeed its authors knew it not, was the legislative father of the Irish Free State'.[11]

After the Dáil government was established in 1919, the large majority of local councils, in the words of the *First Report of the Department of Local Government*, 'challenged the authority of the Imperial Parliament by refusing to recognise the control of the Local Government Board and by making declarations of allegiance to Dáil Éireann'.[12] Of all the Dáil government departments, Local Government was the most successful and least shadowy. In this heady atmosphere, the administration of local services suffered somewhat, a decline that was hastened by the financial disabilities placed by the

British on recalcitrant authorities, by the breakdown in the collection of rates, and by the fact that civil war followed immediately after the Treaty. The combined effect of all this on a local government system that was not in any case working well in the cities and in which committee administration, the democratic power-house of the British system, was patently inefficient in Irish conditions and conducive to nepotism, was to force the new government to suspend some authorities for incompetence or neglect and to consider the whole question of the machinery and procedures of local government. Two decades of reform followed. The result was that, whereas the pattern of Irish local authorities today is largely a late-nineteenth-century creation, the machinery and processes of local government are products of the first generation of independent rule.

IV

The first rulers of the Irish Free State approached local government with the view that as the elected representatives of the Irish people, now come into their own, they had a duty to organize an honest and efficient governmental system and to do so quickly and with no nonsense. Local authorities, for all their displays of national fervour, were in many cases not particularly efficient. Their administration was often sloppy and tainted with nepotism and jobbery, which were anathema to many of the austere and high-minded ministers and their even more austere civil servants. In addition, some authorities, dominated by anti-Treaty supporters of de Valera, failed to carry out their statutory duties just as they or their predecessors had done before independence.

Imbued with the ideals of Sinn Féin and supported by urban middle-class and business interests clamouring for efficient and economical city administration, Cosgrave, O'Higgins, and their colleagues in the first Cumann na nGaedheal governments did not hesitate to think in terms of structures and procedures that were less democratic and more centralized and bureaucratic than what existed. Nor, when the time came, did their Fianna Fáil successors. From 1922 on, a second phase of reforms took place. Between 1922 and 1942, the structure and procedures of Irish local government were transformed from a close and apparently unsatisfactory imitation of those of Britain to a unique system of managerial government and central supervision heavily biased in favour of the counties and undoubtedly more bureaucratic in its operation than what went before.

Although the general trend of local government development after independence was away from the Victorian democratic ideal of the greatest possible devolution of appropriate functions to elected representatives, democracy in one respect was quickly achieved in Ireland. The restrictions on full adult franchise in the 1898 act and plural voting by reason of ownership of property were removed by 1935. Since that date, the qualifications for registration as a local elector have been only adult status (that is, age 21 or over until 1973, and thereafter age 18 or over) and residence.

The Victorian concept of local democracy, which in Great Britain resulted in a two- or three-tier system of authorities everywhere except in the largest cities, was never fully implemented in Ireland, for parish councils were never set up. Indeed, after independence, the trend towards grassroots authorities was reversed, a process that has continued ever since. The poor-law guardians were abolished in 1923, the rural district councils in 1925; in both cases their functions were transferred to the county councils. The smaller urban authorities came under increasing strain and tended to lose or give up their functions and powers. Increasingly, also, town councils were permitted to hand over the actual performance of duties – for example, house building, paving, lighting, and cleaning – to the councils of the counties in which they were situated, and did so. After the introduction in the counties of the manager system, with the county manager being manager for all the local authorities in his county areas, there was virtually a single administration in each county, and it was thus easier for the smaller authorities to give up functions.

This trend reflected the increasing technical, administrative, and financial inadequacy of small units faced with the growing range and rising level of public services. One result was that the county units, including the county boroughs (the major cities, which have county status), came more and more to dominate local government. Local government in Ireland became and is now primarily county council government. Another result is that because there are so few small district authorities, the total number of local councils is small. According to Barrington: 'By the standards of other small democracies, we have very few directly elected authorities, and if we accept that, in practice, we have only thirty-one with a significant range of functions, extremely few by the standards of any other country.' In a comparison of Ireland and eighteen other European democratic countries, he found Ireland seventeenth, with 31,000 people per council. Very few other countries had more than 20,000 people per council, and France as few as 1,500.[13]

Although they are the dominant authorities in the system, the counties and county boroughs have in turn come under strain. Even in 1898, the decision to make the counties as they stood the major units of local government was open to question. However, the counties were there and, although their boundaries were in origin largely the product of accidents, they were accepted without question and without reference to the large differences among them in area, wealth, and population. Population changes, the increase in public services, and scientific and technical advances exacerbated these differences while putting strain upon all, big and small.

By the third quarter of the twentieth century, even comparatively strong county authorities were patently not big enough units for hospital services, and the same was being asserted in relation to other services also. In 1970, the administration of health services generally was removed from the direct control of local authorities and was assigned to Area (that is, regional) Health Boards. Physical planning was also placed on a regional basis, and indeed, as the Institute of Public Administration's report *More Local Government* pointed out, by 1972, regional authorities and administrative units of one sort or another had proliferated. In that same year, the government White Paper *Local Government Reorganization* conceded that the county was less suitable than the region for the planning of many services and for the delivery and administration of some.[14] However, sentiment, both patriotic and sporting, had attached itself to the county units. In the face of this, the government in 1971 – and succeeding governments – shelved the problem, although it was serious, not least in the Dublin area and its immediate hinterland, where there seemed to be a crying need for a new arrangement of authorities for what had become a burgeoning conurbation.

Despite a plethora of studies and policy statements during the next twenty years, no major changes were made. It was not until 1991 that the first steps in a promised programme of major changes were hurriedly taken in advance of the (delayed) local government elections of that year. Dublin County Council and the Dun Laoghaire corporation were replaced by three county authorities.

The democratic element in local government was not only lessened by the concentration of functions in fewer authorities; local government also became markedly more bureaucratic – and more efficient. Bureaucratization took three forms: (1) increasing central government control; (2) the creation of a single local government service, centrally selected by open competition and controlled in many respects by the central administration; and (3), the most important in its consequences, the institution of the manager system. These trends, Barrington thought,

all arose from the assumption by central government of responsibility for raising the level of efficiency of local government according to the conceptions of efficiency in the 1920s and 1930s. . . . The other side of this coin was the subjection of a great part of the day-to-day operations of local authorities to the most intense subordination and control.[15]

Central control by ministerial departments increased steadily from the 1920s until by 1950 it was ubiquitous, though unsystematic and uneven in its incidence. Increasingly, the older conception of local government as a separate governmental system was displaced by the idea of local authorities as agents of central government. Local authorities came increasingly to be viewed as handy field agencies for the administration under supervision of new services. Sometimes, new services occasioned the creation of new single-purpose statutory authorities separate from the local authorities proper, though linked to them by representation. The most important of these were the County Committees of Agriculture (abolished in 1988) and the Vocational Education Committees, each operating under their own statutes and under the supervision of their own sponsor minister. Such arrangements tended to remove the services concerned from direct control by local authorities and to insulate them somewhat. Likewise, in the 1970s, the regional and county development organizations were closely 'coordinated' by a Central Development Committee under the aegis of the Department of Finance: so too were the regional development bodies set up in the late eighties in connection with the National Development Plan being prepared for presentation to Brussels.[16]

Local authorities had of course been objects of central government surveillance and supervision from mid-Victorian times, when a reformed and efficient central bureaucracy was expected by parsimonious politicians to keep a close watch over the poor performance and lax standards of unreformed local administrations. By the time local authorities had become more professional and able to achieve high standards unaided, the tradition of control had hardened. Moreover, a pattern of ever-increasing financial dependence on central funds had been established and led inevitably to central control to protect the taxpayers' interest. (See Table 15.3 for the sources of local authorities' revenue.) Control was the more detailed because grants were often allocated for prescribed purposes and hedged about with stringent conditions, ranging from the need to get prior approval of plans in detail, to payments after inspection or on proof of attaining set standards. In addition, there was stringent audit. This type of detailed control became a permanent feature of local government.

*Table 15.3 **Sources of local authorities' revenue, 1939, 1959, 1979, 1983, and 1991***

	1939		1959		1979		1983		1991 (estimates)	
Source	IR£m	%	IR£m	%	IR£m	%	IR£m	%	IR£m	%
Rates	6.3	50	20.6	40	90.4	20	104.9	11	256.1	23
State grants	4.7	37	22.2	43	265.4	60	613.1	67	502.6	45
Other (mainly rents and repayments for housing; also service charges)	1.7	13	8.8	17	88.3	20	199.3	22	358.7	32
Total	12.6	100	51.5	100	444.1	100	917.3	100	1,117.4	100

Sources: derived from *Returns of Local Taxation* and *Local Authority Estimates* (both published by the stationery office, Dublin), with the assistance of Maurice Coughlan, Department of the Environment. Some amounts have been rounded.

274 The Government and Politics of Ireland

The financial dependence of local authorities on central government was greatly increased, at least temporarily, as a result of the decision – to honour an election promise – to abolish rates on domestic property in 1977. As Table 15.3 shows, whereas in 1959 40 per cent of local authorities' revenue came from rates, in 1979 it was only half that proportion. The consequences of the abolition of rates were immediate and marked. The central government's moves to determine the maximum increases in rates on the types of property that were still liable deprived local authorities of almost the last room they had for manoeuvre in determining expenditure. There were, no doubt, strong pressures on the government in the interests of the national economy to curb the spending of local authorities, which now had less and less incentive to economize, but the results were clear: 'The centre ha[d] virtually taken over local taxation.'[17] The attempt to restore some financial flexibility to authorities by permitting them from 1983 to make charges for services (for example, water, refuse collection, sewage) was a failure. The amounts raised were small, and, clearly, this was a political hot potato that some local authorities could not handle while others would not.

The control of central government extends to supervision not only of performance but of personnel. This takes two forms: (1) selection on a national basis of administrative and professional officers, and (2) control by the Department of the Environment of personnel matters generally. Even before independence, Sinn Féin had indicated its intention of reforming the local government system, which was, in truth, not a single service at all at that time. Local officials were chosen and appointed by the local authorities themselves, and, 'as might be expected in such circumstances, recruitment on considerations other than merit was only too frequent'.[18] Moreover, authorities being separate jurisdictions – many very small – promotion opportunities were inadequate, and consequently morale and incentive were low. Condemning these weaknesses, Sinn Féin promised a national service, appointment by open competition, and mobility.

Such a system was duly instituted, notably by the creation in 1926 of an independent Local Appointments Commission to select and nominate to all administrative and professional posts, and in the creation of a local service code administered by the Department of Local Government. In its annual report for 1950–51, the Department of Local Government could point out that 'over a long period the law has vested in the central authority a tight control over local authorities in staff matters. The purpose of this was to ensure that staffs are properly recruited and fairly treated. Generally that position has been reached.' Once again, however, efficiency had been achieved at the cost of local autonomy, a cost that in this instance few would regard as heavy.

Together, increasing central government control of functions and finance and a centralized control of personnel produced a system that allowed precious little scope for local *self*-government. In 1969 the Devlin Group's judgement was unequivocal: 'The striking feature of the Irish system of local government, whether it is compared with local government systems abroad or with other administrative systems within the country, is the degree and extent of the controls exercised over it.'[19] Despite much talk and even promises of democratizing reforms, successive governments failed to act, partly because 'grassroots' politicians, having a vested interest in retaining a system that suited their local political requirements, did not (and many still do not) want change, and partly because of the strength and tenacity of the departmental tradition of strong central control. In 1980, T.J. Barrington echoed the Devlin Group's verdict given ten years previously: 'Ours remains one of the most centrally controlled local government systems',[20] and, after yet another decade, in 1991 Michael Bannon judged that the government had 'failed to carry through any significant reform of local government'.[21]

V

Central control led to bureaucratization of one sort, for it diminished the discretion of both local councillors and local officials; the creation of a managerial system added bureaucratization of another sort, for it increased the role of the local officials at the expense of the local councillors.

The management system, which was foreign to British local government until quite recently and was therefore not part of the British inheritance, owed its origin to a number of circumstances. Many local authorities before independence were manifestly inefficient and riddled with abuse. The austere rulers of the new state (both political and Civil Service) were not prepared to tolerate this state of affairs, the less so since there was also an element of partisan recalcitrance in some politically hostile councils. Besides, they viewed local authorities as basically administrative agencies. During the twenties a number of councils were dissolved for failure to perform their duties, and it was the satisfactory experience and even popularity of the bureaucratic commissioners, mostly civil servants, who replaced them that perhaps more than anything else led to the adoption of the manager principle. The Report of the Department of Local Government and Public Health for 1928–29 stated that the experience of commissioner government in Dublin and Cork had demonstrated the suitability of managers. They 'brought to the solution of many urgent local problems an absolute impartiality and an understanding of modern developments in city management'.[22]

Because the most insistent pressure for the reintroduction came from Cork, where a group of professional men and businessmen calling themselves 'the Progressives' drafted proposals for a scheme, and because Cork posed a less complicated problem than the much larger Dublin, it was in the Cork City Management Act 1929 that management was first introduced to Ireland. The Cork pattern was followed with minor variations when it was extended to Dublin in 1930, to Limerick in 1934, and to Waterford in 1939. The system was extended to the counties and smaller urban authorities by the County Management Act 1940, and was brought into operation in 1942. Its adoption there, despite the hostility of some government Deputies, 'followed from the perceived success of the city schemes'.[23]

The basic principle of the management system, as it was expressed in the Management Acts of 1929 to 1940, is 'a legal dichotomy of reserved powers of councils and executive functions of managers'.[24] That legislation prescribes the functions of the council (the 'reserved functions') and the functions of the manager (the 'executive functions'). Elected members are to concern themselves with two main types of business: firstly, general policy matters such as the adoption of the budget, the striking of the rate, borrowing, the disposal of council property, the making of local laws (called 'bylaws') and important planning decisions; and, secondly, what might be called representational matters, such as the control of elections, the selection of persons to be members of other bodies, the appointment of committees, and the salary of the mayor (in towns and cities).

All the functions and duties of the council that are not specified as reserved functions are executive or managerial functions. These managerial functions explicitly include the appointment and control of staff, in so far as these matters are not centrally controlled, and the making of contracts, including the letting of houses. Until the removal of responsibility for health and welfare services, they included also the administration of health services and the determination of entitlement to health and other social benefits. Thus, functions that involved decisions open to personal and political influence and that increasingly, as the welfare state developed, required a mass of detailed administration and decisions unsuited to committee procedures were removed from the elected representatives and from committee decision. Since there was no longer any need for a full-blown committee system, councils were made smaller in size.

The manager is an officer of the council or councils that he serves; he is required to keep members informed about business and to aid and advise them in the performance of their duties. He must attend council meetings, and as the Chief Executive Officer he is responsible for the work necessary to implement council decisions. In his own sphere, he must act by formal 'Order' in matters that, had they been council decisions, would have required a resolution of the council. A register of these orders must be available for council inspection. Though an officer of the council, the manager is not chosen by the council, being nominated to it by the Local Appointments Commission. Nor can he be dismissed by his council, which has the power (never so far used) only to suspend him and to request the Minister for Local Government to remove him.

The principle of a rigid division of functions and powers as envisaged in the Management Acts up to 1940 was, however, as little likely to operate in practice as the principle of the dichotomy of politics and administration propounded by the contemporary public administration theorists, to whom the concept perhaps owed something. Inevitably, in the words of a former Dublin City Manager:

|t|he original intention of the legislators to draw a clear line, both in law and in practice, between the Council's reserved functions and the Manager's executive functions has been lost sight of in some degree in the evolution of the system. Managers find themselves involved in business reserved to the Councils. . . . On the other hand Councillors have gained over the years considerable influence in relation to the Manager's functions.[25]

The blurring in practice of the legal distinction between reserved and executive functions was hastened by tensions that arose with the coming of county management in the early 1940s. County councillors, accustomed to administering their own services, which on the whole they did badly, resented the new system. Furthermore, many saw the new managers as agents of the Department of Local Government. Perhaps, also, some of the first county managers were rigid and pedantic in interpreting their powers according to the letter of the Management Act. The Department in circulars exhorted managers to collaborate more with councillors and, under the pressure of public opinion, increasingly insisted on the predominant position of the elected council.

Subsequent legislation, and particularly the City and County Management (Amendment) Act 1955, formally invested the elected representatives with more power. Under that act, the manager is required to inform his council before he undertakes new works, other than maintenance and repair work. The council may, if it chooses, prohibit these works, provided that they are not required by law to be done. Also, members may by resolution require the manager to do any action that is lawful and for which money has been provided, notwithstanding that the action is within the area of the manager's discretion. Thus, for example, although the letting of houses is a managerial function, a council may require a manager to let a house to a particular person. This power, the so-called section 4 resolution, was much used – and so much abused – particularly by councillors in some counties who interested themselves in planning permissions and the rezoning of land that it became a public scandal and was modified in 1991. The 1955 act also provided that, although the control of staff is a managerial function, council sanction is needed to vary the number and rates of remuneration of staff. Likewise, although the making of contracts rests with the manager, elected members have the power to prescribe the procedures to be followed in seeking and processing tenders. Finally, the act gave councils the right, if they wish, to set up estimates committees to take over, formally at least, the preparation of the annual budget. Only a few councils do appoint such committees.

Despite the deliberate attempt to turn back the tide of managerial bureaucracy and to give the elected members the last say even in the manager's own area of competence, the growth of public services and the need to plan and organize complex schemes led to the manager increasingly becoming the major source of initiative in a local authority. Although the council must approve the estimates and vote the rates, the manager, occasionally with committee help, prepares the budget, and it is to him that councillors look to propose and prepare schemes of all sorts.

The growing emphasis on local authorities in respect of planning, zoning, urban renewal, and development generally, including land acquisition and site assemblage, which dates from the Local Government (Planning and Development) Act 1963, led to the managers almost inevitably taking a leading part in the development of their areas. Michael Bannon has pointed to a marked 'expansion of the role of managers into areas of development both within and beyond their statutory role as the chief officer of the local authorities'. They have acquired functions 'in support of the work of other agencies and organizations'. These 'attached' functions, as he calls them, 'have come to embrace virtually every aspect of development in a modern economy and through these functions the manager has been a comprehensive development officer for the territory of the respective authority'.[26] This expansion in the activities of managers has led to the necessity to appoint assistant managers in many counties. They have freed managers from some matters involving much attention to detail and in particular from the need to spend considerable amounts of their time in servicing the smaller urban authorities within their countries.

Although the managers have become the main source of initiative in local government, the councillors have considerable opportunities to influence their decisions, big and small, within the narrow limits for manoeuvre that the central government has left local authorities. Managers are likely to consult councillors about matters involving their own districts or their own constituents (for example, in formulating their road programmes or when letting houses), and councillors expect them to receive representations on matters within their executive powers. Managers even promote the setting up of advisory groups of the council to give them advice on matters within their managerial competence. Thus the roles of councillor and manager have evolved differently from those that were at first envisaged and that the original statutes spelled out. These roles are well understood and accepted.

VI

The role of the councillor as it has developed in the Irish system is a long way from the Victorian ideal of local representatives who decide and administer neighbourhood affairs in the workshops of local government, the committees of the council. As is the case at national level with TDs, the elected member is a consumer representative and more of a factor in the administration of services than a policy-maker or legislator. Of course, local government as a whole is to a large extent administration in any case, in the sense that it is concerned with the provision of services decided upon elsewhere; but even within the area of a local authority's discretion, the manager tends to be the architect of community services.

As is the case at national level also, councillors to a great extent accept this role. Most councillors are far more conscious of being frustrated by some action or lack of action in a central department than by the manager or the managerial system. Yet again, as at the national level, councillors are quite well suited to their role. In any case, they are bound to play it. Their chances of re-election depend upon doing so, and for many this is, they hope, the first step in a political career, the only route to national office, and the only way to make sure of retaining that office once it is attained. To a great extent, local government and national government are, from the viewpoint of the politicians and party activists, virtually one system and not two.

Local representatives, who are overwhelmingly male (only 11 per cent of the councillors elected in 1991 were women), are of course people who belong in the districts they represent. The counties are divided for local government purposes into county electoral areas. A very strong local patriotism, reinforced by a firm – and well-founded – belief that it pays to have a councillor in one's own district, ensures that only people belonging to an area will represent it. Even in the cities, which are divided into wards for local electoral purposes, the neighbourhood appeal is a strong one.

In Chapter 5, we noted that county councils are largely composed of farmers, professional people, and especially teachers, and shopkeepers, publicans, and other family businessmen. The last-named group in particular is greatly overrepresented in relation to their numbers in the community, as it is, together with the professional group, in the cities and towns, where the non-manual working class is also well represented. On the other hand, few people in the manual working class get elected. On the county councils, farm labourers are not represented in the districts where they are to be found in some numbers – that is, in the east and south-east – and the same is true of manual workers generally. Nor are there many of these on the city councils. Only in the smaller urban authorities are they present in some numbers: there, the working class is strongly represented. Only in the small towns, then, is politics other than a middle-class or prosperous farmer activity. But these are minor authorities. In the major authorities, as in national politics, the better-off predominate.

From the point of view of most citizens, however, the predominance of certain occupational groups on local councils probably does not seem important and certainly is not seen as a threat to the proper consideration of citizens' interests. To the citizen, the councillor is a neighbourhood contact man whose duties are to render help with problems such as housing, planning permission, and getting grants of one sort or another, and to secure a good share of new amenities for the district. What is more, citizens are in a position to impose this role, for their votes are at issue here. 'Service' is an important *quid pro quo* for political support in local as in national politics. National politicians are as concerned as the local councillors – and at the same level of public business, for it is primarily local authority services that most often and most intimately concern the ordinary person.

This constraint upon representatives has important consequences. It forces the councillor to concentrate upon relative trivia, and it establishes between the representatives and the manager and his staff a relationship that is rather more that of importunate – though important – clients seeking in their turn to advance the causes of *their* clients than that of a board of directors and their top management. In the council chamber things are different, but many of the matters with which councillors are most concerned, being details, are not effected there. It is possible also for an element of deception to enter into this activity. Sometimes – too often, say some local officials – councillors make requests that they know are impossible to grant, merely in order to appear to be doing a service for a constituent. Similar electoral considerations can also colour their speeches in public debate in the council chamber. Local newspapers give much space and prominence to the monthly meetings of the councils, and councillors sometimes strike public attitudes that are unrealistic and even two-faced, but newsworthy and, they hope, vote-catching.

Most councillors, however, are not only local contact men but party representatives, and, as at national level, the public undoubtedly sees them in both roles. Local government is in fact dominated by the national political parties on the electoral plane and to a considerable extent also in the council chamber. This has been the case since before the state came into existence. From the democratization of local government in 1898, councils were involved in national issues and became foci of nationalism. Subsequently, the civil war split and the deep political divisions that ensued were carried into local government. The tradition established in those days still lingers on.

Because the cleavage in the community over the civil war was so deep, local elections were from the beginning fought on national party lines. Nevertheless, the fact that the election system is the single transferable vote in multi-member constituencies has always meant that, for most, a choice of candidates within one's party is available. Thus it is possible to give weight to local and other considerations without going outside the party. Nor has the domination of national parties at the local level meant that genuinely independent candidates have been totally absent, and we should notice also the appearance in the eighties of the 'Greens', a pressure group turned political party, who were able to establish a foothold at least temporarily, despite party domination.

The effect of this dualism – strong partisanship together with a large element of localism – is evident in the council chamber. The party caucus and party voting are the directing forces, but councillors do not invariably follow the party line, as do their colleagues at national level. Also, it is common to find working arrangements for filling the post of chairman or mayor, or in electing to other bodies, that have ignored party affiliations.

The strong party hold on local government and the single transferable vote system of election have usually produced a high turnout at local elections – lower certainly than at general elections, as in most countries, but high compared with turnouts in the United Kingdom, where low polls and, in the past, large numbers of uncontested seats afforded a poor example of local democracy in practice. Table 15.4 has data on turnout at elections since 1950. (In interpreting this and the following table, it should be remembered that electors in the county boroughs and in the countryside vote to fill seats on a single authority, the city or county council, but those who live in towns with borough, urban district, or town status have two votes, one for the county council and one for the town authority.)

The table reveals, first, a marked contrast in turnout between Dublin, the only big city, and the rest of the country, whether urban or rural. Comparatively, the towns of Ireland other than Dublin are small and have a considerable community spirit; the rural population is likewise strongly orientated to local communities. It is probably the sense of community, together with easier canvassing and a perceived obligation for social reasons in small communities to be seen to vote, that explains the higher turnout there. Indeed, as the table also suggests, there is some correspondence between size of town and turnout: the smaller the town, the higher is the proportion who vote.

The support given to the political parties at local elections confirms the strong party orientation of Irish people to which reference has been made in this and earlier chapters. The data in Table 15.5 suggest that in a rough way there was a correspondence between the support a party gets at general elections and that at local elections. As at national elections so, too, at local, the volume of support for the largest parties placed them in three different leagues, and this pattern of support has remained quite stable over time. The data suggest also that Fianna Fáil, unlike the other two parties, tended to lose support at local

Table 15.4 **Voting at local elections, 1950–91: total valid poll[a] as a percentage of the electorate entitled to vote**

Authority	Elections[b]			
	1950–79 min.	max.	1985	1991
County Councils	60	70	62	57
Urban authorities:				
Dublin County Borough Council	29	51	42	42
Other CBCs (Cork, Limerick,				
Waterford and Galway[c])	55	66	49	53
Borough and Urban District				
Councils	59	67	62	_[d]
Town Commissioners	60	71	65	_[d]

Notes: [a] The proportion of spoiled votes was usually about 1 per cent.
[b] The law envisages that local elections take place at five-yearly intervals. It also permits postponement, and governments have sometimes taken advantage of this because of the incidence of general elections and referenda.
[c] Galway was established as a county borough in 1986.
[d] There were no elections for these authorities in 1991.

Sources: For 1950–67, derived from information made available by the Department of Local Government. For 1974, derived from Local Elections, 1974: Results and Statistics (Department of Local Government, Dublin, 1975). For 1979, 1985, and 1991, from the volumes of Local Elections, Results and Statistics (Department of the Environment).

Table 15.5 **Party support at the central and local government levels, 1973–91: percentage of first-preference votes won by each party**

Election	Fianna Fáil	Fine Gael	Labour	Independents and others
General election, 1973	46.2	35.1	13.7	5.0
Local elections, 1974	38.7	32.6	13.5	15.2
General election, 1977	50.6	30.5	11.6	7.3
Local elections, 1979	38.2	34.0	12.3	15.5
General election, 1981	45.3	36.5	9.9	8.4
Local elections, 1985[a]	46	30	8	16
General election, 1987	44.15	27.1	6.4	22.4
General election, 1989	44.15	29.3	9.5	17.1
Local elections, 1991[b]	37.9	26.4	10.6	25.1

Notes: [a] To the nearest whole number.
[b] County and county boroughs only.

Sources: Derived from official returns.

elections partly perhaps because they were often the party in power and therefore subject to the 'agin the government' factor: their good showing in 1985 when they were in opposition perhaps strengthens this hypothesis. Nevertheless it is, as Michael Gallagher observed, 'puzzling'.[27] Finally, it is evident that candidates of small parties and independent candidates attract more support at the local than at the national level. Of course, at this level the job is nothing like so difficult – fewer than 1,000 votes are required to get a seat in most county council and a hundred or two in some small urban authorities. Many of these candidates are neighbourhood figures; their campaigns are likely to centre upon local grievances and issues; the question of who is to run the country does not arise. It is significant that the appeal of independents and small party candidates is notably stronger and getting stronger with time in the towns than in the rural areas and stronger in the smaller towns than in the larger, as Table 15.6 shows.

Table 15.6 *Percentage of first preference votes won by each party at local elections in 1967, 1974, 1979, and 1985*

Party	County councils	County borough councils	Borough and urban district councils	Towns
Fianna Fáil:				
1967	41.3	34.2	29.2	34.6
1974	41.6	33.0	29.4	35.0
1979	41.1	30.1	31.9	34.7
1985	46.7	39.9	36.7	40.4
Fine Gael:				
1967	35.4	23.6	25.3	29.9
1974	34.9	27.9	25.4	30.9
1979	36.2	30.1	26.8	30.8
1985	31.3	23.0	21.9	24.2
Labour:				
1967	12.3	23.6	17.4	12.4
1974	11.5	18.9	17.8	14.4
1979	10.5	17.9	16.2	10.9
1985	7.3	9.6	11.7	10.9
Independents and others:				
1967	11.0	18.6	28.1	23.1
1974	12.0	20.2	27.4	29.7
1979	12.2	21.9	25.1	23.6
1985	14.7	27.5	29.7	24.5

Source: For 1967, derived from information made available by the Department of Local Government. For 1974, *Local Elections, 1974: Results and Statistics* (Department of Local Government, Dublin, 1975). For 1979, *Local Elections, 1979: Results and Statistics* (Department of the Environment, Dublin, 1980). For 1985, *Local Elections, 1985: Results and Statistics* (Department of the Environment, Dublin, 1986).

VII

Most Irish people almost certainly approve of the idea of local democracy, although to judge by the lack of concern about its emasculation they do not feel strongly about it. Only in the context of a campaign in support of some local demand or a defence of some local institution do politicians spring to the defence of local autonomy; but this they can often do very effectively. Yet the trend towards bigger units, the stranglehold of the central departments over local administration, and considerable bureaucratization all suggest that local government is, in practice, as we have observed, not much more than the decentralized administration of centrally ordained and controlled services.

A number of governments have from the sixties onwards acknowledged the *malaise* in local government. In contemplating reform, some have spoken of the need to succour local autonomy and democracy. However, declarations by governments that they were 'considering' and 'reviewing', and even discussion documents and White Papers all came to nothing. It needed a more radical and vigorous approach than governments and their advisers were prepared to adopt. In the face of the fierce antagonism of vested interests evoked by suggestions for change of any kind, governments simply abdicated their responsibilities.

By the early eighties, it was increasingly accepted that the reform of local government was becoming urgent. The fact that the standards of some services were falling and that cities and towns were becoming increasingly tatty, together with the failure of the service charges system and the *ad hoc* proliferation of regional arrangements, all bore witness to the need. By the late eighties, reform was once again on the agenda. On paper at least promised reforms this time, many stemming from the work and recommendations of the Advisory Committee (the Barrington Committee), did constitute a radical programme.[28] They included:

- the establishment of eight regional coordinating authorities composed of local authority members;
- the replacement of Dublin County Council and the Dun Laoghaire Corporation by three county authorities (already in train in 1991);
- a modification of the *ultra vires* rules to bestow a 'general competence' upon local authorities;
- enabling legislation to allow the devolution of functions from central to local government; and
- expenses allowances for local authority chairmen.

Significantly, however, the critical question of local authority financing was still in the pipeline.

Whether local government will in fact be radically reformed this time round is problematical. The truth is that the system as it is still both suits the central administration, which has it in thrall, and answers the needs of most politicians, who are able to manipulate it to the extent necessary to supply a satisfactory service to their constituents and who therefore block any proposal for reform that does emerge. Given the symbiotic relationship of national and local governments that the Irish political tradition has forged and the election system has underpinned, the difficulties of carrying through major reforms are immense.

Notes

1   T.J. Barrington, *The Irish Administrative System* (Dublin, 1980), p. 49. For descriptions and discussions of regional organizations, see *ibid.*, pp. 49–56; *More Local Government: a Programme for Development*, Institute of Public Administration (Dublin, 1971), pp. 27–32 and Appendices 4, 5, and 6; and C. Coyle, 'Irish local bureaucracies in national and European Communities' policy process', paper delivered at the European Centre for Political Research, Workshop on Local and Regional Bureaucracies in European States, April 1990.
2   Coyle, 'Irish local beauracracies', p. 11.
3   *More Local Government*, p. 28.
4   *Ibid.*
5   *Local Government Reorganization* (Stationery Office, Dublin, 1971), p. 9.
6   Barrington, *The Irish Administrative System*, p. 47.
7   For a complete list, see *Returns of Local Taxation, 1988* (Stationery Office, Dublin, 1991), p. 141.
8   Barrington, *The Irish Administrative System*, p. 44.
9   T.J. Barrington, 'Local government reform', paper read to Statistical Society Symposium, Dublin, March 1991, p. 5.
10 See T.J. Barrington, 'Local government reform: problems to resolve', paper read to the Regional Studies Association, March 1991, pp. 14–15 and Tables 3 and 4.
11 J.J. Horgan, 'Local government developments at home and abroad', in *Studies*, 15 (1926), p. 535.
12 *First Report of the Department of Local Government and Public Health*, 1922–25 (Dublin, 1927), p. 11.
13 Barrington (1) *The Irish Administrative System*, p. 43; (2) 'Local government reform: problems to resolve', Appendix, Table 2.
14 *Local Government Reorganization*, chs 5–7.
15 Barrington, *The Irish Administrative System*, pp. 43– 4.
16 See above, p. 263.
17 C.A. Collins, in *Administration*, 2 (4) (Winter 1954–55), p. 83.
18 D. Turpin, 'The Local Government Service', in *Administration*, 2 (4) (winter 1954–55) p. 83.
19 *Report of the Public Services Organization Review Group*, 1966–69 (Dublin, 1969), p. 48.
20 Barrington, *The Irish Administrative System*, p. 46.
21 M.J. Bannon in *City and County Management 1929–1990: a Retrospective* (Dublin, 1991), p. 52.
22 *Fourth Report of the Department of Local Government and Public Health, 1928–29* (Dublin, 1930), p. 17. The origins of the system are fully explored in E. O'Halpin, 'The origins of city and county management', in

City and County Management 1929–1990: a Retrospective (Dublin, 1991), pp. 1– 20.

23   O'Halpin, 'The origins of city and county management', p. 17.

24   A.W. Bromage, 'Irish councilmen at work', in *Administration*, 2 (1) (spring 1954) p. 93.

25   M. Macken, 'City and county management and planning administration', in *Léargas*, 10 (June–July 1967), pp. 2–3.

26   M.J. Bannon, 'The contribution of the management system to local and national development', in *City and County Management 1929–1990: a Retrospective* (Dublin, 1991), pp. 44–5; see pp. 45–52 for a detailed listing and exposition of these 'attached' functions.

27   See M. Gallagher, 'Local elections and electoral behaviour in the Republic of Ireland', in *Irish Political Studies*, 4 (1989), pp. 21–42 (1989) on this point and on the relationship between voting at national and local elections generally.

28   See *Report of the Advisory Expert Committee on Local Government Reorganization and Reform* (Dublin, 1991) and the statement of the Minister for the Environment on 'Local Government Reform' dated 7 March 1991.

Chapter 16

Controlling the Administration

I

Public authorities, as T.J. Barrington observed, 'exist basically to serve the people, not only The People, but individual people'.[1] In considering the surveillance and control of the administration, this is an important distinction to make. The interests of 'The People' require that there exist effective procedures for finding out whether the solutions devised by governments for the problems the community faces have been effective, and whether the administration has operated efficiently in applying them. From the point of view of the individual, however, it is the openness, accessibility, responsiveness, and sensitivity of government agencies when dealing with his or her particular piece of business that matter. The existence of effective procedures to ensure each of these contributes as much as elections, independent and alert representatives, and adequate consultation to the citizen's belief that he or she lives in a free and just community.

Important though this distinction is, we should notice that not very much was made of it in the institutions and procedures that were developed for controlling the administration. The two sets of institutions and procedures traditionally used tend in the British tradition to be dual-purpose and to obscure it.

Surveillance and control of the administration are effected, firstly, by parliamentary procedures, such as they are, which Deputies and Senators can use to question or criticize at both a macro level (the conduct of business in general) and a micro level (queries and appeals on individual cases). Surveillance and control are effected, secondly, through the courts and quasi-judicial officials attached to the administration itself – namely, administrative tribunals, ministers acting in an appellate capacity rather than as political decision-makers, and designated civil servants endowed with specific statutory duties and powers. These deal with disputes between individual parties, both persons and institutions. If the plaintiff is an individual person, he or she will most likely be contending that a wrong has been done to him or her personally. Thus, as a controller of the administration, the courts and other officials are mostly called upon to act in the interests of 'individual people' and not 'The People', though sometimes an individual citizen goes to the courts on behalf of his or her fellow citizens, usually to question a general policy or administrative practice.

Dr John O'Donovan did this in 1961 when he successfully challenged the constitutionality of the Electoral (Amendment) Act 1959; so, too, did the Murphys, whose contention that it was unconstitutional to tax them as a married couple in such a way that they were charged more tax than two single people with the same incomes was upheld in the Supreme Court in 1980: so, too, did Dr Raymond Crotty when he challenged the constitutionality of the government's attempt to ratify the Single European Act in 1987.[2]

Besides the two traditional methods of challenging the administration, there is a third, introduced into Ireland in 1984 which, unlike the other two, is specifically designed to deal with the complaints of individual persons or bodies. This is the Ombudsman, an institution that originated in Sweden in the eighteenth century – hence the name. It was widely adopted in European countries in the second half of the twentieth century.

Essential to the successful operation of these processes are the mass media. They not only provide information and comment on the major items of public policy and on the government's conduct of business, but also they have the ability to throw light into dark corners and to bring to attention in a compelling way matters, big and small, that, once noticed, call for investigation and remedy. In Chapter 4, we considered the mass media as part of the context within which politics is carried on. In this chapter, we shall be concerned only with their ability to publicize and comment on the actions of public authorities.

II

The traditional forms of control over administrative action in Ireland derive from British practice, involving principles and devices originating in the seventeenth century. Their pattern and the way in which they have operated in Ireland reveal a wholesale acceptance of British constitutional and legal theory and practice as these existed in the early part of the present century, and to a considerable extent continue to exist today.

From the seventeenth century on, it was thought that the legality of government actions could and should be controlled by the courts, which were then emerging to considerable independence, while the political acceptability of government actions would be determined by parliament. As J.D.B. Mitchell pointed out, it is essential to realize that the basic shape and limits of each of these forms of control, legal and political, were established and settled by the latter years of the nineteenth century, *before* the great increase in state functions resulted in a mass of detailed administration and the creation of a myriad of small individual rights and obligations.[3]

Legal control was effected through the ordinary courts, whose main concern was the enforcement of legal rights and obligations, not the fulfilment of public policy. Political control operated through the machinery of ministerial responsibility to parliament. Belief in this system can be seen in the 'steady rise in the popularity of Parliamentary Questions, a rise which reflects both this reliance on parliamentary controls and the need for a mechanism for dealing with individual grievances'.[4] The operations of the emerging welfare state brought the system into difficulties. Its deficiencies as a check on administrative action and for securing redress became increasingly obvious as social and economic legislation began to pour out of parliament.

By this time, however, strong and seemingly almost unbreakable traditions had been established. On the one hand, the doctrine of ministerial responsibility commanded great respect. This respect continued to be accorded in spite of the failure of parliamentary practice to deal effectively with the emergence of strong rule by party leaders that followed the coming of the mass parties and machine politics. In the form assiduously fostered by party leaders, especially those in power, ministerial responsibility came down to two propositions: first, that ministers had to have considerable power and discretion to act and to protect their servants and their sources of information and advice; and, second, that they were answerable only in the House of Commons and, more narrowly, 'on the floor of the House' (that is, in full session) and by the traditional (though increasingly archaic) procedure of the debating hall (which the House of Commons essentially was, and is). Even wide-ranging parliamentary committee investigation and discussion were held to derogate from the principle of ministerial responsibility. Vestiges of this attitude persist to this day in Ireland, where the right of select committees of the Dáil and of the Oireachtas to command the attendance of ministers is by no means conceded, it being held to be contrary to established practice.

On the other hand, for their part, the legal profession in Great Britain and Ireland had developed an unshakeable belief in the efficiency of private law procedures and nursed an insular and myopic suspicion of the development in France and elsewhere of what came to be called 'administrative law' − that is, the branch of public law 'relating to the organisation and working of the public services and the relations of those services with private persons'.[5] At the same time, the courts in their judgements showed a great respect for political controls and a consequent reluctance to interfere with administrative action. This extended to 'the refusal of courts to examine the realities of parliamentary life and, hence, their inevitable tendency to build the law upon the fictions rather than the realities of that life'.[6] Although legislation grew in volume and complexity and ministers acquired rule-making power to an increasing degree (both without corresponding developments in parliamentary procedures to effect adequate scrutiny), the courts continued to give decisions based on the fiction that parliament did in fact control.

Likewise, as the volume of administration increased, a similar myth continued to be accepted in relation to the growing number of disputes in which ministers assumed the role of arbitrators or judges. A judge in an important British case decided during the First World War put it thus: 'My Lords, how can the judiciary be blind to the well known facts applicable not only to the Constitution but to the working of such branches of the executive? The department is represented in Parliament by its responsible head.'[7] It followed from this, went the argument, that 'the individual was not entitled to know or see the individual official who decided (this being, it was considered, immaterial, since the Minister was responsible) and that decisions need not be reasoned'.[8]

The Irish state adopted *in toto* these constitutional and legal principles, myths and all, and the procedures and inhibitions to which they gave rise. For example, the basic statute setting up the central government department, the Ministers and Secretaries Act 1924, declared each minister to be 'a corporation sole' with all that that implied. However, within those confines, institutions and procedures have been developed to improve the ability of the Oireachtas both to enquire into the conduct of business generally and to review individual cases. Also, to an increasing extent in recent years, the decisions of the administration have been made subject to review and appeal, and the courts have become more and more inclined to question administrative action and to exploit the resources of the Constitution to protect individuals from the state. Most important from the point of view of an aggrieved citizen, the coming of the Ombudsman has extended such reviews and appeals beyond questions of legality to matters within the discretion of officials to decide.

III

The surveillance and control of the government's implementation of policies already decided upon are obviously to a great extent matters for the Oireachtas representing 'The People'. Equally obviously, they are inextricably linked with the Oireachtas' role in the *making* of policy. Both when criticizing proposed policies and when urging remedial action, reforms, or new departures, upon a government, parliamentary representatives are quite likely to start by commenting upon policies already being implemented and to draw conclusions from existing situations. These provide them with much of their ammunition and many of their arguments.

In practice, also, the procedures of the Oireachtas tend not to draw much distinction between making policy and making the government behave, to use K.C. Wheare's phrase. Debates on legislative or policy proposals and on the estimates are opportunities to criticize current administration; parliamentary questions may be asked about the government's policy intentions and about administrative action, though most questions are in fact directed to the latter. If Oireachtas committees are largely confined to enquiring into the administration's performance in carrying out policy, it is sometimes but a short step thence to raising policy issues, a step that the Joint Committee on State-Sponsored Bodies, for example, was more and more often taking by 1980, and even more so the short-lived Public Expenditure Committee in the mid-eighties.

Likewise, as was made clear in Chapter 11, the handicaps from which the Oireachtas suffers by reason of the deficiencies of these procedures apply equally to making the government behave as to making the laws. Efficient systems for subjecting the administration to scrutiny developed in only two areas. Within its limitations – and they are considerable – the Public Accounts Committee works well, largely because it relies on the audits carried out by the Comptroller and Auditor General. From 1978, the Joint Committee on State-Sponsored Bodies subjected the commercial enterprises to a searching and systematic appraisal, again because it was well staffed. However, the committees that followed it in the eighties did not establish themselves as successfully. (see pp. 202–204 above) The remedies canvassed in Chapter 11 – namely, the development of an effective committee system covering every area of state activity and the provision of adequate services and assistance – would improve the Oireachtas' ability to vet administrative action as much as it would improve its potential to contribute to the formation of public policy. Above all, as was also argued in Chapter 11, it is the members' own perception of their role as representatives that has led to their poor performance. Their domination by the government is a result of their failure to see themselves as a powerful corporate institution of state with the right and duty as an institution to call the government to account on behalf of the people and to insist on making that right effective.

In theory, the political responsibility of ministers brings them to account in the Dáil. However, as we have observed, the operation of the system under conditions of strict party loyalty and discipline leads to 'responsibility', meaning something different in practice from what constitutional theory suggests. In practice, responsibility comes down to an obligation on ministers to answer questions asked by representatives and to deal with matters raised in debate. Even if it is not very effective, this obligation as it is honoured and carried out in practice is of the greatest importance. It helps maintain public confidence in the honesty of the public service and secure to the individual citizen an opportunity to get a review of administrative decisions and perhaps redress. The practice of political responsibility – that is, the obligation to answer – helps to maintain an environment of questioning and criticism that is accepted as normal and legitimate. Even if it is not likely to involve the removal of a minister from office, it does at least emphasize the subordination of the Civil Service. Both an environment of questioning and criticism and the subordination of the Civil Service are important ingredients of democracy. In states where they do not exist, the quality of public life is very different indeed.

IV

From the point of view of the individual citizen, the obligation of ministers to answer in the Dáil or Seanad is a valuable procedure in its own right and, more significantly perhaps, is important because of what it leads to. Because of it, Deputies and Senators can communicate directly with officials in departments and obtain information about individual cases and transactions; following on, in some cases, they can get action or quicker action, force a review, secure the mitigation of a penalty, or perhaps obtain redress for harm done. (As we shall see, they might also influence an administrative decision in favour of their client: this is a constitutionally much more questionable outcome.) Much the same procedure operates at the local government level, where councillors and officials are in something like the same relationship. Very occasionally, this type of activity uncovers a serious injustice or an administrative mess.

Because the public expects such a service from its representatives and because the operation of the election system obliges representatives to perform it, the volume of such transactions is very large and their range enormous. Because most public representatives at both national and local levels live among their constituents who expect them to 'do a turn' if asked and act accordingly, this service is in practice fairly accessible to the public generally and is comparatively effective. Individuals can in fact get information, action, and a review of their cases. No doubt the accessibility of representatives and the effectiveness of their interventions vary between individuals and perhaps from area to area. The procedure is universal enough, however, for a minister to be able to declare with justice, in 1966, that 'there is hardly anyone without a direct personal link with someone, be he Minister, TD, clergyman, county or borough councillor or trade union official, who will interest himself in helping a citizen to have a grievance examined and, if possible remedied'.[9]

A survey of Deputies in 1981 by Richard Roche found that 'when allowances are made for constituents consulting with more than one deputy on the same issue, the average TD handles approximately 140 representations per week'. If this is sustained throughout the year, 'TDs in toto process close on a million representations per year'. To this we must add the admittedly smaller case loads of 60 Senators and 1,618 local councillors (in 1991). Among the matters most frequently dealt with by this procedure, the 1981 survey found that social welfare benefits topped the list by far, followed by housing, entitlement to health services, agricultural grants and payments, grants made by the

Department of the Environment (roads, drainage, sewage, flood control, and so on), and postal services. 'The vast majority of representations received by Deputies concerned cases of perceived delay.'[10] Help might also be sought and given in matters such as children's allowances and old-age pensions despite the fact that the decisions are routine and a representative's intervention is not needed except perhaps when a delay occurs. Nevertheless, whether the representative can help or not, he or she has to take action and to be seen to be doing so.

The ability of public representatives to intervene in the administration directly has its effects upon administrative procedures and decision-making. To take a minor matter, in order to facilitate representatives some departments send duplicate copies of their replies to members' representations: the representative forwards the copy to the constituent. Again, some ministers and ministers of state have ordered their departmental officials to give them advance copies of their replies to Deputies' representations so that they can be quickly sent to the ministers' party colleagues in the locality, thus perhaps forestalling the diligent Deputy who has done the work. Some Deputies say that efforts by the party in power to exploit their ministers' positions in ways such as this have increased in recent years. When a by-election is pending in a constituency, the number of items of constituency business that are suddenly disposed of rises and so, too, does the proportion decided in favour of those in the district.

There can be no doubt either that representatives' activities extend to trying to influence appointments, though the scope for jobbery is mercifully small and largely (but not wholly) confined to low-level jobs such as cleaners and messengers. There can be no doubt either that many representatives believe the practice to be among their privileges or duties. When, in 1983, the Labour Court found that a former minister 'exercised political influence' that gave a candidate for a job as a lock-keeper on the River Shannon an 'unfair advantage', his reply was: 'Let them keep their snouts out of my affairs.' He had, he said, 'done no more than make representations on behalf of a constituent, as was the right of any TD'.[11]

There is some evidence, too, of representations and perhaps even attempted interference in appointments made centrally. In 1980, the Dáil heard allegations that representations were made in respect of appointments by the Civil Service Commission (which were certainly not going to have any effect whatsoever) and that ministers were requesting information about the progress and results of Civil Service competitions.[12] Two cases mentioned by a civil servant in his memoirs involved ministers.[13] When it comes to senior appointments, it is the Garda Síochána that has been most affected. There, every appointment above the rank of inspector is a cabinet appointment; persons proposed by senior officials have not always been appointed.[14] Appointments to lower rank posts in the Garda Síochána are also regularly the subject of representations. The same kind of thing goes on at local level. Low-grade but much sought, after jobs in local authority services are very often the subject of representations to officials and supervisors by councillors and members of the Oireachtas.

The extension of the activities of parliamentary representatives to this kind of matter and to attempting to influence decisions before they are made goes beyond what is necessary or proper to enable the Oireachtas or local authority to oversee the conduct of the administration in order to further the legitimate interests of individual constituents. For a Deputy or Senator to use parliamentary position in this way is, on the contrary, an abuse of the procedures. Nowhere is this more obvious than in efforts to influence members of the Garda Síochána and the customs service to get prosecutions dropped or quashed and to the Minister for Justice to get fines and other penalties remitted. The representative's ability to intervene inevitably gives the Deputy or Senator a role in the administrative process. The danger of interventions of this sort is that the role will be malevolent.

It should not be supposed that this could not happen, for certainly pressure is exerted upon representatives to engage in this type of activity. Requests for help and favours are part of the daily life of all of them, and the role of contact man is one they readily accept. Survey after survey has found that for most people the preferred strategy for influencing the administrative process is to make contact with an elected representative. It is not the only recourse people have. As we have observed, there are the courts and, more recently, the Ombudsman.

V

Judicial control over government derives from Bunreacht na hÉireann, which provides for courts, including courts empowered with jurisdiction extending 'to the question of the validity of any law having regard to the Constitution'. The Constitution also ensures, so far as it can, that the judges shall be independent. Since, in addition, it contains statements of the fundamental rights of the citizen and of the functions and powers of the various organs of government, Ireland is formally at least provided with a reference point for judging governmental action and establishing authoritatively both the rights and duties of the citizens and the procedures by which such judgements may be made.

Bunreacht na hÉireann is not sacrosanct: it can be amended. To do so, however, the approval is required of both the Oireachtas and a majority at a referendum – provisions that have the effect of giving a final say to the political rather than to a legal authority. Nor, of course, at bottom, does a citizen's protection from the state or the rights he or she actually enjoys depend merely upon their being written down in a constitution. The foundations of legal control over the government lie in a widespread belief – a belief held by many Western peoples – that the law should be obeyed, not least by public officials; that it is the duty of courts fearlessly to say what the law is, even if this involves restraining the government itself; and that the courts should be independent in their performance of this duty and for this purpose need to be insulated from politics and political pressure. Bunreacht na hÉireann provides for justice normally to be dispensed in public, in courts established by law, by judges who 'shall be independent in the exercise of their judicial functions and subject only to this Constitution and the law'. Their independence is ensured by a judge's not being subject to dismissal 'except for stated misbehaviour or incapacity and then only upon resolutions passed by Dáil Éireann and by Seanad Éireann calling for his removal' and by the safeguard that a judge's remuneration 'shall not be reduced during his continuance in office'.

It might be thought surprising, therefore, that the appointment of judges is in the hands of the government and that by custom the Attorney General, a political appointee, who is the government's legal adviser and state prosecutor, is always offered any vacancy to the High Court that occurs during his term of office. Occasionally, an Attorney General has gone straight to the Supreme Court. The results are not surprising. Writing in 1971, P.C. Bartholomew found that, on appointment, about three-quarters of the judges were supporters of Fianna Fáil, the party that was in office for all but six years from 1932 up to 1971. His comment, that 'with rare exceptions, a person named as judge will be one who is favourably regarded by the Government', is as valid today as it was then.[15] It does not follow, of course, that judges appointed by politicians, even judges with overt political affiliations, are politically biased in their professional activities; in fact, there are few in Ireland and none in the law profession who think for one moment that they are. Nevertheless, the practice seems inappropriate to a system that is otherwise insulated from contact with party politics.

Given a politically independent judiciary, what matters to the citizen facing the government is, firstly, the accessibility of the courts and, secondly, the extent of the courts' powers to review the actions of public authorities. To be accessible, courts must be physically near at hand; they must be expeditious in their handling of cases; they must not be so expensive that the poor are at a handicap; and they must not be barred to the citizen by laws that give immunity to any person or, particularly, to the state.

The Irish courts are geographically reasonably convenient, but there are considerable delays in the hearing of some types of cases. As in the case of so many otherwise modern countries, judicial institutions and procedures are archaic and inconvenient. The Irish arrangements are no worse than most and better than some. Partly because of the very nature of the judicial process, partly because of restrictive practices by lawyers and partly because of the parsimony of governments when it comes to financing the administration of justice, the expenses of litigation can be heavy: for most people too heavy and, consequently, they will not willingly go down this road. Clearly, a system of free or subsidized legal aid is essential if the courts are to be available to all equally. Not until 1962, however, was a general provision made, in the Criminal Justice (Legal Aid) Act 1962, for free legal aid at criminal proceedings. Help in civil actions was not given until much later. Only after Ireland had been found in breach of Article 6 of the European Convention on Human Rights (an Irish plaintiff, Mrs Airey, did not enjoy an effective right of access to the courts by reason of the absence of a scheme of legal aid) were more adequate arrangements made.[16] In 1980, a Legal Aid Board was set up to provide free or assisted legal advice and aid in civil matters (with some exceptions) on a means tests where 'a reasonably prudent person . . . would be likely to seek such services . . . and a competent lawyer would be likely to advise him to obtain such services'.[17] The scheme has been consistently underfinanced and has not been able to cope with the demands upon it. It cannot yet be said that this basic service, essential to a truly egalitarian society, is operating satisfactorily.

Until the 1960s, access to the courts was somewhat hampered by the remaining vestiges of the British principle of the immunity of the Crown (that is, the government), which had been carried over into the Irish Free State at independence. However, since then, in a period when the courts began to take a much broader approach to interpreting the Constitution and to cast a more critical eye upon the activities of the administration, decisions in a number of important cases have considerably broadened the right of access. As a result, according to leading constitutional lawyers: '[the capacity of the state to be sued as such (i.e. as "Ireland") is now beyond doubt'.[18] Likewise, a similar whittling away process occurred in respect of state claims to the privilege of not disclosing information. Courts have become ever more reluctant to accept pleas of ministerial privilege or the public interest in order to preserve administrative secrecy.

The principal limitations of the Irish courts in respect of the activities of public authorities are two, and they both arise from the absence of a system of administrative law and courts. Firstly, as the United Kingdom (including Ireland) became a modern welfare state, the increasing need for appellate machinery was met, not by developments in the judicial system proper, but by providing for appeals to ministers, to designated civil servants acting on their own personal responsibility and not under ministerial instruction, or to independent tribunals. In some but by no means all cases, further appeals lie thence to the courts. Secondly, when it comes to administrative action carried on inside the power given by the law, the courts' powers are limited:

Provided an authority entrusted with administrative discretion keeps inside its *vires* and (where appropriate) commits no open breach of natural justice, it may act as foolishly, unreasonably or even unfairly as it likes, and the courts cannot (or at least will not) interfere.[19]

There exist no procedures such as, for example, those in France, where there are courts to review administrative action from the point of *détournement de pouvoir* (the abuse of discretion).

So far as the courts are concerned, this means in practice that in dealing with the claims of citizens, administrators are not bound to follow any given procedures unless the law specifically requires them to, provided that, where appropriate, they act judicially and in accordance with the principles of natural justice. It means also that the development of administrative adjudication by ministers, civil servants, or tribunals has been unsystematic and patchy. The All-Party Informal Committee of the Oireachtas on Administrative Justice reported in 1977 that, 'despite the provision of special facilities in the Social Welfare and Revenue areas, the greater part of the public service, including areas with a high incidence of direct dealings with the public, remains unprovided for'.[20] They thought that if appeals procedures were available throughout the administration, they would be heavily used.

A decade before that, the subject of administrative justice had been taken up by the Public Services Organization Review Group (the Devlin Group). Adopting the report of a study group under the chairmanship of the Chief Justice, it recommended a systematic scheme for reviews and appeals from the decisions of public authorities. The whole system should be subject to review by a 'Commissioner for Administrative Justice', who would, in addition, 'perform the functions of an ombudsman in following up complaints from the public in cases where no tribunal exists or administrative remedies have been exhausted'.[21]

Like so many of the recommendations of the Devlin Group, this proposal was not implemented. The All-Party Committee of the Oireachtas in 1977 found 'great difficulties in its application'. Looking at the needs of the situation from the point of view of the Oireachtas, it thought that 'the institution required is one to review, through the examination of complaints, the operation and execution of the legislative provisions enacted by the Oireachtas and to guard against, eliminate or demonstrate the non-existence of, maladministration in any form'. The All-Party Committee proposed an ombudsman, 'an institution which has operated increasingly in other jurisdictions over the past decades'. In doing so, it recognized frankly that it had 'not dealt with the question of the extension of appellate facilities to areas of the public service where they are deficient at present'.[22] As yet, no comprehensive system has been installed for reviewing the decisions of deciding officers and tribunals.

VI

What the All-Party Committee had done, however, with its proposal for an ombudsman, was to suggest that some provision be made to cover a considerable grey area that fell outside the existing area of review altogether. Following their report, the need for some institution to fill the gap between the reach of the Oireachtas and that of the legal system was increasingly recognized by Deputies and Senators. The Ombudsman Act of 1980 (No.26) provided for the appointment of an officer appointed by, and dismissible only by, themselves and endowed with very wide powers to investigate complaints about administrative actions, delays, or inaction adversely affecting persons or bodies in their dealings with certain public authorities ('certain' public authorities because, as yet, not all public bodies come within the scope of the act). In 1991, the Ombudsman's remit extended to government departments and offices, local authorities, health boards, Telecom Éireann and An Post.

Within his area of jurisdiction, the Ombudsman may investigate any action when it appears to him 'that the action was or may have been (i) taken without proper authority, (ii) taken on irrelevant grounds, (iii) the result of negligence or carelessness, (iv) based on erroneous or incomplete information, (v) improperly discriminatory, (vi) based on an undesirable administrative practice, or (vii) otherwise contrary to fair or sound administration'.[23] Unlike the situation in the United Kingdom and France, where complaints must be submitted through parliamentary representatives, people in Ireland may invoke the Ombudsman's help directly, and he can, if he thinks fit, initiate investigations himself. He has considerable powers to get information and to require the attendance of 'any person'. When he finds that the action he has investigated adversely affected a person, he may recommend to the department concerned that the matter be further considered or that measures including specified measures be taken to remedy the adverse effect of the action. If the response is in his view unsatisfactory, he may report accordingly to the Oireachtas, and, as a matter of routine, he is required to report annually.

The first Ombudsman did not take up office until 1984, a delay that perhaps indicated a lack of enthusiasm in some political and Civil Service circles for the installation of a potentially effective watchdog. No sooner was he at work than there were legal challenges to his authority, perhaps inevitably since the extent of his powers was not laid down in detail and senior civil servants were not accustomed to having their decisions and actions reviewed by an official with the power to examine departmental files and records. The Department of Posts and Telegraphs, Telecom Éireann and the Department of Social Welfare, all authorities with very large numbers of clients or customers, questioned his authority but in each case gave way: so, too, later and with equal lack of success, did medical officers in local authorities, who had argued that the Ombudsman's activities would breach doctor–patient confidentiality.

In the early years, too, according to the Ombudsman's report for 1985, 'there were some difficulties, arising mainly from a misunderstanding of the role of the Ombudsman and the failure by a few senior civil servants to appreciate that the Ombudsman's office is empowered to investigate maladministration at all levels'.[24] The law empowers him to issue a special report to the Oireachtas if a department or other body does not accept his recommendation. This is a last resort, for it is in the very nature of his job to seek a satisfactory outcome in each case. (It is significant that the French Ombudsman has the title *Médiateur*.) He has not yet had to publish such a report, but has come close to doing so on a few occasions. Clearly, when faced with this sanction, departments give way.

More serious, perhaps, were the cutbacks in his budget and staff in 1987 which forced him to reduce his activities and, in particular, to suspend staff visits to regional centres throughout the country, a valuable service to the public, which was much used. It was widely believed that here was another sign that some in government and the Civil Service were less than happy about having an independent official examining their decisions and actions. As a result of the pressure of opposition parties that could not be resisted, the parliamentary situation being what it was at the time, staff levels were restored and increased, and budgets also within two years.

By the early nineties, the Ombudsman seemed to have established himself as a permanent and successfully operating surveillance device. Doubtless, some ministers and senior civil servants will continue to have reservations. In his 1991 Report to the Dáil and Seanad, the Ombudsman still found it necessary to say: 'Not all public servants can be expected to respond enthusiastically to the idea of an institution being set up by the Oireachtas to examine complaints from the general public about their administration.'[25] Also, there has always been, and continues to be, some suggestion that many representatives, national and local, view the emergence of this citizens' complaints service as a rival to theirs and '[see] the very stuff of their existence being snatched from under their noses'.[26] The Ombudsman commented on this matter too in his 1990 report: 'It is necessary, also, to win the goodwill and the support of public representatives who may feel that the Ombudsman is trespassing on their territory.'[27]

Certainly there appears to be a demand, and almost certainly a need also, for this service. The volume and nature of the complaints with which he deals is evidence of this (see Table 16.1). As the figures show, complaints about telephone bills (overcharging) far outnumber all others.

With the institution of the Ombudsman and with more active courts, the position of the individual attempting to challenge the administration is slowly being improved. Nevertheless, the area of administrative discretion is still frighteningly large. In addition to discretionary powers in respect of matters such as aliens, passports, telephone tapping, and opening mail, which all states seem to require, the Irish state has always had a battery of emergency and security powers.

Table 16.1 **Work of the Ombudsman**

(a) *Complaints received 1988–90*

	Total	Within jurisdiction
1988	3,164	2,803
1989	2,948	2,655
1990	3,099	2,727

(b) *Complaints handled in 1990*
(Received in 1990, 3,099: carried forward from 1989, 1,583: total, 4,310)

Civil Service		1,410
Department of Social Welfare	812	
Department of Revenue Commissioners	243	
Department of Environment	109	
Department of Agriculture and Food	60	
Department of Education	57	
Other Civil Service departments	129	
Local Authorities		399
Health Boards		374
Telecom Éireann		2,052
An Post		75
Total		4,310

(c) *Most frequent complaints, 1990*

Telephone accounts (Telecom Éireann)	1,390
Unemployment assistance (Department of Social Welfare	157
Income tax (Revenue Commissioners)	154
Disability benefit (Department of Social Welfare)	132
Old age pension (Department of Social Welfare)	120
Supplementary Welfare Allowance (Health Board)	76
Disabled Person's Maintenance Allowance (Health Board)	66

Source: Derived from *Annual Report of the Ombudsman for the year ended 31 December 1990* (Dublin, 1991)

These powers are the legacy of the war of independence and the civil war, both of which cast inordinately long shadows. In these shadows, there have always been subversive organizations, notably the IRA, and occasional eruptions of violence. From the late sixties, the

Republic has experienced the spill-over effects of civil strife in Northern Ireland. In Ireland in 1990 there existed laws empowering the government to arrest without warrant, to detain without trial, and to try accused persons in special courts that do not have to follow normal judicial processes. In 1990, Special Criminal Courts, which sit without a jury, were operating just as they had been in 1940. Likewise, a 'state of emergency' existed as it had since 1939, thus enabling the Oireachtas to enact any law it wished, however repugnant to the Constitution, provided that such law is said to be for the purpose of securing the public safety. The courts, though, are increasingly prone to question such powers. The Supreme Court in 1976 'expressly [reserved for future consideration whether the courts have jurisdiction to review such [state of emergency resolutions'.[28] It is far from certain what would be their attitude to legislation enacted under them.

VII

The effectiveness of the surveillance and appeal processes which we have been considering in this chapter (and also in Chapter 11–see pp. 200–204 above) depend upon the amount and quality of the information available. There is much evidence that in Ireland the activities of public authorities are not as transparent as they are in some other democratic countries. Undoubtedly, discussion and criticism and the systematic appraisal of the administration suffer most from this comparative lack of openness. Sometimes an individual with a wrong to be righted has been handicapped in the past, though the presence of the Ombudsman and legal aid centres might have lessened the number. The citizen looking for a house or the district for a new health centre is hardly handicapped at all.

To some extent, lack of official information is compensated for by the fact that the country is small and homogeneous. The numbers of politicians, administrators, journalists, and judges are small enough for them to be known to one another and for 'horizontal' communication to be easy. Furthermore, journalists have increasingly developed 'investigative journalism', and, although radio and television were to some extent in the past inhibited from seeking out scandals and exposing the shortcomings of public authorities, Radio Telefís Éireann has a growing propensity and an increasing ability to do so.

What the journalists still do not have, though, is the type of material that an efficient parliamentary system would cause to be routinely produced and published. In Barrington's opinion: 'There has been a great falling off, as compared with the practice of last century, in the information conveyed in the annual reports of government departments, where they still continue to produce them at all.' The result is, he said, that 'operations within government departments and within state-sponsored bodies are almost entirely closed to public scrutiny'.[29] Disclosures in 1991 relating to the affairs of some state enterprises, which revealed the tenuous control that their sponsor departments had over them, let alone over their subsidiary companies, bear out the continuing truth of Barrington's statement.

Above all, Ireland badly needs a freedom of information act requiring officials to make available all material that would not endanger security or unnecessarily expose a person's private affairs. At present, officials are not bound by law to give information except when ordered to do so by the courts in some circumstances. On the contrary, they are inhibited by a rigid Official Secrets Act and by internal regulations that can be, and sometimes are, abused for convenience. Legal provisions providing considerable access to administrative documents have long existed in Scandinavian countries, and, more recently, other European countries such as Austria, France, and the Netherlands, as also Australia and Canada, have adopted such legislation. In the United States, too, there are so-called 'sunshine laws'.

In Ireland, even committees of the Oireachtas have been refused information by government officials, and a minister once told the Dáil that 'government policy on the rights of individuals to know what was held on government files about them was that the Minister in question should be the "final arbiter" of whether to release information or not'.[30] A former civil servant once expressed the Service view and noted its inevitable consequences:

The traditional attitude has been to present as narrow a front as possible towards the public, since from that direction there is little to be expected except mud and brickbats. Consequently information is strictly controlled or channelled – sometimes to the point of ceasing to flow at all. It requires an effort to change so well established a position, which has on the whole been advantageous to the defenders.[31]

Many civil servants would think that this is as true today as it was when he wrote it in 1963.

Of course there must be some limits to the disclosure and discussion of public business, but the limits that obtain in any country owe almost as much to the development of a particular environment and the acceptance of certain practices – which, strictly, need not have been accepted – as they do to constitutional rules or the law. The Irish environment is still, comparatively, one of considerable reticence, even secrecy.

VIII

This review of the surveillance and control of the administration confirms the deficiencies of the Oireachtas to which attention was drawn in Chapter 11. It suggests also that people seeking redress might be handicapped by the absence of a developed system of administrative law, though this has become less likely recently. However, most people will never suffer in practice from these limitations and are unaware of them because they have little or no business with public authorities that is not of a purely routine nature. The handicaps, real or imagined, of the individual facing the administration must not be overestimated.

Most citizens might well be content enough with the situation, though more and more are likely to be sceptical if asked about it. The public representatives busying themselves with their 'contact man' activities, the bolder and more creative attitudes of the judges, and the mediation of the Ombudsman all contribute to softening the administration of public services and lubricating the abrasive edge of government where it bears upon the *administré*. If, as seems to be the case, it is particularly at the macro level (the surveillance of the conduct of business in general) that Irish institutions do not work well, this might not matter much to average men and women with their own jobs to do and their own lives to lead.

Notes

1   T. J. Barrington, *The Irish Administrative System* (Dublin, 1980), p. 171.
2   See *O'Donovan* v. *Attorney General* [1961 IR 114: *Murphy* v. *Attorney General* [1982] IR 241: *Crotty* v. *An Taoiseach* [1987] 2 CMLR 657.
3   See J.D.B. Mitchell, 'The causes and effects of the absence of a system of public law in the United Kingdom' in *Public Law* (1965), pp. 95–118.
4   *Ibid.* p. 99.
5   L. Rolland, *Précis de droit administratif*, 11th edn. (Paris, 1957), p. 1 (author's translation).
6   Mitchell, 'The causes and effects of the absence of a system of public law in the United Kingdom' p. 101.
7   Lord Shaw of Dunfermline in *Local Government Board* v. *Arlidge* [1915] AC 120 at p. 136.
8   Mitchell, 'The causes and effects of the absence of a system of public law in the United Kingdom' p. 102.
9   Deputy C.J. Haughey, then Minister for Finance, quoted in *Irish Times*, 12 Nov. 1966.
10 R. Roche, 'The high cost of complaining Irish style' in *IBAR – Journal of Irish Business and Administrative Research*, (1982) pp.99–100.
11 Deputy Seán Doherty, quoted in *Irish Times*, 14 May 1983.
12 *Dáil Debates*, Vol. 320, cols. 41–51 (29 April 1980).
13 See 'The Peter Berry papers', in *Magill*, (June 1980), p. 46.
14 See article by G. Reynolds in *Irish Independent*, 10 Dec. 1982.
15 P.C. Bartholomew, *The Irish Judiciary* (Dublin and Notre Dame, Indiana, 1971), pp. 33 and 48–9.
16 See European Court of Human Rights, Airey Case, Judgement (Strasbourg, 9 Oct. 1979).
17 *Scheme of Civil Legal Aid and Advice*, laid by the Minister for Justice before each house of the Oireachtas in December 1979 (Dublin, 1979), p. 6.

18   J.M. Kelly with G.W. Hogan and G. Whyte, *The Irish Constitution, Supplement to the Second Edition* (Dublin, 1987), p. 5. For the broadening of the access to the courts, see B. Chubb, *The Politics of the Irish Constitution* (Dublin, 1991), pp. 68–70.
19   J. Kelly, 'Administrative discretion', in *Irish Jurist*, 1, n.s. (1966), p. 40.
20   *Report of the All-Party Informal Committee on Administrative Justice* (Dublin, 1977), p. 37.
21   *Report of the Public Services Organization Review Group, 1966–1969* (Dublin, 1969), pp. 451 and 453.
22   *Report of the All-Party Informal Committee on Administrative Justice* (Dublin, 1977), pp. 17–19.
23   Ombudsman Act 1980 (No.26), s.4. For a description and discussion of the functions and powers of the Ombudsman and a survey of the first five years' experience of the working of the system, see J.F. Zimmerman, 'The office of Ombudsman in Ireland', in *Administration*, 37, (1989) pp. 258–72. See also G. Hogan and D. Morgan, *Administrative Law* (London, 1986), ch.7.
24   *Annual Report of the Ombudsman, 1985* (Dublin, 1985), p. 19.
25   *Annual Report of the Ombudsman for the Year ended 31 December 1990* (Dublin, 1991), p. 3.
26   *Western People*, 19 June 1988.
27   *Report of the Ombudsman, 1990*, p. 3.
28   *In re Article 26 of the Constitution and the Emergency Powers Bill, 1976* [1977] IR 159.
29   T. J. Barrington, *The Irish Administrative System* (Dublin, 1980), pp. 190 and 191. In 1986 only five out of the eighteen departments surveyed by the Consumers' Association of Ireland produced an annual report and another produced a biennial report. (See *Consumer Choice* (March 1986), p. 96.)
30   Quoted by F. O'Toole in *Irish Times*, 31 March 1989. There is a good survey of this subject in articles by *Irish Times* journalists in *Irish Times*, 29–31 March 1989.
31   D. Roche, 'The civil servant and public relations', in *Administration*, 11 (1963), p. 108.

Chapter 17

The European Community Dimension in Irish Government

I

When Ireland joined the European Communities, it became part of a supra-national polity. Accession had the effect of superimposing on the state both a new body of law, including the treaties themselves, and a set of rule-making institutions. Henceforward, Irish politicians and administrators (and other political activists like pressure-group representatives) had to become involved with government at another level. In Chapter 5, we took note of the constitutional consequences of accession. A new dimension was added to the framework of limited government, for Ireland, it was said, 'has two constitutions now' – namely, Bunreacht na hÉireann, the domestic constitution; and the Community Treaties and other primary legislation, the 'off-shore' constitution. In this chapter, we are concerned with the impact of this momentous change upon the conduct of Irish politics and public administration.

II

It required a constitutional amendment in 1972 before Ireland could join the European Communities and another in 1987 to approve new Community functions and institutions embodied in the Single European Act. Article 29.4.3° as amended in 1987, and the provisions of the European Communities Act 1972, provide the legal conduit through which Community law flows into Irish law. A third, to be held probably sometime in the second half of 1992, will be necessary to approve the Maastricht Treaty. What is more, Community law in its own sphere predominates over domestic law. From the beginning, the status of Community law was constantly enhanced by decisions of its judicial arm, the Court of Justice. The position was well summarized by Jacques Delors, the President of the Commission, in answer to a question in the European Parliament: 'It is clear from the wording of the Treaties and from repeated decisions of the Court of Justice of the European Communities that the Community legislation in force takes precedence over national provisions, whatever their nature. Rules contained in the national constitutions are no exception.[1] The supremacy of Community law 'has never been seriously questioned in Irish courts'.[2]

This body of binding law is of two kinds. First, there are Community legislative instruments; second, there are European Court rulings. Legislative instruments take a number of forms. Article 189 of the Treaty of Rome enumerates them:

In order to carry out their task the council and the Commission shall, in accordance with the provisions of this Treaty, make regulations, issue directions, take decisions, make recommendations or deliver opinions. A regulation shall have general application. It shall be binding in its entirety and directly applicable in all member states. A directive shall be binding, as to the result to be achieved, upon each member state to which it is addressed, but shall leave to the national authorities the choice of form and methods. A decision shall be binding in its entirety upon those to whom it is addressed.

Thus, some rules apply without any action of the Oireachtas or other national authority; others require action by the Irish authorities. Even in respect of this latter class – directives – where national authorities have 'the choice of form and methods', they must fulfil the intentions of the Community and must do so without unreasonable delay. Thus, a Community legal instrument becomes a compelling, indeed mandatory, influence on the content of domestically made policy.

As in the case of legislative instruments, so, too, with judicial rulings. The European Court, which has the function under the Treaties of ensuring that Community law is observed, stands alongside, and in some circumstances above, the Irish courts. The Treaty of Rome (in Article 177) provides that where any questions involving the interpretation of the Treaty, or the validity and interpretation of Community law is raised in a case before a domestic court, that court may refer, and if it is a final court of appeal, must refer the matter to the European Court. Thus, the European Court has the opportunity to interpret points of Community law. Domestic courts are obliged to apply the rulings so given. Where there is a conflict of laws, the view of the European Courts prevails.

It should be noticed also that the subjects of this powerful legislative order include not only states, as would be the case in international law, but individuals and other 'legal persons' (for example, companies and corporate bodies). These might, if they consider that their government has treated them illegally under Community law, bring that government before the courts, either at home or in Luxembourg (where the European Court sits). Further, if the European Commission considers that a member state has failed to fulfil its Treaty obligations, it has the power under Article 169 of the Treaty to proceed against it in the Court. Ireland was so arraigned on five counts in the first ten years of its membership and was found in breach on all of them.

These very considerable powers do not, of course, extend to any and every matter but only to the areas mentioned or implied in the Treaties and the Single European Act. These are, however, very wide. The core activities were control of heavy industries for security reasons (iron, steel, coal, and nuclear energy), the elimination of barriers to trade leading to a 'common market' and measures to promote more uniform standards of living. Areas in which Community law and policies have affected Ireland (as also other member countries) include agricultural production, standards and marketing and the size and nature of the farming community; fishing; industrial production; trade and commerce; transport; currency; monetary and tax policies; financial services; company law; working conditions and the health, safety, and rights of workers; industrial relations; professional standards; the right to practise and work; job creation and training; regional and infrastructural development; pollution of the environment; health; social welfare; education and technological development. In addition, the Single European Act (1986) formally legitimized the practices and institutions that had grown up to facilitate the making of common foreign policies and political cooperation. More recently, security and defence issues have come within the scope of the Communities.

The direct relationship between individuals and other legal persons and the Communities is particularly important because of its impact upon the enforcement of human rights and their further evolution. The European Economic Community Treaty itself, though it has no specific rights section, contains statements of rights: for example, it prohibits discrimination on grounds of nationality 'within the scope of the application of this Treaty' (Article 7); it provides for freedom of movement within the Community (Article 48); it enunciates the principle of equal pay for equal work (Article 119). This was only the beginning. Over the years, the Court of Justice identified, expanded, and upheld a considerable collection of rights, among the most important being access to employment, training, and promotion for women equally with men; the right to set up in business, practise a profession, or go to work anywhere in the Community; protection for migrant workers; and competition and the outlawing of discrimination in business.

Even these lists of matters with which the Communities have power to deal are not exhaustive, because there are no set limits to them. The relationship between the Community regime and member states is not a federal one with the functions and powers of each party specified. Each of the Treaties is a *traité cadre* – that is, a 'framework treaty' defined as a treaty that does not only lay down rules but, in John Temple Lang's words, 'provides institutions and machinery by which new legal measures may be adopted and differences of opinion resolved'. Thus, to quote Temple Lang again: 'the boundary between exclusive Community powers and national powers is a moving boundary. Since the Single Act there are now no clear legal limits (no doubt there are political ones) on how far it may move.'[3] So far, this boundary has been shifted in one direction only, in favour of the Communities. The movement has been aided particularly by the Court, which has shown itself more than willing to extend the frontiers.

III

So far, we have viewed Ireland at the receiving end of a great body of law and authoritative decisions, either applying directly or having an irresistible influence upon domestic policy-making and home-made law. This is by no means the whole story. Irish politicians, administrators, and unofficial political activists and experts play a part in the processes by which these laws and decisions are formulated and enacted. They are joined in this by the politicians, administrators, and others of all the other member states in doing business with the officials in the Community institutions. All become part of a European political network, or more accurately a collection of overlapping networks, that is not only highly complex, but also, by its very nature, organic, evolving, and mutating over time. It is the more complex because, in Brigid Laffan's words:

The Community's political system is a curious mixture of intergovernmental and supranational characteristics in which political authority and legitimacy is highly diffuse. Whereas in the political systems of the member states there is a reasonably clear separation of powers in which executive power rests with an accountable government, the Community's political system has no government and therefore no opposition. It is the absence of clear lines of political authority based on a centre of governmental power that makes the EC such a hybrid political system.[4]

It is not intended here to describe systematically or in detail the political institutions of the Communities, how they work, and the relationships between them.[5] It is sufficient to say enough about Community government to permit an understanding of how Irish politicians, administrators, and others are involved with them. Both the linkages between the two and the numbers involved are more numerous than is generally realized.

Although the original treaties provide the constitutional law of the system, the institutions and processes of government and administration have evolved organically. Because the concepts of the founding fathers were so novel, it was inevitable that development so far cannot be explained in the conventional categories and terminology of politics at national level. Whereas the core institutions in Ireland are the government and the Oireachtas and it is the relationships between them and their links with the people that set the character of the system, in the case of the European Communities it is the Commission and the Council of Ministers, and recently the European Council, that are at the centre of the system, and it is the relationships between them that are critical. In the words of Juliet Lodge: 'Traditionally, EC decision-making outcomes have been depicted as the outcome of a Commission – Council dialogue.'[6]

The Commission is a collegiate body of seventeen appointed for four years by agreement between the member governments. Large countries have two members each and small countries one. In 1989, two women were appointed for the first time. Commissioners are usually former ministers in their own countries or persons of ministerial calibre. Legally, they are required to act in the Community interest and independently of the governments of their home countries. In Juliet Lodge's view, however: 'Government expectations of "their" nationals in the Commission have undermined the ideal of the Commission as a collegiate body promoting the EC's "collective" interest, and recruitment and appointment practices reinforce this. . . . selecting the Commission President has been likened to a "papal chimney-smoke".'[7]

The Commission is the driving force of the Community political process, for it has the sole right of initiating policy. It proposes policies and programmes to the Council of Ministers: the Council deliberates and decides upon their adoption, but it cannot act except on Commission proposals. The Commission is also a bureaucracy, a 'civil service' numbering between 11,000 and 12,000 people divided into twenty-three 'Directorates' (departments), each headed by a Commissioner. As is the case with Irish government departments, the Directorates are both policy-formulators and administrators, though the amount of detailed administration and surveillance they carry out directly is far less than most Irish departments. The administration of community policies, notably the Common Agricultural Policy and the various funds through which very large amounts of money are channelled into the member countries, is largely done by the national civil servants for each member state.

In performing both its roles, the Commission is involved in widespread and continuous consultation with representatives of member governments, pressure group spokesmen, experts, the European Parliament, and consultative organizations notably the Economic and Social Committee, a body provided for in the European Economic Community Treaty itself.

By eliciting information from and consulting national bureaucracies, the EP, European and national interest groups and other parties both at the pre-decisional stage of formulating a proposal and thereafter as it begins its passage through the institutions, it [the Commission], acts as *honest-broker* and works towards the production of acceptable compromises.[8]

The role of the President of the Commission, like that of national prime ministers, 'is what its holder chooses and is able to make of it'.

He certainly tends to influence the content and set the pace and tone of the Commission he heads: contrast, for example, the period of office of Jacques Delors, who first took up office in 1985, and that of his predecessor, Gaston Thorn.

The Commission's role as policy-initiator clearly places it at the centre of affairs, but it shares this position with the Council of Ministers, whose chief function is to adopt (or reject) legislative proposals initiated and submitted by the Commission. Whereas the Commission embodies the supra-national principle, the Council is the epitome of the intergovernmental principle. It consists of a ministerial representative, of each member state. A country's foreign minister is regarded as its 'main' representative, but membership varies with the subject for discussion of each meeting. Each country's ministers for agriculture, for example, meet as the Council of Ministers to discuss agricultural business: likewise ministers of finance, transport, economic affairs, industry and commerce, labour, and often social affairs and others meet to consider issues in their own areas and sometimes sit with their foreign ministers.

It helps understanding better if the Council is considered not as a committee but as a system of committees, many of which were not envisaged in the Treaty of Rome. At the top is a body that has come to be known – confusingly – as the 'European Council', a committee of prime ministers not mentioned in the Treaty that has 'summit' meetings three times or more a year. It evolved out of the necessity to have some means of resolving major questions of policy. It first began to meet in 1974 and was formally recognized in the Single European Act in 1986.

The Council of Ministers itself, which, as we have noted, is a collection of functional committees, is in turn supported by a sub-structure of committees and working groups numbering perhaps as many as 200. The most important of these is the Committee of Permanent Representatives (COREPER) – that is, the diplomatic representatives of the member states, for the Communities have ambassadors accredited to them as if they were a state. In typical Community style even COREPER is in fact two bodies: COREPER 1, composed of the ambassadors themselves, who prepare the work of the Council and carry out tasks assigned to it by the Council; and COREPER 2, composed of senior diplomats who prepare the agenda and business for their masters. COREPER is a key, permanent negotiating forum.

The Presidency of the Council is held for six months at a time by each foreign minister in turn. Like the Presidency of the Commission, it came to have a central political role, 'as all member states wanted to ensure that the Community worked reasonably smoothly during their term and that some important decisions were taken'.[9] There has been a growing tendency for states to vie with one another in getting important issues placed on the agenda and brought to fruition in their tenancy. This has led to prime ministers during their period of office visiting their fellow leaders, or at least the most important of them, to try to negotiate agreements.

On the periphery of this complicated process of continuous diplomacy and negotiation, but moving towards the centre, is the European Parliament. Originally called the Assembly, it had a modest start as a nominated body with few powers and little prestige. It gradually became to be known as the European Parliament and its members as MEPs. In 1979, it became a directly elected body. In 1991, it had 518 members, of whom fifteen were elected by Ireland. By the end of the eighties, the European Parliament had acquired some influence upon policy outcomes, and in the early nineties was on the way to acquiring more, as public and political opinion became increasingly uneasy about the less-than-democratic nature of the Community governmental process, the 'democratic deficit', as it came to be called. By 1991, it was consulted on all matters of importance; its opinion was sought on the drafting of Community legislation; it had some powers to alter the Community budget which it could adopt or reject; it could on its own initiative voice its opinion. Its members may table questions for the Commission and Council and raise issues with them for debate.

Whatever may happen in the future, as its powers and role are increased, the European Parliament does not yet have the position of a national parliament. In 1991, Brigid Laffan saw it thus:

Although accountable to the European Parliament, the Commission is not appointed by it. . . . The European Parliament's role in taxation, legislation and budgetary matters is heavily constrained. Although directly elected since 1979, the Parliament does not have the reservoir of legitimacy found in national parliaments. European Parliament elections are akin to 'second order' national elections because governmental office is not at stake.[10]

IV

From 1973, Ireland had to link up with, and take its part in, an on-going system of great complexity that had had fifteen years or more to develop. As we have seen, it was a system characterized by lack of clear lines of authority, a plethora of negotiating centres, and a lack of political accountability as conventionally practised in democratic systems at national level. It might better be viewed as a number of policy networks, mostly organized on a functional basis and composed of the appropriate officials, political and administrative, from the Community and member governments, together with non-official participants, notably interest-group representatives and experts. Not only were the ways of doing business, involving endless negotiation and diplomacy to reach consensus or a majority, foreign to the Irish way of doing things, with its tendency to the adversarial and to strong government by a dominant cabinet, but the then major language of the Community was French and many of the key terms were in that language rather than English. A link-up would not be easy.

As far as the Irish government is concerned, the various ministers involved in Community business operate under their normal conventions. The cabinet as a whole has a general overview and ought to be informed about and favour the policy stance being taken by individual members on all major issues. Occasionally, in the past, cabinet committees have been set up to deal with very important topics. Often at summit level, the Taoiseach and his Minister for Foreign Affairs have had considerable elbow-room as far as their colleagues were concerned. For the ministers most involved, however, notably Foreign Affairs, Agriculture and Food, Finance, and Industry and Commerce, and the Taoiseach himself, Community business has increased the work-load very considerably. As important, it has meant a heavy burden of travelling, the heavier by reason of Ireland's position on the periphery. In 1991, it was widely reported that the Minister for Foreign Affairs was spending two-fifths of his time on Community business outside Ireland – Likewise for their Civil Service advisers, whose responsibilities have increased greatly and whose work routines have become more stressful.

Although each department is responsible for those items of Community business that fall within its ambit on the home front, for there is no Department of European Affairs, coordinating devices do exist. First, from 1987, a Minister of State in the Taoiseach's Department has had responsibility for the coordination of Community Policy, and that department 'plays an important part in setting priorities and in coordinating major negotiations'.[11] The Minister of State chairs a high-level committee of ministers and secretaries of departments. Second, the Department of Foreign Affairs is responsible for the day-to-day coordination of Community business, and for this purpose it has a European Communities Division. There is also the ambassador and his mission in Brussels which, besides foreign service officers, includes officers seconded from other departments that have business in Brussels. In 1991, these included Finance, Agriculture, and Labour.

Apart from these coordinating devices set up to keep the consideration of policy moving along in a coherent fashion and at the required speed, Community business is handled much as is all other business at central government level. In Brigid Laffan's view, there is a distinctive Irish 'policy style' which in some respects contrasts with that of other EC countries. Irish government, she thinks: 'is characterized by a high degree of departmental autonomy. Individual departments guard their policy domains to the neglect of linkages between issues.'[12] The formulation of policy in many issue areas might well involve the interests of a number of departments and so, too, the implementation of Community policies, but rarely are interdepartmental committees or working groups established. What communications do take place are more likely to be informal, as is possible given the small size of the administration. Inside departments,

Community business has been incorporated into the work load of existing divisions and is dealt with in the same way as national or domestic policy. However, the multi-levelled nature of the Community's policy process necessitates the existence of coordinating units in each government department to ensure that the demands of Community business are met.[13]

Yet another feature of the Irish style is evident when it comes to implementing Community policies. In their study of the Irish practice in *Making European Policies Work*, Brigid Laffan and her colleagues described it as follows:

In practice, there is no clear-cut divide between policy formation and implementation. Usually, it is the same official who is involved in Council Working Parties, advises the Minister for Council meetings and subsequently implements the directive. . . . Officials are involved in all facets of the policy cycle on a continuous basis. In Ireland, the administrative body responsible for negotiating a directive in Council is also entrusted with the task of incorporating that directive into law. In many instances, no more than one or two officials assume primary responsibility for a directive or a series of directives. These officials are normally assistant principals or principal officers.[14]

If Community policies involve grants or other payments as they so often do, implementation might well involve these same key officials not only making the rules for eligibility within Community policy guidelines, but also in selecting which projects or schemes will go forward for consideration by Brussels. They will set the criteria and standards to qualify for payment or remissions and decide who or what qualifies. They are thus important 'gatekeepers'.

When it comes to control, it is important to realize that there are two levels. The Community has its own procedures for enforcement up to and including the quasi-legal Court of Auditors and the Court of Justice before whom the Commission may bring recalcitrant member states for non-compliance. There are, also, political and administrative sanctions: a member state, especially a small one, might well find it counter-productive not to cooperate or comply. However, it is important to notice that much control, especially detailed control, is effected by the civil servants of the member states, for it is they who are 'on the ground'. The Commission does not have large staffs in each state. Once again, it is often these comparatively few officials identified above who are likely to be involved in Ireland. The key role they play and the great influence they might exert over a large part of the policy process in these multilevel networks involving two jurisdictions cannot be overstressed. Clearly, it is necessary, in order to understand how government actually operates at this level, to go beyond the constitutional and legal structures and processes and the formal organization charts.

The considerable impact of EC law upon private interests and especially business, including agri-business, means that the activities of the major economic and other pressure groups have to extend to the Community policy process. They seek to influence it in three ways:

1 by putting pressure upon their national governments to pursue appropriate policy objectives in the various EC fora;
2 by seeking to influence Community policy-makers directly and to take a part, if they are let, in formulating and advising on policy;
3 by joining with like-minded groups from other countries in European umbrella pressure groups.

The activities of pressure groups and their role at national government level are the subject of Chapter 7. When Ireland joined the EC, the major agricultural, industrial, and trade-union organizations had necessarily to extend their horizons to Community policy-making. This involved developing contacts and making representations in Brussels and, for those which could afford it, maintaining an office there. One of them, the Irish Farmers' Association, had already done so before accession, and it was followed by the Irish Cooperative Organization Society and the Confederation of Irish Industry which, together with the Federated Union of Employers (now the Federation of Irish Employers), set up the Irish Business Bureau.

Bodies like this, and their equivalents in the other member states are also organized at a supra-national level. The most important of them include COPA (the Committee of Professional Agricultural Organizations), UNICE (the Union of Industries of the EC), ETUC (the European Trade Union Confederation), COGECA (the General Committee for Agricultural Cooperation in the EC), besides a number of sector groups like banking, textiles, chemicals, and pharmaceuticals. The appropriate Irish organizations are members of all these. According to Juliet Lodge, these Euro-pressure groups 'enjoy ready access to EC decision-makers, to each other and to other important actors . . . contacts . . . have been fostered by the Commission and have been seen as especially important to develop two-way communication between the groups and the Commission'.[15]

Given the diversity of interests in every sector, which increased as the six became the twelve, Euro-pressure groups do not always find it easy to aggregate the views of their members to enable them to put forward a common viewpoint. Nor are they the only pressure groups in the field: far from it. Besides the national-level groups at work in Brussels, there are also spokesmen for a large number of non-EC governments, international organizations, and multinational and other giant corporations. 'They also lobby the appropriate Commission DGs along with indigenous EC members' representatives and groups.'[16]

As Laffan and her colleagues have pointed out:

The post-decisional phase of Community policy-making is perhaps even more important to them [the Irish pressure groups] than negotiation, because at this stage the actual content of a directive is translated into Irish law. Frequently, it is the small print and the details of a directive that have greatest implications for an interest organization. Thus they seek to exert considerable pressure on government during implementation.[17]

Here they are operating on the home front, dealing with their own central administration. Often there is considerable consultation, particularly if a department is dependent upon an interest organization for expert advice, or needs its cooperation to administer a scheme or enforce a set of regulations.

Conspicuous by their absence from this extensive policy process are the political parties and the Oireachtas. To a great extent this is inevitable, for they are essentially a part of but, as we have seen, by no means at the centre of the domestic political process. For a number of other reasons, also, they rarely focus their attention upon the European Communities. Most politicians, except perhaps a few leaders, see the EC as 'over there'. Theirs is a view from the periphery. The Community ideals and a Community spirit are not embedded in Irish political culture. Irish interest has always been focused primarily upon economic matters, concentrating on the Common Agricultural Policy (CAP); on maximizing Ireland's 'take' from the EC; and albeit in a more fuzzy way, on preserving neutrality while continuing to get a 'free ride' when it comes to security and defence.

'Irish political parties do not readily fit into the normal pattern of European political families.'[18] The Labour Party automatically joined the Socialists, but the other two major parties had more difficulty finding an appropriate home. To this day, Fianna Fáil seems to fit uneasily with the French Gaullist Party in the so-called European Democratic Alliance. Elections to the European Parliament do not have anything like the status of general elections and are regarded as giving mid-term barometer readings of party strengths. Members of the European Parliament (MEPs) are not linked to the Oireachtas and, with one or two personal exceptions, are not well integrated into their domestic parliamentary parties.

The Oireachtas itself pays scant attention to Community affairs. The European Communities Act 1972 (section 5) requires the government to 'make a report twice yearly to each House of the Oireachtas on developments in the European Communities', but these reports have usually been delayed and have been debated only infrequently. In Brigid Laffan's opinion: 'the standard of debate in the Dáil on EC issues is poor; very few deputies specialize in a policy area unless they have responsibility as spokesmen'.[19] There is a Joint Committee of the Oireachtas on the Secondary Legislation of the

European Communities. Most of its reports have been ignored by the Dáil and Seanad, though, more important, they are taken notice of by civil servants. The Committee's resources were never sufficient and in the early nineties were completely inadequate to cope with the growing volume of EC legislation and the technical nature of so much of it. Consequently, 'the executive is largely unfettered in the management of EC business'.[20]

V

This survey of the impact of the European Communities upon Irish government and politics suggests that Community business has been handled to the greatest extent possible by the ordinary processes of government and administration with little modification of, and few additions to, existing practice. In 1991, Brigid Laffan judged the management of EC business to be 'weak in a number of respects'. The system has 'a limited capacity to evaluate the extensive flow of legislative proposals from the Commission and the balance within and between policy sectors'.[21] Not only is Irish administration segmented, with departments having considerable autonomy, but also there has been little systematic development of coordinating institutions or procedures for long-term, strategic policy evaluation or formulation. 'The "in-tray" "out-tray" approach to policy-making weakens the system's capacity to think in the medium to longer term.'[22]

The result in the early nineties seemed to be that there was little systematic thinking among political leaders or in the Civil Service about a top-level Community agenda that included the functions and powers of EC institutions, particularly Parliament, the impending extension of membership, and the development of economic, monetary, and political union. The Irish government handled the first major Treaty extension (the Single European Act) badly enough. In 1991, it did not look well equipped to handle the second round of major Treaty changes any better.

Notes

1   Written Question No. 2109/87 in *Official Journal of the European Communities*, No. C181/13 (11 July 1988).

2   P. McCutcheon, in *Ireland and EC Membership Evaluated*, P. Keatinge (ed.) (London, 1991), p. 200.

3   John Temple Lang, 'European Community constitutional law: the division of powers between the Community and member states', in *Northern Ireland Legal Quarterly*, 39 (1988), p. 209.

4   B. Laffan, 'An overview of the Community's institutional system', in *Studies in European Union, No.1, Political Union* P. Keatinge (ed.) (Dublin, 1991), p. 241. This chapter relies heavily on Professor Laffan's work.

5   For information on the institutions and activities of the EC, see E. Noël, *The Institutions of the European Community* (Office for Official Publications on the European Communities, Luxembourg); N. Nugent, *The Government and Politics of the European Community* (2nd edn, London, 1991); Brigid Laffan, *Cooperation and Integration in Western Europe* (London, 1992); J. Lodge (ed.), *The European Community and the Challenge of the Future* (London, 1989).

6   J. Lodge, in *The European Community and the Challenge of the Future* J. Lodge (ed.) (London, 1989), p. 27.

7   *Ibid.*, pp. 34–5.

8   *Ibid.*, p. 40.

9   Laffan, 'An overview of the Community's institutional system', p. 245.

10 *Ibid.*, p. 101.

11 B. Laffan, in *Ireland and EC Membership Evaluated* P. Keatinge (ed.) (London, 1991), p. 192.

12 See *Ibid.*, p. 193.

13 H. Seidentopf and J. Ziller (eds), *Making European Policies Work, the Implementation of Community Legislation in the Member States* (Brussels and London, 1988), Vol.II, ch. 6 (on Ireland, by B. Laffan, M. Manning, and P.T. Kelly), p. 385.

14 *Ibid.*, p. 383.

15 J. Lodge, *The European community and the Challenge of the Future*, p. 52.

16 *Ibid.*

17 In Seidentopf and Ziller, *Making European Policies Work*, p. 400.

18 Laffan, in *Ireland and EC Membership Evaluated* (London, 1991), p. 197.

19 *Ibid.*, p. 205.

20 *Ibid.*, p. 208.

21 *Ibid.*, p. 193.

22 *Ibid.*

APPENDIX 1

How the Dáil is Elected
(published by the Department of the Environment, January 1991)

1 Structure of the Dáil

The Dáil (Lower House of Parliament) is composed at present of 166 members representing 41 constituencies. The Constitution requires the total membership of the Dáil to be so set that the national average population per member will be between 20,000 and 30,000. The Constitution also requires that the ratio of population to member must, as far as practicable, be equal in each constituency. No constituency may have less than three members. The constituencies must be revised at least once in every twelve years. In practice, constituencies are revised on the publication of the results of each census of population: a census is normally taken every fifth year. The practice is to establish an independent Commission to draw up a revised scheme of constituencies.

2 Duration of the Dáil

The maximum life of the Dáil is limited by the constitution to 7 years, but a shorter period may be fixed by law and in fact has been fixed at 5 years. The Dáil may be dissolved by the President on the advice of the Taoiseach (Prime Minister) at any time.

3 Membership

Every citizen of Ireland over 21 years of age who is not disqualified by the Constitution or by law is eligible for membership. Members of the judiciary, Civil Service (unless specifically permitted by their conditions of employment), Defence Forces and Garda Síochána (Police Force), as well as holders of certain other offices, are ineligible.

4 Electorate

Every citizen of Ireland and British citizen (as defined by the British Nationality Act 1981), over 18 years who is ordinarily resident in a constituency and whose name appears on the register of electors is entitled to vote at a Dáil election in that constituency. Each elector has one vote only. A register of electors is compiled by the local county council and county borough corporation and comes into force on 15 April each year. A draft register is published on 1 December each year and is displayed for public inspection in post offices and other public buildings. Claims for corrections in the register may be made up to the following 15 January. Claims are adjudicated on by the county registrar, who is a legally qualified court officer. There are 2,483,903 electors on the register for the year 1990/91.

Members of the Garda Síochána (Police Force) and Defence Forces are entitled to vote by post only. Civil servants (and their spouses) attached to Irish missions abroad may also vote by post.

Electors who are disabled may apply to have their names entered on the special voters list and may vote at home. A ballot paper is delivered to them at their residence by a special presiding officer accompanied by a member of the Garda Síochána.

5 General Elections

A general election must be held within thirty days after the dissolution of the Dáil. The Clerk of the Dáil issues a writ to the returning officer in each constituency instructing him to hold an election of the prescribed number of members. The returning officer is the county registrar or in Dublin and Cork, the city or county sheriff. The Ceann Comhairle (chairman of the Dáil) is automatically returned without an election unless he signifies that he does not wish to continue as a member. The latest time for nominating a person as a candidate is 12 noon on the ninth day after the issue of the writs.

The Minister for the Environment fixes the date of the poll, which must be not earlier than the eighth or later than the sixteenth day after the last day for receipt of nominations (Sundays, bank and public holidays are not reckoned). He also fixes the hours of polling, which must be for a period of not less than 12 hours between 8.30 a.m. and 10.30 p.m.

6 Nomination of Candidates

A candidate may nominate himself or be nominated by a Dáil elector for the constituency. A deposit of IR£100 must be lodged in respect of each candidate. The deposit is refunded if the candidate withdraws, is elected or if the greatest number of votes credited to him exceeds one-third of the quota (see paragraph 9 for explanation of the 'quota'). A candidate may include his party affiliation in his nomination paper, if he represents a registered political party. The party affiliation will appear opposite his name on the ballot paper. If he has no party affiliation he may describe himself as a 'non-party' or leave the appropriate space blank.

A register of political parties is maintained by the Clerk of the Dáil. In it he registers particulars of each party which applies to him for registration and which satisfies him that it is a genuine political party and is organized to contest elections.

The returning officer must rule on the validity of a nomination paper within one hour of its presentation to him. He is required to object to the name of a candidate if it is not the name by which the candidate is commonly known, if it is misleading and likely to cause confusion, is unnecessarily long or contains a political reference. He is also required to object to the description of a candidate which is, in his opinion, incorrect, insufficient to identify the candidate, or unnecessarily long. The candidate may amend the particulars shown on the nomination paper or the returning officer may do so. The returning officer may rule a nomination paper invalid only if it is not properly made out or subscribed.

7 The Poll

Polling places are appointed by county councils or county borough corporations, subject to the approval of the Minister for the Environment. The returning officer provides polling stations at each polling place. Usually schools or other public buildings are used. The returning officer is responsible for the organization of the poll, printing of ballot papers, and counting of votes in each constituency. He must send a polling card to each voter, except a postal voter or special voter, informing him of his number on the register of electors and the polling station at which he may vote. He sends ballot papers to the postal voters by post and encloses special envelopes for the return of their votes to him. He arranges to have ballot papers delivered at their homes to disabled electors registered on the special voters list. The postal and special ballot paper envelopes are placed unopened in a special ballot box when returned to the returning officer. Each polling station is supervised by a presiding officer assisted by a polling clerk. A candidate may be represented at a polling station by an agent who assists in the prevention of electoral offences. Before being given a ballot paper, an elector may be asked to produce evidence of identity.

8 Voting

Voting is by secret ballot and on the system of proportional representation, each elector having one transferable vote. The names of the candidates appear in alphabetical order on the ballot paper. The voter indicates the order of his choice by writing 1 opposite the name of his first choice, and, if he so wishes, 2 opposite the name of his second choice, 3 opposite the name of this third choice, and so on. He then places his ballot paper in a sealed ballot box. In this way the voter instructs the returning officer to transfer his vote to the candidate of his second choice if his first choice receives more than the quota of votes necessary for election or is eliminated (through receiving so few votes as to have no chance of election). If the same situation applies to his second choice, the vote may be transferred to his third choice and so on.

9 Counting the Votes

Before the counting of votes begins, the envelopes containing the postal and special voters ballot papers are opened in the presence of the agents of the candidates, and the ballot papers are placed in an ordinary ballot box, which is taken with all the other boxes to a central counting place for each constituency. Agents of the candidates are permitted to attend at the counting place to satisfy themselves that the ballot papers are correctly sorted and counted.

The count commences at 9 a.m. on the day after polling day. Each ballot box is opened and the number of ballot papers checked against a return furnished by each presiding officer. They are then thoroughly mixed and sorted according to the first preferences recorded for each candidate, invalid papers being rejected. The quota of votes, which is the minimum necessary to guarantee the election of a candidate, is ascertained by dividing the total number of valid papers by one more than the number of seats to be filled and adding one to the result; e.g. if there were 40,000 valid papers and 4 seats to be filled the quota would be 8,001, i.e.

$$\frac{40,000}{(4+1)+1}$$

It will be seen that in this example only four candidates could possibly reach the quota. At the end of the first count any candidate who has received a number of votes equal to or greater than the quota is deemed to be elected. If a candidate receives more than the quota, his surplus votes are transferred proportionately to the remaining candidates in the following way. If the candidate's votes are all first-preference votes, all his ballot papers are sorted into separate parcels according to the next preference shown on them. A separate parcel is made of his non-transferable papers (papers on which a subsequent preference is not shown). Each remaining candidate then receives from the top of the appropriate parcel of transferable papers a number of votes calculated as follows:

$$\frac{\text{Surplus}}{\text{Total number of transferable papers}} \times \text{Number of papers in parcel}$$

If the surplus is equal to or greater than the number of transferable votes, each candidate will receive all the votes from the appropriate parcel of transferable papers.

If the surplus arises out of transferred papers, only the papers in the parcel last transferred to that candidate are examined, and this parcel is then treated in the same way as a surplus consisting of first-preference votes. If two candidates exceed the quota, the larger surplus is distributed first.

If no candidate has a surplus or the surplus is insufficient to elect one of the remaining candidates or to affect the order of these candidates, the lowest of the remaining candidates is eliminated and his papers are transferred to the other remaining candidates according to the next preference indicated on them. If a ballot paper is to be transferred and the second preference shown on it is for a candidate already elected or eliminated the votes pass to the third choice and so on.

Counting continues until all the seats have been filled. If the position is reached where the number of seats to be filled is equal to the number of candidates still in the running, these candidates are declared elected without having obtained the quota.

A returning officer may recount all or any of the papers at any stage of a count. A candidate or his agent is entitled to ask for a recount of the papers dealt with at a particular count or to ask for one complete recount of all the parcels of ballot papers. When recounting, the order of the papers must not be disturbed. When a significant error is discovered the papers must be counted afresh from the point at which the error occurred.

10 Results

Having publicly announced the results of the election, the returning officer endorses the names of the elected members on the writ issued to him by the Clerk of the Dáil and returns the writ.

11 By-elections

Casual vacancies in the membership of the Dáil are filled by by-elections. On the instruction of the Dáil the clerk issues a writ to the returning officer for the constituency concerned directing him to hold a by-election to fill the vacancy. Procedure at a by-election is the same as at a general election.

State-Sponsored Bodies in 1991

(Compiled by the author (see p. 246 above)

Commercial (23)

(includes bodies that are partly publicly owned, partly private enterprise)

Aer Lingus Teo
Aer Rianta Teo
Agricultural Credit
  Corporation plc
Arramara Teo
Bord Gáis Éireann
Bord na Móna
Bord Telecom Éireann
British and Irish Steampacket
  Company plc
Coillte Teo
Córas Iompair Éireann
Electricity Supply Board
Housing Finance Agency plc

Industrial Credit Corporation plc
Irish Aviation Authority
Irish National Petroleum
  Corporation Ltd
Irish Steel Ltd
National Building Agency
National Treasury Management
  Agency
Nitrigin Éireann Teo
An Post
Radio Telefís Éireann
Udarás na Gaeltachta
Voluntary Health Insurance
  Board

Marketing, Promotional, Developmental, Research (20)

An Bord Glas
Bord Fáilte Éireann
Bord Iascaigh Mhara
Central Fisheries Board
CERT
Córas Beostoic agus Feola
Córas Tráchtála
Crafts Council of Ireland
Custom House Docks
  Development Authority
EOLAS
FÁS
Foyle Fisheries Commission

Industrial Development
  Authority
Irish Goods Council
Irish National Stud Company Ltd
National Development
  Corporation Ltd
National Microelectronics
  Application Centre Ltd
Racing Board
Shannon Free Airport
  Development Company Ltd
TEAGASC

Administrative, Regulatory, Social Service

The Government of Professions (7)

An Bord Altranais
Bord na Radharcmhastóiri
Dental Council
Medical Council
Pharmaceutical Society of Ireland
Postgraduate Medical and Dental
  Board
Veterinary Council

The Regulation of Economic Activities (7)

An Bord Pleanála
Bord na gCon
Cork District Milk Board
Dublin District Milk Board
Employment Equality Agency
Independent Radio and
  Television Commission
Nuclear Energy Board

The Provision or Administration of Health or Environmental Services (32)

An Bord Uchtála
An Chomhairle Leabharlanna
Beaumont Hospital Board
Blood Transfusion Service Board
Board for Employment of the
  Blind
Comhairle na Nimheanna
Comhairle na nOspidéal
Dublin Dental Hospital Board
Environmental Protection
  Agency
Federated Dublin Voluntary
  Hospitals
Fire Services Council
General Medical Services
  (Payments) Board
Health Research Board
Higher Education Authority
Hospital Bodies Administrative
  Bureau
Hospitals Trust Board

James Connolly Memorial
  Hospital Board
Legal Aid Board
Leopardstown Park Hospital
  Board
Local Government Computer
  Services Board
Local Government Staff
  Negotiations Board
Medical Bureau of Road Safety
Medico-Social Research Board
National Authority for
  Occupational Safety
National Drugs Advisory Board
National Rehabilitation Board
National Roads Authority
National Safety Council
National Social Services Board
St James's Hospital Board
St Luke's Hospital Board

Others (7)

Agency for Personal Service
  Overseas
Arts Council
Bord na Gaeilge
Central Bank of Ireland

Dublin Institute for Advanced
  Studies
Law Reform Commission
National Theatre Society Ltd

APPENDIX 3

The Main Functions of Local Authorities

Source: *Local Government and the Elected Member*, prepared by the Department of the Environment for members of local authorities (Dublin, 1991).

(The powers and functions described in a general way here are not necessarily enjoyed to the same degree by all types of local authority.)

1 *Housing and Building*: provision, management, maintenance, and improvement of local authority housing, including halting sites for travellers; assistance by way of grants, loans, subsidies, and the provision of private sites to persons housing themselves or improving their houses; securing accommodation for homeless persons; promoting and assisting the provision of housing by voluntary and cooperative housing bodies; improvements to private houses as an alternative to rehousing by the local authority; operation of shared ownership system; administration of mortgage allowance for tenants and tenant purchasers; enforcement of standards for private rented accommodation; enforcement of certain housing standards and control; assessment of housing needs.

2 *Road Transportation and Safety*: maintenance and improvement of national primary and national secondary roads, major urban roads, regional roads, county and minor urban roads, regional roads, county and minor urban roads and bridges; Local Improvements Scheme; operation and improvement of traffic management facilities, including traffic controls and public car parks; employment of traffic wardens; road safety education and publicity; registration and taxation of vehicles; licensing of drivers.

3 *Water Supply and Sewerage*: provision, operation and maintenance of public water supply and sewerage schemes; assistance, by way of loans and grants, towards the provision in existing dwellings of a piped water supply and/or sewerage facilities; provision, maintenance, and improvement of public conveniences.

4 *Development Incentives and Controls*: land use planning, including the making of the development plan, the operation of planning control and building by-laws; provision and management of industrial sites;

promotion or urban renewal by, *inter alia*, advising developers, facilitating development wherever possible and carrying out environmental and infrastructural improvement in areas designated under the Urban Renewal Act 1986. Operation of rates remission schemes made under that act; other development and promotion (including contributions to various development agencies), e.g. tourism development.

5 *Environmental Protection*: the carrying out and promotion of environmental improvement and awareness measures; water pollution control (including operation of Local Government (Water Pollution) Acts 1977 and 1990 and oil pollution clearance); air pollution control (operation of the Air Pollution Act 1987); waste collection and the planning, organization, authorization and supervision of waste disposal operations; control of litter (including the making of by-laws under section 4 of the Litter Act 1982); provision and maintenance of burial grounds; ensuring the safety of structures and places (including flood relief and coast protection); fire protection (including fire fighting, fire prevention and miscellaneous emergency services); promotion of civil defence.

6 *Recreation and Amenity*: provision, operation, and maintenance of swimming pools, public libraries, parks, open spaces and recreation centres, art galleries, museums, and theatres; conservation and improvement of other amenities; contribution to bodies concerned with promoting the arts or with providing and developing other amenities; prevention and elimination of dereliction (Derelict Sites Act 1990).

7 *Agriculture, Education, Health and Welfare*: land drainage; animal disease eradication; contributing to the finances of vocational education committees; administering schemes of higher education grants; school attendance, school meals, and contributing to residential homes and special schools; maintenance of certain piers and harbours and contributions towards their development.

8 *Miscellaneous Services*: land acquisition and development; financial management and rate collection; elections, including the compilation of the register of electors and the making of polling schemes; provision and maintenance of courthouses; consumer protection measures, including the operation of weights and measures regulations; markets, fairs, abattoirs, payment of decrees for malicious damage to property, and management of corporate property.

FURTHER READING

General Works

N. Collins and F. McCann, *Irish Politics Today* (Manchester, 1989).
B. Girvin and R. Sturm, *Politics and Society in Contemporary Ireland*
(Aldershot and Brookfield, Vermont, 1986).
J. O'Donnell, *How Ireland is Governed*, 6th edn (Dublin, 1979).

Works of Reference

Administration Year-book and Diary, published by the Institute of
Public Administration, Dublin.
B. Chubb, *A Source Book of Irish Government*, revised edn (Dublin,
1983).
Facts About Ireland, published from time to time by the Department
of Foreign Affairs, Dublin.
A. Mitchell and O. Snodaigh (eds), *Irish Political Documents
1916–1949* (Dublin, 1985).
State Directory, published annually by the Stationery Office, Dublin.
Statistical Abstract of Ireland, published annually by the Stationery
Office, Dublin.

Historical Background

P. Bew, E. Hazelkorn and H. Patterson, *The Dynamics of Irish
Politics* (London, 1989).
J. Bowman, *De Valera and the Ulster Question 1917–1973* (Oxford,
1982).
T. Brown, *Ireland, a Social and Cultural History 1922–85*, 2nd edn,
(Glasgow, 1985).
C. Cruise O'Brien, *States of Ireland* (London, 1972).
P.J. Drudy (ed.), *Irish Studies, 5: Ireland and Britain Since 1922*
(Cambridge, 1986).
T. Garvin, *The Evolution of Irish Nationalist Politics* (Dublin, 1981).
J.J. Lee, *Ireland 1912–1985: Politics and Society* (Cambridge, 1989).
F. Litton (ed.), *Unequal Achievement: the Irish Experience
1957–1982* (Dublin, 1982).

The Earl of Longford and T.P. O'Neill, *Eamon de Valera* (Dublin, 1970).
F.S.L. Lyons, *Ireland Since the Famine*, 2nd edn (London, 1973).
N. Mansergh, *The Irish Free State: its Government and Politics* (London, 1934).
J.A. Murphy, *Ireland in the Twentieth Century* (Dublin, 1975).
T.P. O'Mahony, *The Politics of Dishonour: Ireland 1916–1977* (Dublin, 1977).
E. Rumpf and A.C. Hepburn, *Nationalism and Socialism in Twentieth Century Ireland* (Liverpool, 1977).

Social Structure and Political Culture

R. Breen, D.F. Hannan, D.B. Rottman and C.T. Whelan, *Understanding Contemporary Ireland: State, Class, and Development in the Republic of Ireland* (Dublin, 1990).
B. Brunt, *The Republic of Ireland* (London, 1988).
P. Clancy, S. Drudy, K. Lynch and L. O'Dowd (eds), *Ireland: a Sociological Profile* (Dublin, 1986).
T.P. Coogan, *The Irish: a Personal View* (London, 1975).
Éire Inniu: an MRBI Perspective on Irish Society Today, Market Research Bureau of Ireland Ltd (Dublin, 1987).
B. Farrell, *The Founding of Dáil Éireann: Parliament and Nation Building* (Dublin, 1971).
M. Fogarty, L. Ryan and J. Lee, *Irish Values and Attitudes: the Irish Report of the European Value Systems Study* (Dublin, 1984).
A.J. Humphreys, *New Dubliners: Urbanization and the Irish Family* (London, 1966).
K.A. Kennedy (ed.), *Ireland in Transition, Economic and Social Change Since 1960* (Dublin, 1986).
S. O'Faolain, *The Irish*, revised edn (Harmondsworth, 1969).
M. Peillon, *Contemporary Irish Society: an Introduction* (Dublin, 1982).
J. Raven, C.T. Whelan, P.A. Pfretzschner and D.M. Brook, *Political Culture in Ireland: the Views of Two Generations* (Dublin, 1976).
D.E. Schmitt, *The Irony of Irish Democracy: the Impact of Political Culture on Administrative and Democratic Political Development in Ireland* (Lexington, Massachusetts, 1973).
'Secularization', *Studies*, 293 (Spring, 1985).
'Towards a new identity', *Studies*, 300 (Winter, 1986).
J. White, *Minority Report: the Anatomy of the Irish Protestant* (Dublin, 1975).

The Constitution and Constitutional Law

J. Casey, *Constitutional Law in Ireland* (London, 1987).
B. Chubb, *The Politics of the Irish Constitution* (Dublin, 1991).

B. Doolan, *Constitutional Law and Constitutional Rights in Ireland* (Dublin, 1988).
B. Farrell (ed.), *De Valera's Constitution and Ours* (Dublin, 1988).
M. Forde, *Constitutional Law of Ireland* (Cork and Dublin, 1987).
J.M. Kelly, *The Irish Constitution*, 2nd edn (Dublin, 1984).
J.M. Kelly with G.W. Hogan and G. Whyte, *The Irish Constitution: Supplement to the Second Edition* (Dublin, 1987).
F. Litton (ed.), *The Constitution of Ireland 1937–1987* (Dublin, 1988).
D.G. Morgan, *Constitutional Law of Ireland*, 2nd edn (Blackrock, 1990).

The Mass Media

D. Bell (ed.), *Is the Irish Press Independent? Essays on Ownership and Control of the Provincial, National and International Press in Ireland* (Dublin, 1986).
D. Bell and N. Meehan, 'Cable, satellite and the emergence of private TV in Ireland: From public service to managed monopoly', in *Media, Culture and Society*, 11 (1989), pp.89–114.
Change and Challenge: the Future for Broadcasting in Ireland, issued by RTE Authority (Dublin, 1989).
B. Farrell (ed.), *Communications and Community in Ireland* (Dublin and Cork, 1984).
D. Fisher, *Broadcasting in Ireland* (London, 1978).
R. Pine (ed.), *The Culture and Power of the Media*, Media Association of Ireland (Dublin 1989).
W. Truetzschler, 'Broadcasting law and broadcasting policy in Ireland', in Irish Communications Review, 1 (1991), pp. 24–36.
A. Whittaker, *The Development of the Irish Newspaper Industry* (Dublin, 1978).

Parties, Pressure Groups, and Elections

R.K. Carty, *Party and Parish Pump: Electoral Politics in Ireland* (Waterloo, Ontario, 1981).
J. Coakley and B. Farrell, 'Selection of cabinet ministers in Ireland, 1922–1982', in M. Dogan (ed.), *Pathways to Power: Selecting Rulers in Pluralist Democracies* (Boulder, San Francisco, and London, 1989).
J. Cooney, *The Crozier and the Dáil: Church and State in Ireland, 1922–1986* (Cork and Dublin, 1986).
M. Gallagher, *Political Parties in the Republic of Ireland* (Dublin, 1985).
M. Gallagher,*The Irish Labour Party in Transition, 1957–1982* (Manchester, 1982).

*M. Gallagher and R. Sinnott (eds), *How Ireland Voted 1989* (Galway, 1990).

T. Inglis, *Moral Monopoly: the Catholic Church in Modern Irish Society* (Dublin, 1987).

*M. Laver, P. Mair and R. Sinnott, (eds), *How Ireland Voted: the Irish General Election of 1987* (Swords, Co. Dublin, 1987).

P. Mair, *The Changing Irish Party System: Organisation, Ideology and Electoral Competition* (London, 1987).

T. Nealon's *Guides to the Dáil and Seanad*, published after each general election (Dublin).

C. O'Leary, *Irish Elections, 1918–1977* (Dublin, 1979).

*H.R. Penniman and B. Farrell (eds), *Ireland at the Polls 1981, 1982 and 1987: a Study of Four General Elections* (Durham, NC, 1987).

J.F.S. Ross, *The Irish Electoral System: What It Is and How It Works* (London, 1989).

D. Walsh, *The Party: Inside Fianna Fáil* (Dublin, 1986).

J. Whyte, *Church and State in Modern Ireland, 1923–79*, 2nd edn (Dublin, 1980).

J. White, 'Ireland: Politics Without Social Bases', in *Electoral Behaviour*, R. Rose (ed.) (London, 1974).

*The scope of this work is wider than the title suggests.

Policy Making, the Government, and the Oireachtas

A Strategy for the Nineties: Economic Stability and Structural Change, National Economic and Social Council Report (Dublin, 1990).

B. Farrell, *Chairman or Chief? The Role of Taoiseach in Irish Government* (Dublin, 1971).

B. Farrell, 'Ireland' in *Cabinets in Western Europe* J. Blondel and F. Müller-Rommel (eds), (London, 1988).

G. FitzGerald, *All in a Life: Garret FitzGerald: an Autobiography* (Dublin and London, 1991).

G. FitzGerald, *Towards a New Ireland* (Dublin, 1973).

T. Garvin, *The Irish Senate* (Dublin, 1969).

N. Hardiman, *Pay, Politics and Economic Performance in Ireland, 1970-1987* (Oxford, 1988).

G. Hussey, *At the Cutting Edge: Cabinet Diaries 1982–1987* (Dublin, 1989).

P. Keatinge, *A Place among the Nations* (Dublin, 1978).

P. Keatinge, *A Singular Stance: Irish Neutrality in the 1980s* (Dublin, 1984).

P. Keatinge, *The Formulation of Irish Foreign Policy* (Dublin, 1973).

J.F. McCarthy (ed.), *Planning Ireland's Future: the Legacy of T.K. Whitaker* (Dublin, 1990).

332 The Government and Politics of Ireland

In addition, the following journals contain many articles on public policy issues: *Irish Political Studies, Irish Studies in International Affairs, The Economic and Social Review.* So, too, do the reports of the National Economic and Social Council.

The Administration of Public Services

T.J. Barrington, *The Irish Administrative System* (Dublin, 1980).
City and County Management 1929–1990: a Retrospective (Dublin, 1991).
N. Collins, *Local Government Managers at Work* (Dublin, 1987).
F. Convery and M. McDowell (eds), *Privatisation: Issues of Principle and Implementation in Ireland* (Dublin, 1990).
S. Cromien and A. Pender, *Managing Public Money* (Dublin, 1987).
S. Dooney, *The Irish Civil Service* (Dublin, 1976).
Enterprise in the Public Sector, National, Economic and Social Council Report No.49 (Dublin, 1979).
R. Fanning, *The Irish Department of Finance, 1922–58* (Dublin, 1978).
D.G. Morgan and G. Hogan, *Administrative Law*, 2nd edn (London, 1991).
C.H. Murray, *The Civil Service Observed* (Dublin, 1990).
Report of the Public Services Organization Review Group, 1966–69 (Dublin, 1969).
D. Roche, *Local Government in Ireland* (Dublin, 1982).
Serving the Country Better: a White Paper on the Public Service (Dublin, 1985).

In addition, the following journals contain many articles on public services and on the organization and working of public authorities: *Administration, Seirbhís Phoibli.*

Ireland and the the European Communities

A. Foley and M. Mulreany (eds), *The Single European Market and the Irish Economy* (Dublin, 1990).
P. Gillespie and R. Rice, *Implications for Ireland: Political Union* (Dublin, 1991).
Ireland in the European Community: Performance, Prospects and Strategy, National Economic and Social Council Report (Dublin, 1989).
P. Keatinge, 'Neutrality and regional integration: Ireland's experience in the European Community' in *Between the Blocs: Problems and Prospects for Europe's Neutral and Non-aligned States*, J. Kruzel and M.H. Haltzel (eds) (Cambridge, 1989).

P. Keatinge (ed.), *Ireland and EC Membership Evaluated* (London, 1991).

P. Keatinge (ed.), *Studies in European Union, No.1, Political Union* (Dublin, 1991).

B. Laffan, M. Manning and P.T. Kelly, 'Ireland' in *Making European Policies Work: the Implementation of Community Legislation in the Member States*, H. Seidentopf and J. Ziller (eds) (Brussels and London, 1988), Vol.2.

Index

Senators: occupations of, 208;
    residence of, 205; role of, 292–93.
Serving the Country Better, 239,
    240, 242
Shanin, Teodor, 12
Simon, H.A., 164
Single European Act, 50, 80, 166,
    288, 305, 307, 310, 316
Single Transferable Vote *see*
    Proportional Representation
Sinn Féin, 91–93;
    founding of, 5;
    membership of, 105, 110;
    organisation of, 102–4 *passim*;
    split in, 10;
    support for, 28
Sinnott, R., 11, 141, 142
SIPTU, 111
Smith, Anthony, 63–64, 69
Smith, Patrick, 178
Socialism, 40, 94, 249
Special Branch, 218
State Sponsored Bodies:
    accountability by, 301–2;
    as interest groups, 82;
    creation of, 215;
    control of, 247, 248, 251,
        252–57, 258;
    definition of, 245–46, 248;
    forms of, 246–47, 248, 250–51,
        257;
    growth of, 230, 245, 246,
        249–52, 255;
    Joint Committee on, 202–3, 253,
        259, 291;
    numbers employed in, 217;
    number of, 216, 246, 248–49;
    reform of, 224;
    sponsor ministers, 246, 253–55;
    and Oireachtas, 251, 252–53,
        258–60
Sunday Tribune, 58, 62
Supreme Court, bills referred to, 183

Tánaiste, 171
Taoiseach:
    appointment of, 170–71, 193;
    pre–eminence of, 185–86;
    powers of, 44, 106, 170–72, 186
        ff;
    removal of, 153, 170;
    resignation of, 177;
    role of, 152, 186 ff, 198;

and Seanad Éireann, 197
Teachtaí Dála *see* Dáil Deputies
Television: audience, 24, 66–68;
    control of, 64, 65, 69–70;
    influence of, 29;
    political interference with, 69–70;
    role of, 64–65, 301;
    and elections, 145;
    and independent broadcasting,
        71–73;
    and political broadcasting, 66
Temple Lang, John, 307
Town Commissioners, 269, 271
Treaty, The, 1921:
    constraints of, 40, 42;
    negotiations, 133, 196;
    split over, 10, 18, 92, 280
Treaty of Rome, 50, 306 307, 310
Tracey, Michael, 70
Trade Unions:
    as interest groups, 109;
    ideology of, 33;
    membership of, 111–12;
    and politics, 88, 123;
    and the Labour Party, 105

Unionists, 29, 42
United Nations, 8, 218
United States, 77–78, 92, 139, 161
Urban District Councils, 265, 268–69

Vocational Education Committees,
    265–66
Vocational Representation, 45, 197
Voluntary organisations, 83, 115

Walsh, B., 148
Ward, A.J., 203
Wheare, K.C., 161, 193, 290
Whelan, C.T., 80
Whitaker, T.K., 160, 238
Whyte, John, 16, 118, 143
Wicklow County Council, 154, 165
Women:
    Committee on Rights of, 203;
    and liberation 27;
    position of, 33–34;
        in Civil Service, 241;
        in labour force, 25– 26;
        in local authorities, 84, 279;
        in politics, 84, 174
Workers Party, 93, 98, 102, 105, 138
    see also Democratic Left